The Children of Woot

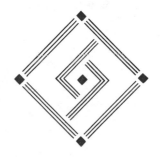

The Children of Woot

A History
of the Kuba
Peoples

Jan Vansina

The University of
Wisconsin Press

Dawson

The ornament on the title page is a
reproduction of the Kuba pattern
named Woot

Published 1978

In the United States and Canada
The University of Wisconsin Press
Box 1379, Madison, Wisconsin 53701
ISBN 0-299-07490-0

In the United Kingdom and Europe
Wm Dawson Sons Ltd
Cannon House, Folkestone, Kent, England
ISBN 0-7129-0830-7

First Printing
Printed in the United States of America
For LC CIP information see the colophon

Contents

Maps

Acknowledgments

The late Daryll Forde guided me and helped me in many ways during the research that led to this book. The late Frans Olbrechts gave me the opportunity to undertake my research, and since then encouragement and further guidance have come from Mary Douglas, Albert Maesen, and many others. Emiel Meeussen and André Coupez not only introduced me to the description of Bantu languages, but taught me how to collect linguistic data and how to systematize them.

Jozef-Maria De Smet has played an unusual role, not only because he was the teacher of history who had the most profound impact on me and my colleagues at the time, but because he, a medievalist, had to convince the "establishment" in 1956 that both oral data and the history of a Central African realm were indeed history, and not anthropology, or perhaps folklore. Without him there would not have been a thesis nor a degree in the department of history.

The Institut pour la recherche scientifique en Afrique centrale sponsored the research. Later the Rockefeller Foundation and the University of Wisconsin's Graduate School funds provided time for more writing about the Kuba, and the Musée royal de l'Afrique centrale at Tervuren and the Frobenius-Institut at Frankfurt granted me generous access to their materials.

The number of friends and scholars who have helped by listening and commenting upon things Kuba is so great that their names cannot conveniently be listed. They include many colleagues and former students. The whole manuscript was commented upon by David Henige, and Steven Feierman read parts of it. Nor should Stanley Shaloff or Andrew Roberts, whose own research often was an inspiration to me, be forgotten. Among others, René Schillings, the connoisseur of Kuba society who helped me set my first footsteps in the field, occupies a special place. So does Elizabeth Evanson, who edited this book and saw it through the press.

But without the help of the Kuba themselves there would never have been a book. Many of them gave their time and restrained their impatience while teaching a hopelessly alien and clumsy researcher the ways of their life. The most generous assistance among them came from Mbop Louis, a full-fledged traditionalist in the 1950s, and Shyaam aNce, who by now has also become an authority on the subject.

The Kuba have attached great importance to their past, viewing it as the force that has shaped their self-identify over the past and the main reason for their present, albeit subdued, legitimate pride. No one exemplified this more than the late King Mbop Mabiinc maMbeky, who died in 1969. But the Kuba are also a critical people who cherish individual expression, as is witnessed in the tales concerning the adventures of the magician Tooml aKwey, or the prankster Kot aMbo. This book is dedicated to all of them.

Jan Vansina

Madison, Wisconsin
July 1977

A Note on Spelling
and Pronunciation

The spelling of African words follows the conventions of the International African Institute, with the following exceptions. In the text, tone markings are not given, and because the seven vowels are represented by five, no distinction is made between mid-high and mid-low tones: ɛ appears as e, and ɔ appears as o. Nouns are given in one form, usually the singular. The special signs for the voiceless fricative and the velar nasal have been replaced by the digraphs *sh* (as in *sharp*) and *ng* (as in *sing* when not in the initial position, and as in *sing* plus *g* when in the initial position).

Names of people are spelled in accordance with these rules plus the rule that the name used must be the one the people uses for itself. These names and spellings were used in my *Introduction à l'ethnographie du Congo* (Kinshasa, 1966), with one exception: the name Mbun has been changed to Mbuun, which is the standard adopted by the Mbuun-speakers themselves, although the vowel is a high mid-vowel rather than a high vowel.

Departures from the usual English pronunciation are limited to the following: *c* is pronounced as in *church*; *p* has a sound that does not exist in English, being a voiceless bilabial fricative that approximates the sound made by pursing the lips and blowing out a candle (it is often described as a sound between *f*, *p*, and *h*); *a* is pronounced as in *calm*; *e* as in *bait* (but shorter), and also as in *pet*; *i* as in *bit*, and also as in *beet*; *o* as in *boat* (but shorter), and also as in *pot*; *u* as in *put*.

Doubling the vowel merely lengthens its sound. For example, *ii* is pronounced like the vowels in *beat*, *oo* like the vowels in *coat*. Double *oo* is never pronounced like the vowels in *boot*.

Special African terms used in the text are italicized only at first appearance. Bushoong and Kete terms that are used more than once in the text are listed in the Glossary.

Part I

Overture

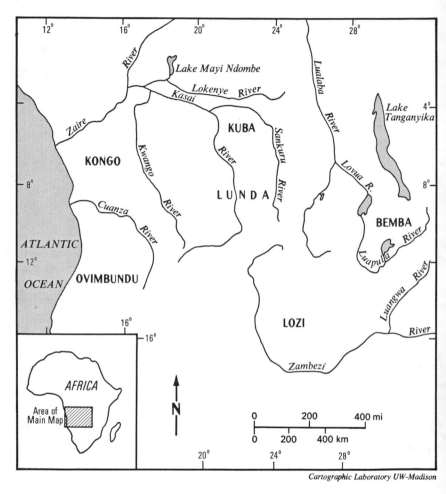

Map 1. The Kuba in Equatorial Africa

Chapter 1

"The People of the King"

"One must nevertheless salute in passing this astonishing achievement of neolithic society."
de Heusch, *Pourquoi l'épouser*

The Kuba of Zaire dazzled the first foreigners and all the ethnographers who later entered "the red halls of the Lukenga's,"[1] the royal court. From Kaxavalla, guide to the traveler Ludwig Wolf in 1885, who compared the reception given to their caravan by the king's son with the splendor of the imperial court in Lunda in past and better days, to Luc de Heusch, the well-known structuralist, no one entirely escaped the magic of this culture. Leo Frobenius, the romantic but sensitive German anthropologist, visited the country in 1905, soon after its rebellion against the Congo Independent State had been put down. Years later, when he cast about for a paradigm to express the essence of African civilization—the civilization of the "blameless Ethiopians"—he chose that of the Kuba. The description of their villages became the epitome of the refined life in Africa.[2] William Sheppard, a black American Presbyterian missionary who was the first foreigner to arrive at the capital, was so struck by the quality of life among these heathens that he became the first to suggest a link with Pharaonic Egypt.[3] And Emil Torday, the first Kuba ethnographer, who tramped over much of southern Zaire, compared the kingdom to Rome under Augustus and its ruler to the Mikado.[4]

Clearly this culture has proven fascinating. One reason is that by 1887 the Kuba kingdom remained the lone witness to the stately courts that had once flourished in equatorial Africa. But even in comparison with others there was something quite distinctive and extraordinary in this civilization, and that is why Kuba history deserves a special niche in the historiography of Central Africa. The state was small: a kingdom two-thirds the size of Belgium or of Swaziland. By 1880 it contained perhaps between 120,000 and 160,000 inhabitants.[5] What fascinated the travelers was not so much its size as its orginality, its complexity, the striking differences with the cultures of the surrounding peoples. The pomp of public receptions and the ubiquitous art first arrested the attention of visitors, who next marveled at the poise and delicate manners of the people, the intricacy of the political system, and, finally, the sophistication of Kuba legal procedures. It is true that the com-

3

plexity of its political organization matched that of any in Africa, while its judicial organization was unique in the whole of the continent. Yet it is also true that much of the Kuba appeal to Europeans stemmed from the cultural preferences of the latter, who recognized the features that they admired in their own civilization.

Still, a society so unexpectedly more complex than its neighbors, a civilization so obviously refined, raised speculation. How did it become what it was? We may disregard suggestions that the Kuba were either escaped Egyptians or Ethiopians, or that they were the unchanged ancestors of the Pharaohs.[6] How then did this society develop? There was a Kuba miracle, and like the "Greek miracles" of our forefathers it must be explained. That is my aim in this book.

Kuba is the name given by their southern neighbors, the Luba, and later by the Europeans, to all the inhabitants of a kingdom that stretched between the lower Sankuru on the north and the Kasai and the lower Lulua on the west. It was bordered on the east by a line located somewhat farther east than the present border of the Mweka district in the province of West Kasai, which is its descendant. The land was forested except for four, or perhaps five, sizable intercalary savannas. It was the southernmost extension of the Great Equatorial Forest. Its environment was unusually rich, for it included no less than three biotopes—the forest, the savanna, and great rivers half a mile to a mile wide. It was well endowed with natural resources, although good pottery clay was mostly restricted to the banks of the Sankuru and the Lulua. There were even some areas especially suited to work iron ore or to grow plants with a high saline content.

The inhabitants used no single name for themselves or their state; they were "the people of the king." By the end of the nineteenth century a number of localized ethnic groups were recognized by them. For practical purposes we distinguish five blocks: the central Kuba, the peripheral Kuba, the Kete and the Coofa, the Cwa, and the Mbeengi.[7] Table 1 and Map 2 give more detail. Map 3 gives the kingdom's place names.

This division of Kuba populations into ethnic groups corresponds only partly to major cultural differences. The Kete spoke dialects closely related to Luba Kasai, the Cwa and the Mbeengi spoke southern Mongo (Nkucu), and the Shoowa speech differs so much from that of other central and peripheral Kuba that it can be as well included with southern Mongo as with Kuba. The Cwa, the Coofa, and the Mbeengi have a different social organization from the others, and also differ greatly among themselves. Central and peripheral Kuba share a common culture; their distinction rests mostly on the basis of different historical traditions. The central Kuba share a single tradition of immigration, whereas the peripheral groups each have their own tradition of origin and settlement.

Ethnic groups were divided into chiefdoms, which were not always adja-

Table 1
Ethnic Groups Composing the Kuba Population, 1953

Ethnic Group	Number of Chiefdoms[a]	Number of Villages[a]
Central Kuba		
Bushoong	1	c. 125
Ngeende	5	c. 50
Pyaang	4 (2 dynasties[b])	13
Bulaang	5	6
Bieeng	1 (independent chiefdom not included)	3
Peripheral Kuba		
Ilebo	1	2
Idiing	1 (part of the Bushoong)	1
Kaam	1 (enclave within the Bushoong)	1
Kayuweeng	2 (enclave within the Bushoong)	2
Kel	6 (2 dynasties)	6
Shoowa	9 (6 dynasties)	17
Bokila	1	1
Ngoombe	3 (3 dynasties)	4
Maluk	4	6
Ngongo	5 (2 segments of dynasties)	6
Kete		
Kete	none[c]	c. 50
Coofa	none[c]	9
Cwa[d]		
Cwa	none	none
Mbeengi		
Mbeengi	none	c. 9

Source: Jan Vansina, *Geschiedenis van de Kuba van ongeveer 1500 tot 1904,* Musée royal de l'Afrique centrale (Tervuren, 1963), pp. 10–12.

[a]In the twentieth century there have been many consolidations of chiefdoms, especially among the central Kuba, the Bushoong excepted. Before 1905 almost every Ngeende or Pyaang village had its own chief. By 1953 villages also had been consolidated to the certain extent. In 1897 Kaam was three villages (according to Samuel Verner, *Pioneering in Central Africa* [Richmond, Va., 1903]); later they became one.

[b]A dynasty is a ruling clan. Several chiefdoms can share the same dynasty.

[c]The Kete and Coofa had only village government. They did not form chiefdoms.

[d]The Cwa were hunters and gatherers who lived in camps all over the territory. Some of them also took up residence in hamlets near other villages. The greatest number roamed east of the Lubudi River.

cent. The Kete, Cwa, and Mbeengi were largely incorporated into the Bushoong and Ngongo chiefdoms, which meant that before 1899, 43 percent of the population in the realm depended directly from the Bushoong chiefdom.[8] This area—including the Idiing, Kaam, Kayuweeng, and even the Bulaang and some Leele who later emigrated to the western bank of the Kasai River—was the nucleus of the kingdom.

The other ethnic units were not united at all and consequently formed a large cloud of satellite chiefdoms around the core. No political cohesion existed among different chiefdoms of the same ethnic group, which prevented them from opposing Bushoong dominance. The chiefdoms of each ethnic group shared a common dynastic clan and common elector clans. Each chiefdom, however, had its own chief and its own electors.

The Kuba, excluding the Cwa, Coofa, and Mbeengi, were organized in matrilineal clans divided into shallow lineages whose depth did not exceed that of extended families. Ideally, marriage was virilocal and men lived with their fathers until the latter died, at which time the sons joined their mother's brother's village. The combination of matrilinearity and the rules of residence resulted in a high geographical mobility; perhaps as many as half of the married people did not live in the village where they should reside according to the "rule."[9] The corporate group involved in most domestic affairs was not the lineage but the clan section—the localized expression of the lineage. It comprised only a handful of lineage members but many spouses and children, married or not, and its composition fluctuated over time. It was the residential unit within the village, and most villages consisted of more than one section. Descent groups had little actual influence in Kuba society. They were potentially important, since they provided an ascribed status and played a major role in marriage, inheritance, and hereditary succession to office. But strict succession to office seems to have been very rare, and inheritance was limited to movable objects. More important, perhaps, was the fact that belonging to a clan meant that one was not of slave status. It was the badge of freedom. Except for chiefs, marriage was monogamous. Female pawns could, however, be held as concubines, and their offspring were then divided among the father's and mother's clans according to formulas that varied for each ethnic group and often according to each pawn contract. Compared to the descent groups, age-grades played a minor role.

This paradigm holds especially for the Bushoong. It does not apply to the Coofa, who were organized in virilocal patrilineal segmentary lineages, nor to the Mbeengi, also virilocal and patrilineal, but who did not live in segmentary lineages. Their lineage structure was much looser than that of the Coofa. Age-grades played a more prominent role among the Shoowa, while small variations in the relevance of descent groups within different situations obtained elsewhere.

In the Kuba cosmology, one or two gods created the world and the first nature spirit. After a man dies he spends a short while as a ghost in the other world and then is reincarnated. If he led an evil life, however, he cannot be reborn and stays in a kind of limbo. Neither nature spirits nor the much less important ghosts kill, and they rarely harm. Misfortune is the sign of evil at work, and evil is the result of witchcraft and sorcery. Diviners played the crucial roles, although the task of priestesses serving the local nature spirits was almost as important. No ancestor cult was practiced at all, and healers, who were neither diviners nor priestesses, remained inconspicuous. Religious movements to smell out evil led by inspired diviners or prophets did exist in precolonial days, but the political authorities kept a watchful eye on this type of development. Ritual rarely involved sacrifice of animal life. It was almost always connected with a charm, whether collective or individual. Cosmology and religion found expression in a wealth of symbols. Rituals involving kingship were much more developed than any others, and the array of symbolic thought involved in them was impressive.[10]

The populations surrounding the kingdom belonged to three different clusters of culture. The west bank of the Kasai was the home of the Leele. The north bank of the Sankuru was inhabited by various southern Mongo groups—including the Ooli, Yajima, Ikolombe, Okpfindu, Pata, and Shobwa—collectively designated as Songo Meno or Nkucu. On the eastern border were the Binji, and on the southeast and south were the Luba (Lulua), Kete, and Bieeng. The southern border along the Lulua was never as clear-cut as the banks of the Kasai and the Sankuru, and some of the Luba, Kete, and Bieeng groups located there were subjected to varying pressures from the Kuba state that made them sometimes a part of the kingdom, sometimes not. Leele society differed sharply from that of the Kuba,[11] but their language and culture were very similar. The southern Mongo were patrilineal dwellers of the forest and intercalary savanna, organized either in tiny chiefdoms or by village, while the Luba speakers, who lived mostly in the savanna, were better organized by segmentary patrilineages (although these were often not very deep) and lived in villages or tiny lineage-type chiefdoms. Nowhere for more than a hundred miles around the Kuba kingdom did any major chiefdom exist, let alone a state comparable to their own, with the exception of the Bieeng chiefdom, just south of the Lulua and east of the Kasai, which had close ties with the realm. No wonder that the Kuba could not conceive of anything more glorious than their kingdom, nor that foreign visitors were so surprised when they reached it. No wonder that the historian asks how this state developed in the middle of nowhere.

Twenty years ago I wrote a Kuba history based on their oral traditions. It was eventually published in 1963,[12] but because it is in Dutch it has remained inaccessible to most readers, including the Kuba themselves. (An English

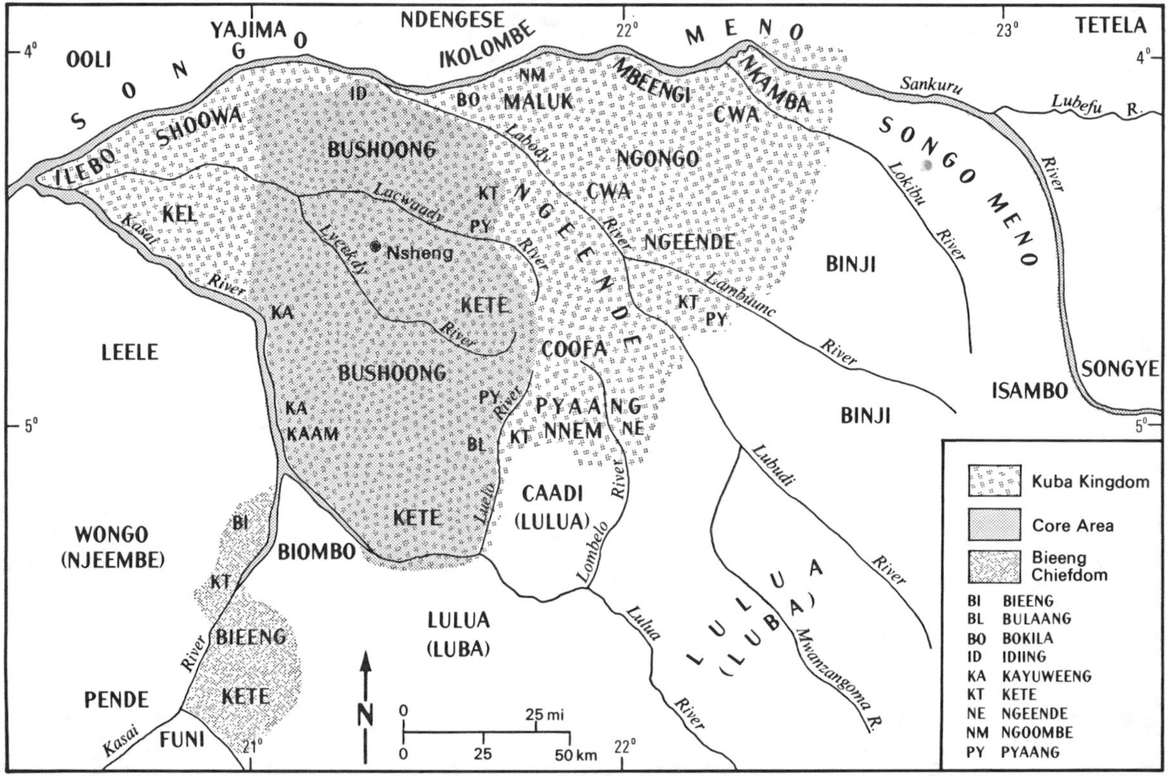

Map 2. The Kuba Peoples and Their Neighbors, c. 1880

Legend:

Kuba Kingdom
Core Area
Bieeng Chiefdom

BI BIEENG
BL BULAANG
BO BOKILA
ID IDIING
KA KAYUWEENG
KT KETE
NE NGEENDE
NM NGOOMBE
PY PYAANG

8

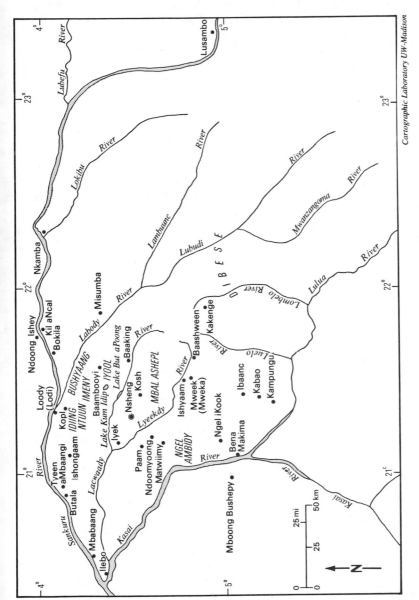

Map 3. The Kuba Kingdom: Place Names

9

summary became available in 1960,[13] and a French résumé was appended to the Dutch publication.) Today the past of this area is much better known, not merely as a result of continued study of the same traditions, but mainly through the availability of new linguistic, ethnographic, archival, and oral data. My previous work provides a repertory of oral traditions and is used as such in this book to document references to oral sources and also to informants.

The present work differs radically from its predecessor. Not merely does it contain revisions or better-grounded conclusions; the subject matter has been broadened because our questions have been broadened and new sources tapped. No longer is this only a political history; still less is it a chronicle. A different history has emerged. Much more than its predecessor, this work constitutes an attempt to use evidence from all the relevant disciplines except archaeology. My own perceptions about history have altered as well, and so the resulting reconstruction differs considerably from the earlier attempt.

What is known about past events can readily be told and results primarily in political history, because that is what the sources make it. But as Fernand Braudel and the school of the journal *Annales* have shown,[14] the flow of events (*histoire événementielle*) is but one of the features of change with which the historian must deal. It occurs at a level of time in which each unit is short. Beyond this, trends (*conjonctures*) appear, which may take half a century or more to run their course. Beyond even these trends, one senses structural changes, which may develop over very long periods and alter the identity of societies and cultures. But there is nothing rigid about the time perspective. The main characteristics of historical time are its variability and the possibility of very long units. There is no single wave-length of time necessarily associated with each structure or institution or culture pattern. Some shifts may take a very long time to reach completion, and hence may be extremely difficult to discern. Thus "nothing" seems to have happened for perhaps a millennium to the basic pattern of Kuba food crop production before a new pattern, based on American crops, began to be introduced in the seventeenth century. This in turn became dominant before the late nineteenth century. The second system took at most two full centuries to develop; the first may have taken much longer or much shorter.

More important, the focus can shift. Trends, which may be cyclical, differ from events, and structural change is something different yet again. As is true for so much of precolonial African history, an analysis of the sources available for Kuba history allows us to perceive trends and even structural change much more readily than events, since so many events have either never been selected for transmission in oral tradition or have been forgotten. But these trends may only be apparent, and may not be the most influential ones that have occurred. As for structural change, what appears is what happened. No major structural change has remained undetected because these phenomena are of such magnitude that traces always seem to remain. In the whole of Kuba history only two such changes have occurred: one when the proto-Kuba became Kuba, and one when the country was knit into a single kingdom. We know only how long the third of the periods that can thus be distinguished has lasted—close to three centuries.

The plan of the present work reflects these new data and the new outlook, as well as another concern. Over the years it has become more and more apparent that there is a fundamental distinction between the way in which the Kuba perceive their past and the interpretation of that past made by the historian when he reconstructs it. That distinction has governed the division of this work into the two parts that follow. In the first I deal with the Kuba approach to history and the substance of their historical knowledge. In the second I interpret and reconstruct the Kuba past.

I am well aware of many shortcomings that still exist with regard to the reality of the past. First, the delimitation of the topic makes it the history of a kingdom rather than any other type of history, such as, for example, a regional history. The impact of political history may therefore be overrepresented. Second, the sources impose limitations. A regional history cannot be attempted because not enough is known about the Kuba's neighbors. No archaeological research has been undertaken as yet in any part of the area. And because of the lack of sources we know little or nothing about personalities and their motivations; as a result the past seems to be dictated by quasi-mechanical forces. The history of ideas, religion, and art is slighted by these sources; the past was undoubtedly much more complex than can be painted here. We lack the kinds of data that could restore the balance. Perhaps more ingenuity will allow a future researcher to do better justice to such themes as intellectual history. Always, though, there will remain a shortage of information and a consequent imbalance in the portrait we can obtain. At least there emerges a portrait in some way related to reality.

Part II

A Past Remembered

Chapter 2

The Kuba and Their History

The first part of this study is devoted to the past as it is remembered by the Kuba. This chapter deals with the Kuba approach to history, and the next two summarize what they remember about it. Chapter Three is concerned with traditions of origin and migration; the fourth retells the chronicle of the chiefs and kings.

The Kuba approach history in a way that differs from that of the scholar. They know what has been in the past, are interested in it, may question the accuracy of one item or another in their oral traditions, even quarrel about it, especially when an implicit consequence of the past represents some advantage in the present. But they do not apply any rules of evidence to it. The historian follows a *method*, which he applies to his sources and his thinking before he concludes that the evolution of a society can be envisaged as having entailed such and such. Because history is thought of as a discipline and historians are trained personnel, it is tempting to dismiss the Kuba attitude toward history altogether; tempting, perhaps, but unwise. The Kuba sense of their history cannot be neglected with impunity since it so profoundly affects their pronouncements about it—that is, their historical traditions. Without understanding their conception of history and their attitudes toward it, we cannot hope adequately to interpret these critical sources. For this reason we must first examine what that attitude entails, what the relevant modes are that help shape their collective thought, and what the different genres of oral traditions are.

Attitudes toward History

Every culture has some sense of history, although it may sometimes be a very weak one. In some cases the past may not interest the living very much; conversely, it may fascinate them. Certainly it did fascinate the Kuba, at least to the extent that they held that one "understands" the why of something if one knows how it began. This by itself explains the existence of a rich body of explicit historical tradition. But why did the Kuba choose to consider something as "explained" once its "origin" was known? I do not know and I did not pay enough attention to it because this attitude was so similar to that of the general public in my own cultural tradition at that time. All we know is that such an attitude is not a universal human response. Many societies are content with a vague "it is the custom" or "it is the way our forebears acted and thought," and look for significance and explanation elsewhere, if at all. Nor will it do vaguely to claim that all states have a developed historical consciousness. Within our own experience the kingdoms of Burundi and of the Tio belie this generalization. More important, it has never been tested.

Such is the compulsion of the Kuba to place everything in a temporal framework that even trickster heroes are located within it. Tooml aKwey, the great magician, who used his powers to play with people (especially those in positions of authority) was, it is said, a real man who lived under the reign of King Kot aNce [7].* The other trickster, Kot aMbo, was not a magician, although he used some magic, and he too is linked to a reign. Indeed, the identity of his great grandsons is pointed out. A researcher can ask about the origin of corn, or the origin of dolls, or the origins of avoiding one's mother-in-law and no one will burst out laughing. An answer will be given. "So-and-so instituted this," the so-and-so usually being one of the prominent cultural heroes: Woot [A], the first man, from whom all others are descended and who created the general features common to all humans, or Shyaam aMbul aNgoong [1], who created the features that make Kuba society and culture so distinctive.[1] Once in a while other names appear and stories are told. Sometimes the question provokes discussion, which ends by the acknowledgment that "we do not really know but it must be so-and-so." Answered or not, to the Kuba it always is a valid question.

Most historical traditions relate to political and social groups—the kingdom, the chiefdom, the village, the clan section. The framework is established by the largest structure: that of the kingdom. Within the political structure certain institutions ensured the transmission of certain traditions. The ruling king; the head ritualist of the realm, the *muyum*; the eldest living son of a king, the *mwaaddy*; the woman who taught the royal songs of the nature spirits to the king's wives—all were required to remember specific traditions. These included a general outline of the overall history of the kingdom entrusted to king and muyum; the royal genealogy, learned by the mwaaddy; the list of queen mothers and the songs, taught by the woman. Some of the other officials were instructed about their predecessors in office, although this was apparently not universal. Could it be that the interest of the Kuba in history stemmed from the ascriptive nature of their political system? Tradition often is an oral archive, a means of legitimation. So it is to the Kuba, but positions in their polity were not always ascriptive. Achievement mattered more than birth, with virtually the sole exceptions of the positions of king, ritualist, and territorial chiefs. The explanation of political ascription

*The numbers or letters in square brackets refer to the place of the ruler in the list given in Appendix A.

will not do. Indeed, why bother with history at all— why not have some other form of legitimation, if legitimation is to be the rationale?

Yet to the Kuba officials, history certainly mattered. I once witnessed a debate, the point of which was to show that title x had been created earlier than title y and therefore x should have precedence in protocol. There was no disagreement with regard to the *therefore*: only about whether x or y was the older title. Lest one be tempted still to link this to the general importance of seniority in the kinship system, of which the offices would be a sort of conceptual extension, one must realize that within the clans seniority of lineages is nonexistent. They are all equal. Moreover, although seniority plays a dominant role in countless kinship systems, this does not necessarily affect ranking of offices by seniority of creation in a state. The history of the Kuba kinship system—insofar as it can be ascertained—does indicate that seniority existed as a principle before the state was created, but nothing more.

Judicial precedent would be a parallel. This too was very important to the Kuba, but not merely as a consequence of the existence of a system of law. Collective representations had to endow precedent with a legal significance. Reasoning of this sort does not explain the fascination with history found here.

This fascination is an attitude of mind that is not automatic. It cannot be dismissed as a dependent variable of organizational principles. True, Kuba interest in history is closely related to their political organization. So is their art; so are their rituals. It goes to show only that political organization is dominant in this society and consequently it is no wonder that their historical curiosity has been given shape by it as well. Still, the predilection for history per se can only be recorded as a "given" of Kuba intellectual concerns. This has an intellectual history of its own, about which all too little is known.

In addition to the official custodians noted above, most narrative traditions were transmitted by *bulaam*, who derived great prestige from their knowledge. They knew the "origins" so they "understood" their society. They were the pundits. The term bulaam was also applied to dance instructors and performers, and refers therefore more to the aesthetic realm than to the historical one.[2] The semantic content of the term suggests that in the beginning the performance brought prestige, and it was only later that the historical substance came to be valued highly—so highly that in the 1950s the greatest admiration was reserved for those bulaam who could rattle off long strings of names without any redeeming performance value at all. Historical content had replaced performance in earning prestige.

Thus, among historical traditions only lists—such as genealogies, lists of officeholders, and lists of place names—do in fact imply that history as such was highly valued. Other traditions indicate only that people liked good songs, poetry, or narratives. When the historical content rather than the performance came to be admired we do not know. It may partly be due to colonial influence. But only partly. A text jotted down by Frobenius in 1905 about the history of the kingdom (which he obtained from a favorite son of King Kot aMbweeky [14]), is structurally very similar indeed to one recorded in 1956 by Jacobs and Vansina, presented to them as "the" official history of the kingdom,[3] and consisting mostly of a catalog of names and praise names. The bulaam are not alone in showing a fondness for names.

What then is the meaning of history to the Kuba? In a substantive way it is the content of what they chose to call history, whether we would agree or not— a *selection* of events, which supposedly did take place starting with the creation of the world. The next two chapters present most of this corpus, which in the 1950s was contained in the royal performance of the dynastic history, in lists of names, sayings, and songs, but mostly in anecdotes to be told when appropriate. How the selection took place was a function not only of the prevailing social institutions but primarily of the prevailing mode of thought in the collectivity. For example, wars were remembered, magic was remembered, organization for tribute was not. Yet clearly the organization to collect tribute was important. In turn oral tradition, including the historical traditions, was a major source for the expression of the prevailing modes of thought.

Concepts about History

The term "history" is rendered by the Kuba as *mooy ma walawal*, "words of yore." A closer examination of the semantics involved rapidly leads us to two sets of notions, one dealing with "words" but involving the concepts of truth and cause, the other dealing with time and space.

A very general term derived from the verb "to speak" includes both noise and speech. It does not include the message aspect of speech. Indeed, the verb differs from another one, "to speak to." When the message is part of the semantic content, either *ikaam* or *dweey* (pl. *mooy*) are used. Both can be translated as "word." Both are proto-Kuba. The first term is found in all Mongo languages (generally, indeed, in zone C of the Bantu languages); the latter is proto-Bantu. They are not synonyms, although their semantic fields overlap. Dweey, the most inclusive term, has been described as meaning "word, voice, decree, statement, message, command, order, ordinance, exhortation, information, news, proclamation, discourse, assertion, speech, sound of music [presumably vocal music only]."[4] It also includes "subject matter" (excluding objects), "event," and "habits." The field of these key terms is so broad that it encompasses many more specialized Kuba words such as those for "habits," "news," "command," and ikaam. It is the term used for "words" in the rendering of "history." Typically for an oral society, "event" and "word" are included in the same concept.

Ikaam, although more limited, still encompasses a broad field, the key elements of which are "a palaver, a statement in judicial court, a cause." The dictionary describes it as "an affair, business, circumstance, palaver, care, cause, responsibility, complaint, concern, reason, object, effect, result, subject, source, purpose, lawsuit, cause, fault, danger, harm, difficulty, deed, doctrine, account, narrative, discourse, debt,"[5] which indicates that like dweey it must be a key concept. Indeed, both are, and both are frequently used. But ikaam is more concerned with "words that have consequences"; it connotes authority. The plural designates "a chief's council or court." Despite its wide field of reference, the Kuba still feel it to be too definite to be used in rendering the concept of history.

Yet the term is closely connected with history. Its intensive form, *ikakaam*, used as a noun or an expletive, indicates "truth"; the noun is always used in the singular. It is the only noun with this meaning, although other expletives exist to indicate "it is so," or "true." The use of ikaam here is suggestive because of its connotation of authority. Is truth what comes out of council or court? As the ethnographic practice indicates,[6] truth does refer to collective agreement. Developing the notion that one witness is no witness (*testis unus*, *testis nullus*), the Kuba took consensus to be the criterion of truth. Nor is this surprising. Other peoples, such as the Tangu from New Guinea, honor the same concept.[7]

Kuba official traditions were not recited before the consensus had been tested and reaffirmed at a preliminary, closed-door meeting of the appropriate council. The practice is known as *kuum*. As a very old notable once told me: "After a while, the truth of the old tales changed. What was true before, became false afterwards." The semantic analysis and the ethnographic observation are in full accord. This conclusion is further reinforced when we observe that to the Kuba "to believe" is "to agree."[8] The relevance of this notion of truth to the historian is obvious. It shows the mechanisms by which homeostasis between a society and its history may occur.[9]

Ikaam is the expression *ikaam imbe*, "because," also means "cause." Other terms designating the base of the trunk of a tree and an intensive form of the verb "to begin" can, and often are, used as nouns with the meaning "cause." But "because" is always "ikaam imbe." The link between important words and their consequences is taken for granted—which is not surprising in a verbal society. The semantics do not take us much further with regard to the notion of cause, except to suggest that cause is linked to beginnings and to the appearance of something. It is suggestive that the Kuba do not speak about the "roots of the matter" but about "where the trunk of the matter appears." Could their notion of change differ? One verb used for "to change" is "to turn over" when applied to objects, answers, and translations; another is "to become" when applied to persons or objects. The semantic evidence allows of no unequivocal conclusion.

The corpus of the traditions makes it clearer. Change is conceived of as an appearance or a putting into place. Kuba do not think about the "flow of history" or the "growth of an institution." Once something—object, institution, pattern of behavior, expression—was created, it existed and was not altered. Very rarely will one encounter the admission that a given institution was altered over time. Even the kingdom appeared full-blown, once it was founded. There were no wars of conquest, only rebellions. And the pattern of rebellions was eternally the same.

Everything has had a beginning, and it is important to know what that was. Moreover, everything that now exists can be *directly* tied to a beginning. Since its creation there has been no change. Behind this concept of cause (and effect, which is *also* ikaam) lies an implicit pattern of thought about the nature of continuity or change and its relation to the "essence" of things—one very different from our own. History is reduced to a statement about origins or to the transformation of an original state of affairs into the present situation. The notion of cause operates homeostatically, since in effect the explanation is conditioned by the present. Yet here homeostasis is not complete, since the origin of institutions or other items now defunct can also be remembered.

History for the Kuba deals then with events (or words), which are authenticated by consensus and which involve a creation unchanged or a single change from the pristine state ("to transform"), a state to which the item can return. This forms a rather static view of the past, and one that will always agree with the present state of affairs. So the Kuba notions about history imply homeostasis.

As in most societies, Kuba notions of time and space are fairly complex, although the computation of time was not. Terms for day, night (which could also mean a period of twenty-four hours), month (moon), season, and year existed, and the parts of the day were also distinguished. Each of the four seasons was named, as was every month of the long dry season. The whole of this computation rested on natural phenomena of a cyclical nature.[10]

Institutions provided units for computation of the week and of periods beyond a single year.[11] These were most often expressed by reference to the shifting of villages or to the reign of a king or chief. Names of the initiation classes could have been used in this fashion, but were not. The term for week indicates the market day, and the three other names for days are derived from it. Given the cumbersome expressions used and their variability, it seems unlikely that a count of days was often used outside the market context. Villages moved every decade or so and the abandoned site usually received a new name. For a while, events could be dated with regard to the abandoned sites; this was done in village histories—just as a lifetime is used with regard to personal reminiscences—but not otherwise. Events in the more distant past were linked to the name of the king ruling then, at least for inhabitants of the core of the kingdom. In the satellite chiefdoms reference was made to the reigns of chiefs, and to kings only when they had intervened in the affairs of the chiefdom. As Alain Delivré has shown, this mode of reckoning time is susceptible to anachronism as soon as the wrong names of rulers are associated with the events remembered.[12] Errors of this nature stem from the similarity or identity of names, from the typing of a king or chief as a character associated with certain types of change ("the warrior," "the magician," etc.), and from the use of certain favorite names with events for which the link has been forgotten. In the Kuba case, the founding heroes Woot [A] and Shyaam [1] are thus used. After much time has elapsed, the risk also becomes great that events or developments will be attributed to the kings or chiefs themselves, when they in fact merely occurred during their reigns. So the Kuba computation of time cannot be trusted implicitly.

One may ask if one time is "better" than another as far as prestige is concerned. For the Kuba it certainly was. The most remote time carried the most weight. We see this in the tale of Kot aMbo, who did not follow customary food avoidances, claiming that what he followed were the original ones—which had been forgotten and replaced by the current set. Or in the argument, already mentioned, concerning whether one title had been created before another one. In this case, rank and speaking order in council were linked to the answer.

An examination of the terms used in relation to time indicates greater concern with the past than with the future in regard to nouns, verbal systems, and invariables. Five out of eleven affirmative tenses have no connection with time. One expresses the very near future (later today, tomorrow morning), another the very recent past; both are used as the "present" form. The present does not exist. The past is comparatively heavily stressed with respect to how long ago an action took place, and also whether the consequences of past action are still with us or not. The distant future is indicated only by the near future tense followed by a generalized timeless narrative tense, the one in fact most used in a sequence of narrated events. Of the negative tenses, two are time-related: one to indicate that the consequence of a past action does not survive and one to negate the recent future.[13] Negation of the past does not make sense because the past has happened. Such negation can, however, be expressed in other ways. That the verbal system is strongly oriented not only toward the past, but toward the effect of past causes in particular, is the most significant finding here.

Apart from nouns tied to the computation of time, the general word used for "time" is "sun," a loan from Kikongo. The term was borrowed in the context of trade and its meaning is limited to "a given moment in time." Before the loan, the same term indicated distance. The loan from Kikongo consists then in a shift of meaning from distance to time, while the old Kuba word for sun was lost. There is no easy way to express a flow of time, although the usual way is a construction involving a noun meaning "times" (French *fois*), as if the flow of time was a repetitive action. This may be linked to the Kuba notion of change, already discussed.

With regard to the past, only the invariable *wal*, "long ago," often reduplicated as "very long ago," is used in time contexts.[14] A set of others relates to time in the past, as well as distance in space. "Very long ago" and "very far way" are the same term. Both time and space are reckoned from here and now, even though no absolute present exists.[15] Since in the nineteenth century distance was calculated by the time it took to travel from one point to another, the link is clear. Time and space were not linked in the Maya sense,[16] where the farther away something is, the older it must be. Because of these terms, confusion is theoretically possible in Kuba texts between something that happened far away and something that happened long ago. But no instance of this type of ambiguity was in fact ever encountered. Still, it may be significant that in the expression mooy ma walawal the invariable, which refers only to time, is used.

Kuba grammar and semantics are much concerned with space location. Nouns, adverbs, one locative preposition, and at least four sets of demonstratives occur. The wealth of demonstratives is unusual even among Bantu languages. Absolute position is indicated by reference to upstream, downstream, up in the air, or down below. The ethnographic material also shows a great concern with proper position on the upstream-downstream axis, and traditions of origin and migration are always expressed with this set of orientations.[17] The most prestigious direction in the past was downstream. Man was created there and so every migration must be seen to start from there. The distortion this implies in accounts of origin and migration is drastic.

So concepts of space imposed a direction, and concepts of time a period (the "longest ago"), as the most prestigious. Moreover, the longest ago has some link with the farthest away. It is no wonder that Kuba history before the settlement starts with the oldest and most extreme downstream place as the paradise of primeval perfection.

The Oral Traditions

In principle, any class of oral literature can carry historical information. For example, a connection between King Shyaam [1] and the Kel lives on in a praise poem about Moyeeng, a minor street of the capital: "the great oil palm, who sent out toward the plain of the Kel," the oil palm being a homonym for Shyaam, the king. The different genres of oral literature must therefore be briefly sketched. By form five classes of sources can be distinguished: songs, mottoes or praise names, sayings or proverbs, lists, and narratives. Special Kuba terms exist for most of these, so that the folk classification corresponds fairly well with mine. Sixteen types can be derived from this main division[18] and are used in this volume. These do not correspond to Kuba categories, but the typology has been made to evaluate the traditions as sources for the historian.

The Kuba will say that their information about the past stems from narratives. But in practice this was not true in the 1950s, when I collected the oral literature described in this section, nor was it so in Torday's time, early in this century. He cites too many sayings as historical evidence and could not have surveyed the whole corpus of sayings (some five thousand, probably) to extract those which have a historical implication. The bulaam picked up materials where they found it, whatever class of literature it belonged to, to elaborate a point, to strengthen it, to deny another point, and mostly to speculate. There was nothing rigid in their approach to information.

The *ncyeem ingesh*, "songs of the nature spirits," praise the monarchy. One song was composed to glorify each king. One, in honor of the royal mothers, lists all of their names, or at least purports to do so. Others are more general. The songs are learned by rote and taught to the wives of kings by a female official of the harem. No variants were found, and the oldest songs claim to go back to the reign of Shyaam. No songs are extant for four kings, although no pattern of systematic amnesia can be detected from this. Since most songs consist of allusions, often in the shape of lists of personal and place names, and the explanation of the allusions is not a part of the teaching itself, it is difficult to use them. Another set, the songs that are only performed within the palace during the night of the full moon, could unfortunately not be obtained. I was told they did not contain any historical material, but at the least they would be truly useful in a study of Kuba cosmology.[19]

Another type of song, the *ncok*, has been transmitted only haphazardly. These songs constitute an art form found only at the court. The only occasion on which they were hummed regularly in 1953-56 was when dancers donned their masks and costumes in the wings. Only one such song from before 1900 contained specific historical information.[20] The remaining older ncok, although at times gems of symbolism, were very general and were sometimes unexplained.

I have used very few sayings or proverbs (*nkwoon*). In regard to mottoes or praise names (*shoosh*), clan mottoes were noted in all the clan sections of the country, and the variations, which can be considerable, were charted for each of them. They were used primarily to determine whether or not clan sections with the same clan name belonged to the same clan or not. By and large clan mottoes contain much less information than the praise names attached to the names of people, places, titles, objects, and groups. Despite the fact that their transmission is rather haphazard and that interpolations occur easily, those that are linked to famous names from the period of Kuba origins, or those attached to ethnic or regional names, were rather often recited. Some yielded valuable data. Those dealing with the royal capitals, which were claimed to have been composed by the kings who founded the capitals, have all been published, as well as those associated with the names of rulers. In general, though, the problems of interpretation were as difficult as they were for songs.[21]

I collected lists of place names, in many variants.[22] I also gathered lists of kings and their genealogies and some of the lists of chiefs or successive incumbents of a given title. Many place names appearing in village histories were also collected, but most village histories go back only a century or so, unless the village was a unit independent of a chiefdom or was a chiefdom in its own right.[23] In those cases, all the data were gathered and published.[24]

A list of persons usually was part of a narrative. But the royal genealogy and a record of the names of the mothers of kings were learned by rote; any candidate king had to know the first while the second was entrusted to the mwaaddy.[25] Since the king steadfastly refused to recite his genealogy for me, I do not know what form it took. Lists of place names were a standard literary form, however, and to judge by the performance of an officeholder who reeled off the list of her predecessors, some lists of persons may also have been a similar literary form.

Most traditions are narratives (*ncik*; *abol ncik*, "to hit a story," *abok ncik*, "to throw a story," to tell a story; *abok* plus a noun is also used for "to think"). Some of them are quite short. Within the corpus of narratives with a historical intent, dynastic tales, village tales, clan tales, judicial precedents, personal reminiscences, and etiological tales are easy to spot. A group of tales about the most remote past within the dynastic corpus belongs in reality to a different genre altogether. Here a cosmology is expounded. So I have dubbed them tales of genesis, or myths.[26] The latter term, however, is so ambiguous that I use it sparingly here.

All of the genres enumerated (with the exception of etiological tales) are fostered by the institution to which they refer and are the official, authoritative record invoked by that institution. With regard to other institutions they may be unofficial, such as a family tradition impinging on a chiefdom's history. Narratives are the single most important corpus of traditions used. The most precious among them are the royal traditions and those that all central Kuba hold in common.

A set of questions peculiar to these sources, especially the dynastic accounts, arises. How in the first place was the *selection* made about events to be remembered and others to be forgotten? An analysis of the extant corpus provides some clues. For the most part, political events dealing with succession, war, law, administration, and the royal personality were remembered. Traditions about later kings help us to see the effect of such selections. For example, a real event during the campaign of a king in 1908 is remembered as an act of magic on his part: while campaigning, he managed to find quarters for all his men in a single house.[27] The essence of the story is no longer the campaign but the magic feat, whatever may have prompted it. Moreover, not all data pertaining to the topics considered suitable were retained. Otherwise the traditions would no doubt be much fuller than they are. Unlike the case of Madagascar,[28] no records written (or dictated) by Kuba themselves exist from before the time when foreigners jotted the traditions down, leaving us with the scanty transcriptions of 1885, 1892, 1905, and 1908 to offer a hint as to the shape of these traditions in the nineteenth century. What was this shape? When, how, and by whom were they told? Was each anecdote separate, as an analysis of the texts suggests, or were all data about a single reign told together? What were the finer criteria of selection?

The practice observed in the 1950s and the rather vague annotations that date from 1908 and 1921[29] seem to indicate that dynastic tradition was told in front of an audience of notables, and could only be performed after the notables, in a private conference, had agreed on the content—the practice of kuum, mentioned before. The political impact of a tale was carefully weighed, at least in the 1950s, when this was indeed necessary in view of the reaction of Belgian administrators to traditions. In case of disagreement, each party offered its own variant. Thus, in 1956 I received a version by a Ngongo chief and then another one by his council. The crucial difference dealt with the identity of one half of the ruling clan. The version of the notables implied that the chief was illegitimate. This sort of manipulation could affect the attribution of achievements to certain clans rather than others, or even alter the toponyms involved in a text about lands, but could leave the rest of the account fairly intact. One may think of kuum as a conservative force since it embodies a minimum consensus. This type of tale was clearly not told for the pure enjoyment of the listeners.

But were there other forces which could alter accounts that had been guaranteed by kuum? For the traditions of genesis, certainly. Newly available information seems to have cheerfully been fitted in when it rounded off an existing theme. This could not have been done in council first. Private storytellers, the bulaam, must have preceded official alteration.

The mwaaddy supposedly kept all dynastic tradition. Moreover, at the installation of every king the muyum, who had his own facsimile court and was the keeper of the national charm, recited the tradition.[30] I have an account by the muyum in 1953. He recited his data alone, without kuum. But is this single account typical for the genre? Another official account was the one the king himself recited at one point during his coronation ritual. This has been taped and published.[31] Very similar in structure and importance to an account given to Frobenius in 1905 by a king's son, it consists of strings of names: "We came from x, went to y," etc.; "B succeeded A and founded capital x with praise name such and such." The pattern is quite clear and is quite similar to that of the muyum and to official chiefdom or village histories, except that most praise names were omitted for the histories, at least by the 1950s. Both the muyum's and the royal account included a few crucial anecdotes in such a way that the whole story was summarized in a sentence or two. The most important anecdote concerns creation of kingship. Longer versions of it from 1885, 1908, 1953, and 1956 are extant but are not present in the dynastic account of 1905 and one of 1953. So the long story was not part of the official presentation. Like any other tale, the longer version was told under the sheds of weavers and smiths by individuals or around the fire in the nuclear family.

Although direct proof is absent, I think that all anecdotes about kings and chiefs have been preserved in this way. Their detail was not official, and they could be embellished by new twists that could spring from the fruitful imagination of a performer or from data brought in from the outside. As it happens, few parts of the dynastic history show evidence of having been even reasonably long narratives. There was therefore limited scope for new twists or further embroidery, with a few exceptions: the tales of genesis, details concerning the choice of the first king, and the adventures of King Shyaam [1] are patent cases. Here we find the marks of the bulaam. The more they knew, the wiser and the more prestigious they were deemed. And so, as performers they spun their tales out. Unfortunately, since the greatest prestige seems to have stemmed from remembering the most names, I suspect that literally hundreds of names in Kuba tradition are spurious and that one should not restrict one's suspicions to a few embellishments of anecdotes here or there. A thorough and comparative critique does help locate gratuitous additions, but certainty about what was added and what is "genuine" is impossible to achieve. We have only a vague idea concerning the style of tradition and its transmission in the nineteenth century, and we must be aware that bulaam could best further their own prestige by looking for more data, preferably genuine. So they have preserved a large corpus of mottoes and other materials, most of which is genuine.

Foreign traditions were freely fused within the framework of preexisting traditional plots when they fitted. The proof of this comes in Kuba traditions of origin. Since the Kuba were in close contact with the Luso-African trade sphere by 1850 at the latest—perhaps actually a century earlier—they had enough foreign stories to choose from, whether these were of Imbangala, Luba, Lunda, or even Ovimbundu origin. And they did. Thus, the mysterious Kash aKol ancestor in the mythical genealogy of the Bieeng, Kel, and Ngongo is nothing but Kakashi Kakulu, "the old little woman" from Luba tales.[32] The Ngongo are probably connected with her because Kol is a name for the Sankuru. The other two are linked to her because Kash aKol stories were first borrowed in Kel and Bieeng territory.

Add to this the undeniable facts that all narrative material is structured by the mind so it can be remembered and that memory either streamlines or tends to symbolize[33] and the full extent of the exegetic problem becomes clear. But it is equally clear that the older narratives are more susceptible to these forces simply because they have been recounted more often over a longer period. Even so, the streamlining or symbolizing tendencies of memory do not necessarily falsify the account, although they are selective and do change emphasis. In practice it turns out that it is not so difficult to analyze most traditions from now back to Shyaam—that is, to the seventeenth century. The anecdotal form, often a terse expression, has preserved many a datum from literary distortion. For the period from Shyaam to now, the tales of wonderful happenings have been those most altered, and even some of these seem to have assumed a pithy, anecdotal, matter-of-fact form as well, such as the one that claims that King Kot aMbweeky II [14], who died in 1896, was a great magician and could make a bell float in the air! How the material has been handled will be evident to the reader by comparing Chapter Four with the succeeding elaborations. Chapters Three, Five, and Six set forth the material antedating Shyaam, all the way back to "creation."

Beyond the tales with historical intent there is a vast corpus of literature not tied to history at all: it is art and wisdom and entertainment dealing with the adventures of men, ghosts, animals, and spirits, and even abstract characters such as Wise Man. Insofar as these creations are handed down through time, they too can be historical sources. The difficulty lies in the chronology, for one does not know at what time period the stories originated. Sometimes they describe customs that died out in the colonial period, and the historian can therefore ascribe them to some period before 1900 but cannot tie them to any particular time. At best, one can use the clues in a story such as that of the slave who bought his freedom by trading for his master in camwood, ivory, and cowries, which dates it to a time when all of these commodities were available in quantity, presumably in the second half of the nineteenth century. But every time the tale was performed it was a "new" production and may have fused new and old elements together much more freely than any intended historical tale would, or any historian would wish. Such sources do tell us a great deal about the situation toward the end of the nineteenth century. And because they portray situations and do not describe change, they differ significantly from strict historical narratives.

The oral data were collected after a general social study of the Bushoong was well underway.[34] All the historical traditions about ethnic groups, chiefdoms, villages, and clan sections were gathered for the whole realm. Other research was more concentrated among the Bushoong and their immediate neighbors. Here most, if not all, the bulaam were interviewed, sometimes over many sessions. Material limitations prevented this research from being carried out over the whole country. Consequently, there still are, especially outside the Bushoong chiefdom, many historical traditions left to be gathered, although most of them relate to the nineteenth century.

As for oral literature in general, samples were taken only for each genre. I gathered perhaps three hundred proverbs or sayings out of a probably five thousand, and a similar number of tales out of a corpus probably just as large, and so on for each genre. All of this collection, with a few exceptions, came from the capital. There certainly remains much more information to be culled from oral literature.

Testimonies were taken down in longhand except for one, the official royal version, which could be taped. Trained Kuba assistants collected most of the village and clan-section histories (1,935 clan-section testimonies alone); I gathered all the others. Originating from 226 major informants, the traditions number over a thousand, excluding variants, and were written down by me in 1953, 1954, and 1956.[35]

We are now ready to look at the content of these traditions. Chapter Three deals with the myths of genesis, ending when the Kuba arrived in the territory where they live now. The fourth chapter tells the story from that time onward.

Chapter 3

Kuba Genesis

A striking aspect of Kuba mythology is that within it many variants live side-by-side.[1] Even to account for the origin of man there are different narratives that form a welter of tales and explanations. The Kuba hold these tales and other myths to be true—in other words, there is a consensus concerning them. Each of the myths offered is accepted, but acceptance of one does not necessarily exclude some of the others. These tales are viewed by the Kuba as not only historical in nature: above all they are the equivalent of scientific or philosophical speculation, a manifestation of Kuba thought.

Among the tales of genesis three sets can be distinguished: those dealing with the creation of the world and of man; genealogies, which deal with a similar theme by explaining how today's ethnic groups are related to each other; and tales dealing with the place of origin and migration to the country now inhabited.

A detailed presentation and discussion of the contents of these tales would pertain more to a study of cosmology than of history. Yet to the Kuba this *is* history, and the tales must therefore be briefly described in order to show why these traditions are not valid for a reconstruction of the distant past, and to demonstrate the attitude toward history that pervades all Kuba historical accounts.

Creation Stories

No fewer than seven myths of creation can be distinguished. In the first, Mboom, also called Mboomaash or Mboomyeec, created the world and mankind either by vomiting or by giving names in thought or utterance.[2] Eighteen such children appeared, including Heaven, Earth, Sand of the River, Sword, Stone, and River Kasai.[3] In daily parlance these creations are still recognized by adding the name Mboom to the word for them: e.g., Kosh aMboom, "parrot of Mboom."

This feature recalls a second myth of origin, for a number of other items are known as "*x* of Ngaan" and are collectively referred to as "the bad things of Ngaan." No one explains why they are "bad." In this myth—and historically it may be older than the previous one—Mboom and Ngaan were cocreators, and the products of each are opposed to those of the other. Ngaan's creatures include chthonic animals and animals related to the water, such as the snake, the tortoise, the crocodile, the hippopotamus, and the iguana. They also include, however, mysterious Siamese twins who had no articulations and who are described as "all rubbery." Their names, Kop aNgaan and Nyony aNgaan, occur also in several praise names, where they act of a kind of fate.[4] Kash aKol, the Kuba transposition of the Luba name Kakashi Kakulu, "the old little woman,"[5] a trickster, is reckoned to be a creature of Ngaan. Among the Luba and Kaniok she also acts as a kind of fate, which gives us a rare glimpse of borrowing from other cosmologies. Mboom and Ngaan were both thought to be kings, each ruling one half of the original world, thus creating the division of villages into right and left parts.[6] But they quarreled over a woman of Ngaan's and left the place of creation. Mboom went to heaven and Ngaan sank underwater. Only then did Ngaan create the "bad things of Ngaan," because he had been slighted.[7] In both these stories the first man, Woot [A], [8] is often mentioned as a creation of Mboom. According to some he even received the power of Mboom's word to continue the creation.

A third story tells about Imbidinginy, "the round thing," perhaps the first calabash. It was androgynous.[9] The gourd broke open and in so doing produced mankind. This narrative is specifically tied to the origin of all mankind, and so is the fourth myth, first recorded in 1892, which held that the first man and woman were let down from the skies by a rope. After they untied themselves the rope was drawn back up. By the 1950s this was given as the origin of a single clan section only, and the rope was described as the thread of a spider, a widespread motif.[10]

A fifth tale revolves around the primeval marsh or water, Shoongl amaash, often linked to Imbidinginy.[11] The round thing created the marsh, which in turn begat Mboomyeec (or, in a variant form, Mboomyeec was a brother of the marsh). This pairs Mboom again with water, just as he is paired with Ngaan in the second myth. The myth is original only in the new name and the stress on primeval water. This myth is even more widely known than the previous stories, and the name recurs in genealogies of origin, especially in those of the Ngongo and the Shoowa along the Sankuru.

A sixth version calls the creator Ncyeem apoong.[12] He created through the power of his word, or by creating Imbidinginy. He began by taking a rolled-up mat and flinging it through the void so that it unrolled and floated at an angle that produced upstream and downstream. This was the image of the earth held by the Kuba. Then he spoke "the things of the world" and the first man, Woot.

In a seventh version, Mboom or the original water had nine children, all called Woot, who in turn created the world. They were, apparently in order of appearance: Woot the ocean; Woot the digger, who dug riverbeds and trenches and threw up hills; Woot the flowing, who made rivers flow;[13] Woot

who created the woods and savannas; Woot who created the leaves; Woot who
created the stones; Woot the sculptor, who made people out of wooden balls;
Woot the inventor of all prickly things such as fish, thorns, and paddles; and
Woot the sharpener, who first gave an edge to pointed things. Death came to
the world when a quarrel between the last two Woots led to the demise of one
of them by the use of a sharpened point. As the archaic character of some of
the names reveals, part of this genesis myth is certainly old, whether or not an
influence from Christian Genesis has been imposed upon it.[14]

Combinations of all those sets occur, which is not surprising, since borrowing and rearranging these matters is freely accepted among the Kuba. In fact,
this is how they speculate about the world, man, the supernatural, and origins.
One example suffices to show how freely borrowing could occur: by 1956 the
story of Eve's creation from Adam's rib was part of the genesis story of at
least one informant, although the names were different.[15]

The northwestern Mongo as well as the central and southwestern Mongo
groups call the creator Mboomba or Mbombianda, Mboomb'iwanda or
Mboomba ibanda, and Mbomb'ikopi: "Lord from whom the world derives its
sustenance."[16] Ncyeem apoong is clearly akin to Nzambi mpungu, known
among the Kongo since the first written records, in the fifteenth century.[17]
Given its distribution to the west of the Kuba, it is likely to have been a later
introduction than the other names, but this does not mean that the myth about
the rolled-up mat itself came from the same direction. Imbidinginy and
Shoongl amaash (Shongl, Shodiky amaash) have been found so far only
among the Kuba. Imbidinginy is linked to Mongo words and has a connotation of chaos; the variability of the second name is unusual, except for the
maash ("water") part.[18] The name may have been misunderstood and forgotten; the variants certainly indicate a fuzzy transmission. One sees only that
water figured prominently, as it does in the first cycle. As for the last myth, its
terminology is all Mongo and therefore archaic in Bushoong, with the possible exception of the name Woot.[19] Since Ngaan also is connected with water
in its other Bushoong meanings ("water put into a container for poison during
the poison ordeal," and archaic "crocodile"[20]) except in the meaning "village, camp," the myth of Mboom and Ngaan may also be old. In fact their
duality may even go back to the familiar one among the Mongo between
landsmen and water people. In short, many elements of all of these myths may
have a respectable antiquity in Kuba thought, whereas others may have been
invented or borrowed or fitted in throughout their history. In either case they
testify to the Kuba interest in the past.

Mythical Genealogies

Genealogies are the product of thought concerning the origin of mankind
and even more of the different sorts of men. The first man for the central Kuba

was Woot. For the Kel, Bieeng, and Ngongo, a woman, Kol, is an ancestor but not the primeval person in all versions. In genealogical logic she may be a back-formation of Kash aKol, whom we have already met. Double Kuba names usually are a personal name followed by the matronymic. Kol, in Kash aKol, would be the mother of Kash. She herself is then seen as a daughter of the creator. The Maluk claim a man, Itoc,[21] who appears also among the Ngongo and Mbeengi. The Shoowa mention a man—Shengdy, Shaangl aMweel, Selenge or Shelyeng, Shengl, and, in Frobenius' notation, Iselenge.[22] The Ngongo know of a woman, Shoringi or Sholoonga,[23] who may be related. A Shoowa name, Shyengl, daughter of an androgynous person, may be added to this list, and reminds one of Shodik or Shoongl amaash, already mentioned. These names occur in genealogies, and some of the doublets occur in a single genealogy, indicating that a desire to multiply the names, and not just faulty transmission, may be involved—the more names that one remembers from the time of creation, the more prestige one acquires. There is, however, no way of determining whether or not all the names of the type Shengdy are variants of a single name, nor can its meaning be detected at present.

These mythical genealogies can be complicated structures involving all manner of names. They are so constructed that the degree of relationship between different Kuba ethnic groups as perceived by the informants is indicated by a corresponding genealogical proximity. At the same time, the genealogies sometimes express the creation of mankind and its evolution from Woot in a kind of shorthand. Woot is seen almost everywhere as the first culture hero, if not the first man.[24] When a simple genealogy wants to express that the Ngongo and Songo Meno (i.e., Mongo from the Sankuru) are more closely related to each other than either is to the Europeans and the Bushoong, it describes them as children of a single ancestress. In strong contrast to this type of genealogy stands that of the Coofa, which knows of no variants and places these patrilineal Luba immigrants in the framework of a segmentary lineage system outside the Kuba realm by indicating a straightforward father-son succession, starting from the creator. Collaterals are not indicated, although those who care to ask will soon find out that these exist and are ancestors to other Luba (Lulua) groups.[25]

In the simplest Kuba genealogy, a creator begot the first chief of a particular Kuba ethnic group.[26] Each ethnic group claims such a founder. All the central and peripheral groups acknowledge Woot as a culture hero and fit him in somewhere, for to be a Kuba is to be a child of Woot. But among the central Kuba, the ethnic founders are the children whom Woot begot in incest with his sister, Mweel. An exception to this is the Bulaang, who are descended from his sister's son—everyone agreeing by this that they were formed late as an ethnic group, after they split off from the Bieeng. The Bieeng, the peripheral groups, and the Kete and Coofa do not claim any *necessary* link with Woot at all. Since not all members of an ethnic group agreed on the founding genealogy (the Coofa excepted), the following list gives the various names of founders according to testimony by members of each of these ethnic groups.

Founders of the Kuba Ethnic Groups

Bushoong
   The first three kings: Nyimiloong, Diambaan, and Miingambeengl (titled *iyol ibaan*, "their captain of war").[27]
Ngeende
   Ishweem (most often a girl) or Mboomiloong.
   Bodimbeeng (Bodimbeeny). His or her child, Ncum aBodimbeeng or Shaakopy aBodimbeeng, is a later but very well-known chief and eponym for Ngeende in poetry.[28]
Bulaang
   Mium; sometimes Byash aKoy.[29]
Pyaang
   Bit aNgom, alias Pyeem Bulaam.
   Kan (rare; connection with Kan clan?).[30]
Pyaang Ibaam
   Mweesh amwaan, "the lucky child."[31]
Bieeng
   Idim aKol, daughter of Kol aMboom, daughter of Mboom.[32]
Kel
   Kash aKol, daughter of Kol aMboom or Mweel. This is a minority opinion: central Kuba migration myths tend to equate all people downstream with children of Mweel and all those upstream with children of Woot.[33]
Ngongo
   Kol aMboom or Kash aKol.[34]
   Etoci.[35]
Ngoombe Itu
   Itoc.
   Woot the sharpener (one of the nine Woots).[36]
Maluk
   Itoc. (Mweel, a sister of Kol, could be an ultimate ancestress, but the people all descend from Itoc.)[37]
Mbeengi
   The founder came from the capital of Etontsi (Itoci).[38]
Shoowa
   Mweelu (Mweel), in two chiefdoms. Also Iweel or Mweelu muKol; also Selenge (Shelyeng, Shengdy), in two chiefdoms; and also Iselenge.[39]

Idiing
Mweel and her son, Shelyeng.[40]
Kete
Loona, or Loon for Poopo groups.[41]
Coofa
Makanda.

Of special interest are Itoci, who is claimed by peoples along the Sankuru upstream from the mouth of the Labody, and Selenge, who occurs downstream. Itoci is still an institution among the Nkucu and Ndengese, and the name refers there to an ancestral eponym as well. Selenge, however, has not yet been attested elsewhere. The woman Kol is found all along the periphery, especially among the Bieeng, Kel, Ngongo, and even the Maluk and Shoowa. Given that the name Kash aKol represents a borrowing from Luba, it is likely that Kol, corresponding to the Luba *kulu*, "old," also is a Kuba back-formation with the implicit meaning "founder."

Legends of Origin and Migration

Kuba tales of origin deal in essence with two topics. The first one centers around the description of their original home, implicitly the original home of all mankind, and around the events that brought about a migration. The second concerns this migration, listing the places and way stations. The direction of this movement always is conceived of as from downstream to upstream, and the means is always by canoe. It is only logical, then, that the ancestral home lay near the widest expanse of water conceivable. So engrained is the pattern of migration that Wharton translated *to ngel*, "from downstream," as "the great emigration." This phrase was the answer that he stated was given to his question, Whence came the Bakuba? The tenacity of the concept of travel by water in the collective representations about migration is shown by the mention of traveling by dugout canoe even when a list of rivers crossed by the migrants is given. This aspect is beautifully expressed by the symbol of national unity kept by the muyum: a paddle on which all the different ethnic patterns of scarification are carved.[42]

Among the central Kuba the place of origin involves two separate sets of actors. The most common version involves Woot and his sister, Mweel. Woot was stricken with leprosy and had to leave the primeval village. His sister went with him to live in the forest. Incest occurred and children were born. After the healing of Woot they returned and brought the children with them. No questions were asked until the pygmies told the story of the incestuous relationship. Woot was so ashamed that he fled upstream.[43] He was furious, though, and caused the primeval village, Buyengl, to burn to ashes and the streams to "break open." The game animals who had been companions of man in this earthly paradise fled into the bush. (Poop [a Kete name], Woot's wife, stumbled against a burnt tree stump while fleeing, felt a soothing tickling in the wound, and thus discovered salt.) Woot took the sun with him, plunging the world into darkness. A spell lay on the country, blanketed in perpetual night. Mweel had to send messengers twice before he would restore light and fertility to the country.[44]

A variant was recorded in 1905 from the Idiing area by Frobenius, who glossed Iselenge as the moon and Ooto as the sun.

Iselenge [Shelyeng] and Ooto were children of one mother. They migrated with many people and came in the country between the Lulua and the Sadi [Kasai]. They all passed the night in a huge house. Iselenge and Ooto slept on the floor, each on his side. At night Ooto crossed and slept with Iselenge. A rat came out of the bush and said to Ooto: "You are a chief; your sister is a chief. How can you sleep with your sister as a chief?" Ooto said: "I have no other woman." The rat: "That was evil of you."

Iselenge stayed there. Ooto, however, went with people in the area of the Bapende. All the people of Iselenge became ill in the arms and legs and many died. That is why Iselenge sent the fly, the dog, and the turtle to call Ooto back. Ooto sent word: "I will come tomorrow." But the next day Ooto did not come. Ooto did not come for a week. Then Iselenge sent the dog again to Ooto. Ooto sent word: "I will come tomorrow when the cuckoo sings." And the next day Ooto came and every one became healthy.[45]

Clearly the variant is a less elaborate version of the Kuba tradition, which was recorded later. For instance, in other versions of the Kuba tale the dog, the tortoise, and the fly were refused the sun because they had stolen Woot's meat, wine, and tobacco—obviously a later addition, since tobacco has been cultivated here only since the seventeenth century. Then the woodborer was sent to Woot. The spell was broken when the morning birds could again call forth the sun, for Woot's spell had lain on them. Nevertheless Frobenius captured the rationale for the incest that is still given during the boys' initiation ritual: "there was no other woman." When other women became available, the "women that God gave us [mothers, sisters]" became taboo and had to be exchanged. This variant is merely given here as an illustration. Its two paragraphs correspond to two stories, which can be linked or separated in other cases.

Before Woot left, he wanted to leave the chieftainship to his favorite son, the ancestor of the Ngeende. So he put the emblems in an old, tattered basket, which he was to hand over to the first person he met on the morning of his flight. A pygmy had noticed the basket and told the ancestor of the Bushoong to come first. Hence he was the one to receive kingship. Not surprisingly, in the Bieeng version it was the Bieeng ancestor who received it.[46]

Woot did not depart alone, but took emigrants with him. His route over hills and rivers—always upstream and by canoe—is still enacted during the boys' initiation as an event in mythical time.[47] On his way he created the landscape, plants, and animals; and he left people along the route. Before leaving them he twisted and poured a charm on their tongues, and they began to speak other languages. Pursued by Mweel and her companions (who later became the central Kuba), he blocked the road first by leaving behind him the bodies of a lazy man and of a witch, and later by dropping huge boulders in the river to prevent pursuit. He then disappeared in the east, toward the rising sun; one source calls this direction *Taangwa dika.*[48] Woot never died. Mweel abandoned the pursuit, and the Kuba in turn settled on their land while Mweel disappeared into the waters of what probably can be identified as the Kasai River.[49]

In an obviously later variant of this tale, Woot and Mweel planted bamboo thickets between the primeval water and the land in order to keep the Europeans separated from the Africans. But the Europeans had excellent knives and cut through the bamboo, whereupon Woot, Mweel, and the people fled, sometimes after a battle lost, sometimes not. This story is completely incompatible with the first account of Woot's travels. Its relevance is to attribute the motive for the migration—there had to be a motive—to another cause: the incompatibility of Europeans and Africans.[50] It is an instance of speculation about the world and how this is fitted into a larger mythical framework of existing theory about the origin of mankind.

A complete alternative myth, a second cycle, exists, however. According to it the first people lived along the shores of the primeval water. Shodiky amaash (of the water), the mother of all people, and Bwiilangady, the father, always lived in the sea. The children would venture out to play on the beach, and ultimately their father told them to stay on land. So they remained to play on the hill Ibaang and buried their dead in Iyuushdy, "the flowing down of the water." The deceased returned to the ocean, where they continued to exist as doubles of the living. The first village was NcaaMatudy, the sea Mbup, and the land Mput.[51] This myth echoes the widespread conviction that after death a person returns, often in the form of a grasshopper, to a place located as far downstream as possible.

In this cycle another motive for the migration is used: the war between Europeans and Africans—a war triggered by the greed and the will to dominate of the Europeans, a telling comment on how the Kuba perceived Europeans in the nineteenth century, when the tale was created. Explanations are added as to why people are black. All people originally were white, but the leader of the Europeans made magic and turned people black, or, in another version, the Africans turned black to disguise themselves from the Europeans, a comment on the presumed inability of the Europeans to recognize African faces. Some informants rejected these tales and argued that blacks simply became black as a result of the sun's action.[52] Whether this is influenced by European popular beliefs or not does not matter; the point is that it shows again how speculation is expressed in myth. The theme of Noah's curse on his sons is also used to explain why Africans are black.[53]

The war with the white men—called Albinos, Whites, Portuguese, or even Imbangala—was called the War of the Throwing Knives (though one informant claims the term used refers to the swords of the Europeans), or the War of the Imbangala. They fought with knives, or, as a variant, whites and Africans sat back to back and threw sand or water on each other. The throwing produced the sound *puu, puu, puu*, and a Ngeende song recalls the war as "the war of *puuku puuku, iyele*." The tale has authentic details. The whites wore armor and helmets, were shod in leather or bark, rode on horses, wore several layers of clothes, and had straight swords not unlike the royal sword. The terms Mbup and Mput are used in this tradition. Mbup means the ocean and Mput is widely referred to as Portugal.[54] One informant even added anachronistic steamboats and white women to it. And yet the tradition is untrustworthy.

If these traditions are really old, they imply that the central Kuba lived at one time near the kingdom of Kongo and that the war could have been fought with the Imbangala. But the Imbangala were not near the Kwango at all before about 1620, and on the grounds of general Kuba chronology a date so late for a Kuba presence in that area is impossible.[55] The Kuba must have borrowed the stories about the Europeans from traders in the west, and in the earlier nineteenth century the Imbangala were among the first such traders. They may well have told such stories in the markets of the middle Kasai (Mai Munene), where the Kuba went to trade, and at home the traders related it all under the heading "Imbangala wars." Some of the data are quite old, as indicated by the references to armor and helmets.[56] Why were these tales incorporated? Because they fitted well in the generally accepted framework of the Kuba collective theory of the origins of mankind.

But if such data were borrowed from peoples so far to the west, it is quite likely that the story of the drunken king (Noah) and the description of the destruction of paradise, as well as the discovery of salt by a wife turning back to see the primeval town burn, also stem from there. Missionary teachings in lower Zaire and Angola could well have reached the Kuba in such forms. If so, the tales would have become common with the intensive missionary efforts after 1640 and would have reached the Kuba via the traders sometime later.

Is this whole war then to be dismissed as a recent addition to a seemingly old conception about the cradle of mankind? That conclusion may be rash. One element, the throwing knife, is undoubtedly old.[57] A "war of the throwing knives" may well have occurred in the dim past of the ancestors of the central Kuba, or the ancestors may have heard a story relating to the knives and their use north of the equatorial forest. The term *poom*, used to describe Europeans, is probably connected with *pombeiro* and *mpumbu*, the market at Okanga or at Malebo Pool, even though Poom is the name given by at least one source for a war between the Cwa and the Kuba ancestors. But then that war is also called by several other names that suggest a savanna north of the Sankuru.[58] Mput, which now means Portugal in the whole of western Zaire, is used in Yans traditions with the meaning of "country of origin, the man's side." The term, I believe, is indeed derived from the west but replaced the notion of "original home." Its praise name indicates this:

> I go to Mput,
> wish of my mother,
> downstream of the river.
>
> I go to Mput,
> to eat the plantains of Mput,
> downstream of the river.

The plantains are described as a major food in ancestral times. And in the same set of tales the Kel and the Bushoong remember that they wore bark cloth—as they still do in mourning—in their ancestral homes. Obviously, older notions have been transferred under the new name Mput.[59]

The second cycle, then, I take to antedate the introduction of certain European elements. Those elements were introduced because they fitted the myth. The original myth recognized a war as a reason for leaving the cradle of people, a war having to do with throwing knives and *perhaps* with the Cwa, and it knew about the older staple food, the plantain, and the old dress, bark cloth.

The original water itself in both cycles was called NcaaMatudy, Ipuk, or Ndoong Takut, according to the tales of the central Kuba. The water was "the river that exhausts a bird [that wants to cross it]," or simply "the big river." The first expression refers to a widespread cliché, which, among the Tetela for example, is used to identify the Zaire River at the mouth of the Lomami River. It is also a more general Mongo motif. The water is also called Mbup or Mbu, a term which traders probably brought to the country. Mbup is often described as including the ocean beach, tides, and waves. All these details about the primeval water filled out and "proved" the correctness of the original theory, so they were incorporated.[60] There are many other names for the water, however, and in descriptions among peoples along the Sankuru it is added that the original water was not flowing but turning in circles. This, I believe, was the old conception: at the extreme downstream point, water could not flow farther and, as flowing is a characteristic of water per se, it had to turn in circles. Names associated with circling primeval water are the

Matudy River, Lubirik (Lubirika, Imbirik), and Etemeri (Itemberi, Etembere); Matudy is closely linked to the central Kuba traditions.[61]

These are not the only places associated with origin "before the migrations." The Shoowa mention Bolongo Mpo and Nsanga Lubangu. The first is well known among the southern Mongo as a prestigious place where chiefly power was divided when this group split off from the other Mongo. The second is given as their ancestral home *upstream* by all the Luba of Kasai, including most of the Kete.[62] These prestigious place names have been borrowed. One northwestern group of clans consistently gives Me, while other names occur but once—such as Mboncoongo, the Okooncola River, or Posh.[63] Only more research north of the Sankuru will determine whether these names too are stereotypes, and if so, of what.

Migration narratives list names of various places along the way: villages founded or rivers crossed, or sometimes intercalary savannas where the migrants resided. Savanna "plains" are most often mentioned by those who claim to come from upstream, mostly the Kete and the Coofa, who in this follow a convention current among the Luba of Kasai. Cwa traditions either follow a pattern associated elsewhere with village or kinship tradition or copy the stories of their agricultural neighbors.

There are strong presumptions that informants attempted to make their lists as long as possible to bask in the admiration of their audience. They were not loath to borrow names. Perhaps the clearest illustration is the exploitation of a praise name for the Matudy River (Ncaa Matudy) among the central Kuba:[64] *Aloong katudy aKamany kapish, kody mapish,* or *aloong lamatut amamany mapish.* Some informants changed Loong Matudy and Kamany aPish into villages. *Maan amaan* (sand and sand), which occurs in the royal version as *Kashep kamaan amaan, kaka nyeeng,* "a little savanna of sand and sand [nothing but sand] and without reeds," a description of the ocean shores, is also used in this fashion.[65] Other names may have been invented in this way or in others: e.g., by transferring names of spirits to places and vice versa, since spirits are associated with places. The general confusion is illustrated by the king's public recital.[66] After Mbup, "the ocean," comes the primeval village on its shores. This is Nshyaang aMboom (the creator Mboom). Then Buyengl (the paradise that Woot fled) is mentioned, followed by the names of rivers and spirits. Then Woot returns to Buyengl, now apparently the first village, and following is a set of river names, among which Nshyaang aMboom occurs again. No geographical sense can be made out of this list of rivers, but the utterances about the last two contain complete praise names that involve other rivers in the vicinity of the present country, referring to the Kasai between the Sankuru and the mouth of the Lulua for one name and to the Loange for the other. The praise names make sense, but their sequence does not.

As might be expected, vast divergences exist among the tales of different informants, even among the central Kuba.[67] A version of genesis recorded by Frobenius, unpublished to date, is as follows.

Long, long, long ago there was no Lukengo [king]. There were many chiefs. This however is long, long, long, long ago (*kalle kallekallekallekalle*). Nimilongo came with his wife from the direction (20° right: i.e., NNE). They crossed the water Mbubba and settled then at Bolombo [the only post downstream from Bena Dibele on the Sankuru in 1905]. They left Bolombo and went to Bijengele. In Bijengele they settled. Bijengele was destroyed by fire without any (military) reason. Because of this they left Bijengele and came to Ipuku. In Ipuku a white man made war (!?) upon them. They fled and went to Yekka.

Nimilongo and his wife crossed the Sankuru. His wife was his sister, but she was also his wife. In Bolombo she gave him a child, a son Nimi, but Nimilongo died at Yekka. His wife gave Nimilongo (so the informant asserts contrary to all that follows) only one son. That was Nimi. Nimilongo died. Nimi dropped his name and called himself Yambamba [B]. Yambamba was the chief of the Bussonge (suddenly many people) at Yekka.

In those days white people came to Luidi [a commercial station on the Kasai near the confluence with the Lulua, founded c. 1891, existing in 1905] and so the people of Luidi came to Yekka and fought the Baschi Bussonge. Therefore the Baschi Bussonge left and went to Imenia. Yambambe had died at Yekka. His brother (!?) Mschumbo Matschamb [C] said: "I am the head of all." [The tale of the hammers and the anvils follows.][68]

The general impression left to the analyst by this indigestible welter of divergent tales is that only those place names can be trusted whose locale is still known—that is, those in the general vicinity of Kuba country. Names of rivers must be handled with extra caution because as they became known to the Kuba the names of any rivers "downstream" from the Kasai were readily inserted. None of these beyond the very last river crossed by the forebears of the Kuba can be trusted.

With this rule for a guide, the situation becomes clearer. All of the central Kuba claim to have originated from the Iyool savanna, south of the Sankuru and west of the lower Labody. Before that only the Bushoong claim to have crossed the Sankuru from the north, a tradition that is also widespread among the peripheral Kuba living along this river.

The reader may be surprised to note the absence of a structural analysis of the tales or even a commentary on the symbolism involved. This is not necessary to the purpose of the present work. I have demonstrated well enough which elements in all of this are credible and have expressed my conviction that active speculation about cosmology among the Kuba produced paradigms early on that were later fleshed out or altered to incorporate newly acquired relevant knowledge.

Immediate Kuba Origins

After mentioning the rivers crossed, the king in his recital went on to describe the Bushoong situation north of the Sankuru as follows.

Those who had arrived before us were the Ndengese. The Ndengese before us had not come for nothing. And when Lakoin had killed an elephant, the Bushoong said about that elephant: "Let us bring it to ... nyim [their king]." Itoc [*sic*] said: "Let us ..." The Ndengese said: "Let us bring it to ... Itoc." The Bushoong refused. They took the tusk and brought it to nyim.

The Ndengese said: "We leave you, you do not have nice customs. We go to follow Woot there where he went upstream." They followed Woot and we remained to follow them. We did settle at the edge of their village. The custom of the Ndengese had disturbed us and we did no longer agree well with them anymore and we returned from there, very far away. [Other data make clear there had been a battle in which the Ndengese were defeated by the eastern people, the Nkucu, probably in the lands of Bolongo Itoko.]

We arrived ... at Ngwel [*sic*], that plain of Ngwel over there. And when we arrived at Ngwel, when we were there, we were there with ... Nyimilong [chief]. Mingambengl took over and left. Nyimilong left us in the hands of Mancumashyaang. From the riverbank [of the Sankuru] we came with Mancumashyaang to Iyool.[69]

Others mention a battle at Ngweel or Pwoon, Pweeng, or Poongi between some Cwa and the Bushoong. The royal version implies that the Bushoong had in fact been tributary to the Ndengese and their chief, Itoci, since he was entitled to the royal tribute. This is confirmed by the praise poem of the Bushoong that starts out:

> The Pil, the people of the sun,
> They who wear raffia skirts and bark belts,
> The people who can curse,
> They are the warriors [*iyol*, a title] of Itoc.[70]

The name Lakoin is a Yajima title, so the king posits a close relationship between the Bushoong and these people. A major informant, Mbop Louis, added that each king went to the Lakoin of the Yajima to learn how long his reign would last. He always took the same route, crossing the Sankuru at Mbabaang, not far from its mouth.[71]

Still, the Bushoong are said to have followed the Ndengese, going *up-stream*, until something happened to make them turn back. The whole tale is not as fanciful as it might appear, for among the Nkucu groups Ohindu and Nkamba, just east of the Ndengese, there still are people known as Bosongo, or Bushoong. And the Ngongo clearly come from the same area.[72] Furthermore, when a king was to be crowned he sent messengers to Ndoong Ishey, the "home of Itoci," to get kaolin—white porcelain clay—for the ritual of installation. The Ndengese claimed this, as stated in a 1929 report from their administrator, and the king admitted as much, adding that a monarch sent for kaolin only when the existing stock was exhausted. The king also stated that the messengers then crossed the Sankuru at Kil aNcal and that Ndoong Ishey was not a special name, only the name for the crossing. They returned with a quantity of kaolin sufficient for several reigns. The Ndengese seemed to imply that it was the name of the capital of Itoci, which was placed by all informants near the Lokenye, well upstream from Dekese. To fetch kaolin from there meant to be inferior to whomever had inherited Itoci's rights. But the king justified the need for kaolin by the fact that the former abandoned villages of the Bushoong had once been located in that area.[73]

Certainly there was a connection between the Ndengese and the Bushoong. As late as 1974 the former claimed to have once been ruled by a single paramount called Itoci, and among the Yajima his paraphernalia are still kept.[74] The Ndengese version has it that during the great migration they too had crossed the Sankuru and defeated the local inhabitants, who sued for peace. Victory was celebrated, but during the celebration the victors were surprised and defeated by the "Kuba." In the colonial period *Itoci* were aristocrats among the Ndengese, the name being a title that could be bought and that brought with it certain rights such as wearing certain specified emblems. The title was linked to the "division of power" on the locally famous intercalary savanna Iji, in the northwest, from where the Ndengese claim to have come. Others held that the title was of Ngongo origin in the days when the Ngongo were still living north of the Sankuru in the Ohindu area.[75] The Ohindu recall the Ngongo as the first inhabitants of this area, not counting the Cwa, who are known to be autochthons of the whole forest. When the Ohindu mixed with the Ngongo on the savanna of Yumbi, north of the Sankuru, they exchanged some of their Nkucu ways for Ngongo customs among a population called Ulungu Ituku or Bolongo Itoko, which still lives near there, at Bolongo Itoko, far to the north of the Lokenye.[76] One must only add that all Kuba are called Bakongo by their northern neighbors, who do not distinguish between Bushoong and Ngongo. Some of the Ohindu reminiscences may therefore have involved ancestral Bushoong as well.

A common praise name for the Kuba king is "the great canoe in which the Diing and the Koong have crossed," or "the great river crossed by the Diing and the Koong."[77] The king is the river or the canoe, an image that often recurs; the Diing are the northern Bushoong (the *I* in Idiing is a prefix of locality); and the Koong are the Bushoong. All of this was definitely not invented during the 1920s as a ploy to deal with Belgian administrators. The kings were reticent about their northern connection, but could not deny it.

Their own praise name affirmed it, even though it remained either cryptic or unknown to the administrators. The only group among the central Kuba who denied any stay north of the Sankuru were the Bieeng, whose official tradition steadfastly maintained that they came from the Loange, in the west, where their chief at that time was Toci [Itoci]. The other central Kuba all stress that they originated from a place downstream, without comment about the Sankuru at all.[78]

The peripheral Kuba along the Sankuru all claim to have crossed from the other bank, and some Kete traditions affirm this. Among favorite Shoowa emigration clichés one finds *okap*, *bokap*, *ikap*, "the division,"reminiscent of *Bokapa ikopo*, "the division of the chieftainship," a universal southern and southwestern Mongo cliché. The least this shows is the prestige of the Mongo among the Shoowa. The Idiing situate the capital of Itoci upstream from Dekese. The Maluk claim to be fairly recent immigrants, and the Ngoombe are even more recent. They hold that a fraction of their group still lives along the Lokenye in the general area of that former capital of Itoci. The Bokila, a small group, stem from just across the river. The complicated Ngongo wanderings are placed mostly upstream, between the Sankuru and the Lokenye, and they mention Bolongo Itoko. Whether they merely borrowed the name from the Ohindu we do not know. If they did, they show great respect for their northern neighbors, a strange behavior since otherwise they hold them in low esteem. The Kel have no Mongo clichés, and their sites of migration lie on the south bank of the Kasai River, but not as far downstream even as the mouth of the Loange. In the same area one finds sites mentioned by the Ilebo and the Kayuweeng.

Obviously these traditions do not apply to all the central and peripheral Kuba people: they apply only to the ruling houses, and there are many of them. For these, Sheppard's summary of what he learned in 1892 stands: "From all the information I can gather, they migrated from the far North, crossed rivers and settled on the high table land."[79]

In the 1950s I believed that there had been little borrowing from the outside and that the references to Europeans and Imbangala in the traditions of origin indicated Kuba connections with them. So in a complicated compromise, I tried to reconcile the different versions.[80] Now there is no need for this. Kuba "origins" lie to the north. But which origins? For how many Kuba? Origins in which sense? Certainly not for all, since some clans or villages or groups claim to be autochthons.[81] The historian's concern is with society and culture, not with the physical ancestry of persons. When he talks about origins he must remind himself that he means antecedent situations of a particular society and culture.

Once the question is put in this fashion, the language affinity between

Mongo and Kuba becomes even more relevant. Language is the means of communication that transmits culture. Whether or not linguistic affinity implies that most of the population is also genetically related is not as important. Language certainly refers to the sources of culture and society. The Kuba languages are all essentially Mongo, except for Kete and Coofa, which are close to Luba. A southern Mongo origin for Kuba culture and society is therefore practically certain. Kuba distinctiveness grew out of a common, southern Mongo stock. The evidence from tradition that has been cited now confirms this view.

It permits us to say something more. The chiefs did not come alone. Indeed, the clans Ilyeeng and Iyeeng are specifically mentioned as having accompanied the first king, who was the warrior leader of Itoci.[82] All aristocratic clans in every chiefdom likewise claim that they came with their dynastic clan. A suspicious number of nine, eighteen, or twenty-seven such clans (multiples of nine) is found in each chiefdom. The claim may not be true for all of them; still, a great number of chiefs and followers were no doubt involved. A substantial part of the population may well have immigrated from beyond the Sankuru.[83] Indeed, immigration on the scale of infiltration continued right up to the 1950s.[84]

The Bushoong leader was not the first to cross; he was probably the last of the central Kuba to do so. The process has lasted for centuries—at least three, probably four or more, since it began long before King Shyaam [1] in the seventeenth century, and it was still going on in the 1950s. A gradual Mongo expansion southward carried people over the Sankuru in small numbers, village or hamlet after village or hamlet. They found places to occupy in a territory then sparsely populated by pygmoid hunters, the real autochthons, and by some Kete. Even some Cwa crossed the river from north to south. The movement was so slow and continuous that it must have seemed to the migrants that they were just making one more move, as every village does once in ten years on the average, when the lands nearby are exhausted. But gradually villages left their old territorial lands for new domains. Then one day either a chiefly settlement followed and claimed allegiance from the commoners who had preceded it, or a chiefly settlement set the example for others to follow, or one of the new settlements invoked old custom and established a chieftainship by imposing it on their fellow immigrants. These were processes that had occurred countless times north of the Sankuru as well. This is the picture, then, of a true population movement: slow as a glacier and as vast as a tidal wave.

In fact the process was so slow as to be almost unconscious. Political leaders excepted, there should be no memory of it. The only memorable aspects were the shifting claims over people and land. Even the political leaders would not remember for very long where their clan had once been. Only the most recent residences where they had exercised some political role would be remembered. Hence it is in fact normal not to find trustworthy or precise traditions about migrations except for the last stages before the migrant chiefs set foot on the territory of the kingdom.

The picture outlined above explains why we greet the migration routes proposed by such authors as Boelaert or Van der Kerken with skepticism.[85] They trace the Bushoong as Bosongo back to Bolongo Mpo, near Bomate, beyond Iji, and as far north as the Ruki near the present Mbandaka. The time span implied in such a long journey must be enormous, given the slow rate of movement. Much of the data are cosmological genealogies that do not reflect history but group relations and, perhaps, the wishes of the administration at the time of their collection. All mention the creator. One even has the eponymic Mongo and the two heroes of the famous Lianja epic, Lianja and his sister Nsongo, even though the southern Mongo do not know the epic. One cannot accept the premise that any genuine genealogy of so remote an antiquity would have survived for so long by people who were so little aware of their migration and had so little need for this type of genealogy.

But, it may be argued, perhaps the Kuba actually came from downstream. That would explain why they stress this in their cosmology, their perception and organization of space, and the like. After all, the Leele claim to come from upstream and associate space and cosmology with this claim. And they are likely to have come from upstream once they crossed the Lulua and the Kasai, moving from the present southern Kuba country or even farther south. The Luba Kasai claim to come from upstream but have not organized their customs around that claim; downstream is consequently their place of honor.[86]

Even if the Kuba collective memory had correctly retained the general movement of expansion, it would not help us much. For between the valleys of the Lokenye and the Sankuru, downstream is west, toward Lake Mayi Ndombe and the lower Kasai. But north of the Lokenye valley—where at least the Ngongo once lived—the rivers flow northwest to the lower Tshuapa and the Ruki. This is just what Boelaert and Van der Kerken postulated. And it is the route that links the southern and northwestern Mongo in the most direct and satisfactory way. One can even argue that the terms Mboom and Ngaan represent land people and water folk, just as those terms are opposed to one another among the more northwesterly Mongo. And the primeval water or marsh could even refer to the Ruki marshes, the greatest in all of Africa.[87]

All this is not impossible. But it remains speculation—and fruitless speculation, unless it can be proven or disproven on better grounds. At this distance in time, in space, and in vagueness of formulation, certainty cannot be achieved.

This chapter has shown that Kuba society and culture has its roots north of the Sankuru, that Kuba culture is an offshoot of southern Mongo cultures. How the amazingly different Kuba way of life grew out of the more pedestrian southern Mongo world is the theme of our story. The traditions telling it now follow.

Chapter 4

Tales about the Kings

Dynastic history as it is related by the Kuba traditional historians and more particularly by the bulaam of the Bushoong is presented in this chapter according to the chronological order of reigns. But no traditionalist would ever tell it in this way; to him the chronology does not matter. It is only in the special accounts of the king and the muyum that a framework for the whole past is given. The chronology adopted here is derived from those accounts and from lists requested by administrators in our century. The succession of leaders or rulers has been established from these data and has been confirmed in part by the royal genealogy, in part by a list of queen mothers conserved in a ncyeem ingesh song, and in part by the internal evidence of the matronymics.[1]

The ordinary bulaam, if he was sufficiently skilled, knew most of the data that have been woven together into a single narrative here. But he also would never relate them this way, because this was not the way traditions were handed down. He told anecdotes about king x or king y, following them up with other anecdotes about the same king or perhaps about another one if the tale reminded him of another anecdote. And he would tell them as a tale, a true tale, a tale complete in itself. He also knew certain sayings and obiter dicta relating to the past and might interject or explain them as he talked with other sages or when he was telling the story.

This chapter therefore summarizes many anecdotes in an order which the Kuba accept but which is not their own. Through summarizing, some of the flavor of the originals is lost, even though I have tried to preserve the character of storytelling. The whole forms a body of data that is the necessary starting point for any further elucidation of Kuba history. All efforts at interpreting early Kuba history must start from this corpus of oral traditions, and later chapters are mostly interpretations of data mentioned here.

My exposition, even here, does go beyond the traditions insofar as it is necessary to explain an allusion to some major development. Because such an allusion is often obvious to the Kuba listener, there is justification in providing a gloss. In some cases, however, I have gone even further. The discussions of the origins of the foreign king or of the muyum are instances in which the explanation presented here goes beyond the commentaries of most

47

traditional historians. This is necessary to pave the way for the analysis in later chapters. But I have kept this intrusion to a minimum, and what follows is mostly the point of view of the traditions.

After genesis and migration stories are completed, most central Kuba tell that their leaders competed on the Iyool plain and that the victor, a Bushoong, became the first *nyim*, or king. (The term king is used throughout this chapter even though, as I argue in Chapter Seven, the kings before Shyaam were only chiefs.) Beyond this each of the ethnic groups has its own traditions. The next highlight, however, is known all over the realm. It is the saga of King Shyaam [1], the great culture hero. With him a new period clearly begins: his reforms and those of his immediate successors establish the Kuba state. There follows a long span of time during which only snippets are known about successive kings; then clan, village, and personal histories begin, adding more detail to the events of the last century.

The pattern of oral history is fairly complex. A few names of chiefs, and even of clans, have survived from the indeterminate hiatus between the migrations and the competition at Iyool. The latter theme legitimizes the political order and hence is widespread. Its character as a political charter is demonstrated by the fact that it was the first oral tradition to be recorded by Wolf in 1885. After this event the list of kings falters and another hiatus occurs, ending only with the cycle of anecdotes about Shyaam. Furthermore, close analysis reveals that even for the period after Shyaam traditional specialists began to waver about the order of succession for certain kings or forgot their very existence. A third hiatus was clearly in the making. The data were written down just in time to prevent the opening of another chasm. These hiatuses in Kuba traditions conform to a pattern universally found in bodies of oral tradition.[2]

Structural gaps are even more pronounced in the chiefly histories of groups other than the Bushoong. After Iyool and the names of the founding ancestors, the next remembered chiefs are those who presided over the main divisions Pyaang, Ngeende, Bulaang, Ngongo, etc. of what was once—it is held—a single ethnic chiefdom. After the divisions are established, gaps are evident (down to) the recent past, when tales about other subjects come to the rescue. These patterns betray a mental image so familiar to most Kuba that they are not even aware of it. One thinks from founder to founder, and because gaps cannot be tolerated in any systematic account, if only because of the legitimacy of succession, telescoping must occur.

From this it follows that the competition at Iyool and the arrival of Shyaam stand for two real and profound structural changes in the society. Hence Kuba political history is divided into an archaic (pre-Shyaam) and a later period. Because the drying up of information occurs not after Shyaam himself, but after the reign of his second successor, these two reigns are included with his and are set apart from what follows. This produces three eras: the archaic period, the rise of the kingdom, the classical period. This is the built-in, if implicit, view of the traditional corpus that will be followed in this chapter.

These structural gaps make the list of rulers before Shyaam and his predecessor useless for chronological purposes. As set forth in Appendix A, Shyaam certainly ruled in the seventeenth century, perhaps as early as 1620. After him the dates 1680 and 1835 can be linked to kings ruling then by the mention of an eclipse of the sun and the passage of Halley's comet, respectively, and written data begin in 1880. Before Shyaam we have only the name of a single king of the second dynasty, the ruler he ousted, and before this we have only the names of the first and last kings of the first dynasty. It is noteworthy that the story about the dramatic end of the "first" era has almost become a prologue to the Shyaam cycle, practically obliterating a whole era. No one knows when the nyim title was created, and no one knows when Itoci of the migration period ruled.

The Bushoong immigration, which took place before the archaic period, ended at the latest in the sixteenth century, but it is unlikely to be that recent because the gaps would then be assumed to be extremely small. If all the ruling clans before the Iyool episode are to be counted as "dynasties," a long time elapsed, presumably during the immigration itself. Some of these claims would go back not only to the time when Itoci ruled but presumably even before. When the first Kuba crossed the Sankuru will never be known. Excavations around existing sites at Iyool are the only means of acquiring even a very approximate date for this event. And kindred sites could be found north of the Sankuru for the period before that. It would not surprise me if the northern sites date well back into the first millennium.

The Archaic Period

The Hammers and the Anvils: Kingship Invented

The account about the events at Iyool is known in shorthand reference as "the hammers and the anvils." Its locale is Lake Kum Idip and the plains to the east that form an intercalary savanna called Iyool, which extends eastward to the terrain around Baambooyi. Wolf and Sheppard recorded the story in 1885 and 1892, respectively. Wolf's account follows.

When, generations ago, so tells the oral tradition of the Kuba, the whole area around Ibaanc and the capital to the Lulua was still an impenetrable forest, the Bena Bussongo [the Bushoong] lived as a small tribe under their chief Lukengo [Luba for "Kuba king"] together with the more powerful Bena Bikenge [the Bieeng] on the left bank of the Lulua [where they lived in 1885], who were also Bakuba. One day the chief of the Bikenge asked tribute from Lukengo, who refused with the remark that he was equal to the Bikenge chief and not his subject. Finally they believed they had found a means to decide who among them should be paramount in the future. Bikenge and Bussongo would each fashion a copper plate in a given shape, and the chiefs would throw them at the same time into the Lulua; he whose plate would float should be recognized as paramount. In the evening before the day of decision the young wife of a Bikenge, who came herself from the tribe of Lukengo, heard that her husband and his tribesmen planned to cheat. They had taken a bit of palm wood and covered it with such a thin layer of copper that it was not heavy enough to sink. She made up her mind on the spot and during the night succeeded in secretly removing the false plate. She ran with it to Lukengo, whom she told about the planned deception. The plates were then switched: the young woman took Lukengo's plate and put it in place of the one she had removed. Early next morning, Lukengo with all his followers was at the Lulua and called for the Bikenge, who saw themselves now outdone. Then Lukengo threw the light plate into the Lulua and, since it did not sink, declared himself paramount of all the Kuba. He did not choose to remain a neighbor of the Bikenge, but crossed to settle on the right bank of the Lulua, where he founded a kingdom in the middle of the forest and extended his rule in time to the northeast, over the Batua [Cwa] and Bakete [Kete] who were living there. The young traitress fled the vengeance of the Bikenge and of her husband to go to Lukengo, who as a reward took her to be his first wife and issued a law that in remembrance of her patriotic action his followers only be allowed monogamous marriage with Bakuba girls. Hence every Mukuba [Luba: sing. of Bakuba] may only have one legal wife from his tribe, and his other wives, whose number is unlimited, cannot be Bakuba but have to be slaves.[3]

Note that the locale is different, that the story is told originally in Ciluba, that monogamy is a reward, that the objects are plates rather than anvils, and that this version closely follows the Bieeng account, recorded by Sheppard.

A great national dispute came between Xamba [Shyaam] and another supposed heir to the throne. The different factions had fought and still the matter was not settled. So it was agreed that the two contestants make iron axes [hammers, or anvils] and proceed to the lake nearby and that the one whose axe floated would be counted king. Xamba (so they said) made his axe out of wood and covered it with thin iron. On the day of the test before thousands of anxious disputers the axes with befitting ceremony were thrown into the lake. Xamba's axe floated and while the people shouted and fought Xamba was borne on the shoulders of his strong men to the capital and crowned king of the Bakuba.[4]

Here the founding of the state has been equated with the arrival of Shyaam [1] and iron substituted for copper. Miniature anvils sewn on the top of caps are preserved in the Musée royal de l'Afrique centrale, at Tervuren, and are said to be "emblems."

The tale constitutes a genuine political charter of kingship, as the following summary of the other known versions shows.[5] At Iyool the ethnic groups of the central Kuba, including the Bieeng, parted from each other as a consequence of their dispute over paramountcy. The leaders of each group—the

Bieeng, Ngeende, Pyaang, and Bushoong—agreed to throw hammers (or anvils) in the water of the lake. The Bieeng hammer had been cunningly fashioned by a Kete,[6] who had covered a wooden core with a layer of copper. The wife of the Bushoong leader was the sister of the Bieeng leader. She stole her brother's hammer, which ensured the outcome. The Bieeng did not accept the victory. Their leader discovered the theft before the throwing and just waited, leaning with his hand against a tree. Its imprint is said to be still visible on the very tree! Meanwhile the hammer of the Bushoong leader Mancu maShyaang [C], alias Mboong, as he now called himself, floated. Proudly Mboong shouted a praise name and asked: "If I have been chosen by rights, is there no spirit upstream and downstream of the river, is there no one?" Miracles began to happen. The water colored itself in turn red, yellow, and white.[7] The trees began to shake and a crocodile appeared. Mboong stood on its back and ventured out on the small lake with it. All these miracles, except for the appearance of the crocodile, had been performed by the Cwa, whom Mboong had bought off. The crocodile was a genuine manifestation of the spirits. Then Mboong returned to shore, pulling all the trees sideways so they did not grow straight. (This is in fact so today, perhaps because of a depression in the slope.) In the evening there was a dance of such triumph on the plains—perhaps the dance of enthronement—that the earth gave way under the weight of the massed dancers, creating a depression still visible today and shown by the local sightseeing guide, who also shows the three ravines which, it is said, were then created along with the three villages that lay nearby: ravine Shyaanc Bacwa of leader Mbodimbeeny, the Ngeende; ravine Ngwoong Labey of the Pyaang Ibaam; and ravine Lakwey of the Bushoong, whose village was Bumumyeeng of Chief Mboong. Hence the praise name for the Iyool plain: "Hammers and anvils at the pit of Iyool, the circles on the plain. If you pass Iyool, you will hear the words of the Ngeende, the circles on the plain."

A war with the Bieeng ensued. According to the Bieeng the ethnic groups fanned out from Iyool as a result.[8]

It is intriguing that this story is not the only one justifying kingship. As has been told in the account of genesis, Woot [A] wanted to leave the emblems of command to his favorite son, a Ngeende. But, helped by the Cwa, the Bushoong ancestor arrived first in the morning and chose between a beautiful chest and a tattered basket. He took the basket, which contained the insignia. Thus he succeeded Woot.

The Woot story is probably older than that of the hammers and the anvils. It claims succession by seniority and in the *patrilineal* line, which is contrary to Kuba practice. When asked about this in the 1950s the Kuba were quick to point out that these children were the issue of the incestuous relationship between Woot and Mweel, which made the succession matrilineal as well.

But the story does *not* stress that point. And the fact that most of the neighbors of the Kuba are patrilineal, of which the Kuba are well aware, does not explain the story either. It clearly deals with the legitimacy of the Bushoong chief in relation to other chiefs. Because of its similarity to the hammers and anvils story, I take it to be an older tale of legitimacy going back to a time when the Kuba were patrilineal.

Another tale explains matrilineal succession. One day Woot was drunk. In his intoxication he lay naked. His sons saw him and mocked him, but his daughter fetched a piece of cloth and, walking backward to avoid gazing at him, covered him. When he came to his senses Woot disinherited his sons and instituted matrilineal succession.[9] The same theme of the drunken king is also used to explain why black people became black, as we have seen in the stories of genesis. For this reason the proposed structural analysis does not seem convincing as it stands. I believe, on balance, that this story spread after the seventeenth century from the lower Zaire and came to be integrated in the boys' initation as an explanation for matrilinearity, no doubt because it evoked themes consonant with the dominant evocation there.

All sources agree that a new institution, kingship, was created at Iyool, and all concur that the Kete and Cwa were in the country before the Kuba. An analysis of variants discloses that the other central Kuba preceded the Bushoong; they lived under the rule of their own chiefs, except for the Ngeende, who had split into at least two groups. The Bieeng claim that their chief was overlord but was expelled by the Bushoong. This overlordship, however, is not supported by any other variant. A likely tale stems from the muyum, keeper of the national charm and of the most official tradition. The first ancestor of the muyum was a certain Matady, who ruled over the central Kuba. A later ancestor of the muyum was a certain Matady, who ruled over the central Kuba. A later king, Ngol a Woot, "older brother of Woot," married a Bieeng girl. Their son murdered his father and the Bieeng succeeded—again, note, in the patrilineal line—to the kingship. This happened well before the hammers and anvils episode. Given the muyum's position, it is plausible that his clan once ruled over the first group of central Kuba, ancestral to the Bushoong and the Bieeng. The muyum's clan history shows that group to be of Ngeende or Pyaang origin. Still other tales are told to account for the muyum's position, his special court—a replica of the royal court—and the fact that neither the king nor any chief can enter any clan-section settlement of the muyum's clan.[10]

Occupying the Land

It seems clear that most of the central Kuba had immigrated south of the Sankuru before kingship was created and the Bushoong claimed leadership. When they made that claim, fighting broke out, and the fact that only the

Bieeng fought indicates that the Bushoong dynasty claimed rule only over the Bieeng-Bushoong groups. Gradually the Bushoong managed to drive the Bieeng west and south, and the Bushoong occupied the center of the country. North of the Lulua a pitched battle resulted in a Bushoong victory, aided by Pyaang archers, over the Bieeng, who, driven south of the Lulua, went on a long march southward until they met the Lunda in the area between the Kasai and Loange rivers. Driven back by the Lunda, they met the Pende and returned to their present habitat, where they encountered only Bushoong, after the founding of the kingdom.[11]

The other central Kuba all tell of migrations away from Iyool, listing the names of chiefs and capitals until the migrants reached areas where they settled and split into chiefdoms. In fact the expansion can be seen as gradual, the Bushoong moving south and west and the Ngeende expanding to the southeast along the valley of the Labody River. Most of the Pyaang (one group broke off early and stayed near Iyool) preceded the Ngeende in this movement to the southeast. Their traditions mention generations of fighting with the Cwa and assimilating the Kete. Some Pyaang "turned into" Kete, as happened at Kampungu, and vice versa. But the Pyaang continued to be a single chiefdom, with the exception of the small group left near Iyool, until their eighth chief. The Ngeende broke up almost immediately. It is curious that there are no tales about Ngeende Pyaang relations although they "should" have been in almost continual contact and even though an early Pyaang chief had a Ngeende father.[12]

I studied the Bushoong tradition more carefully, which may explain why it is much more tidy. The principal reason for its greater clarity, however, may well be that Bushoong dynastic tradition was tied at all stages to the prerogatives and the obligations of kingship, a kingship that was not diluted by any divisions.

Near the Iyool plain the king's sister died and a meteor fell on her grave. The first clash with the Bieeng also took place nearby. Then the king moved south, across the lake, that is formed by the Lacwaady River and is called But aPoong, to occupy the lands between the Lacwaady and Lyeekdy rivers on the plain of Mbal aShepl, where he remained. The ethnic name Mbal given by other Kuba to the Bushoong may be linked with this place name. Since the kings remained in this area, further expansion by their Bushoong subjects south and northwest is not a topic for more tales.

Several tales deal with the crossing of But aPoong. The best known claims that when the Bushoong arrived at the Lacwaady River the man named Pyeem kapul, from the clan Ilyeeng, one of the two clans that had come with the royal dynasty from Itoci, declared: "Let no one cross this river before the king. He who does will be killed, for no one can pass the small quick fish *shing* [it is too fast], no one can lift a stone with a thread of raffia, no person can precede the king." The people camped on the bank. In the middle of the night they saw a light on the other side of the river. The next day they crossed, the ruler leading, and they found Pyeem. The ruler asked him why he had crossed first. He answered: "Here is my head; lop it off." The notables then killed him, after the ruler had refused to do so personally. That was the first man killed at the behest of a king. And a teller adds: "Many would follow."[13]

In another story the king killed someone who was rude to him. Afraid of the consequences, he fled to a spot near a spring not far from But aPoong. The Bushoong believed him dead. While they were looking for his body they met a Kete named Loon (eponym of the Kete Loon group), of the clan Iyop. "Did the king pass here?" they asked. "No." But they searched his house and found an iron staff and kaolin, two emblems of kingship. "Loon, he is here!" The Kete asked them to wait and went to tell the hidden king that they were looking for him, not to kill him but to ask him to be their king once again. The king refused to come out of hiding, but asked that his mother bring him pulses because he was hungry. When she brought them and he ate, the Bushoong located him, for they had followed the mother.[14] They then crossed But aPoong and the Kete man was rewarded with the title *tataam*, "head of the harem." The last sentence is not the whole point. The story first stresses the exceptional nature of kingship, for kings can kill with impunity; it stresses also the aboriginal character of the Kete; and the episode about pulses and hunger probably also conceals a meaning.

Tataam is also connected with the But aPoong crossing in another tale. The Bushoong were afraid to cross this lake because its name means "mention of the eagle's feather," the emblem of chiefly power. They thought that all would die in the crossing because a lake with such a name must possess magical power, and indeed, in the twentieth century it is reputed to have such power. The king ordered the crossing. On arriving at the other bank a man shouted "We are alive!" (*te mony!*). And the king gave him the title tataam. Variants add that he carried the king across on his shoulders and that the latter added: "From now on you will be the guard, cook, and keeper of the eighteen women given to me by the aristocratic clans."[15] The story implies that there were aristocratic clans who each gave one woman to the king and who probably formed a council. This is possible, for such clans are found in all Kuba chiefdoms and each gives a girl as wife to the leader in each chiefdom. This part of the story may, however, simply be an anachronism.

There was a battle at But aPoong. Some say it was a fight with the Bieeng, who were the victors; the Bushoong then had to hand over a sister of the heir to the throne, whom the Bieeng took with them. This seems to be a cross between a Bieeng story and the following traditional tale. To cross the big lake the Bushoong divided into two parties, each of which went around to either end where the lake was smaller, and crossed there. One party was led by the king, the other by his twin brother. Because they were royal twins, the elder was named Eagle, the younger Parrot. When the parties reunited a quarrel broke out. One day Eagle nicked the nose of Parrot. Being no longer physically whole, the younger twin could no longer succeed to the kingship. In another version, Parrot fell ill because of magical action taken by Eagle. Both versions have a similar ending: it was decided that thenceforth no descendants of the twins' sisters *except for those of the eldest sister* could ever succeed the king. The descendant of any other sister could become *cikl*, the ranking official of the country in those days, and could wear the parrot feather. The tale sets forth the rules for succession: matrilineal, by age, and restricted as to collateral succession. It also explains why cikl belongs to the royal clan but is in a different branch. Its use of the title may be anachronistic, however. Only one of the versions adds the expected conclusion that twins are a problem for succession: it states that since that time twin births have not been accepted in the royal lineage and twins have been killed at birth. The original point of the story probably was that because age is the predominant criterion for succession, the denial of seniority implicit in twin births is disruptive. [16]

After crossing But aPoong, the king stopped first near Kosh, where the muyum still lives, keeping the national charm in the forest that lies between his residence and the lake. A few more tales about two battles against the Bieeng in the southern part of the Bushoong territory and the role played in them by representatives of the aristocratic clans conclude this set of narrative traditions.

One other item is told about Iyool. A king's son, Shaambweky, announced that thenceforth clothing of raffia would be worn and bark-cloth clothing would be restricted to use during mourning. The anecdote points either to a connection between Iyool and raffia textiles (presumably the Bushoong learned to weave them from the Kete) or between Shaambweky and raffia cloth. If Iyool is but incidental here the information loses much of its relevance. [17]

The first king, Mboong [C], settled successively in two capitals on Mbal aShepl: "the falcon" and "the slow forest bird," both symbolic evocations and allusions to situations or events now lost. Bieeng tradition calls the Bushoong king at Iyool "Mbobobo,"[18] and claims that Mancu maShyaang [C] was only his successor. Their exodus was spread over two reigns. I think that two or even three kings may have been involved, and central Kuba expansion was probably a fairly slow process. The Cwa were repulsed everywhere but at the same time they were indispensable for the installation of chiefs and kings, because they were deemed to be the oldest inhabitants. Some Kete moved with the Pyaang or became Pyaang; other Kete were subjugated by the Bushoong, who did not assimilate them but created a new pattern of political subjection. But the expansion of the central Kuba went on until it reached the rich iron deposits of Kabuluanda, in the southeast near the Mwanzangoma River, still in the deep forest.[19]

Among the western Kuba groups, the Kel and the Shoowa migrated during the same general period as the central Kuba. The Ngongo may have begun to occupy their extensive lands across the Labody River in this period or a little later. Like the Bokila, they came into contact with the central Kuba at a later time.

Clearly all these movements were but a part of the general expansion of the southern Mongo. Once this is evident the implausible feature of a major population concentration at Iyool stands out. The reason for the myth is another Kuba collective perception: just as migrations before must have been by canoe and upstream, so later migrations of central Kuba must start from Iyool. It is even a cliché in some clan and village traditions, a political figure of speech. The historian visualizes an expansion over a broader front, all along the Sankuru and parts of the lower Kasai. The Leele crossed first, then the Bieeng and the Pyaang, then the Ngeende, and then the Bushoong. But this must remain conjecture because changes in the affiliation of ethnic identities among the populations involved are unknown, although such changes did occur, as shown by the Pyaang who became Kete and the Kete, Pyaang.[20]

The Early Bushoong Kings

The next traditions about the archaic period deal with a queen, Ngokady [D], who, like another queen, Labaam, belongs perhaps to the set of migration stories.[21] Neither of the two names may correspond to a historical person, although informants have a tendency to attribute more to Labaam, whose praise name is associated with building (which is the etymology of her name) and rivercraft. The only clear tradition linked to the queen begins by stating that she ruled because there was no male heir, a principle also enunciated by the formula recited at each royal enthronement. To hide the queen's monthly indisposition the cikl built the high wall known as *nkop* around the palace. One day, while presiding over the council in the palace, the queen was shamed when the councilors noted the menstrual blood. They decided that in the future no woman could come into the square used for the council nor could women be rulers. Two customs are thus explained. The tale has its equivalent in the Lunda empire, where menstrual blood was also given as the reason why women could not continue to rule.[22]

According to one source, Labaam "invented" one of the initiation masks, *nyeeng*, which was supposed to accompany the king when he appeared in the main square of the capital. Today the mask plays no role in the boys' initiation.

The mention of these queens occurs in a natural place for tradition to fill a void, the hiatus between the first and last kings of the Mboong dynasty. As *king* the Bushoong know only about Lashyaang [E] and his demise. Informants are uncertain whether there were three or nine Lashyaang, both ritual numbers, the latter more perfect, and both indicating "many." Later on, the name Lashyaang was sometimes used almost as a title for whoever happened to be ruler. In the songs for the spirits sung for the king who died in 1939 the royal wives called themselves "the women of Lashyaang." "The counting of Lashyaang" means to ascertain who is supposed to be the successor after the king's death, and in one of the songs for the spirits the dynasty is "the line of Lashyaang." Of the three known full names of Lashyaang kings, one belongs to the later king Shyaam. And since *lashyaang* means "seed," the other two full names could be understood respectively as "the seed of the kaolin of the Mbal" (Mbal being an alternate name for the Bushoong), alluding to the sacred kaolin, and the other "the seed promises the fruit," which sounds suspiciously like a saying. The whole could have been a praise name chopped up this time not to furnish place names for the migration, but for the purpose of providing kings' names to fill a hiatus. So King Lashyaang, the last of his line, may well be in fact an unnamed king x,[23] the personification of an entire era.

Frobenius was told that Mancu maShyaang [C] had two brothers named Lashyaang, both half brothers having the same father, and that after Mancu's death they fought for the throne. The people of Imeny (a northern district associated with Iyool[24]) killed one of them; the other one and the people then migrated to Shyaam Mbak, near Kosh.[25] Another version has it that the first Lashyaang [E] committed adultery with his younger brother's wife and had to resign. The quarrel was settled by a clever woman who was rewarded with the title *mbaan*. The same king is said to have replaced the title of his first notable, the *kin mimbaangt*, by *kikaam*, a title borrowed from the Ngeende. Both anecdotes at least indicate that according to the tradition these titles antedated the last dynasty.[26]

The "second" Lashyaang founded two capitals, whose names are part of the same praise name—supposedly the praise name for the villages but clearly composed after his death, since it runs: "the absence of the head, the hitting of the anvils, the legs remain downstream," which refers to his defeat and decapitation.[27]

His demise occurred as follows. One day Woot, far upstream, sent some of the Kete and/or Pyaang to the court of the Bushoong king for camwood and food. They took with them yams and small bananas as presents. The messengers were well received and good meat was prepared for them. No one noticed that flies had settled on it. When they began to eat, the messengers saw the flies and left, growling: "This is not meat; these are flies." The next day they were brought the best buffalo and warthog meat, but this did not help. They complained to Woot, who sent a large group of Kete or Pyaang to punish the king. A battle took place near Kosh, the king was killed and decapitated, and on the spot where he fell a giant tree, Shyaam Mbak, grew. The invaders spread all over the country, and the Bushoong had to hide. Ncoom Lashyaang, father of the deceased king, collected his son's head on the field of battle. As a reward for having saved and treasured the head, still part of the national charm, they named the father muyum.[28] In variants such as one given by Frobenius,[29] the meat was skin and rubbish and the food the messengers took was millet, the Kete staple, rather than yams. The story makes it evident that the chiefdom was overrun by a force from the east, indicated by the mention of Woot, the Kete, and the Pyaang.

All other anecdotes about this king have some connection with his death. According to some informants Woot sent the richly attired muyum from the east. But he arrived too late: the Bushoong had found a new one among the Leele. So the muyum stayed at Kosh. The story tallies well with the eastern origins and distribution of the muyum's clan, and it is as likely that the muyum were the successors of the kings of the next-to-last dynasty than that they were, as they claim themselves, the first dynasty that preceded all others. Most informants stick to the father-of-Lashyaang version because the skull is addressed in prayer as Lashyaang and is kept by the muyum.

Other traditions claim that the present mourning customs were introduced after the death of Lashyaang and that the important title *mbyeeng* was created to honor a king's daughter who had sounded the alarm in the capital to warn of invasion by the Kete and Pyaang. Her son received the title. In another setting the title is linked to the visit at an indeterminate time of an anonymous stranger who told the Bushoong how to set up the office of mbyeeng.[30] A variant of this version links creation of the title to the time of the demise of Lashyaang. Both these traditions are ascending anachronisms—i.e., the attributed date is too recent. Undoubtedly mourning customs are older than the death of Lashyaang, and at least at the village level the title probably is also older than his death.[31]

The historians do not tell us what happened to redress the Bushoong fortunes. They simply state that Mishe miShyaang Matuun [F] succeeded to the throne. Most sources say that he was a Leele, whose ruling clan is the Ntuun. The Bushoong summoned him to be king. A revealing variant links this to the first king, Mboong [C] who sent his seventy (a cliché number) sons to the Leele to find a king. The messengers first asked an older brother, Ngup aShyaang, who refused because he preferred to draw palm wine. They returned and met the younger brother, who was about to set out hunting, armed with bow and arrow. They said: "Put your bow down. The king does not pass with his bow and arrows." Mishe miShyaang understood the message. In memory of the event the praise name says: "The king does not pass by with his bow, he has passed to the sound of the anvils, of the staffs of office *malooncy*, attentive to the business of state, attentive to the court case."[32] In fact this ruler probably came from the east, not from the Leele.

When this king arrived at the capital he did not know proper etiquette. He was taught not to sit on the bare ground, not to carry weapons when coming to a council or court, not to look at blood or a wound. He is portrayed as the wild, foreign hunter who becomes civilized, a theme well known from the Luba-Lunda area. The previous tale also deals with etiquette. As there are good grounds to believe that the king did not come from the Leele, the first tale is probably only an attribution, perhaps taken from a folk tale, and the second may be one as well.

Mishe miShyaang Matuun [F] was the last (and perhaps the first as well) king of his dynasty. He was destined to fight Shyaam [1] and be killed by him. The creation of the second title of the harem, *mashingady angady angwoom*, "who dresses up like the queen mother," is linked to his reign in the following story. The king continually lost weight from lack of appetite. His wife sent to the Leele for pepper, thus introducing the chili plant and its berry, and spiced his food with it. He liked it, gained weight, and bestowed the title on his clever wife. Again there are reasons not to take the anecdote too seriously,[33] but the king actually did rule. He is said to have founded three capitals; two of them share a praise name, the usual mark of historicity.

The Rise of the Kingdom

Woot [A] created human culture; Shyaam [1] created civilization, Kuba culture proper. He is the best-known monarch of the past, and more anecdotes are attributed to him than to any other king. Frobenius merely stated that his accession was regular, but also mentioned a trip taken by Shyaam during which his "brother" Mancu maShyaang [C] wanted to seize the throne. Shyaam was recalled immediately and killed him. "Shyaam ruled only for a short while and died from natural causes."[34] Despite Frobenius' lack of attention to Shyaam, we know that his fame antedated 1905 by the fact that Sheppard attributed the throwing of the anvils to him and, in Frobenius' own account, by the mention of Mancu maShyaang, the hero of the anvil episode elsewhere. Even Frobenius begins his account with Shyaam.

The Coming of Shyaam

Shyaam was the son of a slave woman, Mbul aNgoong. During his youth he went west with three slaves who were to help him gather the wisdom that he would acquire from his travels. He visited the lands of the Leele, the Ding, the Pende, and especially the Mbuun, where he stayed longest. There he learned all manner of things. Interested by the plan used among the Mbuun in building capital towns, he set out to measure them. (Later he built his capital on this plan and all capitals since then have followed it.) The Mbuun became suspicious of this and resolved to kill him. Moreover, he committed adultery with a woman named Shaash. Discovered, he fled, pursued by the Mbuun shouting *"shaash, shaash."* That is why to this very day the same shout is given when an adultery is discovered. In running away he had forgotten his clapperless bell. So he quickly fashioned a charm and returned. The effect, we are told, was that the Mbuun could not ask him anything and therefore could not accuse him. It was dusk by the time he reached the house of Shaash, and when darkness fell the charm lost its power. The Mbuun wanted to capture him now, but could not because of their rule that no prosecution could be initiated during the night, a rule that still exists among the Bushoong. In the middle of the night Shyaam escaped through the roof of the house and returned home. The event is commemorated in the words of a song: "the night of the Mbuun has arrived." This firmly ties the anecdote to the Mbuun rather than to any other group.

Shyaam brought many things with him: maize, the technique of making palm wine, the Bushoong hat, the stick used as a mnemonic device to remember the amount of fines, the oil palm (which bears his name), initiation of boys, tobacco, carving, cassava, millet, sorghum, palm nuts, the dance *makieky*, the *mwaandaan* belt of office, the royal charm *ncaam mashok*. His wife invented the mask *mukyeeng,* fire, palm oil, the white embroidered woman's dress, and perhaps other items. Shyaam introduced the ceremonial knife *ikul*, which he wore at his waist when he fled. Torday also attributed to him introduction of raffia cloth from the Pende, embroidery patterns from the Kel, and the board game *lyeel*, "African checkers." According to Torday, the Ngongo attribute to him the introduction of the friction drum and the manner of wearing one's cap on the top of one's head; obviously, as Torday stated, all the inventions and arts for which no other origin is known are ascribed to him by the Kuba.[35]

Shyaam returned from his travels with the Ngoombe and the Maluk. Ngoombe and Maluk historical recollections do not agree with this at all. The tradition is based on the saying *Idiing iShyaam, Ngweemy* [the Ngoombe] *Shyaam*, which can just as well refer to their subjection by the king.[36] Shyaam had also learned about many powerful charms while traveling. When he came back he went to the capital and claimed the kingship. Mishe miShyaang Matuun [F] was afraid and proposed to leave power to Shyaam's sister's son after his death. Shyaam refused and fled. Before he left he told the king that as a sign of his power he would cause twins, a symbol of overpowering fertility, to be born as soon as he had left the capital. And so it came to pass. Hence one of his ncyeem ingesh songs:

> Come out, come out *aa*, come out *aa*.
> You come from the corner of the village, come out *aa*.

He rests at Mbooy, open *wooo*,
When the child of six months was born
Twins have come into the world, *u, u, u*.[37]

Shyaam was hidden nearby in the house of a friend, Kaan aKambady, because the king was looking for him everywhere with intent to kill. One day Shyaam's faithful dog was noticed, and the king was told about it; a slave was sent to fetch him. Shyaam, however, had foreseen this, had had a pit dug, and there hid with his dog, thirty cowries, and provisions of maize. By chance Kaan had given him the cowries just before Kaan's mother prepared a meal of maize for him to eat. Later, after Shyaam became king, the mother asked him for the return of her loan in cowries, but the king had forgotten all about it. She said: "I gave them when we had maize for a meal," and then it came back to him. Hence the habit of accompanying a loan with a meal, as is still done now. Shyaam had taken the thirty cowries into the pit because it was the custom to bury a corpse with that number of cowries; Kaan could then swear that Shyaam was in his grave and could undergo the poison ordeal to prove it. All of this happened, we are told; Kaan was vindicated and the royal slave killed.

Still it became too dangerous there and Shyaam fled to the Kel in order to obtain more charms because he felt himself still too weak to challenge the king. But Bushoong traders in that area heard talk about him, and his extradition was requested. The Kel promised: "Listen, tonight we have a big ball and you can see and catch him there." Shyaam went to the dance but remained invisible either because he had rubbed himself with kaolin or because he had a shield made out of the hide of the hippopotamus. Nevertheless his host was summoned to the capital, whereupon Shyaam advised him to flee. Shyaam hid himself elsewhere in the area and married the daughter of a famous medicine man. In this tale, then, the Kel are said to be part of the Bushoong realm.

The medicine man wanted to test Shyaam's magical ability. He forbade him one evening to sleep with his wife and the next morning had him sacrifice a fowl in his presence. That evening he brought Shyaam to a spiny *ndweem* tree, calling "Is there nothing more?" He whistled on a leaf and behold, a very shy black antelope stepped out of the forest and stood stock-still in front of them.[38] Shyaam, obeying his orders, went to it and caught it barehanded. He killed it and brought the skin to his father-in-law, who concluded: "Truly, now I see that you are able to be a famous medicine man."

When he felt strong enough Shyaam returned to the capital. His father-in-law had asked him to visit a pregnant woman along the way. Shyaam did so, and she bore twins. He gave medicine to the mother and the babies and three cowries to the mother, as is still the custom. While still in Kel country, he cured a man bitten by a snake: he blew on the ground; the soil boiled; and Shyaam made a paste of it and rubbed it on the snakebite. Nearing the capital, he met the wife of his friend Kaan. She was harvesting peanuts and had left her cooking pot against a tree. She told him there was a great famine in the area and requested some food. Shyaam dug up a parasol tree (*Musango smithii* R. Br.), cut its roots in pieces, and placed a *kwoong* (*Sarcophrynium macrostachyum* [Benth] *K Schum*) leaf on the bottom of a rectangular pit with the root pieces on top. He bound the leaf and root pieces up and filled the pit with sand. Then he beat the ground with his staff, shouting "*laaml poo.*" And lo, when the woman dug up the package, the roots had turned into good cassava. She said: "Good, now we have food, but what about the relish?" Shyaam went to the tree where the cooking pot rested, looked up, and shouted: "*He*, men up there come down." And a great many caterpillars came down into the pot. Thus he invented the use of caterpillars as a relish. When he had finished he declared symbolically: "All the Bushoong are in my belly."

But Shyaam still lacked one thing to gain the throne: the blessing of the royal clan. The Bushoong give this by spitting on the person to be blessed. So one day Shyaam went to the capital and hid near the entrance of the palace under a rubbish heap. The king passed by, saw the rubbish and spat on it in disgust. Now Shyaam was blessed.

Shyaam wore the nyeeng mask and hence could spy on the king without being seen. This mask accompanies the king whenever he appears on the main square, and wearing it allowed Shyaam to be near the king. At night Shyaam hid charms everywhere. In this way he created a huge cloud of crickets, a Kuba delicacy, and had it land on a plain near the capital (one version names Iyool as the plain, but that is too far away). Dressed up in royal attire, seated on a royal litter, he hid in a small woods. No sooner did the news about this manna from heaven spread in the capital than everyone went out to take part in the harvest, the king and his two sons accompanying them. The people found Shyaam in the woods and exlaimed: "Here is the new king." One of the sons of the previous monarch warned his father in time, and they fled. But one son fell into a hunter's trap and was killed. Shyaam had him buried. Mishe miShyaang Matuun hid in the forest near the spring, Bwoon, of the village Paam. Soon, however, a farmer noticed someone was stealing his palm wine, caught the former king, and brought him in his house. He warned Shyaam, who had him thrown alive in Bwoon. One of our best informants, Nyimiloong, commented that Shyaam became the first true king because he could not be deposed. Before his reign kings could be proclaimed and deposed at will.

What can be accepted as true in these tales? First, that Shyaam was a foreigner. To the Kuba this is apparent because many sources claim that his mother was a slave; those who claim only his father was a slave give him the name Mbul aNgoong, which is a matronymic. They merely want to emphasize the continuity of kingship by claiming a continuity in the matrilineal line, which is now the line of succession and inheritance. Since the notions of slave and foreigner are related, the message is clear: a foreigner founded a new dynasty. This is reinforced by the stress laid on his travels, which must be seen as the influx of Western cultural influences. And perhaps the first kings of this dynasty were not reluctant to remember their Mbuun origin,[39] though Shyaam was seen as a successor to the first Kuba dynasty by being given the name or calling himself Lashyaang laKady andek, "the seed promises the fruit," an allusion to King Lashyaang.

Shyaam's saga casts him in the role of an archetypal medicine man. That explains why he could wrest kingship away and be himself the greatest king in Bushoong memory. But he is also connected with trade. In addition to what is described above, he is also said to have fought to protect trading caravans on their way to the Lokenye River. He could be seen as a Mbuun trader, the Mbuun being themselves by then connected with a branch of the Atlantic trade via the Kongo. But there are difficulties in this interpretation. How did he overcome the incumbent ruler? The traditions make it clear that this was a long process, even though the chiefdom was not particularly large. Several possibilities exist. The stories all involve the support of a party among the Bushoong. Perhaps the previous foreign dynasty from the east was still unpopular? Perhaps his status as a foreigner without any ties in the country allowed him to rally several factions against the dynasty? Perhaps the new things he brought with him gained him support because he was seen as wealthy? We do not know how it happened, but Shyaam did succeed in establishing a new dynasty.[40]

The Reign of Shyaam

His reign was prosperous. Shyaam was peaceful and wont to say: "I am the oldest of all villages," implying that while all owed him respect he would protect others as younger brothers are supposed to be protected by their elders. Yet he waged war. One informant claims that he incorporated all of what came to be considered the Kuba ethnic groups except the Ngongo. This is an exaggeration. One anecdote, remembered in detail because it involves the newly introduced tobacco, deals with a war against the tiny group of the Ilebo at the confluence of the Kasai and the Sankuru. The Bushoong had occupied an island in the Kasai. The enemy attacked and killed the two most famous Bushoong warriors because they would not fight before they had finished smoking their pipes. That is how tobacco became famous in the country. There is also mention of his war against the populations north of the Sankuru, where traders bought camwood and ivory in the area of the Lokenye. It is said the whole region recognized his overlordship. Torday stated that Shyaam abolished the use of spears and throwing knives as weapons because he was so peaceful. This, however, is flatly contradicted by one of my informants, the *shesh*.[41]

Shyaam's magic became too powerful and absorbed all his reproductive power, making him unable to procreate. One source claims that in Mbuun country he had been offered a charm enabling him to beget many children when he became king. But the giver had added: "If you bear children, the royal clan will not, and you will have no successors." Because he refused the charm, Shyaam had no children and the dynastic clan Matoon had many. This was a great sacrifice in a matrilineal society where the father-child link is strongly accentuated emotionally. Then the people decided that the capital was Shyaam's wife and gave his name to all the children born there. So his name has been perpetuated. The men of the capital also procreated children with Shyaam's wifes, and in gratitude Shyaam ruled that henceforth the title *mbeem* would only be given to a natural child of a royal wife. In variants he is said to have invented the title, but the function already existed. In any case he did change the pattern of succession (which had previously been restricted to members of the Ndoong clan, one of the eighteen aristocratic clans) by extending it to the children of *any* royal wife. Some attribute the creation of the corresponding title mbyeeng to him as well, and all claim he created many other titles and offices.

Shyaam's younger brother, Mboongl a Shimy,[42] wanted to seize the throne. When Shyaam went one day to a village to obtain medicine to strengthen his hold on the kingship, the people there told him to give three cowries and one calabash of palm wine to the first person who knocked on his door by the next morning. Shyaam did so. The person was Mboongl, and he was given the objects. Nothing happened. Some time later Shyaam learned from another brother that Mboongl was arousing the people against him. He ordered Mboongl killed. An aristocrat of the Mitoom clan shot him dead, and perhaps killed another brother of Shyaam as well. Then the king declared this clan fallen from its status because it had killed royals, but he gave the clan the office of *kol mat*, or secret police.[43]

After Mboongl's death Shyaam was given an arm of the deceased to eat. As a result the king's belly began to swell and he became mad. While in this condition he invented the "songs for the spirits," climbed a palm tree feet first and head down, and when he had come down again shouted: "If I am not a *ngesh* [nature spirit] why would I then climb the palm tree?" He sent someone to the Nkucu, north of the Sankuru, to fetch some medicine to cure him. The components of the charm were the liquid of an eye and a human finger. Before it could be administered it was necessary to carry the *nkolakol* drum through the streets of the capital at night. The king would then be healed. The ritual was fruitless, however, until he managed to acquire a charmed, small bell which he hung from his belt. When the bell fell it took the insanity with it. It fell off in a well-known woods, and anyone who today enters those woods is supposed to become mad because Shyaam's illness remained there. Some time later Shyaam's friend Kaan aKambady died. To convince the people that he was innocent of this event, Shyaam had the nkolakol drum carried around at night and thus established the ritual that is still observed today.[44]

Mboong aLeeng: The Hawk

Shyaam was succeeded by Mboong aLeeng [2], his mother's sister's son, who had been on bad terms with him. Mboong aLeeng is remembered and stereotyped as a warrior. This stereotype is confirmed by the praise names of his capitals: "The assembly of weapons: one weapons surpasses all, that of the king," and "The gliding of the hawk: he sees what there is to eat." He is said to have fought the Ngongo, the Bokila, the Nkucu, the Ngeende, the Bena Caadi (a Lulua group near the Lulua River), and above all the Pyaang and the Bieeng.

The war with the Ngongo was provoked by one of Mboong's sons who committed adultery with a wife of the king and then fled to the Ngongo. The king defeated the central forces of the Ngongo.[45] The conflict with the Bokila came about when the king heard that their chief was wearing brass, a royal prerogative. Despite his admonitions the chief would not desist, so he had a sister of the chief kidnapped when she was at the market in Ngeende territory. The chief continued to refuse submission "because he had not participated in the hammers and anvils contest," which, it will be remembered, had already occurred. The king waged three campaigns against the Bokila before securing the payment of tribute. Some of the prisoners of war were settled in the village of Mweek and were instructed to fight a guerrilla war against the nearest Pyaang chief. After a while the king found them not eager enough and sent the inhabitants of a Kete village to raid them. This they did, but the people of a neighboring Cwa village thought it their duty to defend Mweck and destroyed the Kete force. The leaders of Mweek then went to beg pardon from the king. The king also established a small village near the village of Bokila for surveillance and allowed a group of Songo Meno to settle in yet another village near Bokila.[46] This example reveals much concerning the tactics and the scale of fighting as well as the means taken to subdue and incorporate an enemy.

Wars with the Cwa and their Pyaang allies were much more serious for the Bushoong. One tale tells how the Cwa and their leader Iloong (Ilunga) attacked the Bushoong capital one day when everyone was in the fields. Finding only one old man, who was playing the guitar, and the king's sister, they took them prisoner. Ever since, the inhabitants of the capital have not been allowed to farm. After a while a man from the prestigious Iyeeng clan found the royal sister in a Pyaang village and fled with her to a Kete village, Baaking. He sent word to the king, who had her brought back and granted the clan Iyeeng tribute rights over the village. But the royal sister gave birth to an egg, which fled by itself to the muyum. The egg is supposed to return to the capital to kill any tyrant king. After he has died, the egg will jump on his brow and the dead man will set upright and confess all his crimes. In effect the egg—and what looks like a kaolin egg is one of the items of the national charm—acted as a deterrent against excesses of power.[47]

The military might of the Pyaang was broken when their main chief Mashaal was defeated and fled eastward to Lusambo. One Pyaang tale tells of a curse put on Mashaal by another Pyaang chief. As a result Mashaal became insane, murdered his mother, and wore her ashes in a little bag of genet skin around his neck. He then made war upon the Kuba king but lost, and, sitting backward on his litter (the equivalent of a throne), he was carried away from the kingdom by his companions, who became the Isambo. The Bushoong have no detailed recollections of this war against Mashaal. In any case Pyaang power was broken and the main chiefdom was split in several parts, although the Bushoong still had no firm hold over it.[48]

Mashaal's flight was not the only emigration to the east. Mboong aLeeng is said to have "invented" the friction drum used for the boys' initiation and hence the initiation itself. One day half the population of the initiation camp fled the hardships they were undergoing and settled in the east of Binji.[49]

Toward the end of his life Mboong aLeeng was told that the Bieeng had been sighted south of the Lulua. He decided to attack them to recover the offspring of a royal sister captured by the Bieeng after the events of "the hammers and the anvils." He defeated them in their new territory, but was ambushed by a Kete group when returning and was killed near the Luebo River. Nevertheless, the Bushoong brought a Bieeng princess back with them and founded at least two settlements with the Bieeng captives. At least four other tales are told in connection with this war. One attributed Mboong's victory after years of fighting to one of his wives, a Bieeng who told him how he could overcome and kill her brother and his friend, the two main war magicians for the Bieeng. Another is a tale about the prediction of a Bushoong victory by a war magician who before the battle caused wooden mortars, used to pound cereal, to hit each other until one was knocked down. A third tale tells of chiefs who challenged each other to a duel during the battle and killed one another, after which rainbows appeared in the south and the north. In the fourth story, the Bieeng captured a member of the Bushoong crown council, who before he was killed put a curse on their custom of wearing mwaandaan belts. From these tales one learns that the outcome of the battle was long undecided, and that in the end the Bieeng were ambushed in the woods and their settlement(s?) occupied. They had to capitulate "to ask for the fire." After

Mboong aLeeng's demise the acting Bushoong leader proposed peace, even though he had the advantage. He asked for the head of the major Bieeng warrior; when it was brought he threw some of the ambassadors who came with it in a ravine and took the others as captives to the capital. The war was certainly memorable insofar as the two most famous medicine men of the Kuba, Tooml aKwey and Shyaam aNdoong, are portrayed as participating in the conflict as war magicians of Mboong aLeeng. The whole cycle for one of these men is associated by some informants with this war.[50]

Mboong aLeeng is further credited with territorial reforms. He created a new, small province for his main successor, reorganized the harem by asking and receiving one wife from each Bushoong clan rather than just one from each of the eighteen aristocratic clans, and founding captive villages. These reforms enhanced not only his prestige but his economic power as well.[51]

The King Who Would Not Die

The succession to Mboong aLeeng's throne seems to have been disputed. Several contenders, among them Shyaam Mbweeky[52] and Myeel, are mentioned but did not rule. Myeel's mother invented decorative motifs for textiles, and she also invented blacksmithing [sic]. Myeel is remembered as a royal personage and the best smith there ever was. He forged iron statuettes, a boat with its crew, and a miniature house. Every old remarkable piece of metalwork is credited to him. One informant also had him invent weaving and carving. When Myeel was proposed as king, the Bushoong refused because he was too strict: once he had heavily fined a village that had ruined some ore he had left to dry in the bush, an event that the Bushoong remembered, and so they refused to accept him as king.[53] In reality, Myeel may not have lived at this time.

One contender for the throne was the elder brother of MboMboosh. The brother was killed because he was a witch and MboMboosh [3] won the power struggle.

He is remembered as a beautiful man—very dark and very heavyset. He was a great warrior as well. He conclusively defeated the Pyaang and overcame a Luba group near the Mwanzangoma River, at the limit of the kingdom in the southeast. With the help of the main Shoowa chief he repelled a major Ikolombe or Yajima attack that was led by one of his sons whose mother was an Ikolombe or Yajima. With the prisoners of his wars he settled more villages, and his authority over the Shoowa came to be firmly established.

Within the realm most of his difficulties stemmed from within the royal lineage. He tried to counterbalance the influence of its male members by increasing the prestige and the power of his own children. MboMboosh became very old, ruling forty years says Frobenius,[54] and founded nine (which means many) capitals. The people grew tired of him because he was so old and was no longer fit to rule. His younger brother roused the population against him and MboMboosh was sent to the Ngeende, but they returned him. He then defied everyone by having a huge basket filled with tiny millet seeds, saying that he would eat one of these each year and not die before they were all eaten up. The outraged inhabitants of the capital decided to burn the palace down. The king was warned by his daughter, who had given herself to a slave in order to learn the secret plan. MboMboosh fled in time by a side entrance, still known as "the footprint of the king," and suddenly appeared in full regalia before the blazing palace. He rewarded his daughter and his children in general with a set of privileges regarding marriage and adultery: if wronged, they were to receive much more than others in adultery cases; in contrary cases they were to pay no damages at all.

But MboMboosh was finally killed. Those who were waiting to succeed him convinced his favorite wife to slip a noose around his neck one night and then push the other end of the rope through the wall of her house. The heirs pulled and the king was strangled.

A Bieeng woman introduced the cultivation of cassava, or else only the preparation of cassava porridge, *kat*, during his reign. This is the last introduction of an American cultigen to be mentioned.

By the end of MboMboosh's reign the kingdom had almost reached its present size and, more important, the key internal institutions had been created. The Kuba kingdom was a reality; the Bushoong chief was no longer considered to be merely *primus inter pares*.[55]

The Classical Period

Little is remembered about the kings of the classical period beyond the names and praise names of their capitals, their songs for the spirits, and some of their own praise names.[56] The known anecdotes follow in chronological order.

Mbakam and His Successors

Under the reign of Mbakam Mbomancyeel [4], strange things happened. There was an eclipse of the sun, snow fell, huge caterpillars invaded houses and cooking pots, and a corpse that had been lying in state disappeared. Mbakam also is said to have killed his mother, which may be connected to the other events. He lived in three capitals, sleeping in whichever palace was indicated by a flock of weaverbirds, who would leave one tree and fly to another in the courtyard of a different capital. This seems indeed miraculous when one realizes that weaverbirds will not leave a tree where they are nesting in great numbers. The three capitals together constituted his power, according to his praise name: "the bow, the bowstring, and the arrow." It is possible that they were but three quarters in one town.

His mother wanted to kill him because she preferred his younger brother Miingambeengl. She gave him a deadly charm hidden in a necklace, but, forewarned, the king gave the jewel to Miingambeengl, who died wearing it the same day. Later, Mbakam invited his mother to a party and made her drunk. While she was intoxicated he killed her with a tusk. Since then, a tusk has been placed on the tomb of each deceased king. Because of this incident, the tusks are called "ivory forks."[57]

It is plausible that it was Mbakam who finally vanquished the Pyaang, where his name is remembered.[58]

Most Bushoong have nothing to say about Kot aMbweeky ikoongl [5] except his praise name, the name of his capital, and its praise name. One of the best informants, the shesh, knew that under this king the men of the royal lineage became so difficult that he had their settlement, Mweengt, stormed, and many were killed. The king gathered the remainder and established them at the capital in the quarter called Ngel aMbiim, where they lived surrounded by the royal slaves. A Bieeng tradition mentions that one of his sons by a Bieeng mother ruled over them south of the Lulua, but because he was too subordinate to the Kuba kingdom, he was deposed. One Idiing source recalls that this king burned the village of Loody and thus subdued it for good. (One of his predecessors had done the same, but the village later refused tribute.) The royal praise name stresses the size of Kot aMbweeky's capital and the number of his children and grandchildren, which, given the political importance of royal children, is worth noting. Perhaps it was under this king, if not before, that the Bulaang immigrated from the Bieeng. (The Bulaang were originally Bieeng, and left for unexplained reasons.) Pyaang tradition remembers a Pyaang chief who went to war against the Caadi and the Bulaang and died in Bushoong territory. His predecessor had fought Mbakam, and he therefore may be contemporary with Kot aMbweeky.[59]

Virtually nothing is told about Mishe miShyaang maMbul [6], whose song for the spirits stresses the great number of his subjects.

The House of Nce

Under Kot aNce [7] the territorial power of the Kuba seems to have reached a high point. He dared depose certain heads of chiefdoms, the eagle-feather chiefs, and relegated them to a remote Bushoong village, where they were executed. He defeated the Ngongo in the battle of Mbong aMbidy at Ishaamisheng, their easternmost settlement, after they had refused tribute. With the prisoners he established a village named "peace," and he appointed one of his sons by a woman of the proper dynastic clan as ruler of Misumba, the main Ngongo chiefdom. But his most famous war was defensive. The Caadi and another Luba group, perhaps the Bena Cishiba led by Kabamba, had driven the Pyaang away from the rich iron deposit at Kabuluanda, near the Mwanzangoma River. They were driven away by Kot aNce after a struggle in which one hero is still remembered to have worked wonders. At some later date, however, the site fell in the hands of the Luba.

Kot aNce was also a great magician who cut a river in two with his sword (the Red Sea motif), cut off his own head to delouse it, and silenced the weaverbirds who were twittering away during a council meeting. More personable is the tale that he invented a tall, pointed hat because he was short and wanted to be more impressive. He died as the result, it is said, of magic wrought upon him by Tooml aKwey, whom Kot aNce had executed: the king died when he was pricked by a hair on the skin of a dead elephant. As part of the same magical vengeance the capital was afflicted by an epidemic of tropical sores.[60] The ncok song from this reign mentions beads for the first time, and also cowries, if the mention of cowries during the reign of Shyaam is anachronistic.

Of the next monarch, MishaaPelyeeng aNce [8], all that is remembered is that he improved the razor blade; hence his nickname, Lukengu (razor blade, in Luba), came to be applied by the Luba to all Kuba kings. As the tradition has it, the story is linked to the explanation of the Luba term and perhaps expresses an interest in technical innovation. But the tale may also be a reflection of the King's ruthlessness, which perhaps earned him this name among the Luba, although there is no evidence for this. The following story is attributed to his brother and successor, Mbo Pelyeeng aNce [9], but may really be his work: the king killed seventy[61] sons of Kot aNce [7] when they came to the palace to weave, as had been their habit during their father's reign. Thus a reigning king openly challenged the power of the royal sons of one of his predecessors. It would be more logical to attribute this to Kot aNce's successor, as some informants do, than to the second successor. Whoever did this soon after died of remorse or of nightmares. Mbo Pelyeeng aNce is remembered as an excellent smith, an outstanding farmer, and a rather puritanical man who would not dance, as kings should, and forbade the Bushoong to do so. He killed the "nine" (actually eight) ethnic national spirits: three of these were Bushoong, one each was Kel, Ngeende, Bieeng, and Pyaang, and one was from the small Ibo region near the Kasai, inhabited by the Leele. In addition to providing the names and the number of the spirits, this tale may reflect a memory of the abolition of cults that honored the spirits. The bolstering of ethnic identities of the different groups in the kingdom was a menace to its unity and had to be abolished, which could only succeed if the ethnic self-identity of these groups had already weakened. The kingdom was now clearly more important than the chiefdom, and the status of the king as a spirit was enhanced in his praise name: "I am not a nature spirit; yet I dug a pond." The story associated with the motto concerns the valley of Kok aNgency, near the present capital. A medicine man gave the king a laxative, but the monarch did not heed the ritual avoidances that pertained to it. The resulting flood of excrement could not be stopped and dug a whole valley and the spring of the brook. The sources clearly have difficulty in distinguishing between the two brothers—for instance, why would the good smith not be the one who perfected the razor blade?

The House of Mbul

With the reign of Kot aMbul [10], around the turn of the nineteenth century, more information becomes available. Before he succeeded, a major succession dispute took place. A certain Mbakam was to succeed Mbo Pelyeeng aNce [9] but was opposed by a nephew who claimed seniority either by virtue of his age or because his mother belonged to a segment of the lineage that had already produced kings, whereas his uncle came from a more collateral line. Either of these two situations pertained to the rules of succession, which ranked heirs by seniority of age and forbade collaterals to succeed. Mbakam committed suicide after cursing the nephew, who was probably the older brother of Kot aMbul. The nephew died soon after. Mbulape, the nephew's mother, became regent. In memory of these events a house was thenceforth maintained on the main street of the capital as "the house where one hangs oneself"; it was built to help resolve future succession crises of the same nature by pressuring one of the contenders to do away with himself.[62] Another version of the succession dispute has the surviving contender die because the curse of Mbakam made his mouth lengthen into a snout like a mouse so that he could neither eat nor drink. This is an interesting case of a fantastic tale being tacked onto a historical reality.[63]

Kot aMbul is remembered as a warrior. The residents of a northern Ngeende village killed one of the king's sons when he came to request either service or tribute. A punitive expedition was led by two other sons, which is recorded in his song for the spirits. During this reign the Coofa immigrated into the country. In fact, the migration may have taken longer and it certainly involved clashes with the Pyaang and the Bushoong. The Bushoong claim to have fought a group of Pyaang who were between them and the Coofa, thereby obstructing the Bushoong's ability to resist the newcomers. Kot aMbul's army attacked one Coofa settlement after another and, in true cliché style, the prisoners were "crushed" to death in mortars and the children were strung up. In other words, he used terror as a means of rule. While not preventing the immigration he did succeed in making the Coofa tributary. Some Luba influence on his court can be deduced from the praise name for one of his capitals, which is the translation of a Luba (Lulua) praise. His martial disposition is shown in all the praise names related to him and his two capitals. In one he is "the fire that burns in the Maluum woods; the hunter who does not hunt with dogs [i.e., who hunts people down]." He was an outstanding war magician: it is told of him that when a bolt of lightning struck he picked it up and threw it into the bush.[64]

The major achievement of Miko miMbul [11], the next ruler, was to marry a slave girl and to cause such marriages to be recognized. The matter affected the status of children born of a slave wife more than the status of the wives themselves. In memory of this, his dynastic statue has at its base a carved head representing his slave wife. Elements from his song for the spirits stress agricultural production, although one testimony claims that he was very lazy, meaning perhaps that he introduced few innovations. He did maintain royal power. On his orders a rebellious village in the northern part of the Bushoong chiefdom was subdued by another village; the report of the outcome stated that thirty-one rebels were killed, and six hands were brought in to prove it. Another source relates that a royal son killed a Kete for insulting the king and then went into hiding. The king sent some Cwa to locate him, but the Cwa claimed they did not find him. In another version the son was found and congratulated, and a village was named for him. This last story comes from several lineage traditions, as does one claiming that the king settled a friend in a village to have him near at hand, and from this a clan section grew; in another tradition the king made a village tributary to one of his sons. The lives of two great medicine men are placed in his reign. One of them was his own son, "small with a great beard," titled *kayen*, who was named Kopangaan, but nicknamed Kishdy. He quarreled with his father, who could not succeed in having him killed; all attempts were foiled by the marvelous use of magic. In some sources he was not the king's son; instead, the other magician was. This medicine man is portrayed as a trickster and a social rebel.

Mbop Mabiinc maMbul [12] succeeded about 1835. He is remembered for his use of terror and is usually labeled a "bad king." He was still living when Wolf visited the country, but died in 1885 or 1886.[65] During the last part of his reign he was paralyzed. The traditions give evidence of the development of trade during his reign: slaves were bought for the king, and an allusion to the great market Ibaanc appears in the royal song. As is discussed in Chapter Ten, outside sources expand this and clarify trade developments after 1875.

He fought the Ngeende, Pyaang, Bulaang, Kel, Shoowa, Bieeng, Leele from Ibo, Ngongo, Ngoombe, Bokila, and Caadi in an effort to increase royal control and the flow of tribute. Scarcely any non-Bushoong group escaped attack. Clichés of "crushing" men to powder in mortars, cutting women open, and holding mass burials for executed people stress his ruthlessness, especially with regard to the Ngongo. Terror was not unrestrained: not all captives were killed, and the Ngongo and Luba captives were settled in three villages within the Bushoong chiefdom.

He had many sons—perhaps three hundred, as Torday claimed—and used them as his agents. Several stories concerning them exist. One indicates that the king could order a son to be killed even in Bieeng country, south of the Lulua, as if that area was becoming part of the realm. A detailed tale deals with clashes between his own sons and those of his heir apparent: the king had the leading son of the heir apparent murdered, but the heir apparent managed in turn to kill the king's son. During his last years the situation deteriorated. When the king was struck by paralysis the heir apparent, Miko Mabiinc maMbul [13], had him moved from the capital to Ngel aKook, a village in the south, while the second in line to succeed prudently moved away to Ibaanc. It was even suspected that the king wanted to leave his title to a son rather than a brother or a sister's son. After 1886 a civil war broke out between the potential successors, and the female members of the royal lineage fled north. The war's course was, however, rather desultory, and it ended upon the natural death of Miko Mabiinc maMbul sometime before 1892. In fact this may not have been untypical of previous succession crises.[66]

One tradition about this period holds that Mbop Mabiinc maMbul [12] and Nyimiloong, a son of his predecessor, apprehensive about the arrival of Europeans and the disasters they might bring, decided to commit suicide. A woman who overheard them was also to die by magic. They all left the capital and a few days later their deaths were announced. When the bodies were brought to the capital a dispute erupted between two royal sons, one the son of Miko miMbul [11], who wanted to give precedence to the corpse of Nyimiloong, his brother, and the other a son of Mbop Mabiinc maMbul who wanted his father's corpse to enter the capital first. As a result of the quarrel both cursed each other and died in the ensuing civil war (1886–91?).

Although this tradition seems to use the names of real people, it cannot be correct, because the paralysis of the king, known from Wolf, Frobenius (1905) and most other sources, contradicts the first part of the story. The tradition took shape sometime after 1891–92, and since the official version then was that the king had been paralyzed as a result of poisoned palm wine given by the heir apparent, this tale must be even later. At the earliest it crystallized around 1896–99 and probably can be dated somewhat later because it expresses implications of the disastrous effect of the European impact, which became apparent only after 1896. King Mishaape [15] (1896–1900) closed the country to Europeans in an attempt to isolate his realm. Indeed, one version of this tale replaces Mbop Mbiinc maMbul with Mishaape, and has the king complain outright about the racist feelings of the Europeans. It may be that Nyimiloong, the woman, and the king died in quick succession, one after the other, and a civil war occurred afterward. This example indicates some of the factors affecting the creation of a tradition and how it becomes crystallized. Its most important testimony deals with the roles of royal sons in the politics of the state, and in this its general tenor is correct. On the other hand, it is also invaluable as a document concerning the reaction of the Kuba to the European penetration, but here it is anachronistic.

The first Europeans are remembered in Bushoong traditions. In one, Silva Porto, who arrived in 1880, is named Cingom, "the firearm," and is believed to have had a flowing beard. After this point traditions continue to be formulated and are accompanied by written sources for the succeeding reigns. Several of them mark significant episodes of the reign of Kot aPe [18] (1902–16), especially those connected with fighting, and add miraculous occurrences that are the kernels of the traditions. But dynastic traditions do not explicitly refer to the reign of terror instigated by the rubber policies of the Compagnie du Kasai and lasting from 1902 to early 1911; only private reminiscences and family traditions recount those events. Some of our informants were eyewitnesses to this whole period and recalled the battle against the Zappo Zap in 1900, when the capital was stormed and sacked.[67] A major reason that the Compagnie du Kasai is not preserved in tradition is that no outstanding events were perceived as being obviously linked to them, in the way wars are. The compulsory requirement that the people gather rubber developed gradually, and tradition could no more cope with this evolution than it could with the great trading movements that had occurred before and about which only scattered traces are to be found in the oral heritage.

The tales of the kingdom constitute only one layer of historical evidence. It is the Kuba view of their own past. The substance of this chapter is known to any good Kuba bulaam. Having suggested the nature and the texture of these materials, we must now adduce fresh evidence and approach the subject from other perspectives to try and overcome the restriction imposed by the Kuba selection of what is worthy of remembrance, or what happens accidentally to have been preserved in sayings, songs, and poems. The remainder of this study is devoted to that task.

Part III

A Past Interpreted

Chapter 5

The Means of Interpretation

This chapter examines the means of interpreting Kuba oral traditions and serves as a preface to the interpretation itself, which is the subject of Chapters Six through Twelve. Those chapters present reconstructions of the proto-Kuba period, followed by political and social history and then by economic, religious, and artistic developments.

We are now acquainted with the perceptions the Kuba have of their own history. The task ahead is to reconstruct their past—I am tempted to say "as it happened," but that cannot be done. We are dealing with a *selection* of data about the past, and many events are lost to us. But even if we had complete information concerning all events affecting every person during every day we would be forced to bring some order into the perplexing chaos of life. We must interpret, and there are as many ways of interpreting as there are historians. Every historian carries his own set of assumptions. Each has approached and discovered his data in a way different from others, and as a result has acquired a different outlook with regard to his data. Writing history is a dialogue between the historian and his data, the traces and voices of the past.

For this reason it is not sufficient to discuss the sources alone. I must also clarify, briefly at least, my methodological premises about society and culture, and my encounter with the data—especially here, where the sources are scarce and the lacunae loom large, to be bridged by my assumptions. This chapter therefore deals first with the sources and second with the methodology. Even so the reader cannot expect that all of my implicit presuppositions are set forth. Many of them I am not even aware of, and in any case they will become evident from the reconstruction itself.

The Sources

Sources for history can be classified in several ways. The most meaningful approach distinguishes between two classes of data: sources that assert that such and such happened, and sources that document a situation. The first group encompasses oral traditions and written records. Their assertions must be my first hypotheses. The second group entails such sources as languages or cultures. They do not assert anything about change in the past, and with them I start out using my own hypotheses to describe a situation. The first type of source is more directly informative, albeit less objective. The second, while more objective, is also less stimulating.

The first type consists of data that historians are trained to cope with. The statements offered can be turned into propositions to be tested, and can thus help historical reconstruction far more than the relatively inert sources of the second class. The usefulness of the second type of data stems first from their ability to provide checks on the initial proposition, then to modify it to more satisfying explanations. For these data the skills needed are essentially anthropological and linguistic, although other types of data can be relevant.

During my research it became evident that oral tradition (our only source of the first type before 1880), linguistics, and ethnography form a natural triad because data from any one of these fields have a direct bearing on the other two. What oral tradition tells us is in its way ethnography; ethnography allows an understanding of the implications of traditions (serious risks of anachronism being granted here); and language not only allows us to understand the traditions, but can also be used as a control. Besides this cluster there exists a biological data cluster, and there should be an archaeological one, probably closely linked to the biological one.

Archaeological data, priceless as they would be, are unfortunately not available, for Kuba country is still virgin territory to that discipline. Thus we lack the means for dating the earlier periods of history and to test and improve the chronology inferred for the seventeenth to the late nineteenth centuries. Once digging begins, however, the results should help to provide a revealing check on the overall validity of the reconstruction put forward here, which should therefore describe the kind of objects that may be found and the layout of the settlements in terms immediately understandable to the archaeologist. The transition from archaeology to the first cluster comes by way of comparative ethnographic data, especially artifacts.

A more detailed discussion of the written records and of linguistic and ethnographic data follows; data from the biological cluster are briefly discussed afterwards. Oral traditions have been discussed in the previous chapters.

Written sources are scarce until the early twentieth century. Only three documents—dating from c. 1619, c. 1624, and 1756—may have a bearing on earlier Kuba history.[1] Direct reports are available only after António da Silva Porto reached Kuba country on August 8, 1880,[2] although his was not the first Luso-African caravan. In his wake the 1881 expedition of Paul Pogge and Hermann von Wissmann met some Kuba, but it was only in 1885 that Ludwig Wolf entered the country to sign a treaty with the king's son whereby the Kuba relinquished their sovereignty to the Congo Independent State,[3] a fact that the Kuba did not realize until 1899. By the end of 1885 Europeans were living at Luebo, on the southern border of the kingdom, but not until the summer of 1892 did William Sheppard penetrate the kingdom to the capital, of which he has left us an extremely valuable account.[4] The same year several commercial posts, whose records have been either lost or were never available, were established on Kuba territory. From then until 1899, when a force of mercenaries from the Congo Independent State stormed the capital, a few brief data are available.[5] After 1900 the most valuable materials for Kuba history were those gathered by Emil Torday in 1908, although some were collected by Leo Frobenius in 1905. The Congo Independent State was taken over by Belgium as a colony in 1908. In 1910 the Belgian administration established a post at the capital and more data became available. Starting in 1919, ethnographic material and many items of traditional history were collected by the administrators, among them Lode Achten, René Van Deuren, and Pierrot. During my period in the field I was allowed to peruse the records of the local area (territoire) and those of the district, Luebo, to which it then belonged. A massive file of Achten's work (1919-29) is available at the Musée royal de l'Afrique centrale.[6]

In 1953 I was able to find Torday's main informant in the area and to check all of Torday's published materials not only with the informant but also with his elders. This allowed me to reconstruct the way in which Torday had gone about his research and how the Kuba court had used his interest in history to further its own aims. Torday's work is fundamental, for it profoundly influenced the early administrators and such later Presbyterian ministers as Wharton.[7] It may also have affected some of the younger Kuba, for I found one short manuscript history that was clearly copied about 1940 from his major work of 1910. Later administrators relied more on the leads provided by Achten. Since no Kuba had access to their archives, that material did not have a direct influence on them. But because different administrators kept asking similar questions, the need for the Bushoong to give the "same answer" certainly led to a hardening of tradition. Some of the administrators or their clerks may have orally communicated information which they had read in the archives, but evidence for this is almost nil. Since I had access to all the records and checked for this possibility of feedback, we can be positive that there was very little except that, as noted above, variants tended to be suppressed.

Catholic missionaries were in the kingdom from 1904 and recorded some information but did not disseminate it among the Kuba. It was only during the 1930s that much valuable material was collected by Prosper Denolf, a missionary active in the eastern part of the realm.[8] Most of it was published in Dutch, so no direct feedback occurred. The missions were in fact not interested in the detail of Kuba history and exercised little, if any, influence in this regard.

It is remarkable that the impact of writing on the oral tradition up to the 1950s was so slight. The fact that until the 1950s very few Kuba were educated beyond the lower grades of primary school is an obviously important factor in this situation.

The Bushoong language exudes a flavor all its own. A few decades ago it definitely did not conform—at least on the surface—to the image of a Bantu language, and even Althea Brown Edmiston, the author of a grammar and dictionary, had to be assured by Alice Werner that the language was in fact Bantu. A proof of the scanty phonological knowledge of the recorders was the current complaint that "the Kuba spoke very badly and shamelessly admitted it themselves."[9] Brown Edmiston states: "I met with many perplexing problems, esp. in the conjugation of the verb, the pronunciation and the spelling of words." But her perception was so obscured by the model of other Bantu languages that she provided nonexistent final vowels to all her words.[10]

Even when it became clear that the Kuba idiom was Bantu, its place in the classifications varied. Before 1953 Bushoong and other Kuba languages related to it were linked with those of the north, among which Mongo was and is the best known. But it was felt that the language reflected influences from another linguistic group, perhaps a substrate.[11] My data were responsible for taking the language out of the northern grouping, Guthrie's zone C, to link it with zone B languages, spoken to the west, on the basis of its particular phonology and a few shared items.[12] (Maps 4 and 5, pages 86 and 87, show the locations of peoples.)

By 1966 lexicostatistical counts clearly showed that the language does after all belong to zone C, despite a heavy phonological influence from zone B. It was then noticed that these B features were not equally present everywhere but fanned out from the capital in more or less concentric circles. This shows that the B phonology was a court innovation.[13] It is sufficient to know that oral tradition claims that the founder of the last dynasty came from the west to explain the phenomenon, which in turn supports this aspect of Kuba tradition.

The same tradition also solves the mystery about another language, *lambil*, once spoken at court.[14] On the basis of the few words available, Harry Johnston thought that lambil was not Bantu at all. Later it was declared to be Bantu, and analysis of the term shows it to be akin to two other terms, *mbil* and *ibil*, applied to territory dependent to the Bushoong. Brown Edmiston concluded that the term was applied by the Bushoong to the other dialects and languages of their group to denote "certain variations in accent and pronunciation."[15] Torday was in fact told that people at the capital formerly spoke in the same way as those of what were then the dependent territories.

Once all of this was realized, an attractive strategy for making use of this linguistic history presented itself. All Bushoong words fall into a few categories, or sets: (1) those that are shared by many languages and go back to proto-Bantu; (2) those that are shared only with languages of zone C and may go back to the ancestral language of the Kuba; (3) those that are shared only with the Luba languages (zone L) or Luba Kasai, of which Kete is a dialect; (4) those that are shared with the western languages (Diing, Mbuun) of zone B; (5) those shared only with other western languages, such as Pende (zone K) or Kongo (zone H), or a combination of western languages; (6) innovations; (7) words whose distribution area does not conform to any of the above sets, such words having an aberrant distribution; and (8) words that defy comparison.

Since for set 2 the rather remote northwestern Mongo languages were used for a comparison, it can be assumed that this set, along with set 1, really represents the ancestral speech of the Kuba. In many cases the presence of similar items in other C languages strengthens the proposition, and makes certain that no recent loanwords from an adjoining zone C language (Ndengese, Tetela) have been included. The set can be used to reconstruct the way of life of the proto-Kuba just before they became differentiated from the southern Mongo—before they became Kuba.

Set 3 includes both items taken over from the Kete, who were earlier inhabitants of what is now the realm, and later loans from the Luba. It is therefore not always easy to interpret. In some cases it can be shown that the loans went from Luba to Kuba or vice versa because a phonetic filter is available. But the date of the loan cannot be established by linguistic evidence alone.

Sets 4 and 5 indicate loans from the west, set 4 being an earlier set that can be dated by the arrival of Shyaam and the last dynasty, and set 5 being a somewhat later set, most of whose terms were presumably transmitted by traders.

Sets 6 and 7 require special explanation. Innovation occurs when the language needs a new word. That need indicates change, since new words are needed for new objects, situations, attitudes, or behavior. As for aberrant sets, they indicate an individual change in a single cultural or social feature or a group of associated features. Only set 8 contains no historical clues at all. In all the sets phonetic correspondences should be regular, and if not, the irregularity should be explainable in terms of patterns of borrowing—i.e., no explanation valid only for a single term can be accepted.

This strategy of employing sets for comparative purposes was applied to Bushoong words and the results are set forth in Appendix B. The most obvious result is the confirmation that Bushoong indeed belongs to zone C. Thus, hypothesis is now backed not only by basic grammatical criteria but by lexical data as well. The significance of the results will unfold as we proceed, for they permit the main outlines of the proto-Kuba society to be sketched. The results indicate not only that loanwords between Bantu languages can be detected by the comparatist, but that the endeavor is rewarding. In this study linguistic evidence has been especially useful not only as a control on oral traditions but also to provide new data and to suggest lines of thought not adumbrated by tradition.

Ethnographic data are the very stuff of history. All history deals with change in culture and society. To claim that institutions and culture do not change is to deny history altogether. Yet is is only insofar as they do *not* change that ethnographic data can be a source for historians. Some items, such as the use of the hoe in agriculture, may have changed little over long time periods.[16] The crux of the matter is to know which features can be viewed as "retentions" from the past, and unaltered retentions at that. Comparisons with neighboring societies and cultures give us the main clues here. Either the Kuba practice differs from that of a society such as the Leele, which shares the language and overall cultural features of the Kuba—and one must account for this—or the Kuba practice is similar to that of neighboring societies, whether or not they presumably shared a common ancestral culture and society. Data from the first situation seem better than data derived from the second, for one may postulate evolutions of the features from a common ancestral form to the different forms found in the ethnographic record. One explains by invoking change. Explanations based on the second situation are much more ambiguous. Similarities may be due to a common origin and a lack of change since those remote days. But they may also be due to a later diffusion, even when the feature existed in some form in the common ancestral culture, for that feature may have been altered or lost in some cultures and then have been reintroduced in another form from another source. The only test to determine whether diffusion has taken place is to indicate that the designated features are found only in a group of societies that are known to share a common ancestral way of life, or on the contrary, that they are found in other societies as well. In the latter case some diffusion, at the very least, has been at work. In practice almost all my arguments rest on differences among features in societies that stem from a common ancestral society, or on similarities among features in societies that do not share a common ancestry.

I have used comparative ethnography rather sparingly, and then most often as an adjunct to semantic items or oral tradition. In part this results from a lack of distribution studies. Where such studies are available, as they are for musical instruments, certain agricultural techniques, raffia weaving, the division of labor between the sexes in agriculture, and matrilineal distributions, the data have been considered.[17] It is clear, for example, that certain musical instruments have long been used and that the xylophone is a later addition. But this is clear mainly because the distributions agree closely with other—primarily lexical—data.

Distribution studies are useful to help discard explanations that are too particularistic. The Kuba are matrilineal: they belong to the matrilineal belt that crosses Central Africa from the Atlantic to the Indian Ocean, but they form a bulge in the pattern and are sandwiched between patrilineal Mongo on the north and patrilineal Luba on the south. Their eastern neighbors are also patrilineal. The hypothesis that the Kuba were once patrilineal and then became matrilineal (itself to be proved by other means) cannot be explained simply by stating that they started requiring the groom to work for his bride's parents and hence caused temporary uxorilocality. An independent "invention" is unconvincing, and the particular explanation must be abandoned. The Kuba "borrowed" the institution, and one must concentrate on the conditions that made them borrow it.

The central Kuba are culturally close to the neighboring Leele even though specific social institutions differ widely. Both groups know about this relationship and enshrine it in their cosmology.[18] That situation warranted a close comparison of their ethnographies, all the more so as the best explanation is that the Kuba and the Leele once belonged to the same general ancestral society. Mary Douglas carried out an explicit comparison relating to the economies of both societies, which led to the conclusion that although there are major differences in economic production, the inferior Leele techniques were known to the Bushoong. Douglas further established a connection between differences in social organization and level of economic achievement.[19] It is tempting to see the Leele as an archaic culture out of which Kuba society has grown. But by comparing Leele society with their neighbors it becomes clear that the development of their typical age-grade villages and the associated features are a unique Leele innovation. Leele characteristics "spill over" into neighboring fringe areas but do not completely cover any other ethnic group. These features are what make the Leele unusual in comparison with the Kuba, and just as the Kuba have a history showing how they formed a kingdom, the Leele have one that involves the creation of their institutions. They are not "archaic Kuba" but a society that has developed. And the data from both societies dovetail nicely when a common ancestral society and culture of a general southern Mongo pattern is presupposed.

Beyond the Leele, for whom ample evidence has been collected, only scattered data are available for the southern Mongo themselves.[20] One must regret that these peoples have not yet been studied by a professional anthropologist, especially since it appears that once they shared a common ancestral culture with the Kuba and the Leele. Data permitting more detailed comparisons are available for the northwestern and southwestern Mongo, the Luba Kasai, the Luba of Shaba, the Pende, the Yans, and the Sakata. Useful, if less detailed, are reports for all the western groups, including the Ding, Ngwii, Mbuun, and Tsong, and for the Tetela and Songye to the east of the

Kuba. Their immediate eastern neighbors, the Binji, have not been studied. Information combed from all these sources has been moderately useful, usually as an adjunct to linguistic data.

Within the confines of the Kuba kingdom, ethnographic variability among the major institutions has been fairly systematically recorded. This allows arguments to be made about the antiquity of such institutions. One argument is to claim that they remained unchanged over long periods of time (retention or survival); another, the age-area argument, is that the variant found in the center of the distribution in space is younger than the peripheral variants of such institutions. These arguments were only adduced when other data— usually oral—had already suggested the results. The patterns strengthened other available evidence, but I did not dare use them as valid testimony on their own, nor in fact did I need to. In some respects the non-Bushoong chiefdoms represent a more archaic stage of the society as a whole, but in others their situation in our century has been influenced by the fact that they have belonged to the kingdom for a century or two. Only one chiefdom, that of the Bieeng, lies outside the kingdom and might be presumed to retain the organization and social life that existed "before" there ever was a kingdom. Here again, however, close links to the kingdom do exist, and the Bieeng situation has been used only sparingly, even though I believe that they have some "archaic" value. They have not been studied in the depth that is necessary before this line of inquiry can be confidently pursued further. We have only their own official history, travelers' reports, which date mostly from 1896 and ethnographic notes collected during a few days in 1956.

Iconographic materials from the seventeenth century exist. They consist of a few raffia textiles now in museums in Stockholm, Copenhagen, London, and Ulm. The textiles come from the former kingdom of the Kongo. They belong to a class of products called "Kasai velvet," which only the Kuba produced by the late nineteenth century. A comparison of the decorative patterns between the Kongo and the late Kuba work shows very similar patterns of ornamentation. There clearly exists a link between the two, which is supported by oral and linguistic evidence. Other iconographic data valid for the nineteenth and perhaps the eighteenth century can be obtained from the royal statues.[21] Ideally such data should be matched against archaeological material, but this is still lacking. The closest finds are in northern Angola, Zambia, and at Kinshasa itself, but these sites are too far away to have much value for this study.

A study in human biology has confirmed the differences between the Bushoong and the Cwa,[22] and general knowledge about the biological origins of cultivated species of plants has been used to distinguish between American cultigens and others. The only remaining problem lies in differentiating American beans from European pulses, and deductions from this particular line of inquiry have not been made. Data about the relative resistance to blight by sorghum and maize in a wet environment that is marginal for sorghum proved useful. There is wide scope left for detailed studies on the effect of cultivation and consumption of staples not only on economic production and agricultural technology but also on nutrition and even human demography. Further ecological studies of the various biotopes and their changes could in time throw much-needed light on the relative prevalence of major fly-borne diseases. But this sector of research could not be pursued for lack of data and sufficient expertise. Questions such as whether sleeping sickness existed in earlier centuries, and if so what effects it had must be left aside. It may be mentioned in passing, that a solar eclipse (1680), the passage of Halley's comet (1835), and a cold wave in the late seventeenth century, all mentioned in the tales about kings, proved priceless in establishing the chronology of the kingdom.

Methodology

Despite the disparity of the sources mentioned it was possible to follow a pattern in using them during research.[23] Oral traditions were my starting point but are no longer the only, or perhaps even the main, sources of information about Kuba history. Linguistic data and ethnographic materials have yielded a great deal of information. My concern with establishing Kuba history began with collection of the abundant oral data, which quickly led me to the local archives and to earlier published accounts. Next came a reconstitution of Kuba history from this corpus. By and large, the interpretation followed an implicit model of Kuba society that was mainly inspired by the then-prevailing functional models of British social anthropology. The role of the model was to classify the data according to "relevance," and to guide the reconstruction accordingly.

Then followed a moratorium (after 1957) while other questions about the Kuba and other societies preoccupied me. When I came back to the problem of Kuba history in 1965 it was with the realization that the colonial situation had not merely distorted a few features of traditional society but had affected them fundamentally. The discovery by Stanley Shaloff[24] of a critical early source that I had not found and the chance to use some hitherto closed archives led to a study of certain aspects of Kuba life during the colonial period, a study that broadened as it grew. The new sources were not the main motivation for this interest: it stemmed from the Kinshasa school of history, then led by Bogumil Jewsiewicki and Jean-Luc Vellut. Their attitude toward the past prompted me to formulate new questions and to look for the type of document that contained the answer. This quest for a history of the Kuba during colonial times is not over; it is now at a stage where more archives

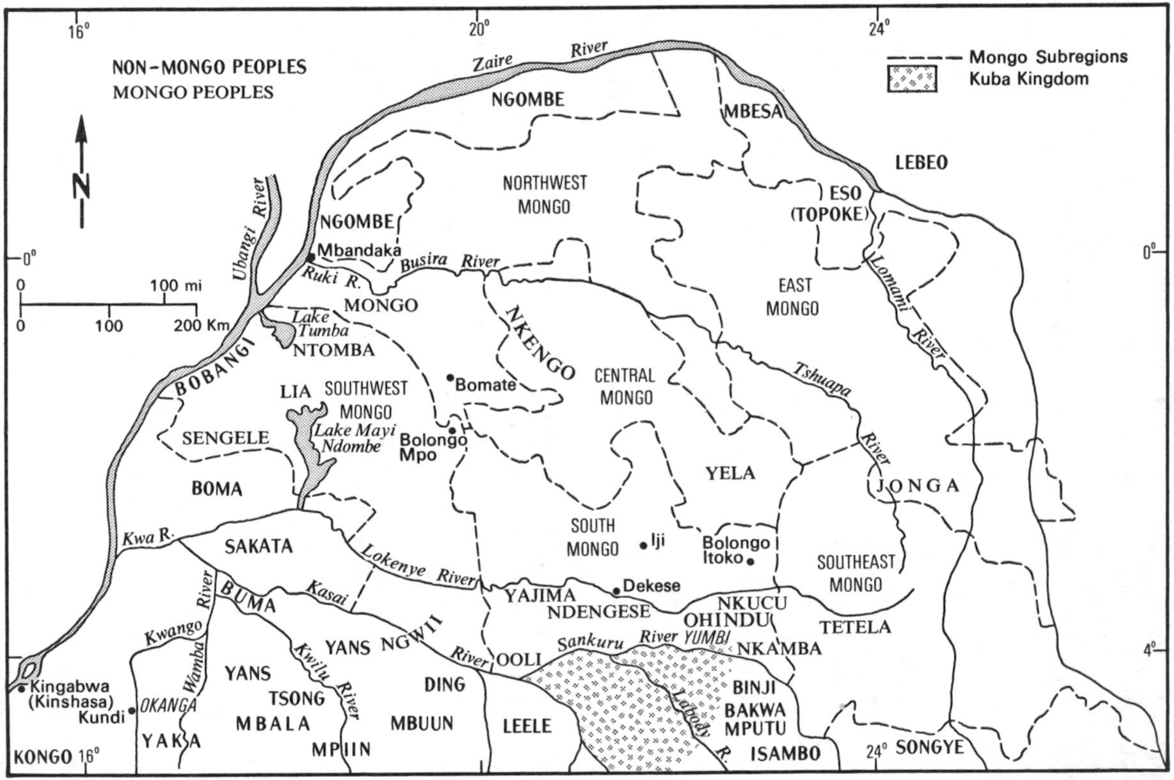

Map 4. Peoples to the North and West, c. 1880

NON-MONGO PEOPLES

MONGO PEOPLES

Mongo Subregions

Kuba Kingdom

NGOMBE

MBESA

LEBEO

ESO
(TOPOKE)

EAST
MONGO

JONGA

Lomami River

Tshuapa River

NORTHWEST
MONGO

YELA

SOUTHEAST
MONGO

TETELA

Bolongo
Itoko

NKUCU

NKAMBA

NKENGO

CENTRAL
MONGO

Iji

Dekese

OHINDU

YUMBI

BINJI

BAKWA
MPUTU

ISAMBO

SONGYE

Bomate

SOUTH
MONGO

NDENGESE

YAJIMA

Lubody R.

Sankuru River

NGOMBE

MONGO

Mbandaka

Busira River

Bolongo
Mpo

OOLI

LEELE

Zaire River

Ruki R.

LIA

SOUTHWEST
MONGO

Lake Mayi
Ndombe

NTOMBA

Lake
Tumba

Lokenye River

ILA

YANS

NGO River

DING

MBUUN

SENGELE

BOMA

SAKATA

Kasai

BUMA

YANS

TSONG

MBALA

MPIIN

Ubangi River

Kwilu River

BABANGI

Kwa R.

Wamba River

Kwango River

OKANGA

YAKA

Kingabwa
(Kinshasa)
Kundi

KONGO

N

200 Km

100 mi

100

0

0

16°

20°

24°

4°

0°

16°

0°

Cartographic Laboratory UW-Madison

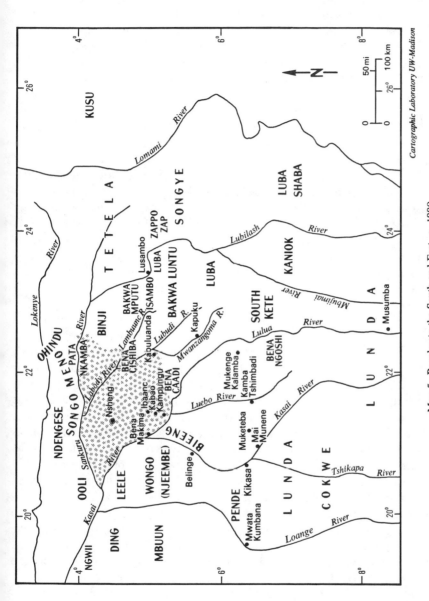

Map 5. Peoples to the South and East, c. 1880

87

must be tapped. Evrard's confirmation of the Kuba-Mongo link led to more specific work on the linguistic clues that could yield historical data.

About the same time the results of the work done by Joseph C. Miller made it clear that at least on one crucial point the Bushoong dynastic traditions were incorrect. His work implied a major challenge. Meanwhile, research by David Henige concerning the chronology of oral traditions led to the realization that the traditions still held fresh insights for those who had fresh minds.[25]

In 1971-72 I began more active research. By then I was in a much better position to know what the society and culture had become by 1892, before the European impact had grown substantial but after the impact of the Luso-African trade had permeated the society. My base line from which to probe the past was more secure. There were new questions to ask, questions voiced by other scholars concerning other societies. The more I learned, the more questions could be put to the Kuba data. A nagging dissatisfaction with a history almost completely confined to the deeds of kings, and one clinging scrupulously close to the "the source"—a product of my early training—was also gaining ground. I reopened the case, and this work is the result. There is no reason to believe that this book constitutes a definitive history, and indeed I would argue that it does not. Why should other major sources of information, including, I hope, archaeological research, not become available in the next twenty years?

The method followed here has been an ongoing interaction between the data and the historian[26] that has continued until it appears that those questions which can be tackled given the existing documentation have been considered. The general framework governing the design of this "history" remains a sort of social anthropology concerned with process and conflict as well as with balance, with nonintegration as well as with integration. I have retained the conviction that Kuba institutions are only loosely integrated with one another, so that Kuba society forms a loose system, and that political organization has been the dominant influence in it. The search for systemic characteristics has led to a stress on trends, among them economic change which my earlier study seriously underestimated. My stress is upon the primacy of the political evolution and the interaction between it and economic development. A sharp concern with intellectual history and art history has never been absent, despite the scantiness of the data. My view remains that basic perception about the ultimate reality of the world and fundamental affective and cognitive patterns as expressed in symbolism and art change very slowly indeed. Proof for the precolonial period is lacking, but this conviction is borne out by the slow rhythms of change in these realms during the otherwise hectic colonial period. I consider this a valid indicator of the precolonial pace.

Overall, then, this model is not entirely structuralist. It also repudiates the position that history is a blind, inexorable march (forward?) dictated by im-

mutable laws hidden somewhere inside a society. There are historical accidents as well as incidents. While no transformation can be achieved if the time
is not ripe, the ripe time without the right person will miss the opportunity for
change. The model used here recognizes social units as elements in an open
social system. It recognizes relationships between the units, "relationships of
relationships," accidents, and functions—an accident is but a function gone
awry. In the end it still looks like some sort of functional model, but one in
which the impact of every element on the whole is recognized because the
parts are ultimately interdependent, while nothing is claimed a priori as to the
effect of this impact. Each element can fit or clash with others, and over time
it can alter. In short, no total integration exists, but there is coexistence and,
as a result, a measure of interdependence and compatibility.

Chapter **6**

The Forebears

Our earliest glimpse of Kuba history is in the sixteenth century or perhaps even much earlier, at a time before there were any Kuba. An ancestral society common to the Kuba, Leele, Wongo, and all the southern Mongo then occupied the country between the Sankuru and the watershed on the north, formed by the valley of the Lokenye. Only an archaeologist would be able to tell how long that society had existed there. When it disappeared is hard to say. The southern Mongo societies today may well be its least changed descendants, and perhaps their way of life until recently reflected much of what was already in existence then. My reconstruction is not, however, founded on this assumption as much as on the data that emerge from a comparison of linguistic and ethnographic data common to the southern Mongo and the Kuba.[1] The results are a sketch of a way of life which is important because it represents a starting point that can itself be compared with the situation existing just before the incorporation of the Kuba kingdom into the colonial world. The differences between the two situations are the cumulative result of change and must be accounted for in my further reconstruction.

The area was part of the equatorial forest, characterized by a tree canopy overhead but surprisingly sparse undergrowth. Here and there, especially on the flatter and higher elevations, intercalary savannas appeared. Such savannas could be very long and were usually narrow, as was the main one between the Sankuru and Lokenye watersheds, which extended for perhaps fifty miles or more and was ten to twenty miles wide. Or, like the savanna of Iji, northeast of the Lokenye, they might consist of only a few square miles punctuating the forest. Temperatures in the forest were around 27° C (81° F) through most of the year, but rose much higher in the open spaces. Rainfall occurred during much of the year, the dry season not exceeding two months at the most in June and July, with a little rain even then; the bulk of the precipitation occurred in two periods: October-November and March-April. It was relatively dry from late December to early February. Four seasons in all could thus be distinguished.

In addition to the forest and the savanna, a third biotope was formed by the major rivers. The Lokenye was not wide enough to have sandbanks or to make much of a break in the canopy, but the Sankuru was almost half a mile wide, had glistening sandbanks when the waters were low, and caused a riot of light to burst through the gap it made in the forest cover. From July through September, when its waters were low, was the best time for fishing and perhaps also trading at places located several days' journey from home.

The rivers and the savannas, landmarks that are remembered in the traditions, provided alternative environments containing different flora and fauna from those in the forest. The area as a whole was more attractive than the lands farther north, where intercalary savannas were rare and where a triple environment was absent. The Sankuru was larger than any other river to the north and was rich in aquatic life; its products complemented those of the savanna just as the latter complemented those of the forest. It was a good country to live in.[2]

Men made their living from hunting, trapping, fishing, and agriculture. The last may have provided more food than the others, and the women spent most of their time on it, but the men cared little for it. The occupation that carried prestige for them was the hunt. Among the various types of hunting, the pursuit of elephants stood apart because it was so dangerous and required great agility and presence of mind. Perhaps it was already practiced primarily—as it later would be—by the Cwa.

There were various methods of hunting. Monkeys were pursued with sharp poisoned arrows without iron heads,[3] birds with blunted wooden arrows, antelope with nets, toward which a group of drivers sent the animals, where they were then stabbed with spears. Antelope were also hunted with bow and arrow. Sometimes a few hunters, aided by tracking dogs wearing little wooden bells, would go on a running hunt. A single hunter might lie hidden a few feet from a waterhole or a path indicated by the spoor of game animals. The running hunt may have been intended mainly to catch warthogs (*Phacochoerus, Potamochoerus, Hylochoerus*), which the Kuba, at a later time, preferred over all other meat.

There were dangers in hunting. The buffalo of either forest or savanna variety was often deadly if provoked, and the leopard might attack even when unprovoked. Individual hunting was not favored by any except the Cwa; the forebears of the Kuba preferred to hunt in groups. In the dry season they would move for days through the intercalary savanna, driving the game into nets, camping in temporary shelters.

Although hunting was exciting and psychologically rewarding, more animals were caught by traps than by pursuit. A wide variety of traps existed, ranging from the simple sliding noose for small antelope to the spring traps of bamboo that were used especially for squirrels and were placed on branches, to a massive roof set up near water to catch warthogs and designed to cave in when the trigger under it was disturbed. The technology of trapping was as well developed as that of hunting. Collective labor was also required for it, but only for such semipermanent devices as the trap roof and perhaps pits and fences constructed with trap openings. The Cwa lacked an extended technology of the more permanent types of traps because they moved so much, although centuries later, after 1900, they were renowned for setting crocodile traps.

Fishing methods resembled hunting with traps or with a net. Fish traps were set all year around. When the water was low, by means of collective labor weirs were placed in the major rivers, sometimes extending almost across the Lokenye or entirely across inlets. Later, Kuba fishermen on the Sankuru would build permanent dikes running out into the river; these had gaps where traps were placed and over which a little house was built to allow a watchman to operate along the whole dike day and night. But the usual method of fishing on the main rivers involved use of a net, which was thrown out and then trawled by two canoes. Hook and line were also used. Along the Sankuru certainly, and perhaps also along the Lokenye, there were specialized fishermen who would travel far in the dry season, catching as much fish as possible, drying it on the sandbanks and smoking it, perhaps even salting it if they had enough salt. Fish would spoil so easily at those prevailing temperatures that some conservation process would be necessary when a big catch was made. It is quite likely that while traveling during the dry season a fisherman traded with other fishermen and with the landlubbers who bought not only fish but pots, for the good clays for pottery are found only along the Lokenye and the Sankuru. One spectacular but rather rare occupation for fisherman was to go after hippopotamus with harpoons and floaters. This method was not very developed, however, and its technology was not comparable to that on the lower Kasai and the Kwa, where it later (and perhaps even then) was much more frequent.

The trade in fish with landlubbers during the dry season may not have been as extensive as it was at other times because the landsmen also spent much time fishing then. They threw poison into fenced-off sections of the small streams and caught the stunned fish by hand or in baskets. It is even possible that they followed the later Kuba practice of excavating artificial ponds near small streams for that purpose. For the rest of the year they fished with hook and line or with baskets used to scoop up the fish. Scooping was woman's work: the women went every day to the spring to fetch water and therefore had more opportunity to fish by this method.

The basic agricultural technology presumably involved three types of fields. The first type was cleared within the forest, where all trees except the real giants were cut down within a given area. The branches were cut from the fallen trunks and were burned, then the ashes were hoed into the ground by the women, who did the planting. The main staple was the plantain. Two crop rotations were possible: either the grove was kept up for as long as possible, which certainly was the case near the clearings where hamlets and villages

were located; or plantains were grown for one year and beans the next,[4] and
when the beans were harvested yams were planted.

The second type of field lay in the intercalary savanna. It was easier to
prepare because a clearing already existed. Here the rotation was sorghum or
perhaps millet followed by beans and *Voandzeia*. Secondary plants, among
them eggplants, were also grown. After the yam harvest in the forest or the
Voandzeia harvest in the savanna the fields lay fallow to regenerate. Perhaps
then oil palms and even raffia palms were planted in the clearings.

The third type of garden consisted of the small plots located behind the
houses in the village. Clearing and maintaining them was women's work
exclusively and the plots were only a few feet away from the place where
women pounded the cereals or plantains and cut up the yams for cooking.
Here they grew gourds, calabashes, medicinal plants, and perhaps yams.

The only domestic animals were dogs, fowl (more for meat than for eggs),
and goats (for meat only). No special food was given to them nor were any
shelters provided. The dogs slept in the house, the poultry under the eaves,
and the goats where they could.

The yield derived from gathering is unknown compared to agricultural
yields, but was of major importance. It provided all building materials,
firewood, material for ropes, tools, and furniture, as well as many sorts of
leaves and roots used for condiments and sauces. Different sorts of
caterpillars—each in its season—termites, and wild yams were welcome
additional snacks. Trees of the fig variety were important, for they provided
the bark cloth used for dress. A legion of basketry objects was woven from
materials gathered in the wild. Perhaps honey was also gathered; at the most
hives were placed in the trees to encourage bees to settle there.

The main crafts were iron smelting and smithing, woodcarving, basketry,
plaiting, saltmaking, pottery, and a little raffia weaving. Pottery and ironwork
were dry-season occupations, the latter because the ore was dug up from
stream beds and had to dry in the open, the former because low water uncov-
ered the best clay and it was in that season that most trade occurred along the
two main rivers. Salt was obtained by burning the male inflorescence of the
oil palm. It was a task for women, as was the manufacture of pottery. All the
rest was left in the hands of men. Iron smelting was a craft requiring
specialized knowledge, as was smithing, although to a lesser degree. The
skills for the other crafts were widely distributed, and almost any man could
carve wood, plait, or weave. The only task that required some collaboration
among several men was iron smelting, and the master smelter was the epitome
of the craftsman. The major tools of his trade, hammers and the anvil, as well
as such products as the double bell, probably were already major emblems of
chieftainship.[5] Whether or not smithing was a hereditary occupation and
whether smiths were shunned or admired is unknown. It is likely that their

shed stood on the village plaza not far from the shed for weavers or plaiters, and that both were then, as later, the places where people gathered to gossip.

The limiting factor in production was certainly labor. Given a very likely low density of population, land was plentiful; the only land that may have been crucially limited in areas north of the Lokenye was the intercalary savanna. Rights to hunting and fishing were vested in territorial units and were quite specific. Certain parts of certain animals, such as the tusk of an elephant, had to be given as tribute to the "chief," as in the story of Lakoin, cited in Chapter Four. Capital investment was of major importance only to fishermen, who needed craft of various sizes. The boats were individually owned but were built and manned by crews. Their other tools—and they needed many—were fashioned and were kept in good repair by constant labor involving everyone in the fishing settlement. Technical knowledge in production was esoteric only for medicine men and iron smelters.

The crucial importance of labor is shown by the basic rules of ownership, which stated that the person who had expended labor on an object or a plot of land was the owner for as long as the object lasted or the land produced, fallow land included. Division of labor by age and sex was clear-cut. Children helped to gather food or carry water, shooed the birds away from the sorghum fields, threaded raffia, and probably helped with the preparation of bark cloth. They also shot birds and trapped small mammals. Elderly persons stayed in the village, tended the babies, and gave formal and informal advice. Elderly men generally ran the community. They also benefited most from the efforts of others, and in this sense the society was a gerontocracy, in which the relations of production were dominated by the elders. Women took care of the kitchen and the very small babies, fetched wood and water, and did most of the work in the fields once they had been cleared. They may even have been entirely responsible for clearing fields in the intercalary savanna. Men cleared the forest, hunted, fished, and made war when necessary. Cooperation among men was limited in the agricultural villages to communal hunting or perhaps the building of heavy traps, whereas in the fishing villages it was a sine qua non for their main activities. Collaboration among women may have involved helping one another in the fields and in dry-season fishing, perhaps the only occasion when all the inhabitants of a settlement worked together. The unit of production therefore was very probably the polygynous household, which was also the unit of consumption. If so, the likely goal of each unit was to plant enough to serve its own needs and to calculate the amount of labor necessary for this according to yields of the worst agricultural year in recent memory. Since yearly variations do not seem to have been very great in this climate, production probably totaled at best a modest surplus and at worst just enough to subsist.[6] Whatever was produced beyond that was a function of demand, either by the community as a whole or by political authorities. Since the political structure was minimal, I believe that each hamlet acted as if all its constituent households formed a single unit of consumption, which would raise the output slightly but would not produce either a significant or a reliable surplus.

Anything affecting the distribution of labor, or cooperation among laborers, or the health of the workers immediately affected output. Without alteration of any of these conditions a small potential for surplus might exist, but to obtain impressive surpluses more collaboration and more involvement of men in agriculture would have been necessary. Concerning the history of health we can only speculate. On the whole the situation may not have been very different from that which prevailed at the end of the nineteenth century, before European diseases such as smallpox were introduced. Given the fact that we do not really know whether or not trypanosomiasis was endemic in the area at all, nothing more can be said about the population than that the nutritional balance, especially with regard to protein, was better than it is in our century. The average life-span could not have been very great given the prevalence of malaria, helminthiasis, dysentery, and pulmonary diseases during the dry season. Still, the society reproduced itself, and we may even accept a small increase in population leading to later territorial expansion. On the whole it is sufficient to state that the population was almost in equilibrium with the biotope. There are no reasons to believe that vast changes occurred.

We can describe the rudiments of the process of production,[7] but much less is known about exchange. We do not even know whether or not markets existed. Some redistribution of goods and services was customary among kin or among residents of a hamlet or a village, as a result of marriage (bridewealth) and judicial action (fines). The political system beyond the village level was probably not elaborate enough to create channels for a redistribution of goods and services. There is some indication of intervillage trade in the vocabularies, but in any case not all villages were endowed with resources for making iron or pots. Later on, the Ohindu in this area would receive their iron from the Yela (Lomela zone).[8] Pottery and fish were certainly traded in locations away from the two main rivers, and a symbiotic exchange between pygmoids and agriculturalists is likely. It is also hard not to imagine that camwood, *Baphia nitida*, which grows abundantly here, was in demand south of the Sankuru and the Kasai. And why would salt, which was much more efficiently produced south of the Sankuru, not have been a traded item as well?[9]

The ancestral southern Mongo lived in villages composed of at the least several family units and several hamlets, whose leading men were all related as members of a single patrilineage. Residence was certainly virilocal, and men lived in the settlements of their fathers. The main doubt concerns the mode of descent. Was it matrilineal, as it was among the Kuba or patrilineal, as among the southern Mongo later? One might argue that the matter is of small importance[10] since unilineal descent relates merely to a limited number of rights and obligations that vary from one society to another, and bilateral tendencies are strong in all Mongo groups.[11] In those groups marriage is virilocal, and residential groups are mainly composed of patrilineal kin with their families and retainers. Lineages are patrilineal and have a common name and a common food prohibition. They were responsible for the conduct of feuds to defend their members or to avenge them. They could hold political rights over lands, and when collective labor was required it could be organized by the lineage directing the settlement or by the larger lineage including several villages.

Except for the cooperation among villages, southern Mongo lineages all fulfilled these functions. And their ancestors, who were ancestors of the Kuba as well, did the same. They were patrilineal, organized in lineages. A comparison of Kuba terminology and Mongo patterns shows that special terms existed for persons four generations removed, from ego up and down, which would fit a deep lineage system. Why otherwise would a term such as great-great-grandchild (still preserved in Bushoong) and its converse even be needed? The Mongo did not have a system of alternating generations, which could point to shallow lineage depth, and the Kuba have alternating generations only in ascending generations, whereas the Leele have a complete alternating system. The Kuba then stand between the Mongo and the Leele.

By themselves, shallow generations are not indicative of matrilineality. The Kongo and the Pende have deep lineage structures and yet the Pende use alternating generations. Today the Kuba have shallow matrilineages, but one can conclude that they once had deep lineages, which were probably patrilineal because of the correspondence of some of the implicated terms and of the general structure of the terminology with Mongo practice.[12]

With regard to marriage and bridewealth the terminology informs us only that in-laws were seen as "persons to be avoided (almost ritually)" in the Mongo set while in the Luba set they are "the persons to be paid." Mongo and Luba both have a special term for bridewealth but the Kuba have none, although in the nineteenth century they paid bridewealth and may have performed some bride service as well. Tentatively, I would suggest that the ancestral southern Mongo paid bridewealth, but to a lesser extent than that which was practiced among the ancestral Luba. Polygyny was common and was more widespread among wealthier people, such as lineage elders, than among others. After all, the elders did control the community. The Mongo term *nkolomo*, "old person, notable," evolved in the Kuba language to mean "dignitary" and among the Leele to mean "pawn." The Leele opposed it to a political term, *kum*, whose original meaning everywhere was "chief." The content of that notion became to them "master of, owner of," while the original meaning was preserved among both the Kuba and the southern Mongo.

Each patrilineage lived in its own hamlet, which formed part of a village. The Mongo term for such a hamlet, *etuka*, has been preserved to the present in some Kuba expressions. It is unlikely that all the hamlets of the village were occupied by related patrilineages forming a lineage of a bigger size corresponding to the village. The Kuba king in the 1950s described his Bushoong as living on the fringes of the Ndengese village, and they were certainly not related. Although it could be an anachronism, the fact that in most southern Mongo villages lineages of different origins and different clans live together is significant. These villages are directed by councils, composed of all the heads of the constituent parts, which conduct common village business, and something like this was already in existence in ancestral times. Perhaps client lineages or individuals lived side-by-side with their masters.

Other social features remain very dim indeed. No age-grades seem to have existed. Twins were singled out for special status, but since that status has changed so much among the Bushoong it is difficult to visualize what it might have been in the old days. Namesakes had special friendly relationships one with the other, justified probably through the practice of keeping personal names in the lineage, so that namesakes "should be" related. Other names were used as well, however, since a whole stock of Kuba names—including common ones such as Mbop or Kot—do not mean anything in the language now. Or are these the remnant of the old lineage names? Whether the ancestral southern Mongo kept slaves, or pawns in temporary servitude, or hostages remains unknown because no common terms have survived. If they did, these statuses were very different from the ones later found among the Kuba.

Chiefdoms, however small and unimpressive, existed. There were dynastic lineages, and the chiefs ruled over a territory which may have comprised as little as a single village. The mystical power of a chief such as Itoci was linked to a ball of kaolin[13] which constituted the principle of authority known as *ekopo*[14] among today's Mongo: an authority based on control over territory, and not derived from kinship seniority alone. Emblems pertaining to it, such as the leopard skin or the double bell or legitimacy in the form of a designation by nature spirits (the hammers and the anvils tale), are linked with this status of *nkum* to such an extent among the southwestern Mongo, and less clearly among the southern and central Mongo, that the whole complex must be considered very old. Legitimation of the dynastic line was provided by a charter myth claiming the gift of ekopo, the *bokapa* ekopo, which also occurs as Bukap and similar names in western Kuba traditions.[15] For the Ndengese the last bokapa ekopo took place at Iji, north of the Lokenye and, according to some of their versions, the Boshongo, ancestors of the Bushoong, received legitimacy there.[16] This theme may have been borrowed from the southwestern Mongo, as perhaps did the concept of nkum; if so, it happened even before the period we are describing. Some insignia such as the eagle's feather, the royal drum, the royal palisade or hedge, and the placement of the chief's residence at the head (downstream?) of his capital are also present in Ndengese practice.

Chiefs bore titles. Itoci was the title of the chief of the Ndengese. Later, Lakoin is known as the title of a Yajima chief, and in the royal account of the migrations this may mean that the ancestors of the Bushoong were closer to the Yajima. The present Ngongo title Yeli Ngongo corresponds to that of the chief of the Ntomba of Mayi Ndombe. Other titles that seem to go back a long way[17] are Longomo, Lokwa, and Welo among the Ooli and Yajima. The whole region was apparently divided into numerous small chiefdoms, each having its own title.

Chiefs ruled directly over villages. There were no subchiefdoms. If they existed at all courts were very small, and authority, although based on the notion of territory, was also tied to kinship. What turned a lineage leader into a chief was perhaps more the size of his village and the cohesive powers it provided than any abstract notion of common territory or rights derived from a framework of kinship. The kum were in fact still the leaders of stateless societies in the strict sense.[18] Dependents were perceived as clients, and their status was justified not by the fact that they lived on the chief's territory but by fictive matrilateral ties, as has continued to happen among the southern Mongo. On the other hand symbolic tribute was paid to the chief as "owner of the land." This was what caused the rift between the Bushoong and the Ndengese: Itoci was not paid his tusk.

There is no evidence concerning genuine political power. Did chiefs curb private feuds? Could no one be killed except by their leave? Was the court a genuine center for the flow and redistribution of tributary goods? True, there were some political institutions. The head of the warriors was an *iyol*, and a medicine man for war charms, the *ilweemy*, was found at every court, perhaps even in every village. Assemblies may have existed— distinct from village councils—when the chief controlled more than one village, but all the terms referring to this are derived from verbs "to assemble," "to gather," so they do not prove anything. Ethnographic evidence suggests only that there was a capital or a court, the later *nsheng*. It is probable that the elders at the court, the nkolomo, were seen as inferior but complementary to the kum, which explains the semantic drift of those two terms together everywhere, especially among the Leele. So the chief may have ruled with the elders of his village.

The ancestral southern Mongo had a cycle of legends to account for the world and its peculiarities. It had been created by Mboom (Mbombianda) alone or assisted by another creator, Ngaan. The pygmies were the earliest inhabitants. They were said to have come out of trees. The first couple committed incest. Alternative explanations at the time may have involved a descent from heaven and an emergence from a primeval marsh. What mattered in daily life was not creation but the nature spirits, the ancestral spirits, and one's fellow men. Among the latter there were witches, who were always kinfolk, and sorcerers who used charms. An oracle, *bukaang*, existed to detect such people, and it is highly likely that the poison ordeal was used to test suspected witches. Every village had its own collective charm and its own medicine man for war. Of rituals we know only that ritual acts and objects were always accompanied by prohibitions, especially food taboos. These may in turn have been linked to concepts of pollution, although no linguistic evidence pertaining to the question has yet been discovered.

The nature spirits were localized; they had their territory and hence a relationship to chieftainship—and ethnicity. Nothing is known about their cult, which I suspect was the cult connected in each village to its collective shrine. Some ancestors, the Leele *nkadi* or Mongo *bokali*, helped the witches or sorcerers. One apparently archaic representation the Kuba have maintained is the notion of a place where ancestors go, the ilweemy, which recurs as *Ilombo* in Mpongwe. Perhaps, then, this was part of the collective representation in these times as well.

Tales were no doubt spun, sayings and proverbs coined, praise names and poems composed, songs sung. A few bits of the poetry, I believe, survived from that period. Yet none of the Kuba terms for these genres of oral literature corresponds to Mongo terms at all, suggesting that the perception of genres and their taxonomy must have altered considerably since those days. As for music and art, all the musical instruments used, except the xylophone, belong to the Mongo types even though certain instruments have been refined, whereas the Kuba style in visual art is ultimately not Mongo, even if it is found today in part among the southern Mongo. Details of decorative patterns and the like must await the excavation of pottery.[19]

In ancestral southern Mongo times the lands between the Sankuru, the Kasai, and the Lulua, similar to the lands to the north but with larger rivers, more savanna, and hence more biological diversity and attraction, were inhabited by the pygmoid hunters and a few Kete farmers. A Cwa leader from the far west of the area remembers their old way of life as follows, the description containing probably only one anachronism: the title of their leader, "king of the vine," clearly a later Kuba denomination.

We were always wandering around in the forest, in what is now the land of the Kel, after their arrival near Budiashep and Butala. We changed residence every time an ethnic group [of farmers] settled in the neighborhood. The Cwa have always known only one leader and one title in contrast to the elaborate hierarchy of the other Kuba. We only knew the *nyimmwaan*. We were roving in the forest and showed the way to the others. We were wandering, the ones to the right, the others to the left [an allusion to their motto].[20]

In the west the Cwa have become almost totally acculturated, but not in the east, where they have succeeded in preserving their own language, Locwa, and their own culture despite some acculturation. They were until recently—and still are in parts—nomadic hunters of the forest,[21] living in round shelters, clothing themselves with leaves, and hunting individually with a dog and bow and arrows. They had a bilateral social structure in which clans were unknown. The band could have been described as an extended family with hangers-on, but its main characteristic was the fluidity of its composition, there being a constant flow of individuals in and out of bands. Among the Cwa marriage was endogamous, which explains why Hiernaux could find such marked differences from the Kuba.[22] No bridewealth seems to have been paid, and we do not know if they practiced straight exchange of sisters or not. Of their religion we know nothing, and of their arts we have only the faintest hint of their naturalistic style of drawing in sand or of engraving wood.[23] In later times the Cwa obtained their iron (and they used very little, since they relied more on poisoned arrows than on metal arrowheads) from their farming neighbors, who also exchanged vegetables for meat. There is no reason why this should not have been practiced in the early days. Their right to steal food is associated with their status as autochthons.[24]

Traditions stress the differences between them and other Kuba. Some sources (including even a Cwa) obviously see them as the first rung on the evolutionary ladder. They "invented" all the important contributions, such as fire, cooked food, palm wine, and according to some, even chieftainship.[25] This is but the flattering side of a coin whose obverse reads: "The Cwa were savages and we civilized them." Either Woot or one of his children found the Cwa, who were naked. He took their women away and the men followed. "We" taught them to live in houses, "we" gave them Kuba food and dress. These attitudes are reminiscent of those of the farmers and of the Twa in the north, who form different castes which despise each other thoroughly.[26] Cwa were not unknown north of the Sankuru in ancestral southern Mongo times, and from the Kuba point of view, they lived in a state of dependence on the farmers. When they crossed the Sankuru, the farmers took little if anything from the Cwa south of the river. The poisoned wooden arrow may have been their only contribution, and even so, it may be that the Cwa north of the river had them as well. Reports that the Cwa had potters, saltmakers, and blacksmiths are as incredible as the one that they invented the five political titles found among all the Kuba, two of which are tied to a regular village organization. These stories simply make the point that these crafts and titles are very old indeed.[27]

Kete society was different. They were farmers and hunters, and they knew the crops the southern Mongo cultivated. In addition they had sugarcane and a variety of banana, both of which may have been unknown north of the Sankuru. Perhaps they were better farmers: millet is always associated with them. Their material culture was fairly similar to that of the ancestral southern Mongo, and their woodcarving was much better, as was their salt production. They burned marsh grasses and filtered the ashes. In later times, and perhaps even in earlier ones, this led them to cultivate the best grasses in the marshes. With the crystallized salt they made tiles or blocks, which later (and perhaps earlier) were used in trade. They also kept some sheep, an animal unknown north of the Sankuru possibly for ecological reasons. They not only used bamboo but, as in the case of marsh grass for saltmaking, are believed to have planted clumps of the plants. They had more palm trees, especially raffia palm, than their northern neighbors. Perhaps this was due to the higher proportion of savanna—the Kete lived in the open, intercalary savanna—or it may be due to more intentional planting. More raffia trees meant more raffia. They wore raffia garments, and perhaps their loom was more efficient than the Mongo loom. In any case, on all these points they influenced the Kuba when the two met. In technology the only superiority the southern Mongo may have had lay perhaps in the art of smithing. And even here some Kuba traditions recall that it was the smoke of a smithy that betrayed to the Kuba the presence of a Kete settlement on the Iyool plain.[28]

The Kete are now matrilineal, and were probably so in the past. Their term *bulungu*, "matriclan, matrilineage," is isolated in the Luba world, and is presumably old. They may have represented the most distant extension of the Central African matrilineal belt. It would be dangerous to speculate from their present practice what their precise kinship organization was in early times, because of their centuries-long symbiosis with the Kuba. Still, the presence of a strictly alternating nomenclature of kinship as well as special terms for "sister's son" (*mwipu*) and "mother's brother" (*manseba*), which are old features because they occur over the whole area of Luba languages, fits in well with former matrilinearity and shallow lineages or clans, though it does not necessarily imply the existence of preferential marriages. It follows that the Luba Kasai, whose terminology is practically identical, also once were matrilineal. One retention can still be seen in their practice of having bridewealth paid by the mother's brother of the groom in certain cases, and in other rights that the mwipu has in relation to his manseba.[29] The Luba became patrilineal in an unknown past and adapted the "of *buikulu*" ("of the quality of a distance of two generations or more") modifiers to their outlying generations to make the terminology applicable to their new lineage system.

Kete descent groups were known as *Baa* plus the clan name, corresponding to the Luba (Lulua) practice of *Bakwa* plus the clan name. No organization beyond the village was known, and even in a village each clan section may have kept to its own, although a general council met from time to time. Villages may have been small and did not cooperate with each other, which would explain why the incoming Kuba found almost no difficulty in setting among, and later in overcoming, the Kete.

Like the ancestral southern Mongo, the Kete practiced some form of nature spirit worship, although their cult and representations for and of death were different. The dead could return to harm or help, and were supposed to be more active than among the ancestors north of the Sankuru. The Kete were excellent sculptors and carved pillars and statues for their spirits, as well as at least one type of mask. All were carved in what is called the "Kuba" style, which belongs to an area stretching from the middle and upper Kasai (all Kete country then) well into Angola.[30] All in all, the Kete were better farmers than the ancestors of the Kuba and better artisans perhaps, but their political organization was much less coherent.

If this reconstruction of ancestral southern Mongo society is correct, archaeological work should be able to corroborate it. At the edge of savannas located between the Sankuru and the Lokenye, village sites should be found with a rectangular plan, the houses bordering a plaza, the streets oriented downstream to upstream wherever the terrain allows it. Possibly gaps can be found on each side of the street, denoting the boundaries of hamlets. And remnants of the chief's palisade, or hedge of *Dracaena*, would be on the short side of the plaza, downstream. Within the palisade should be found the house of the chief, and perhaps a shed, and a few houses for his wives and his kitchen. On the upstream side, outside of the village and beyond the limits of its clearing, on the left as one looks upstream from the chief's end, should be the rubbish heap. It should contain the bones of goat, fowl, fish, game (especially warthog), palm nuts, remnants of iron tools, and perhaps slag. On the plaza there should be traces of the smithy and perhaps another shed. The houses should be rectangular, presumably no wider than two palm ribs in width, with a door to the front (perhaps not traceable because the sill was raised above the soil). The kitchens behind the houses facing the plaza might give evidence of polygamy: there should be several that served as both dwelling and kitchen for one woman and her children behind each polygamist's house. They should contain shards of pottery. Probably graves would be found all over the site, since everyone was buried in the village of his birth; usually burial would take place long after the village was abandoned, assuming that villages shifted as much then as they did later. Perhaps the tombs included such items as arrowheads, anvils, hammers, rings, spears, although most would be only modestly supplied. The tombs should be rectangular, containing a side chamber only for the more important people. Coffins would have been made out of mats stretched over a framework of sticks or a similar material. Kuba kings later were buried in coffins that were the size and shape of a small house and were referred to as dugout canoes; perhaps early coffin shapes came closer to the canoe. Iron should be found, but no copper. Copper would indicate that long-distance trade was much more developed than I think. The pottery could be very similar to what is found today along the Sankuru and Lokenye, both with regard to types—especially for the basic cooking vessels—and to decoration: geometric, but less profuse than later. The cooking pots may resemble either Kingabwa or Lungebungu ware.[31] If careful research is possible, the gardens behind the houses should yield pollen of the plants described. Sites of former fields, if found, would be much more convincing, however. What exactly would be found on a foundry site I do not know, although I suspect a shaft furnace was used, burning charcoal made of very hard wood. Salt-processing sites should have broken crockery, pottery filters, and potassium salts.

Not all of this will be found, for several reasons. The acidity of the soils will have destroyed much evidence. The reuse of the site as a cemetery and later as a field, and then perhaps as a village again, may make it very difficult to interpret the finds. Unfortunately it is not likely that an archaeological expedition will want to prospect and excavate what are predicted to be small village sites of relatively recent age. Should it be carried out, however, it is probable that the finds will entirely follow my description. Any good excavation will certainly improve our knowledge about this period, anchor its chronology more firmly, and provide a link between wholly archaeological "cultures" and those that can be reconstructed backward from more recent situations.

Chapter *7*

The Age of Chiefs

The next three chapters interpret the social and political history of the Kuba after their appearance south of the Sankuru. The Kuba claim that the kingdom was founded at the beginning of this period, but it is my argument that a kingdom, as distinct from chiefdoms, began only with the last dynasty. Before then the chiefdoms remained totally or largely autonomous. Hence I distinguish the Age of Chiefs from the Age of Kings throughout.

A major trend in the history of the Mongo has been their expansion southward, a slow process that left traces from the Zaire River in the west to the Lualaba in the east. It was a process that began before the first proto-Kuba crossed the Sankuru, and it was to continue until the colonial period. When the whole movement began cannot be ascertained. But it was a very long time ago, and the trend may have lasted for a millennium, perhaps more.

The first to cross the Sankuru were the forebears of the Leele and the Wongo, in enough numbers to impose their speech in the lands where they would finally settle. They must have remained for some time among the Kete, then crossed the Lulua and the Kasai Rivers to arrive in the area where they live now.[1] Some of the original migrants may well have lingered south of the Sankuru and were absorbed by the central Kuba and the Kel, who followed them. Why was the Sankuru crossed? It may well be that the event took place because there was more savanna and more lakes and rivers, which meant a more diversified and more generous environment. It may be because the proto-Kuba were pressed by others who were moving south from the central Mongo area, where the people felt that the population density was becoming too high. Perhaps both of these factors played a role. This does not explain the huge, long-lasting Mongo movement southward, nor does it explain why the forest fringes should have been less populated although the environment there is much better than farther south. Indeed, it does not fully explain why the Leele and the Wongo would have left the better environment of the Sankuru-Kasai area for the drier, more open, and less fertile lands they finally occupied. Other factors, now lost to us, must have played a role.

When the central Kuba began to trickle over the Sankuru, settlement after settlement, they formed a minority among the Kete. Their sociopolitical organization was on a slightly larger scale than that of the Kete and gave them some, but not an overwhelming, advantage. Adjustments between the communities, immigrant and autochthonous, were bound to occur in the form of alliances, probably cemented by marriages between these groups, and ultimately a stable though rather unequal relationship of power was established. Out of these accommodations grew a new society. Its social and political features are the subject of this chapter.

Social Organization

Terms to designate clans, or the largest descent group, are usually similar over large portions of equatorial Africa. Even though some terms such as the Kete bulungu, "matriclan, matrilineage," may be rare, they can be shown to have great antiquity.[2] So it is rather odd that the Kuba *iloonc*, "matriclan, matrilineage," is only found in the Kuba group of languages and in related form among the neighboring Ndengese, where it is *donji*, "patriclan." Its etymology remains obscure. In Ndengese the term is rarely used and may be an import from their southern neighbors or an archaic expression. The whole situation leaves the impression that the Kuba dropped the usual Mongo term and that this was prompted by a profound change in the nature of the kinship groups.

The suspicion turns into near certainty on examination of the kinship terminology. The patrilineal proto-Kuba became the matrilineal Kuba. The clearest indication of such a change is their borrowing of the Kete term "mother" for "grandparents" and in general for "our ancestors."

The pervasiveness of Kete influence on the terminology can be seen by comparing Kuba, Luba (Lulua), and Mongo terms, since the Luba (Lulua) is practically identical with Kete. Among the terms adopted by the Kuba are "my mother," "my father,"[3] and new derivations from these for "father's sister" and "mother's brother." The special Luba and Kete term for mother's brother was not borrowed. The Kuba usage expresses the old Mongo classification, using new words. In this generation only the expressions "your, his, their, our father" and "your, his, their, our mother" were retained with their Mongo roots.

In ego's generation most terms were altered, but once again the Mongo principles of classification were kept. This is evident in the use of a single term to designate a sibling of the opposite sex, a conceptual category that does not exist in Kete or Luba. The term meant "sister" in Kete and occurs from the Atlantic coast all the way to the Kuba and Kete. In Luba, however, the same root means "both breasts" in the expression "her breasts are developing." The Kuba may have kept the appropriate Mongo term, but they probably did not because the new term that was borrowed is very frequent in the expression "sister's son," "heir," and in many languages to the west even "matrilineal relative." This is presumed to have been early Kete usage as well.

In the generations below ego the Kuba kept the Mongo conceptual scheme so that there are special terms for great-grandchild and great-great-grandchild. Their terminology in descending generations is therefore not alternating, unlike the Luba and the Leele. While it is impossible to state whether "child" is Mongo or Luba, a tonal quirk allows us to be certain that the term for "grandchild" is derived from Kete.[4] On the other hand, the roots for "great-grandchild" and "great-great-grandchild" are the same and are identical to the Mongo root. The first of these two is a clear correspondent to Mongo. The second is prefixed by an element that has not been traced and may be an innovation.

The terminology for affines underwent considerable change as well. Here the Mongo conceptual scheme was discarded but the Luba scheme was not adopted. Considerable innovation took place. The general term for affine in Mongo was dropped. The Leele coined one with a meaning "those who cause to give birth," and the Bushoong replaced it by the Luba term. As for specific Kuba terms, "husband" is a loan from the Luba term "male," while "wife" is a new formation probably meaning "she who causes gifts," an obvious reference to bridewealth, as is the general term for affine.[5] The former Mongo term for wife subsists, but is used only for female pawns. New terms for "co-wives" and "co-husbands" (persons entering into a corporate descent group use these terms for other such persons of the same sex) were innovations as well. They were made up from Luba stems meaning "groin" and "vagina." The groin item designates women who share the same groin, and the vagina men who share the same vagina. We do not know if the terms once existed in Kete. They have not subsisted. The pattern of classification exists there as among the Luba.

A special Kuba term found neither in Luba nor in Mongo designates brothers-in-law ("sibling-in-law of the same sex as ego"). This term, *nshaam*, can be used by either women or men provided that it refers to persons of the same sex as ego. If the sex differs, the husband-wife terminology is used. Mongo has a single term designating all affines: viz., all affines of the first ascending generation (father-in-law, mother-in-law) and the men of ego's own generation (brother-in-law). Luba also has a single, general term for affine, but its term differs from the Mongo. In effect the central Kuba sorted out two groups of in-laws: on the one hand those who belong to the first ascending generation to whom the general term for "affine" refers, and on the other hand those of ego's generation. The principle of generation was thought to be of such importance that it had to be reflected in the terminology. The term nshaam seems to be derived from a verb and would mean "those who unite," quite appropriate for this class of in-laws.

A study of bridewealth circulation throws some light on the terminology. By 1892 bridewealth was essentially given by the father of the groom to the father of the bride. But since the Kuba were then matrilineal, this means that every marriage actually involved four clans; two in the ascending generation who transacted bridewealth matters, and two in the lower generation who were allied through the marriage. Hence the etymological stress on "paying" in the older generation and on "uniting" in the lower one. It is hard not to see the pattern for bridewealth transfer as a retention from the days that the Kuba were patrilineal, since the practice is logical in a patrilineal setting: two clans exchange persons and transfer goods. The Kuba *practice* is scarcely sufficient grounds for an assumption of retention, but the *terminology* is. Both the anomalies of transfer and terminology taken together leave little room for doubt, especially because fathers and brothers-in-law reside normally in the same settlement.[6]

Bridewealth matters were complex in the late nineteenth century. First, it was possible to acquire a female pawn[7] for a very high price. The children of such a union all belonged to the man, or else the contract specified how many of the offspring would belong to his clan and how many to hers and in which order of birth. The linguistic evidence suggests that the development of this institution can be ascribed to the period before the kingdom was founded, although, as usual, a later origin cannot be completely excluded. The practice led to the necessity of coining a new term for wife. The old term for wife remained as the designation for female pawn. The main implication of pawnship, a widespread practice in southern Zaire,[8] is the existence of great inequalities in wealth or power. Such inequalities are evident in the nineteenth century, but in the archaic period there is little evidence for inequality of wealth. Inequality of power may have been more relevant, although again this could not have been very great among the Kuba at the time. One suspects that in time a disparity developed between Kuba and Kete and that many a Kete wife was acquired with bridewealth on condition that her children be transferred to her husband's lineage and clan. This explanation fits the general picture, and probably the first such women were acquired by chiefs and elders. The heavy bridewealth was a way for central Kuba to escape some of the consequences of the shift from patrilinearity to matrilinearity. The term for "wife" in the patrilineal setting stuck among the Kuba to what are in effect "patrilineal marriages." A new term was coined for "matrilineal marriages," even though these became the norm.

Ideally a suitor undertook to perform bride service for his mother-in-law and sisters-in-law during at least one agricultural season (or year). More often than not in later times he was able to buy himself out of these obligations. But in a less mercantile age this was probably not so, and in the archaic period most younger men about to marry or recently married presumably lived for a

year or more with their in-laws. This would complicate residential patterns
even more and increase residential mobility even further, which may account
for dropping the general term for affine from the Mongo heritage.

In the nineteenth century it was held that anyone who performed bride
service had to pay little bridewealth. But the situation did not really obtain
then as we know both from accounts telling how Bushoong boys acquired the
goods required[9] and from the way Bushoong tales portray marriages. Practice
may have been closer to the norm in earlier days. If bride service rather than
bridewealth was involved, it implied that men could marry relatively young
and that consequently polygyny was relatively restricted. The early situation
may have combined common bride service with the acquisition of additional
wives on a limited scale by elders or chiefs through pawnship and perhaps
through inheritance of wives. But even then, bridewealth for all marriages
cannot be ruled out since the Kuba chose to designate affines in general and
affines of the first ascending generation in particular as "those who are
paid"—i.e., who received the valuables paid for a bride.

What was paid as bridewealth during this archaic period? In later times the
payment was in trade goods, and this may have been true earlier. The goods
must have had an economic value and were not just symbolic objects such as a
dish (the practice among the Cokwe) or an arrow (the first payment of a set
among the Mongo). This economic significance of bridewealth seems to
exclude preferential marriages altogether. Preferential marriages are those
between partners having a mutual kinship relationship—e.g., cross-cousins.
Their kin not only favor such unions, but penalize those who choose partners.
Preferential marriages did arise later among the Leele from the pawning
system and perhaps from the age-grade organization, but not as a primary
feature of kinship organization. This is the case only among peoples west of
the Leele. There bridewealth was paid only if no preferential partner was
available at all.[10]

The change from patrilinearity to matrilinearity very probably occurred
during the archaic period. Evidence of remodeling and innovation in the
terminology supports the natural assumption that the change was a gradual
one. The changing rules of descent and alterations in the patterns of residence
certainly triggered some changes in the actual patterns of behavior among
different sets of kin. A change in terminology did not in itself bring about a
change of roles, but changes in patterns of descent and residence almost
certainly did. The new terms came to correspond to new attitudes and new
norms of behavior.

The Kete influence must have been quite pervasive, considering that even
the expressions "my father" and "my mother" were borrowed from them.
But unlike the Leele, the Kuba did not completely adopt the principle of
alternating generations: they did so for the ascending generations but not for

the descending generations. This implies that lineage depth must have shrunk. By itself the depth of a lineage can hardly be deduced from this pattern of nomenclature, but certainly a loss of specialized terms implies a loss of interest in precise genealogical calculation and hence in both depth and scale of kinship grouping. To cite an instance of the reverse trend, the Luba of Kasai, who are patrilineal now and have deep segmentary lineages, felt the need for distinguishing generations beyond the second one, up or down, and did so by adding ''of buikulu'' to distinguish them from the first and second ascending descending generations.

But why, then, did the Kuba keep the complete set of terms in the *descending* generation? It can only be because in certain contexts descent in the male line was important. The terms indicate automatically how many steps a person is removed patrilaterally from certain matriclans. The main use of this mode of reckoning probably was to calculate the distance between a person and an ''important'' lineage or clan, such as clans of chiefs and founding clans. This is supported by practice in the rules of succession to certain offices, which are reserved to men or women one or two generations away from a dynastic line or clan. A parallel over four generations is still found to the far west among the Sakata and Boma, who are also the product of patrilineal Mongo immigrants and matrilineal locals. A similar case, but for two generations only, is that of southwestern Mongo such as the Ntomba and Sengele, who are matrilineal, like the Kuba.[11] It is not surprising to find this type of reaction when Mongo are involved, given the strong sense for bilaterality that is found among all Mongo.

So far the data indicate that the proto-Kuba became matrilineal, that their lineages became shallower, that bridewealth was retained or became more prominent than before, and that there were leading lineages. But why did the proto-Kuba turn to matrilinearity at all, and what were the general effects of the change?

When patrilineal and matrilineal people mix, the impact of change in choosing one of the two modes of descent can be set forth as follows. When a Kuba male married a Kete female, by the *patrilineal rule* the child belonged to the Kuba clan; by the *matrilineal rule* the child belonged to the Kete clan. When a Kuba female married a Kete male, by the *patrilineal rule* the child belonged to the Kete clan; by the *matrilineal rule* the child belonged to the Kuba clan.

The rules of descent are not the only variable to consider. Later, and presumably at the earlier time, Kuba residence was viripatrilocal until the death of the husband's father. In later times the family went to live in the husband's mother's brother's village after the death of the husband's father, unless a special position was given to the husband by the village leaders of his father's village.[12] So residence is an important variable. Moreover, among all the groups involved, whatever the mode of descent, men exercised authority;

therefore any child considered in the above paradigm should be male if we try to see the advantages of switching rules of descent for both Kuba and Kete.

It is not easy to use demographic considerations to explain the shift in mode of reckoning descent. No doubt at first the totality of the Kete outnumbered the inhabitants of the early immigrant villages, but not all of them had contact with the Kuba. Moreover, marriages between immigrants and autochthons were but a small fraction of all marriages, each group preferring to marry within its own kin. Because they came in village groups, the immigrants had no great shortage of women, and the movement was slow enough so that the early immigrants could always obtain needed wives from their relatives north of the Sankuru. Both groups, we can assume, were well aware of the demographic implications of exchanging women and would not be willing to part with their women unless it was to cement alliances between villages or leaders. Therefore only a small proportion of the women of either Kete or Bushoong were affected.

At first the Kuba stuck to their system of descent and the Kete to theirs. This meant that a man born of a Kuba father and a Kete mother would be raised in his father's village and would enjoy all the rights of an heir there, at the same time enjoying full rights as a sister's son in the Kete village. The son born of a Kete father and a Kuba mother would not enjoy full status in either situation. This again raises the question: Why should the Kuba have ever changed?

When the different marriage combinations, outlined above, are examined it appears that none of them offers a strong incentive for the Kuba to change the rule of descent, not even when the Kuba were giving far more women than they received (the case of the Kuba female married to a Kete). In that case a number of men without full status anywhere emerged as living with their fathers in the Kete village, going to the Kuba village of their mother only if it had more to offer. But that would mean that the Kuba were better off, and in that case why would they agree to hand over more women to the Kete than they received? What is clear finally is that by preserving virilocality as the key factor the Kuba could make the transition *without losing much by it*. The principle of *descent* must have mattered more to the Kete than to the Kuba, whereas *residence* mattered more to the Kuba. This does not explain why the change, which must be traced to Kete insistence, occurred; it explains only why the change was acceptable to the Kuba.

The effects of the new system were considerable. It increased the mobility of families. Almost any husband could now lay claim to residence in the village of any of his grandparents and even that of his wife. Political leaders had to take this mobility into account if they did not want to lose their supporters to competitors. The new system undid the homogeneity of the village because the male members of a descent group could no longer stay together, since their mothers now resided in different villages. At best only older men whose fathers had died could return to the original home of the descent group. Previously each lineage had formed its own village; now men of all kinds of lineages lived together around a minuscule core provided by the "founding lineage" of the village. First there were the women and children of those men who, with them, formed the local clan section. Then came the descendants of sons who had been persuaded to stay on after their father's deaths, the sections called "children on top," and "on top of" those the sons of these sons and their families. In time such patrilaterally linked clan sections became large and had to be granted a voice in village affairs. Village government was reorganized to represent all the bigger clan sections in a common council, *malaang*. Another effect of the development was to increase the average village size—at least as compared to single clan-section villages, although not to villages in a patrilineal virilocal system.

Some such evolution did occur, and as a result Kuba clans are scattered all over the country among many ethnic groups.[13] Inspection of Kuba village names indicates that many among them are the names of clans, as would be expected if single clan sections settled apart. But by the 1950s there were almost no such Kuba or Kete villages left, and the few exceptions were tiny hamlets. Sheppard gives an indirect indication of the size of settlements. Most, if not all, he saw in 1892 were too big to contain but a single clan section.

In time kinship groups, except for the localized clan section, lost much of their significance and almost all their corporate functions. Villages took the place of descent groups and became the basic social units in matters of land tenure, local defense, and local political organization. The village became in fact the cornerstone of the whole sociopolitical structure not only among the Kuba but even more so among the Leele. It therefore was not the growth of political institutions that destroyed the descent system's usefulness, because there is no overarching political structure among the Leele. It was the compromise arrived at between the matrilineal Kete and the patrilineal Kuba or Leele. It not only created strong villages but also opened the way for a stronger political organization.[14]

The development of the village council, malaang, led to recognition of the corporate personality of the village itself. This existed from the outset through the appointment of a headman, the *kubol*. In the nineteenth century he was usually the oldest man. He had no authority, but he represented the village and was responsible for its actions. From the earliest days both Kuba and Kete villages had headmen. Although they did not copy one another they exercised mutual influence. The Kete term for council, *kibanza*, clearly refers to a chief's court or council in other Bantu-speaking societies of the southern savanna, while the Kuba malaang is derived from a Luba verb "to argue, to exhort," and may have been used by the Kete at some time. Kubol is a straight combination of two terms also found in Mongo and means "head of the village." *Shanshenge*, the Kete village headman, "father of the capital," is composed of a Luba group, *sha*, "father," and a Kuba word, *nsheng*, "capital," itself derived from Mongo *bosenge*, "the patriarch's place." Since Kete villages were independent they were all "capitals."

From the outset another role existed in Kuba villages, that of spokesman. This still exists in Leele villages as *itembangu*,[15] messenger and spokesman, a younger person. The early similar Kuba title was probably mbyeeng. But soon a division in two parts arose because the Kuba built their villages along each side of a street, and each village half elected its spokesman for life. His authority within his half of the village was much more real in daily affairs than that of the village headman. He saw to it that the decisions of the council were carried out, and he led his half in the council. The origins of the two names, mbeem for the half that had precedence and mbyeeng for the other, are unknown. Analogues are the *mbeengi* of the Ooli, who ruled the village along with its headman, and the Ngwii *mbeam*, who was the headman of the second most important village in a cluster within a chiefdom.[16] Even the notion of village moieties may go back to proto-Kuba times, for other southern Mongo have preserved traces of it. The Kete certainly had nothing of the sort. Besides these officials, many villages also had an official medicine man, the ilweemy,[17] and among the clan sections there may have been some that were more honored than others because they were the "founders," the *mbaangt*.

The processes described in reorganizing the social structure in this epoch took a long time to unfold. A changeover from one type of descent to another need not take centuries.[18] The effects could have been felt almost immediately, although a stable form of social organization emerged only gradually. Once the new system was constituted, however, with its rules of descent, residence, and marriage, with its recruitment pattern among villages, including the gradual character of upward social mobility, these small-scale institutions were not to undergo any radical outward changes for centuries. They were the foundation for other institutions, which in turn shielded them from further change. Following Fernand Braudel's approach, one might claim that these phenomena belong to the long term (*la longue durée*).[19] An upheaval occurring during the archaic period may have taken an indeterminate but perhaps a fairly long time, one which could be reckoned in centuries rather than in years or decades.

Still, one must not be too confident that there has been little change since those days. There is no a priori proof for a long term. And since we do know that the basic patterns of production were later altered, we may well wonder how this may have affected the basic social organization itself. I believe the outward form was left largely unaltered but that later the operation of the family units changed considerably. With it, roles and attitudes changed as well, and the whole social system must have felt the effects.

Early Chiefdoms

The story of the hammers and the anvils that was told in Chapter Four implies that even before the Bushoong leaders crossed the Sankuru there were other chiefdoms in the area. Despite the explicit meaning of the story, no kingdom was founded at Iyool. What came to be the great event to Kuba traditionalists was no more than a minor episode in its time, affecting merely a single chiefdom. Examined closely, the tradition states that the Bushoong wrested the chieftainship from the Bieeng. When the plot about the capture of the anvil was introduced and the tradition was fashioned, we do not know. The oldest theme in it—the fight between two factions within what was the Bieeng chiefdom—goes back to the period itself. The complete tale possibly dates from the reigns immediately after the kingdom was founded. It legitimized the Bushoong claim to overlordship for as long as a Kuba state would endure. This explains the importance attached to this myth, and also the fact that it was the earliest one foreigners heard. When compared with the tale of how nyim seceded from the realm of Itoci, an event of comparable significance, the contrast is striking. Only the Kuba king told this one in the early 1950s, and he may well have borrowed parts of his information from the Ndengese, whose accounts confirm this story.[20]

Given the character of the hammers and anvils tale as a legitimizing charter, it is not surprising that when a new ethnic group appeared among the central Kuba, it was listed among those who had participated in the competition at Iyool. The Bulaang are such a group. They claim to be a late offshoot of the Bieeng, a claim no one disputes, and yet the king included them in the list of those competing at Iyool. Iyool is also a widespread cliché origin in many village and clan histories.[21]

In view of this it is tempting to hold that the references to the Ngeende and Pyaang are also later insertions, their names having been added when they came under Bushoong rule. Plausible as this may seem, it raises the question of why they were so singled out and not the Kel, Shoowa, Ngongo, or any others except the Bulaang.[22] It may be that since only Ngeende and Bushoong villages, plus one Pyaang village, exist near Iyool, these groups have been tied to the event merely because of proximity to the site. The locals point out ravines associated with the three groups and indicate where the original villages of each of these three groups were located. The praise name of the plain recalls this. In these versions the Bieeng and the Bushoong occupied the same

settlement, which once more shows the close link between these two, rein-
forcing the feeling that the basic struggle for the chieftainship occurred between them.

On the whole my interpretation is that a titleholder under Itoci arrived near
the lake called Kum Idip, "the chief of the lakes." He had refused tribute to
Itoci and disturbed existing relationships among the Bieeng, Pyaang, and
Ngeende, particularly since he claimed an already existing chieftainship. The
latest immigrants and the allies they made within the Bieeng chiefdom were
called the Bushoong. They either invented the title nyim or wrested it from the
Bieeng. A large portion of the population did not side with them. The ensuing
war between Bieeng and Bushoong affected the nearby Ngeende and Pyaang
chiefs, which is why the latter have been incorporated into the tale.

Ndengese sources confirm some serious upheaval. The Ndengese saying,
"Itoci is the upper jaw, nyim the lower" and "If you don't accept Itoci, cross
the river and join nyim" recall the earlier separation.[23] Beyond this some
Ndengese state that during "the great migration" they crossed the Sankuru
and overcame one group of locals after another until the autochthons sued for
peace. A celebration took place, but during the feast the Ndengese were
attacked by surprise and defeated by the Kuba, whom they since have been
obliged to serve. The banquet attack may well be a cliché, and yet the import
is that there were one or more sizable attacks on the local chiefdoms.[24]

Yet no kingdom was created. During the archaic period the Bushoong
dominated only some Kete villages in the southern part of their chiefdom after
the villages were wrested from Bieeng hands. They also claim to have controlled some of the Cwa. Besides the hammers and anvils tradition there is no
evidence of any *claim* of paramountcy by the nyim, let alone any *real* overlordship over the other chiefs, the *kum apoong*, "chief [who wears] the eagle
feathers," during the whole period. During the Age of Chiefs then, the
Bushoong chiefdom was but one among many, even if one of the two biggest
units.

Its political organization was no doubt similar to that of the others. Thus the
internal organization within those chiefdoms at the close of the nineteenth
century helps us visualize the Bushoong organization before the seventeenth
century, although it must be emphasized that both their later dominance and
the passage of time must have altered many features in those organizations.

How had these chiefdoms arisen? In some cases a kum, "chief," crossed
the Sankuru only after commoners had already done so. Or a budding patriarch among the migrants might claim the title of kum, perhaps obtain inves-
titure from a kum north of the Sankuru, and be accepted by other migrants.
Some settlements may have asked for a kum to lead them, as to live without a
chief was not thought proper: "All would not be well."[25] In the Bushoong case
and perhaps in others, a kum migrated because he had broken with his over-

lord and, foreseeing no chance of staying, he had to seek new opportunities to the south. In all cases the political institutions of the southern Mongo were simply carried south.

In the new environment, however, such institutions could not remain unaltered. The matrilineal Kete lived here, and as matrilinearity became the rule chieftainship inevitably changed. From being a kum who was a particularly honored patriarch, the chief became a kum whose authority was exclusively based on territorial ties. No longer did he rule both because of his *mpifo* (Mongo: quality of senior in a lineage or clan) and his ekopo (Mongo: territorial tie.) Only the ekopo counted.[26] Intellectually the migrants were prepared for this, for they knew of territorially based authority. But social reality had to be adapted. Earlier the kum had drawn his support mainly from the different lineages of his own clan, whether living in their own villages or in quarters of settlements. Their heads were his lieutenants and recognized as such by the common designation of nkolomo, "elder," and in the case of some by titles such as iyol, "warrior." With the appearance of matrilineal sections the nkolomo were no longer tied by kinship to each other or to the chief. Some of them remained the main supporters of the kum, but he had to share authority with them in order to maintain his legitimacy. Entirely unrelated groups who offered support to the kum were also welcome, and their leaders or nkolomo achieved the same position. The matrilineages of these supporters came to be known as the "founding clans," or mbaangt. The same term applies among the Leele to the first, core lineage that has founded a settlement and claims more rights, especially ritual rights, than others. It is not certain whether among the Kuba mbaangt clans developed first at the village level and then at the chiefdom level, later disappearing from the villages, Perhaps the early situation was similar to the one still prevalent among the Ohindu and some other Nkucu, where any large village was de facto self-governing and acquired its own chief, whose territory was restricted to the village. The only evidence concerning this question for the early central Kuba indicates that there were some large villages, with several nkolomo, recognizing a single chief. It does not tell us whether or not the chief controlled other smaller villages, although I believe he did. Those nkolomo resident at the capital became representatives of mbaangt clans, and the term came to mean "aristocratic clan" or "elector clan," since the council of mbaangt at the capital acquired the right to nominate or to depose a kum provided candidates belonged to the dynastic line.[27]

Kuba traditions picture the leaders of the mbaangt as companions of the chief, "who *came* with him." If this is taken not to refer to migration at all but to the formation of a matrilineal chiefdom in which the power of the kum depended on the size of his capital, "who *lived* with him" would be more accurate. Traditions claim there were nine, eighteen, or twenty-seven of these leaders. But nine and its multiples are expressions of the perfect number. In the colonial period nine, eighteen, and twenty-seven clans were indeed found (sometimes with difficulty), although there was one case of twenty clans. The numbers could vary, and had certainly varied before. Fewer mbaangt clans would have sufficed to back up a claim to a small chieftainship. Eleven out of eighteen Bushoong mbaangt clans, fourteen out of twenty Pyaang, and fifteen out of twenty-seven Ngeende mbaangt clans do not even claim to have immigrated with the ruling clan, nor are they autochthons. They claim to have begun in another ethnic group, whether central Kuba or not. So only a minority of the claims conforms to the generally accepted cliché of "mbaangt clans coming with the kum."[28]

The situation in the 1950s suggests a dynamic evolution of the status of mbaangt clan itself. Some clans must have *achieved* aristocratic status without having been linked even patrilaterally with chiefs at all. They were his core followers. Some mbaangt clans may have lost that status later on; one instance is known of this. Other mbaangt clans were not "founders" at the beginning of the matrilineal chiefdom but attained the status later, when their support was needed or conceivably to round off the numbers to eighteen or twenty-seven. At the foundation of the chiefdoms the maximums of mbaangt clans were seven for the Bushoong, six for the Pyaang, twelve for the Ngeende; the minimum for the Bushoong may have been two, which are specifically said to have accompanied nyim from Itoci, probably as junior patrilineages of nyim's patrilineage.[29]

The kum was not alone in seeing the foundation for his authority altered when the society became matrilineal. The elders of the supporting junior lineages saw theirs weakened as well, since the new clan sections spawned others "on top" of them as time went by, and could split off when they were numerous enough, achieving direct representation on the village council. This weakened the leadership of the original head of the clan section, but by moving to the chief's court such a head could achieve the status of mbaangt clan, thereby strengthening the chief's hold over the chiefdom. That hold was directly dependent on the ratio of the inhabitants at his residence to the average number in the dependent villages. The move strengthened the lineage head because in return for his crucial support he claimed privileges that could not be denied. The mbaangt thus formed a council (*ibaam*, among the Bushoong), which nominated, deposed, and advised chiefs. Power was effectively shared now, and each partner exercised more power than he could have achieved by himself. The mbaangt clans were privileged in that they could depose the kum but he could not depose any of them. So crucial was the unity between them that the notion of ethnic group came to be linked in time not to a single chiefdom but to a single set of rulers; one dynastic clan and its mbaangt clans, whether they ruled one or several chiefdoms. The term nkolomo, later *kolm*, came to be restricted to the leaders of the mbaangt before it was extended again to all notables, whether they were leaders of clan sections or not. Thus one sees certain mbaangt groups as originating among the clan sections that had been at the chief's court even when the chiefdom was still patrilineal. Other clan sections were co-opted later, when they moved to his residence.

The alliance between mbaangt clans and rulers was strengthened in new ways. At a kum's accession each of the mbaangt clans gave him a wife in return for a gift that was not considered to be normal bridewealth. When a chief was deposed, the women scattered like grasshoppers. Hence their name, "grasshopper." The process then began all over. The kum had to be wealthy, since these gifts were due at his installation. But he collected wealth from the mbaangt clans, since any new nomination to the council of the mbaangt clans, whether a new clan section was added or whether a deceased incumbent was replaced, was accompanied by a gift to the kum. Hence a network of marital ties and the exchange of gifts knitted rulers and mbaangt clans together. It also ensured a certain stability for the chieftainship, since the mbaangt leaders were not eager to depose a kum if there was no wealthy candidate available to take over, but the kum became wealthy only after his accession and his wealth was inherited after his death by his lineage successor. In time though, and in some cases apparently relatively early, this was not a sufficient safeguard, for the kum's wealth came to be seen as part of his office rather than as personal wealth, and it was used to pay the installation gifts.

The wives bore children who belonged to mbaangt clans and yet were children of the ruler; thus they represented the union between the two basic elements that made up the strength of government. As children they remained loyal to their father but not to his potential successors, thus helping to stabilize their father's rule. As members of their matriclans they remained loyal to the mbaangt clan and helped preserve its power. This also explains in part the stability of most of the early chiefdoms.[30] An additional element in the alliance between kum and mbaangt clans involved other marriage politics. The daughters of the ruling lineage's women were married to members of the mbaangt clans. Their sons were potential successors, but the fathers of these sons were members of mbaangt clans. Their daughters continued the ruling line itself. Such marriages created a web of kinship between all the matrilineages involved, which was limited only by the rule of exogamy. Then as now the rule may have prohibited anyone from marrying any kin with whom genealogical ties could be traced, thus forcing lineages to broaden the range of their alliances relatively rapidly.

The sisters and female parallel cousins of the chief were married only to inhabitants of the chiefdom, at first no doubt to members of the mbaangt clans. But if that was not possible because of the rules of exogamy, the offspring were still linked by their ancestors to the chiefdom. In time the practice of choosing commoners became more widespread. In part this may have been the result of a rule that considered morganatic marriages indissoluble and monogamous. But the advantages to the kum were great as well, since such a marriage ensured that the father of a kum in the next generation was not a member of a mbaangt clan and that commoners could consider the kum as "their man." The aristocratic clans favored such a development for fear that the influence of any mbaangt clan to which the kum's father belonged would exercise undue influence.

The above is but a rough sketch, for we know nothing about marriage politics in the early chiefdoms and must base our conclusions on later practices, such as the one dictating that kum's sisters marry commoners exclusively or at least preferentially.[31] Specific marriage policies for each chiefdom may explain why some were more stable than others.

The kum's residence was organized like any other village. Its daily affairs were regulated by the village council, the malaang. The most important officers on the council were mbeem and mbyeeng, and all the main clan sections were represented by their elders, also termed kolm. This council was fully as important as that of the mbaangt precisely because the strength of a chiefdom lay in the numbers and the will to fight of all the inhabitants at the court. At first the aristocratic clan sections dominated here as well, since they had been the first core followers of the chief. In time, and despite the marriages between mbaangt clans and chiefs or among mbaangt clans themselves, new sections of commoner descent began to appear "on top" of the older ones that were mbaangt. Perhaps some of the later mbaangt originated through such a development, when a section "on top" of a mbaangt clan was considered a mbaangt clan, but this process could not go on indefinitely. As the commoners gained a stronger voice, they formed a third force countervailing that of the ruler, the ruling clan, and the aristocrats. This allowed the kum to assume a mediating position with regard to the other forces.

The parallelogram of forces cannot be reconstructed accurately, but we can be fairly certain that it involved three blocs of people: the ruling clan, the aristocrats, and the commoners. The chief was a member of the ruling clan, but his interests opposed those of his heirs, who wanted him deposed. He was supported first by his sons, who benefited from his status only as long as he was chief. Rivalries among the mbaangt appeared as they attempted to capture certain kolm titles. Such titles had existed before the matrilineal chiefdoms even existed, and they developed further within the village council at the chief's court. Under the circumstances politics could scarcely be a straightforward, simple set of predictable oppositions. The balance of power tilted differently in different chiefdoms and it shifted over time in any given chiefdom as well, which helps explain why chiefdoms such as the Pyaang, the

Bieeng, and the Bushoong did not break up in early times[32] whereas the Ngeende and others did.

Instability does not mean only a rapid turnover of chiefs. Deposed chiefs often tried to regain their position by appealing to clan sections of those mbaangt clans who happened not to be the lineages that held the office. With their help and that of a part of the public, a valid countergovernment could be set up and, if the support was large enough, this might lead to the splitting of the chiefdom. This process occurred on a large scale in most chiefdoms during the nineteenth century, but was infrequent during the Age of Chiefs. The traditional cliché that describes the process states that the court was split apart because of quarrels between the mbeem and mbyeeng halves. During the colonial period many chiefdoms were found to belong to clusters having the same ruling and mbaangt clans as each chiefdom in the cluster.[33] This confirms traditions that view all chiefdoms in a cluster as having hived off from a single parent chiefdom. In this view there was once a single Ngongo, Pyaang, Ngeende, Bulaang, Kel, etc. chiefdom, and the ethnic history is but the hiving off from the ancestral chiefdom.

Some ethnically united groups, however, constitute more than one cluster of ruling and mbaangt clans. The Pyaang and Ngeende consist of two clusters each, although the second one is only one village; the Kel also have two clusters. The splinter groups and one of the Kel clusters seem to have been autonomous smaller groups, which were later made subject to a bigger chiefdom from the main cluster, thus acquiring their ethnic label. Later on they recovered their autonomy.[34] The main exceptions to the overlapping of cluster and ethnic label are the Shoowa and the Ngoombe. Here, as among the Kete, the label refers to a common language and common customs differing from those of the Kuba. The Shoowa and Kete languages still exist, but the Ngoombe lost their specific southern Mongo speech. The Cwa label refers to a separate language and a very different way of life.[35]

The main titles were at first carryovers from southern Mongo practice. Others are of Kete, and perhaps ultimately Luba or Songye, origin. The most important one was the leader of the kum's residential council and head of all notables. At first he was called kin mimbaangt among the Bushoong, who later reserved this title for the presidency of the council of mbaangt and replaced it by *kin ikaam*, "leader of the council," or *kikaam*. Earlier than the last title they used the more descriptive *nkyeenc makaam*, "the commander of the council." Among the Ngeende this function was labeled *mell* or *mel ibaanc*, a term connected with the council of the mbaangt.[36] The title could not be reserved to a given mbaangt clan; if it had, it would almost have given rise to a second ruling clan. The practice of requiring that officeholder to be the son of a kum and mbaangt may be quite old.

Among the kolm of the twentieth century, a crucial group consisted of the

kolm matuk mabol, "notables of the corners of the village," in which the
Mongo term etuka, "part of a village" (inhabited by a common patrilineage)
appears.[37] The expression is old, but that does not imply that the first four
titles to which it applies are equally ancient. The four, by 1950 found in all
chiefdoms, were the cikl, *ipaancl*, *nyimishoong*, and *nyaang*, in that order.
Cikl may be of Luba origin and was reserved among the Bushoong to the
temporary replacement of the chief during the interregna. The incumbent
always belonged to a nonruling branch of the ruling clan and the first to hold
the title was, it is said, the twin of the first king, appointed after their quarrel
at But aPoong.[38]

The second title, ipaancl, is clearly related to *epanzula* and *epanshula* of the
Luba and Songye along the uppermost Sankuru. Among the eastern groups it
immediately follows the kikaam. According to a tale noted by Frobenius in
1905 among the Kuba Isambo of Lusambo, it was the title of the very first
chieftainship, at least in this group. Given the proximity to some Songye and
Luba groups, where it also occurs, it may have derived from them. It has no
meaning in the Kuba idioms. But was it older than the foundation of the
kingdom by Shyaam [1] or not? One episode of the migration from But
aPoong is associated with the creation of the title, but that may be an anachronism. The title rotated among the clans Ilyeeng and Nshoody, both mbaangt
among the Bushoong.[39] Nyimishoong and nyaang are more recent titles and are
not found everywhere.[40] Among the Bushoong, but not elsewhere, the four
titles are associated with the governorship of provinces. I believe the first
two titles to be older than Shyaam, but the functions may once have been
quite different. The titleholders very probably lived at the chief's court.

Besides the titles mentioned, all chiefdoms had mbeem and mbyeeng for the
halves of the chief's residence and the military titles iyol and shesh, one for
each half of the court, as were two titles for women, mbaan and *katyeeng*. The
term shesh is of Luba or Songye origin as a name, and seems to refer to the adze,
which is an emblem of office. Katyeeng is Luba in origin and was first used as
an honorific for mothers of successors—the women of the chiefly lineage who
have given birth. This was still the case in the eastern chiefdoms in the 1920s.
Mbaan is of Luba origin as well, although traditions claim the title to be either
very old or to date from events connected with the death of Lashyaang [E].[41]

The oldest title of all, along with iyol, is *mbyeemy,* a title vested in the clan
Iyeem, which is also the muyum's clan. The mbyeemy was the ritualist for the
court, just as the muyum was the ritualist for the kingdom. His duties in the
archaic period consisted mainly of making offerings to the spirit of Ngaan on
behalf of the chiefdom at a river or lake.[42] Tataam, keeper of the harem, may
not be a very old title despite the fact that folk etymology connected it with the
crossing at But aPoong, whereas *iyok pyeemy,* "the washing with kaolin,"

the chief's first wife, certainly goes back a very long way. Kaolin, white porcelain clay, has long been the most important emblem of office, with ritual connotations, among the Mongo. The Bushoong kings continued to obtain it from sites north of the Sankuru. The title refers to a specific episode during the ritual of enthronement, a ritual that can be taken to be equally old since the kaolin from north of the Sankuru was used for it.[43]

The ideology of chieftainship is well known for later periods, but can only be inferred from praise names and comparative ethnography for the early period if we assume, as I have done, that all mentions in narrative texts may be anachronistic. The installation of a chief was the manifestation of the ideology. The mbaangt paid homage by having each of their representatives prostrate himself before the chief, who placed his foot on the representative's head while the crowd chanted:

> Hit, trample [tura, nyeka]
> the mothers of the clan,
> the clans, yii, yii.

In recent times this was done only in the Bieeng chiefdom, but the Bushoong have kept the name "hit, trample" for the homage ceremony in general. At an earlier point in the ceremonies the mbeem stated:

> Woot's elect [and he asks him to show his clan and his children],
> you alone, you are king;
> let go of your kin.
> You belonged to your mother's clan,
> now you are your own clan.
> Kill your father [renounce your father],
> Kill your mother [renounce your mother],
> What is forbidden is a female king.[44]

During these rituals mbyeemy played a role among the Bushoong. The chief was initiated into his function by the kikaam, who kept him in seclusion for a ritual nine days. The ritual anointing of the chief along with ritual intercourse between him and iyok pyeemy were the highlights of the ceremonies. Beyond this, and the general appeal to subjects to pay the noble tribute—i.e., the tribute that counts as homage—the rituals differed from chiefdom to chiefdom, but the Cwa autochthons played a role in all of them. Besides the kaolin, one or more charms were essential to government, the anvil being one of them. In the tales they are represented as being kept in a house of charms, but such houses no longer exist east of the Loange River. For the Bushoong the charm is said to have been Inam, consisting of scales of the crocodile of Woot, collected at But aPoong nine days previously and presented to the chief by the representatives of the eighteen (two times nine) mbaangt.

It will also be recalled that a miraculous sign was needed to indicate which of the potential successors was acceptable to the spirits, as had happened at Iyool. This, the texts cited above, and the rituals give an excellent idea of the ideology of chieftainship. The chief, the chosen of the spirits (or Woot), rules by virtue of their help and the help of magic connected with them. He must foreswear all his kinship connections. Hence the rumors that incest was part of the ritual, for he was the chief of all and all equally. In the praise poems the earliest king is equated with the sun, as Woot had been. Not only is he Woot's successor, but just as the earth cannot live without the rays of the sun which give life, so the people cannot live without the chief. The sun metaphor is not only presented in the praise names but is also carved on boxes.[45]

The main emblem of the aristocrats was the cane of office, connected with Woot among the Bushoong and with the area north of the Sankuru (where they came from) among the Ngongo. For them it was Itoci himself who was opposed by the first kikaam, who instituted the position of mbaangt. The cane of office was highly respected later on in the east, while in the west more respect perhaps was paid to the special belt, mwaandaan. The Bieeng mbaangt however, do not wear the belt. Tradition relates that they lost this right through being cursed by one of the Bushoong mbaangt. The historian may well wonder if the mwaandaan is not a later innovation, perhaps coming from the Kwilu people.[46]

In addition to the objects mentioned, chiefs also carried important emblems which were not sacral by themselves, items such as the leopard skin or the eagle's feather, the anvil, the double bell, a throne perhaps. Many, if not most, of the uncounted royal emblems are more recent, but all the above seem old. They are not only mentioned by traditions but are found among the southern Mongo.[47] The kolm of the period certainly began to acquire some insignia modeled after those the chiefs wore. Thus the cikl may have worn a parrot's feather and the kikaam an owl's feather. But the elaborate system of feathers as precise insignia of rank, which came to prevail later, was probably not yet organized. The symbolization of hierarchy in a systematic fashion, making use of all insignia, is almost certainly a product of the period of kingship.

The chiefdoms were small, the duties and privileges of titleholders not quite clear, and power probably remained fairly diffuse. Control over subject villages was perhaps limited to one collection of tribute a year. In judicial matters only cases involving murder or bloodshed may have come to the chief's court. In the beginning there must have remained a strong tendency for individual villages to avenge murders by outsiders. The chiefs had to overcome this feuding spirit and could do so only by attacking the offending villages. At the outset the chiefdoms were tiny, sometimes a single big village and a few hamlets. With the passage of time some may have grown to about twenty villages, but later figures cannot be trusted, especially since a great deal of internal migration has since occurred. Shifts of "ethnic" allegiance were also occurring, and the earlier villages were smaller than the average in the nineteenth century. In all but two cases, the Pyaang and the Bushoong, the chiefdoms were miniscule.

Development of the Bushoong Chiefdom

The oldest chiefdom founded south of the Sankuru was ruled by the clan Iyeem, led by a chief whose title was the muyum. In a struggle over the chiefdom this clan lost its position to the Mwey clan, which relegated the muyum to a ritual position. He maintained his court and began to exercise the usual inalienable rights of first occupancy. Before him the Cwa alone had been recognized as first occupants. A member of the muyum's clan, the mbyeemy, was attached directly to the Mwey court to propitiate Ngaan, perhaps at the lake Kum Idip.[48] The position of the muyum's clan as a ritual senior is also evident from its status in other chiefdoms, such as the Pyaang in the east or the Ilebo in the far west, where the clan occurs. No chief could enter their settlements or village sections, impose tribute on them, or order them about. Like the Cwa they were, however, indispensable for any installation.

Then the iyol of Itoci came, ousted the Mwey, and took the title nyim. He received the support of the mbyeemy, who was made president of the council of the mbaangt while the muyum's position remained unaltered. Once settled in the heart of the Bushoong chiefdom in the savanna of Mbal aShepl, the muyum guarded what was now considered the most sacred lake, But aPoong. The unusual development was not the takeover; there are signs that this had occurred in other chiefdoms. It was the split of the ethnic unit: the Mwey clan refused to accept their ouster and mustered enough followers to wage a protracted war. This resulted in the origin of the Bieeng and the Bushoong. Before this both the Bieeng and Bushong may have been called Bambal, although Bushoong as a general term refers back to the earlier age. During the war the Bushoong received aid from the Pyaang, at least in its later stages, when they were fighting in the south. The main effect of the long and drawn-out fighting—probably lasting more than one generation—was to keep the Bushoong united. When all Bieeng had left the center of the kingdom, the chiefdom had expanded to fill an unusually large territory. A rule that restricted succession to the children of the oldest sister had been imposed after a civil clash near But aPoong, during the Bieeng war. This internal strife nearly destroyed the Bushoong leadership.[49] The rule made the opposition of different lineages within the dynastic clan impossible and prevented future splits. It may be that as the first king challenged some of his notables the rule was established that no king would be deposed. At least the tales of the notable Pyeem kapul and of the hidden king imply this. Yet later one of the several kings referred to as Lashyaang may well have been deposed.[50] On balance we cannot be certain at all that these two tales prove that the kum was installed for life. The balance of power in the chiefdom left the mbaangt in a powerful position, but not as powerful as would have been the case if several dynastic lineages had competed for the chiefdom.

Unlike the Pyaang chiefdom, where the immigrant Kuba assimilated the Kete and in some cases were assimilated by them, and unlike all other chiefdoms, which seem either to have left the Kete alone or driven them out or perhaps assimilated some of them, the Bushoong began to dominate Kete villages. They probably began this process in the southern part of their chiefdom. They also attempted to control the Cwa groups they encountered. In general, they regarded these two groups as inferior subjects. Two offices were developed to deal with them. A tribute collector, *paangl* (*paangala*, in Kete), was installed in each Kete village to supervise the collection of tribute and corvée labor.[51] This was a choice position, because part of the tribute remained in the hands of the collector, and the chiefs no doubt gave office to trusted supporters. In much later times similar offices went mostly to sons of kings, but in this early age some paangl may well have belonged to mbaangt officers. But the offices were not hereditary nor attached to any special clan. The official in charge of collecting tribute and supervising labor from the Cwa was the *meshoosh*, and there was probably only one such office during the whole period. The hunters could not easily be pressured; if tribute was paid it must have been irregularly and without leaving much to the official.

The territorial organization may have developed toward the end of the archaic period. Later, the land was divided into nine provinces. Mention of one province occurs in a tradition related to King Mboong aLeeng [2], who founded the smallest province, Ntuun, for his successors and his lineage.[52] The rest existed before that time. The map of the provinces shows that at one time the cikl ruled over the whole territory except for the center, where the chief had his own province. If, as I believe, ipaancl was the next territorial title to be created, the lands in the south were granted to him, perhaps during the Bieeng war and certainly to counterbalance the holdings of the cikl. The provinces of the nyimishoong and nyaang were later taken from the cikl's territory or from the royal region. This may even have occurred as late as Shyaam's reign.[53]

Provinces were further subdivided into counties. Unlike the provincial chiefs, the heads of counties did not reside at the court but in the center of their county, where they represented the king. Their status precluded their working in the fields, and they had to be fed and housed by the residents. They judged small cases arising between the villages of the county and transmitted orders from the provincial chief when he did not send a messenger to all the villages or come in person. No tradition tells us when any of the counties were created. Since the county chiefs restrict the authority of the provincial chiefs, the county chiefs could be a later creation.

The Bushoong expansion was viewed with some alarm by the other central chiefdoms, especially by the Pyaang, who had evidently built a powerful chiefdom themselves. Nor did the Kete take kindly to the imposition of tribute. In the end Kete rebels in the central area, backed by Pyaang, defeated the Bushoong, killed the chief, overran the capital, and imposed a new dynasty, leaving the muyum in what was by then his time-honored position. There are no clues as to how the Bushoong mbaangt reacted. All that is evident is that the chiefdom was not merged with that of the Pyaang. Nor do we know which clan took over the chiefdom. The second dynasty is only known by the name of Mishe miShyaang Matuun [F]. During the reign of the second Mishe miShyaang [6] this name was interpreted as maTuun ("of the clan Ntuun"), known to be a prestigious Leele clan, and it was surmised that Mishe miShyaang Matuun came from the Leele and from the clan, despite the grammatical evidence.[54]

How long the second dynasty ruled we do not know. If it was but a short time one may imagine that the Bushoong inhabitants had not accepted their new situation and rallied around the stranger Shyaam [1] to overthrow the dynasty. If it was a long time such motivation may not have been important. In any case they did rally around Shyaam in sufficient numbers to cause the fall of the dynasty.

During this long Age of Chiefs, other chiefdoms were being formed in the Sankuru-Kasai-Lulua area and were expanding into unoccupied territory. One or more early rifts prevented the Ngeende from establishing a strong chiefdom, but they expanded. In the west a Bieeng splinter group mixed with local inhabitants to form a Kel chiefdom; other Kel had already formed another chiefdom between the Lacwaady and the Kasai. North of the Lacwaady a number of small chiefdoms were formed by people who were known as Shoowa and who came across the Sankuru after all the central Kuba and the Kel had left. In their expansion on the intercalary savanna they met Bushoong who had settled to the northeast of Mbal aShepl. Other Mongo groups kept crossing upstream. Among them one big chiefdom, the Ngongo chiefdom, grew first on both banks of the Sankuru, later mainly on the south bank. Some of its members even went beyond Lusambo, upstream, and some returned from there. Later the Ngongo chiefdom, like the Ngeende one before it, began to suffer from several rifts which finally wrecked its power.[55]

The immigration of the central and the peripheral Kuba resulted in the development of a new society. Kinship was weakened as the key criterion for ordering public life because matrilinearity was accepted. The chiefdoms came to be based on territory alone and, at least among the Bushoong, the Kete were not integrated, with the result that social inequality developed in a new dimension, opposing citizens to subjects. This had existed in the opposition of Mongo and pygmoids, but the latter were too elusive to develop and harden the relationship. Social inequality also grew as the novel distinction began to emerge between commoners on the one hand and rulers and mbaangt clans on the other. The geographical scale of the chiefdoms may not have altered very much from the previous period, with the exception of the Bushoong and probably the Pyaang, but the internal organization was completely different, and elaboration was possible. Centers could be strengthened, titleholders could become administrators, etc. A kingdom was definitely a possibility, especially after the Bushoong defeat by the Pyaang. But none arose at that time. The Pyaang could have fused the two large chiefdoms into a single state, but they did not. Concomitantly with the sociopolitical changes, adaptations in the realm of economic production had also taken place, in small part due to the slightly different and better environment, in large part due to the merging of Kete and Kuba traditions. Other cultural fusions occurred between Kuba and Kete, to be discussed in later chapters.

The evolution described in this chapter ended well before Shyaam—that is, before the end of the first quarter of the seventeenth century. Such an evolution could not have occurred overnight; at the least it took several generations. Frankly I cannot imagine this being compressed into less than a century. The processes and events discussed in this chapter occupied most of the sixteenth century and the early seventeenth century at the least, but may have taken a much longer time. This means that the proto-Kuba period, before any emigration took place, probably ended before 1500. It ended, I believe, well before then, and I consider that the description given in Chapter Six belongs to the first half of our millennium.

Chapter 8

The Age of Kings:
Administrative History

Shyaam [1] and his successors turned a congeries of chiefdoms into a kingdom ruled by the Bushoong. The general institutions and conditions of the realm are fairly well known from the extant descriptions of 1892 and 1907.[1] The traditions claim that the kingdom began with Shyaam, but given the tendency of folk history to idolize this king, it is difficult to determine which innovations are to be attributed to him. There is no doubt that he was a real person, that he was an outstanding personality, and that he took the throne. If he had not been so remarkable, folk history would not credit him with being "the innovator." Malagasy traditions did this for Andrianampoinimerina, and the few existing written documents bear them out.[2] Yet not all the institutional transformations were achieved by this Merina monarch alone; many must be attributed to his successor, Radama. Similarly, the innovations among the Kuba cannot all be attributed to Shyaam or to the period of his reign. Nor did he conquer all the other chiefdoms: credit for that should also go to his successors. In an indirect way such credit is given in the selection of feats attributed to those kings. The tendency is to cast Shyaam in the role of the perfect innovator-inventor, the "magic king." His successor, Mboong aLeeng [2], is cast as the ideal "warrior king." Despite this idealization, at least one famous anecdote involving both power politics and some administrative change was attached to the name of MboMboosh. If Kuba traditions are taken as a literal guide, the period of the creation of the kingdom ended with him.

Periodization is misleading, however. On closer scrutiny it is clear that some informants, but not those who were best informed, attributed a crucial reform to MboMboosh although it was actually carried out by Kot aMbweeky ikoongl [5][3]—namely, settling the dynastic lineage, including the potential successors to the throne, at the capital under close daily control. Furthermore, most of the sociopolitical institutions initiated during this "period" did not develop fully until later. As a structural change in time, the formation of the kingdom should be viewed in a single sequence beginning with Shyaam and ending with the colonial era.

Shyaam is credited with a basic innovation: the founding of the capital as a bureaucratic center. Even in this case, Mboong aLeeng, his successor, completed the task.[4] The creation of a capital implies establishment of an administrative framework, and Shyaam also began the military operations that were to fuse the chiefdoms into a single state. He ushered in a new period, the Age of Kings, which I distinguish from the preceding Age of Chiefs in the following chapters in order to underline the fact that before him there existed a group of chiefdoms but not a kingdom. He began the task of building a genuine state. In describing that state I will first examine the development of the whole administrative framework to 1892; then I will trace the evolution and the institutionalization of power relationships. For this I must work backward from the period of the 1890s using the known institutions and relationships, which are the basis of the descriptive sections of this and the following chapter. The main subdivisions deal with the notion of office and its development, with the development of the administration, the development of the executive—a concept that does not seem to be clear in Bushoong parlance—and with councils and courts, which formed one set of institutions designated by the same basic vocabulary (ibaanc, ikaam) and which were served by the same personnel. In this descriptive typology then, the "executive" dealt with the administrative organization of the territory, which was its major task, with the collection of tribute, and with the execution of orders as well as with the physical means of coercion used to ensure compliance.

Office

Shyaam took over a unified chiefdom, which had some titled offices. He and his successors made a bureaucracy out of those by creating new titles that complemented the existing offices and by developing the idea that all the titles together formed a single, overarching system. In doing this the rulers developed not merely a territorial organization but a set of coherent, central institutions at the capital. They were so successful that in time the bureaucrats, the kolm, formed a power bloc in their own right[5] and became the backbone of a new social class, the patricians. The pattern of social stratification was profoundly altered and social-class formation became more pronounced.

By the late nineteenth century there were three categories of office: that of the king; that of the ngwoom incyaam, members of the crown council; and that of the kolm. We do not know when the king claimed to be a monarch—i.e., when the chief of the Bushoong claimed lordship over all the other chiefs. Whether it was Shyaam, as I believe, or one of his successors, no one could have made a convincing claim without the military victories that were provided by both Shyaam and Mboong aLeeng. Royal power grew so fast that by the middle of the eighteenth century King Kot aNce [7] could exile and execute eagle-feather chiefs with impunity; the former equals of the Bushoong chief had become inferiors. Shyaam introduced the notion that the king was a nature spirit, ngesh. This is the message, obvious to every Kuba, in the anecdotes about his madness and the invention of the ncyeem ingesh songs. In a similar way[6] priestesses of ngesh spirits become possessed by their nature spirit. After their return to normality they teach villagers the songs and dances taught to them by the spirit. But Shyaam was more than the priest of a nature spirit: in later times, and perhaps in his own day, he was considered a spirit himself. His own motto ends with the affirmation "Shyaam, the eldest [first] of kings." The ncyeem ingesh songs originated with him.

Royal symbols and etiquette developed throughout the period, as can be gathered from praise names and songs, but these sources do not allow us to posit a clear evolution. At most they give the impression of an increasing wealth of symbolic material attached to kingship. Pageantry stresses the king's unique position not only as head of the bureaucracy but as a person sui generis, deriving his legitimacy only from kingship itself: "My kingship stems from Nyony aMboom. This kingship, God gave it in my hand."[7] The king embodied the kingdom; the realm never acquired a name distinct from that of the king's title. By 1880 the king's spriitual and worldly power and his wealth far exceeded that of anyone else. His arbitrariness and his right to be arbitrary were stressed and praised, and his innate sense of justice was paradoxically affirmed at the same time.[8]

By the nineteenth century the selective use of terror in warfare against non-Bushoong peoples was common, whereas only a generation earlier a king was said to have died from remorse at having killed the "seventy" sons of his uncle, a former ruler. Royal power and perhaps callousness had increased considerably since the seventeenth century. By 1880 the king could arbitrarily impose a fine, called ishyeeng itaan, "fifteen," against whoever displeased him. Upon learning that he was labeled a malefactor, the accused could hang himself or else give fifteen cowrie shells to the royal messenger to protest his innocence, after which a court trial was held. If the accused was found innocent the king had to atone by making gifts; if found guilty the accused committed suicide, holding kaolin and a stem of sansevieria grass to bless the king before dying.[9] An accused person who did not either request trial or hang himself was sacrificed at the king's death if he was still alive at that time.

The uniqueness of kingship was demonstrated in the rituals accompanying the burial of a king and the installation of a new monarch.[10] By the end of the nineteenth century these lasted for a full year and involved every segment of the population. It was made repeatedly evident that the king epitomized the realm, that without a king society would wither and "civilization" disappear. By his initiation rituals and a symbolic act of ritual incest the king was detached from common mortals. He no longer had any kin (which was the meaning of the incest), and he stood above others as a true nature spirit. This preternatural quality may have been instilled by "incubation" with (i.e., sleeping next to) a statue, at least in the latter eighteenth and nineteenth centuries[11]—a statue that had absorbed its royal "mana" from the deceased king. In the 1950s some subjects believed that this rite had taken place in earlier times. Others did not, but attributed supernatural power to the royal control over the most powerful charms in the kingdom.[12] The introduction of terms, originating in the area west of the Loange River, for "medicine man" and "royal basket of charms" makes it plausible that this aspect of sacred kingship goes back to the beginning of the kingdom. Shyaam was, after all, remembered as "the magic king."

Even though we lack clear evidence as to the growth of the complex of institutions, practices, and ideas surrounding kingship, there can be little doubt that as the real power of the kings increased, the notion of kingship was correspondingly enriched. The rituals of accession were so complex and so many social groups played a role in them that they must have undergone considerable development since the early days. The same must be true of the items of royal adornment. The great royal costume, which weighed about one hundred fifty pounds, by the end of the period was used only for the enthronement and the burial of the king. A detailed study of this icon of ideology has not yet been made, but each part of the costume, each decoration stitched or painted on it or attached to it, held a specific message. The meanings indicated that the king was unique, was the embodiment of his bureaucracy, and was the embodiment of the people. The luxuriance of symbolism in the costume could not have developed in a short time; it must instead have grown throughout the period. The abundance of the costume's imagery reflects the unfolding of a collective dream and shows that kingship stimulated the imagination of the Bushoong to the point of creating a fantasy world around the king. In that world, they never tired of adding to previous achievements.[13] Perhaps only a few understood all the evocations inspired by the details, but all Bushoong, and to a lesser degree all the other ethnic groups, reacted to some of these and were overawed.

The eighteen crown councilors, titled ngwoom incyaam, "medicine man of the basket," were the representatives of the mbaangt. The title originated in the west. Their authority was primarily a collective one, exercised in the crown council, the ibaam. Their position remained essentially ascriptive. They were the representatives of the aristocratic clans, nominated as such by their clan's section at the capital and confirmed by their peers. Shyaam may have introduced their special belt, the mwaandaan, which the king also wore.[14] When they met in council with the king they could and did veto any of his proposals by moving their belts up and down. If Shyaam introduced this, it means that he confirmed or increased the powers of this group. There is also evidence, however, that he and his successors carefully whittled away at the group's privileged position by limiting their access to the titles that existed when Shyaam came to power.

The ngwoom incyaam as individuals retained authority and power up to the 1880s. Each of them could condemn a whole matrilineage to slavery by breaking his belt or his staff of office. In practice, however, that power was channeled insofar as it could only be validly exercised when the ngwoom incyaam were acting collectively. Apart from recruitment, the main differences between them and the kolm was that the kolm held their titles individually and the authority linked to each title was precisely circumscribed, differing from every other title. By the 1880s an important kolm title was valued more than the general status of ngwoom incyaam. This marks a reversal of relations in comparison with the pre-kingdom era.[15]

Each kolm held a different title, a different office, wielded an authority different from that of the courts or councils he might belong to, and exercised different functions. No single person in the political arena could own two titles, nor abandon one to gain a more important or less important one, and no two persons could share the same title. Recruitment was based on achieved status. Kolm were proposed by the king or, in other chiefdoms, by the eagle-feather chief. For the more important offices they had to be accepted by their peers in council, and some of the more important offices required that the kolm belong to a category of ascribed statuses as well (an aristocratic clan, the sons or grandsons of a king, a particular aristrocratic clan, or a combination of these). Less important titles were awarded by the king, and thus were entirely achieved statuses.

Although the statuses and associated roles of kolm were highly differentiated, they all belonged to a single administrative system, which underlay all political institutions. Without a grasp of the overall organization of political office, the structure and functions of any of these institutions cannot be properly appreciated. The systemic character of the offices was exteriorized by insignia, the main one being the wearing of the feather of a designated species of bird. Different kolm had different feathers, and the feathers were grouped in sets: e.g., birds of prey represented officers attached directly to the king, or the same feather could be worn on the head by one kolm and at the corner of the mouth by another one in the same set. By the end of the period at least one hundred and twenty different titles were in use at the capital alone. And yet it was easy to identify a titleholder by the nature of his feather, which acted as an insignia of rank.

Unlike kingdoms that have been and can be described as segmentary, the Kuba state was so conceived that no office at any level was a miniature replica of any other, as happens when authority is delegated undivided.[16] There were territorial officers, but their authority was carefully circumscribed and was not a blanket delegation of royal or chiefly authority. The authority of the provincial Bushoong chief over each village in his province was limited by that of the special representative for each village at the capital, and by that of many kolm who held jurisdiction or special authority with regard to matters of tribute, information gathering, or justice. This situation developed primarily during the eighteenth century.

Any free man could become a kolm and acquire the corresponding prestige. The offices became so numerous that any man over forty had a good chance of holding at least a minor title. By 1953 one quarter of the men held a local title and half of the men in the capital—virtually all older men, excluding slaves—were kolm.[17] The proportions were similar in 1892, since only a few titles were created during the early colonial period. Every man over forty therefore stood one chance in two of becoming a kolm. By that time titles had proliferated even more in the smaller chiefdoms, where almost every man held one, but the content of the offices had eroded to the point that many were no more than honorific distinctions, like decorations in France. Despite their large number, titles were highly desired as a public recognition of success. Their prestige justified the ambition and struggle involved in obtaining one. Support for the regime followed from that. The bureaucratic system thus had the side effect of interesting most or all men in the operations of the administration and of generating enthusiastic acceptance of the regime. Undoubtedly the complexity of the system by 1892 was partly the outcome of this participation. The system allowed the Kuba to become so intoxicated with organization, and above all with public honors, insignia, and pageantry, that the "mirage of the feather" had become the central value in the political culture. Each title had its praise name, emblems, and symbols, and the most important ones even boasted their own funeral and installation rituals. And, of course, each had its own ideology.

These ideological elements were linked in parallel or hierarchical sets. One part of the ideology, the ceremonial or the emblematic part, was common to many titles, and another part of it was unique. The combination of these elements was always unique. The appearance of each kolm evoked the whole system and its ideology, and at the same time it identified the individual title as well, placing it in the several hierarchies represented in that particular nexus. A single example illustrates this.

At the capital, the nyaang, a provincial governor, had to be from an aristocratic clan. He commanded the region Ncol, just as other governors commanded other regions. He wore a white oxpecker feather, as did two of the three other governors and as did the king when he wore the hat of his grand costume, which included this feather and all the other feathers used in the system. Nyaang wore a special hat, as did the other governors, and carried a wooden staff like the staffs of the ngwoom incyaam, although his was of a lower rank. He wore a red copper hat needle, which two other notables were entitled to wear. An adze was worn over his shoulder, and two tiny bows were worn under his shoulders, as they were by other governors; other kolm wore bowstrings, as did the king, who wore hippopotamus tusks on his shoulders. Nyaang's belt of bark belonged to a set that included the higher-ranked mwaandaan of the ngwoom incyaam, and a lower-ranked embroidered belt worn by lesser kolm. The back ornament he shared with all the main kolm and the king. Rings worn around the wrists and ankles recall sets of rings and baldrics of different metals and of raffia, sometimes studded with cowries, all varying according to rank.

Nyaang's insignia were identical to those of one other governor, the nyimishoong, who preceded nyaang in rank: he was placed before him in public processions and just after him in the speaking order at councils. Nyimishoong's iron staff and the blades of his adze indicated the difference between them: nyaang's adze resembled a rake with four teeth; nyimishoong's had two entwined blades of a different shape. One look at the adze told the observer where nyaang ranked among the provincial governors.[18] His praise name differed from that of anyone else. I did not record any anecdote associated with his title, but one may well have existed; if so, we can assume that, as in other cases, it related the title to other titles and to the king. Whatever the particular ideologies were, they merged to form a global political ideology. This explains why the latter was so rich that no single person could remember all of its ramifications and why its splendor and intricacy were deemed to be the essence of civilization. It is also evident that no single king could have established such a complex system. It grew from the time of Shyaam to the colonial period.

The rank of every notable was established by the rank of his title, and for titles of the same rank, by seniority of nomination. Rank was manifested by the place a notable held in the succession of speakers at all councils. The main Bushoong hierarchy is set forth in Table 2.

In other chiefdoms the group called *kolm matuk mabol* had variations for the last title (nyaang) among the *kum ashin*; many variations occurred in the other titles in this group.[19] In the third and fourth groups, most titles varied from chiefdom to chiefdom or equivalents could not be found. New titles were added to group four well into the twentieth century.

In each chiefdom the eagle-feather chief dominated the hierarchy. The king was the eagle-feather chief of the Bushoong and therefore was at the top of their hierarchy. The Bushoong chiefdom ruled the kingdom, but there was no system of titles common to all chiefdoms. For example, the kikaam at the capital represented only the Bushoong kolm. No one represented all the kolm of the country or all the eagle-feather chiefs. The only title common to all was king, nyim, which is also the special chiefly title held by the king among the Bushoong. He alone theoretically linked all the chiefdoms, villages, and

Table 2
The Hierarchy of Bushoong Kolm (Notables) in the Twentieth Century[a]

Group 1: kikaam

A single person, the representative of all kolm living at the capital. Named by the ngwoom incyaam (crown council), not by the king.

Group 2: kolm matuk mabol (literally, "notables of the corners of the village")

First rank: kum ashin	Literally, "chiefs of the lands" (provincial governors).
cikl	Chief of three lands (provinces).
ipaancl	Chief of two lands.
nyimishoong	Chief of one land.
nyaang	Chief of one land.
Second rank: no special name	
mwaaddy	The representative of royal children and grand-children.
nyoom	The representative of the potential successors to the king.
kikaam angel abol	The representative of the government of the town area of the capital.
ipaancl ikikaam	The deputy of the kikaam angel abol.
Third rank: no special name	
mbyeemy	A ritualist, named by the ngwoom incyaam; a member of the muyum's clan.
seven different titles	Each title was ranked by seniority of nomination.
Fourth rank: no special name	
mbeem	Called "the father of the king"; the representative of one half of the capital.
mbyeeng	Called "the father of the capital"; the representative of the other half of the capital.
shesh	The chief military officer for kombeem, mbeem's half of the capital.
iyol	The chief military officer for kongweemy, mbyeeng's half of the capital.
katyeen	A woman; the representative of the women of kombeem.
mbaan	A woman; the representative of the women of kongweemy.
various deputies for the male titles in this rank	

Table 2 (*continued*)

Group 3: kolm bukwemy	
twelve kolm	Those kolm responsible for collecting tribute and supplying corvée labor. Each was ranked by seniority of nomination.

Group 4: *no special name*	
sixty or more kolm	Each kolm was ranked by seniority of nomination.

[a]The order of titles is the order in which members of the ibaanc council spoke at council meetings.

hunters together in a common hierarchy. He alone was *ncyeem nkwoonc*, "God on earth."[20] Although his insignia showed him to be at the top of the Bushoong pyramid, and although by his eagle feather he was the equal of other eagle-feather chiefs, an abyss lay between the king and all the others. The eagle-feather chiefs were the highest in rank in their own chiefdoms, but their prestige and rank at the royal court was low. At best they were seen as equivalent to the kum ashin.

Shyaam organized the core of the kolm matuk mabol, using the previously existing titles kikaam, cikl, ipaancl, mbyeemy, mbeem, mbyeeng, iyol, (shesh?), mbaan, and perhaps katyeeng, which was at first an honorific for the mothers of potential royal heirs. He is credited with altering the recruitment criteria for mbeem and mbyeeng and increasing their importance by giving them a crucial position on councils.[21]

The attribution of the creation of any title to a particular king has not been remembered in the traditions. This is much less important than the general evolution of the system, which permitted the content of existing titles to be altered. Since titles were conferred for life, but could not be changed, a person named to low office was confined there, and under such circumstances an enterprising individual could increase his status only by trying to expand the privileges and responsibilities of the office or by increasing his personal influence as a favorite of the king, "a king's friend." The latter approach could result in additional attributes being given to the title he held, which is what happened to the mbeem and mbyeeng of the capital. The converse could also occur. A case in point seems to be the office of mbyeemy. Once very influential, he alone performed the royal rituals and presided over the crown council when it acted as a court of justice. Even though this council may have been instituted by Shyaam, the mbyeemy's influence waned when a second title, *pok ibaan*, "their [charm] pot," was created. This titleholder was appointed by the king and was in charge of making medicine for him. Almost half of the responsibility of the mbyeemy was taken from him by the creation of the new title. Similarly, cikl, who was chief of all the "lands" (provinces), lost influence whenever a new "chief of the land" title was created. That erosion of provincial authority ended only with the creation of the last title, nyaang.

A similar process affected many offices as the multiplication of titles from the seventeenth to the late nineteenth century reduced the responsibilities, authority, and significance of the earlier titles. In the Bushoong system as a whole, the multiplication by successive kings of titles in groups three and four (see Table 2) increased the royal power over kolm in groups one and two. The process is also evident within groups three and four, where titleholders were in charge of collecting tribute and supplying corvée labor. The multiplication of titles here led to a tighter control by the king over his revenue, which may have expanded his income and decreased the importance of older titles in those groups.

Obviously the system took time to grow. The creation of rules of succession limiting certain titles to children or grandchildren of the kings must have taken at least one or two generations after Shyaam to become fully established. Those rules came to apply to the most important titles. Children and grandchildren of kings as separate social categories are first mentioned under Kot aMbweeky ikoongl [5],[22] suggesting that only for his reign can we infer the probable existence of the succession rule as a regular practice. Under Kot aNce [7] many offices were created, as is evident in the praise name of his capital, "Asking the meaning":

> They repeatedly ask about the words,
> The reparation: they repair the people;
> *The Bushoong give offices to the people,*
> The chasing away: they chase them from the corners* of the town. [italics added]

The last line indicates that creation of offices was intended to diminish the power of the mbaangt and it may even be correct to understand that offices that had been reserved to mbaangt were now given to others. This slender bit of evidence does not allow us to deduce that this king initiated the policy of extending the kolm system, perhaps to accommodate his many sons;[23] it merely indicates that existing or new offices were being used by the king to attract supporters. Both before and after him, kings altered requirements for eligibility to office and created new positions. As stated earlier, some titles existed before Shyaam. He or perhaps one of his successors built a system of offices, using existing ones as a start. The system probably was continuously enriched thereafter. Its effect was to attract more income, more supporters, and more authority for the king.

*mbaang, the place for the mbaangt.

The Administration of the Executive

The territorial organization of the Bushoong chiefdom was either created or perfected by Shyaam [1] and Mboong aLeeng [2]. The last province was created by Mboong aLeeng, and the kingdom began to take organized shape during his reign. The traditions tell us that Shyaam brought back from the Mbuun the idea of a capital. Since the concept of a chief's court (*bosenge*, in Mongo) is older, than Shyaam, the traditions must refer to the layout of the capital. One of its features, the great palisades surrounding each ward, appears in Kot aMbweeky ikoongl's [5] praise name.[24] Palisades imply dignitaries, since only dignitaries are entitled to such enclosures: outside of the Bushoong chiefdom and among the Mongo, only eagle-feather chiefs and senior patriarchs can have their own enclosures.

Evidence of the development of the capitals can perhaps still be discovered by archaeological digging[25] which should at least reveal their respective sizes. In 1892 the capital was a striking sight, its outer wall consisting of a palisade nine or ten feet high, the wall enclosing the palace standing over twelve feet. The town had its streets, plazas, and special buildings. It was a true city, housing about 10 percent of the population of the core of the kingdom, 5 percent of the total. Most of the inhabitants were notables, artisans, or traders. Some of them farmed, although according to an explicit tradition, ascribed to Mboong aLeeng's [2], they were forbidden to do so. This was the economic and political hub of the realm. Even though it was moved at least once during each reign, it remained within the same general area, which measured about seventeen by six and a half miles, and it retained the same rectangular plan. A special official carefully preserved the overall measurements and the details. Most elements of the houses and walls were movable. There was only one capital at a time, even though King Mbakam Mbomancyeel [4] is said to have lived in three at once. These three simultaneous capitals may have been invented later to account for his praise name, "Mbakam, of the bowstrings at Ngwi, the arrows at Malaam, and the bow at Tal."[26] If he did try to occupy three towns at once, none of his successors followed suit.

The plan of the town area of the capital was essentially the plan of any Bushoong village. The palace area was completely different, however. Other precolonial palaces, such as those of the Lunda or Kongo, contained palisades for chiefs and a maze of walls, courtyards and plazas.[27] This idea and perhaps some of the actual layout was what Shyaam brought back from the Mbuun, who could have invented it, but it is at least equally likely that the idea comes from the Lunda or Kongo. The Mbuun had a trading connection around 1620 with the Kongo,[28] and later their chieftainship was heavily influenced by the Lunda.[29]

The king's palace included his meeting halls, storehouses, harem, personal dwelling, and the courtyards used for assemblies. Around it his ritualists—mbyeemy, pok ibaan, and cikl—had their quarters, as did the potential successors, the royal slaves, and all male twins born among the Bushoong. Such twins had to come and live in this quarter; their leader became spokesman (*muyesh*) for the king. The most important drums were housed in or around the palace. It and the surrounding wards formed one half of the city plan. Many of these elements date from Shyaam's reign, but he required a less elaborate plan, for he had only a harem of aristocratic wives and may not have had a pok ibaan. He brought plans for the inner palace proper; later expansion is linked with the growth of the realm, specifically the quarters occupied by the majority of the royal slaves, the pok ibaan, and the potential successors.

More important than the palace itself was the notion that the kolm should reside at the capital and their clan sections along with them, which meant that the capital's population outnumbered that of any other village many times over. This was the basis of the strength of the kingdom. Shyaam's elevation of the mbeem and mbyeeng of the town area of his capital to very high rank provided a unified government. The terminology of praise associated with these officials, "the fathers of the king," makes it clear that in this matrilineal system they were to be devoted to him and not to kingship in general, which was the role of the "maternal uncles of the king," the *kum ashin*.

Shyaam moved his capital three times, as did his successor. After a raid from the Cwa Iloong,[30] which caught the town by surprise because everyone was in the fields, Mboong aLeeng [2] ordered that the inhabitants would no longer be allowed to farm. This tale reflects the change from a farming community to a real city—a change that did not occur all at once. It presupposes that enough food was grown by captives in the surrounding villages and was brought in from greater distances as tribute or as market produce. Mboong aLeeng may have started this process: he is remembered for the creation of different types of dependent villages and clearly was the initiator of much of the territorial organization.

He is said to have introduced the custom that all Bushoong clans provide him with a wife which meant that instead of the eighteen wives of the mbaangt the king had hundreds of women, and a bigger harem meant a bigger capital. Again it is hard to imagine one king alone completely implementing this policy, but he may have set the rule and his followers saw to it that it was followed by all clans. Shyaam already had founded the mbweengy, a quarter in the town area of the capital, for some of his wives. Here royal wives could bear children fathered by anyone, and the king remained their sociological father. This presupposes that even Shyaam had more wives than the women received from the mbaangt.[31]

MboMboosh succeeded Mboong a Leeng and was reputedly the most long-lived of all Kuba kings. He founded nine (the perfect number) capitals. Anecdotes attached to his name and reign indicate the existence of wards for royal slaves and mention a street named "the footprint of the king" around the compound of the king's most trusted favorites.[32] Two reigns later, Kot aMbweeky ikoongl [5] created the ward for the potential successors and surrounded their quarters with those of his royal slaves. By then, at the beginning of the eighteenth century, the royal slaves were numerous enough to guard the king and supervise the activities of his dynastic lineage and its servants. This was the last major addition to the palace area of the capital. Most kings after him are remembered as having built only one capital each, although during a half-century of rule Mbop Mabiinc maMbul [12] occupied four, not including the one he inherited from his predecessor.[33]

With regard to rural organization, Shyaam created a special police, the kol mat, who numbered at least one per county and one per province. Those in counties reported information directly to the king or to the kol mat of the province. Their role was to check on all activities, especially tribute collection and collectors.[34] Free Bushoong villages also had their kol mat. In addition to their role as informers, they could also be ordered directly by the king to kill designated persons accused of being rebels.[35]

Mboong aLeeng [2] not only created the smallest province—an enclave in one of the provinces of the cikl as an appanage for his successor[36]—but organized (or reorganized) the payment of tribute, in part as a consequence of claiming a wife from each clan. This meant that in time children of mothers from all the villages were living at the capital, and each village had at the capital a son or grandson by a royal wife. By the nineteenth century these descendants were held formally responsible for the annual basic tribute from their village. In this role they replaced the kum ashin. They also provided the king with information about their villages, duplicating the role of the kol mat. This system seems to have developed during the eighteenth century.

A further check on the power of the kum ashin came at some unknown time as a result of the creation of the counties, *nnung*, or, if a county already existed, by altering the method of appointment of county heads. These officials were now directly appointed by the king, with confirmation left to their own village council. Their functions were mainly judicial. By giving the king direct control at this level and its mainly judicial functions, the measure reduced the authority and the power of the kum ashin and strengthened the centripetal forces within the Bushoong chiefdom.

From the time of Mboong aLeeng at the latest, villages came to be classified as free or unfree. The latter were called *matoon*, the name of the royal clan. They had no titleholders and were subject to a headman, the *kubol matoon*, who lived at the capital.[37] The inhabitants were essentially considered to be prisoners of war. Two types were distinguished: the *bubaang* villages, located around the capital, which delivered the daily requirements of firewood, palm wine (bubaang means "palm wine" in royal language), and food for the palace; all other matoon villages were appanages of the king, his mother, and his heir apparent. A very few were endowments intended for a lifetime and more. In matoon villages the beneficiaries could require much more tribute and services than was usual in free villages. Villages became matoon because they were settled by prisoners of war or because they were convicted collectively of a more or less serious crime. Ndoomyoong became matoon after its inhabitants were convicted of the theft of a supply of cowries belonging to the king. Some Kete villages were similarly dependent. Mboong aLeeng created all the variants of the village system. The king introduced a new form of initiation: all matoon villages had to send their boys to the capital, where at least one son of the king was initiated with them and became their age-grade leader.[38] Many of the later kings created new matoon villages with prisoners of war. At least one, the Kete village Baashween, became an appanage of a female of the royal lineage, but the majority of matoon villages remained attached to the king himself. Only one ever went to a mbaangt,[39] and none went to a kolm. After the first grant by Mboong aLeeng, none went to potential male successors. As a result the material base of groups which could challenge the king's authority remained restricted while that of the kings expanded.

All free villages paid tribute once a year, toward the end of the dry season, adding one antelope for the use of their representative at the capital.[40] The kum ashin was called upon only when tribute was withheld. He then went himself to collect it or inquire in person as to why it could not be paid. Tribute consisted of food, usually maize, from a special field in each village (the *shash anyim*), and of dried foodstuffs such as yams, cassava, plantains, dried meat, or smoked fish. Other products such as raw raffia cloth, salt, iron, knives, hoes, pottery, camwood, carved objects, baskets, etc. were added according to local resources and specialty. The main requirement was food, and the main guideline was "Eat the fresh food, bring the preserved to the king."[41] The amount of tribute requested in the 1950s was low. Before 1951 the village Mboong Bushepy was asked each year for one raffia cloth per adult man, two dwarf antelopes, and an antelope for the king's child at the capital. When the king received the tribute at the annual gathering he gave part of it (probably the meat) to the provincial governor and to his favorites. He stored the rest.

Free villages also paid special tribute when there was need for their particular products at the palace or when there was an urgent need for everyday items. The latter were collected directly by the provincial governor, who went from village to village to raise the amount imposed, and who kept a part of the proceeds. This was exceptional, whereas the levy of special products occurred more often. It was done by certain kolm whose office required that they be informed about supplies throughout the chiefdom. These special officers and their deputies existed for most "rare" natural resources, such as iron ore, salt, or clay for pottery. The *tancoon* and his deputy, the *cikl tancoon*, were in charge of iron ore. Mboong Bushepy had a mine in its area and paid whenever the tancoon requested it, the assessment for every adult man being five to ten standard-size balls of iron (*tol*, nominal class 12). In a similar way the *makaan* collected camwood, the *nyim lakaang* palm oil, the *nyabashoong* game, the *nyimancok* elephant products, the *nyibin* carvings and decorated mats, etc.[42] If a village was the seat of a regional market, a kolm was appointed to maintain order, administer commercial justice, and collect a tax from traders. The market in Ngel aMbidy county was in the charge of the *kyeemk ngel ambiidy*, who raised the tax there. Like the special tax collectors, these officials were also allowed to keep a portion of the proceeds for themselves. If they took too much, regional or local kol mat informed the king of it.

Corvée labor was also required by the capital. Each building in the palace area (the harem excepted) and public buildings and enclosures were assigned to a specific village for building and maintenance. The provincial governors were in charge of labor recruitment; once at the capital, the laborers were under the command of the official in charge of repairs. When a new capital was built or sections were moved, the official architect supervised the operations. Two stewards of the royal household assessed the daily maintenance requirements for the palace and sent their orders daily and directly to the bubaang villages. When free villagers had completed their job, the king provided them with palm wine as if the corvée was nothing more than a working bee like those that women organized to hoe their fields.[43]

Special offices were created to procure the services of specialized performers, just as kolm existed to supply special products. The *mwep ngom* was responsible for supplying drummers for numerous official occasions. He requisitioned them from the villages where they lived. Other officials acted similarly when musicians or dancers were needed.[44]

Governors could also draft labor to build vine-suspension or other bridges and to keep the paths cleared in their domains. This was done very rarely, if at all, there being evidence of only one bridge in the whole realm. In times of general mobilization—of which no memory remains—the governors called out the men from all the villages in their "lands" to provide an army.

Inhabitants of the capital did not pay tribute. Artisans were called to the palace by the appropriate official when their special services were required (e.g., to carve posts or beams), but this happened infrequently. Many of the free male inhabitants were kolm. In each of the wards the head was responsible for the upkeep of fences, houses, and courtyards. The streets and squares were kept clean by prisoners.[45] The *tataam*—who, incidentally, was not a eunuch—supervised the harem, while pok ibaan and *kum adweengy* (a wife of the king) supervised the work required from the royal wives, who had to build and repair their own houses and were expected to embroider cloth, to dance, and to sing every day, especially during the new moon or at special feasts. Kum adweengy was the fifth wife of the king in rank. The royal wives who lived in mbweengy were supervised by the *men mbweengy* and his deputy, and the *nyibit idiing* ("king of war for the slave quarter") supervised requests made of the royal slaves and led them in war. Other officials, some of them slaves themselves, acted as a constabulary or as messengers for the king. By 1892 the king recruited labor for these purposes among his slaves, led by one of his sons, who carried a knife as a mace or proof that he was a royal messenger.[46]

In time the nonterritorial titleholders all came to be conceived of as representatives of the people they were taxing.[47] Since these kolm advised the king on the resources or services pertaining to their office, they quite naturally became spokesmen for the craftsmen. The tendency to see them as representatives of the crafts grew to be so engrained that the mbyeemy in charge of relations with the nature spirits came to be seen as the spirits' representative.

Since the bubaang and other matoon villages were more heavily taxed than others, it is not surprising to find rules prohibiting men from leaving the bubaang settlements without royal permission; the same was probably true of all matoon villages, all the more so in that kings could, and sometimes did, decide where any of their subjects should reside.[48] If we discount an ambiguous tale concerning Shyaam, the earliest account we have have concerning forced residence dates from the reign of Miko miMbul [11].

With regard to the other chiefdoms, villages, and settlements, the taxation system was different. Taxes continued to be levied on every Kete village by a paangl, usually a different one for each village, and a meshoosh taxed Cwa settlements. Both kept part of the proceeds for themselves.[49] Subject chiefdoms were represented by an *ibwoon* at the capital. He was a Bushoong official who would go to "his" chiefdom to collect the tribute paid at the end of the dry season. Tribute was light, and consisted of meat and special products.[50] Special assessments included one woman for the king whenever a new eagle-feather chief was elected, and tribute in goods when a new eagle-feather chief was installed, when a king died or was installed, and when a potential successor to the king died. For instance, two Pyaang Makesh villages paid twenty-five pieces of raffia cloth for the funeral of a potential successor and thirty for the election of their chief. No corvée labor was required. Payment of tribute varied according to distance and over time, as well as according to the size and internal cohesion of the various chiefdoms.

All territorial heads in the kingdom, whether Bushoong or not, paid homage to the king. To refuse was to announce open rebellion. Homage was paid not only by the kolm at the accession of a king but by all subjects through the mechanism of the "noble tribute." Anyone killing or finding a "noble" animal was to send either the whole or a prescribed portion of it to the king through hierarchical channels. The sole noble domestic animal was the sheep. Only the king could keep sheep, and he kept two or three herds in matoon villages. Noble game included the black genet (*Atilax paludinosis*), the tree-dwelling pangolin, the civet cat, and the giant pangolin. The portions of noble animals that were required were the skin and feathers of the eagle; the skin of the leopard; one horn of a buffalo; one tusk, the tail hair, and nine blocks of meat of an elephant; one tusk of a hippopotamus; a haunch of a warthog; and a portion of five different types of caterpillars from the seasonal harvest. In the chiefdoms these items were brought to the chief, who sent them to the king.[51] Among the Bushoong the finder or killer, accompanied by his headman and the appropriate chief of the "land," went directly to the king. The noble tribute had nothing to do with wealth: the point was homage. Wealth could be involved, however; by the nineteenth century, and probably before, a tusk was the equivalent of bridewealth, and was thus an item of high value.

Homage is mentioned in the traditions, perhaps anachronistically, as early as the split between Itoci and Lakoin. Given the ubiquitous ethnographic distribution of the practice, and indeed given both the variety and the distribution of most of the animals cited, this may not be anachronistic. Details about tribute do not appear at all in the traditions, which only mention "rebellions," presumably meaning the nonpayment of either noble tribute or general tribute. Presumably the earliest system before Shyaam's reign, and perhaps during that reign as well, was payment of a basic tribute and corvée to the provincial governor. The rest of the complex system grew up beginning with Mboong aLeeng [2]. Shyaam or Mboong aLeeng was also presumably the first to request tribute from subject chiefdoms.

Military organization was not nearly as intricate. The principal military offices were the *nyibit* ("king of war"), the iyol and shcsh of the capital, and the nyibit idiing. The residences of these officers in the capital corresponded to their position in the order of march: shesh and iyol in the vanguard (right and left), nyibit in the center, and nyibit idiing with the troops surrounding the king. The iyol nyibit, first deputy of the nyibit commanded the rear. There is no information on the marching order used in war during the nineteenth century, but one account dates from 1907.[52] The grand army was perhaps last called out in full array under Kot aNce [7] to fight Luba groups in the middle of the eighteenth century. Before that it had not been summoned—if the traditions can be presumed to be complete—since MboMboosh [3]. There are some indications, however, that MboMboosh and Mbakam Mbomancyeel [4] dispatched strong armies against the Pyaang.

Of interest is the description of the order of battle in the campaign of

MboMboosh against the Nkucu: "King, your tactic of fighting in two lines and .defying the enemy will not avail with the Nkucu, who are guerrilla fighters; fall upon them at night and unaware while they camp and you will overcome them."[53] Battle lines and more or less formal defiance appear in tales relating to the Bieeng wars and the campaign of Kot aNce against the Luba.[54] All these references, as well as earlier ones referring to battles follow-ing the hammers and anvils episode, may be anachronistic, but they can at least be taken to reflect nineteenth-century practice, and the names of military heroes and war magicians may well be from earlier times. The size of the armies on the battlefield and the number of casualties in battle and in war generally remain unknown. The impression gained is that in most encounters these were not impressive: the Kot aNce war against the Luba may have involved not much more than a score of victims,[55] certainly less than one hundred. Troops were recruited from the capital by shesh and iyol and eventu-ally by the nyibit from villages lying in the line of march. The theoretical possibility of mobilizing all men in all provinces, or even in one province, may have remained entirely theoretical during the last two centuries.

Other sorts of military expeditions were more frequent. The king some-times ordered a Bushoong village to attack a target enemy village; he even in one case ordered a Kete village to attack a matoon Bushoong settlement. In one tale Mboong aLeeng [2] ordered the people of Mweek to wage guerrilla warfare against the powerful Pyaang. When success was not forthcoming, the king judged this to be rebellion and ordered a Kete village to attack Mweek. The Kete did so, but the nearby Cwa of Ishyaam, who had not been told about the order, fell in turn upon the Kete, killing some of them.[56] This type of action continued until late in the nineteenth century, when Mbop Mabiinc maMbul [12] asked the Caadi, who were not even a part of the state, to attack Bulaang villages, which were.[57] But the Caadi preferred to pay slaves as indemnity rather than fight. Earlier, in the reign of Miko miMbul [11], Mweek was sent to destroy the distant village of Kopl. This was a relatively bloody operation: thirty-one people of Kopl were killed, and the iyol of Mweek brought the hands of six enemies as proof. The men of Mweek suffered no losses.[58] It is plausible that this type of operation was practiced from the earliest period, for the first story about Mweek under Mboong aLeeng indi-cates that the Cwa were confused by it because it was an innovation.

For some expeditions people in the capital were used, mostly royal slaves under the leadership of one or more of the king's sons. But the "army" also included many inhabitants of the town area of the capital. A song of Kot aMbul [10] (c. 1800) tells of his sending two of his sons out to avenge the murder in a Ngeende village of one of their brothers, who presumably was there to levy tribute. The campaign against the Ngeende that Torday witnessed in 1907 involved primarily men from the capital (whose population was by then reduced) and was led by the nyibit, perhaps because the king went in person.[59] Most small expeditions were led by royal sons, war magicians, or the nyibit. This is clearly attested as early as the reign of Kot aNce [7] in his campaign against the Ngongo, although he himself led the army against the Luba.[60]

Kings did lead coercive operations outside the Bushoong chiefdom. These have special technical names and some occurred well into this century. For example, when a chiefdom was held to be in a state of rebellion, the king would go on "inspection" with a large armed retinue, settle in the rebellious court, exact tribute, and return only after having secured a formal submission.[61] In these circumstances the *nkweemy nyeeng* was in charge rather than the nyibit. In the latter part of the nineteenth century a maximum of five hundred men—all of the king's male slaves—were involved in these operations. Although they are not mentioned, such actions may have taken place in earlier times. They probably are not mentioned because they did not rank as "wars" for the Bushoong, and detailed accounts from most of the other chiefdoms are still not available. Preliminary accounts from the other chiefdoms do not indicate any, but very little was remembered in those areas.

Sheppard leaves no doubt that in 1892 the Bushoong chiefdom had a police force led by a son of the king and consisting of forty men. The leaders wore special insignia and were sent to arrest the headmen of recalcitrant villages.[62] This pattern may well have developed in the eighteenth and nineteenth centuries, when royal power was no longer really challenged in the villages of the chiefdom or by the Kete. It probably grew out of the practice of sending royal sons with an expedition, as has been noted above.

In this period it is clear that some military titles were added to the older ones. The cases of nyibit idiing and nkweemy nyeeng seem evident. In general, however, it should be noted that no proliferation of military offices occurred. This sector did not yield rewards as rich as the offices responsible for the collection of revenue. One can also argue that military titles are old. Some go back to the proto-Kuba period, and most of the others to the early kingdom of the seventeenth century. This implies that the military organization was completed early on and was found sufficient to its task. A small force went a long way because of the organization at the capital.

Councils and Courts

In 1892 five councils existed at the capital, only three of which seem to date back to the Age of Chiefs. Shyaam [1] may have organized the others himself and in so doing transformed the existing ones, or initiated their transformation. He certainly created the ibaam, the crown council, by transforming the former council of mbaangt and giving a new title, ngwoom incyaam, to the members. The basket (*ncyaam*), of which they were the medicine men, was a new royal charm, the term being Kikongo. Its content may have been that of the old charm Inam, though presumably it included new ingredients. By 1892 the crown council met to install a king, a kikaam, and a mbyeemy, and presumably it had done so from the beginning. Perhaps also from the beginning its members initiated a new king for eighteen days (one for each mbaangt), the first such initiation being either that of Shyaam or, more likely, Mboong aLeeng.[63] The council also met—although infrequently—to rebuke the king. In view of the general erosion of the power of the mbaangt, it might be inferred that such meetings were more frequent in the seventeenth century than later. The ibaam was internally divided into a "downstream" and an "upstream" section, each with nine members. Its duties were mainly religious. At each new moon the men sang the songs of the nature spirits, another of Shyaam's innovations. They did this in the area also called ibaam, an open space on the righthand, upstream side of the capital, outside the walls. They also kept a small round drum which was covered with an iguana skin and which was beaten when they sang the ncyeem ingesh or another song aimed at spiritually strengthening the king and kingship.

Members presumably were chosen by their peers. They had to belong to a particular aristocratic clan, and they were members for life. They could also be made kolm. In 1953 the shesh of the capital was also a ngwoom incyaam. In Shyaam's day the council must have wielded considerable power, if only because it served to legitimize the new dynasty. The king belonged to it but did not preside over it, that being the role of the *kikaam mimbaangt*. When members were displeased with royal proposals they shook their mwaandaan belts; when pleased, they lifted them. Open rejection was not believed proper, but the members did hold veto powers. All deliberations were secret, all members could speak up, question, and even upbraid the king. Only a direct rebuke in answer to a royal speech in the council was deemed improper. In addition to its ritual sessions, the council could call the king to attend a political meeting whenever it chose, and the king could summon the council for the discussion of serious matters. The frequency of and the reasons for the meetings certainly varied over time.

The former chiefly council eventually became the present *ishyaaml* after the king was excluded from it and it lost its judiciary powers. The name ishyaaml is very old, being used for chiefly councils everywhere, and the former chiefly council was no doubt called by the same name. At the later ishyaaml no king could be present, and meetings were held at the kikaam's residence. Members were the kikaam, the four kum ashin, kikaam angel abol and his deputy, the mwaaddy, and the mbyeemy. Without the presence of the first six members, no business could be concluded. This gave them, in fact, veto power over the agenda, and in the 1950s they used it. These members spoke first, and the other titleholders who were part of the council followed. Even the seven "who follow mbyeemy" could appear and speak. These included tataam, *men mbweengy,* pok ibaan, nyibit idiing, and *nyim sheky,* the guardian of the poison oracle. Deliberations were secret. The council met frequently, although attendance varied according to the points on the agenda. Meetings were called by the kikaam, who sent the mwaaddy to notify the members. The king could send muyesh, his spokesman (the leader of all male twins), or pok ibaan or *cikl mbeem,* deputy mbeem of the capital, to request the kikaam to call a meeting. The council could refuse to discuss any matter brought up by the king and could block royal projects by doing so. It used this power in 1907 and in the 1950s.[64] The council had to reach a unanimous decision—a requirement for all Kuba councils—which was transmitted to the king via the cikl. If the king rejected the decision, the kikaam and the four kum ashin visited him at night and attempted to convince him. If they failed, they sent the iyol and shesh of the capital to signify their refusal to support the royal point of view. Then the king had to call the *mbok ilaam* council to take up the question. These procedures of the 1950s show that by that time each of the parties involved had developed elaborate means to arbitrate conflict without losing face. The power of the kolm was balanced by that of the king. A refined balance of power among the different groups competing for decision making was also established through overlapping memberships in other councils and in the representation in ishyaaml, another council, of all the groups involved except the potential successors.[65]

During meetings of ishyaaml, the first five members and mbyeemy each had an empty basket, said to be "the basket of wisdom," which was the emblem of the council and on which they leaned one elbow when speaking. These resembled the royal basket *yiing*, although the latter was covered with beads and cowries and the former were plain. The kikaam presided, seated on a tiny podium, an emblem he shared with the eagle-feather chiefs.[66] These emblems and the oxpecker feather were specific to the council and expressed its elevated rank.

The procedure and the composition of ishyaaml evolved after its creation. This council was created when the kolm were successful in eliminating the presence of the king. That occurred when the kikaam, the provincial governors, and mbyeemy (as the leading kolm) felt that the earlier council, now represented by the mbok ilaam, was no longer effective. Since the feather indicates that the council's first role had to do with territorial matters, this reinforces the view that it is a creation of a full-fledged kingdom. The council was strongly loaded with mbaangt members. It represented organized opposition to the king, a need which arose only after the ibaam and the provincial governors had lost power and control over the income from the provinces. This cannot be ascribed to Shyaam's reign, since he presumably had to rely heavily on his mbaangt to be legitimated. The creation of the council represents a counterweight to the developed power of the kings and must therefore be presumed to date from the late seventeenth or early eighteenth century, certainly, I believe, before the reign of Kot aNce [7]. It involved the kolm, which were the oldest titles and, excluding only nyaang and nyimishoong, had been in existence before the creation of the kingdom itself. The kikaam angel abol, the mwaaddy, and the seven "who follow mbyeemy" are later additions. They reflect both the further growth of royal power and the growing influence of "the Bushoong," that is, the settlers of the capital.[67]

Mbok ilaam, "the way of the kitchen" or "the way of tribute,"[68] grew out of the former general council of the chief's settlement before ishyaaml became specialized, but its name dates from the creation of the present ishyaaml. It was a council for current affairs, and met in a square named for it within the palace walls. All the kolm were members, but not all could speak. The king presided over it. He called the meeting through the muyesh, who sent the twins from their quarter next to the palace to notify the notables.[69] At the meeting only the king and the kolm bukwemy (higher ranks) spoke. In Bushoong terms, the feathers of the birds of prey and those of the guinea fowl (the capital) were added to those of the oxpecker. The former group, birds of prey and guinea fowl, were the king's men especially the military; the latter were mbeem and mbyeeng, who occupied a special position insofar as procedure dictated that they spoke last. The order of speech was, first, exposition by the king through his spokesman, the muyesh; then the members of ishyaaml, according to rank; then the others in reversed rank. After mbeem and mbyeeng had spoken, the kikaam and then the king summed up. The last speakers had the advantage, and the king's summation was supposed to give the sense of the meeting. The king presided with his back to the wall of his inner palace. He sat on a throne or on the back of a slave who crouched on all fours. The muyesh sat in front of and below him, with his back to the king. On the right side of the king, at a 90° angle, the members of ishyaaml were seated by rank. Opposite the king sat the other kolm. In front of them sat mbeem and mbyeeng, on the right and left respectively. They thus occupied the upstream side, and the king was downstream. The fourth side (left) was the "gallery," reserved for kolm who could be present but not speak. In the 1950s the meeting could be open to the public, in which case that side was open to them.

Before the debate began and after everyone was seated, the king's hornblowers announced his arrival. He entered through a special door at the inner palace side and was presented with a big charm, covered by a white cloth, which was called the royal *ncyeem*, "God." The king controlled the meeting because he first outlined the question and often suggested the answer. No one could contradict the king in this council; the result he desired had to emerge. If the kolm disliked the item proposed or the suggested solution, if any, they could filibuster by asking for more information or by quarreling about procedure and hierarchy or by absenting themselves. A council meeting could last several days. At night the five leaders of ishyaaml would let the king know their real opinions. If the king persisted and brought the session to an end despite filibustering or other obstruction, the ishyaaml could reopen the question and reach a decision; a new mbok ilaam session was then called and met until a compromise was reached or one side gave in. The decisions of mbok ilaam were publicly announced in the squares and streets by male twins who, as mentioned before, lived at the capital, and who were employed as town criers. This was the situation I observed in 1953, and I believe that it was the same in the late nineteenth century. How the procedure developed remains unrecorded. Obviously, however, it is related to the whole balance of power, the object of the next chapter.

Another procedure could also be followed, and perhaps this should be viewed as yet another council. The personnel was the same but the meeting place was the *iyoot* square, deeper within the palace grounds.[70] The king spoke in person or through the muyesh. After him mbeem and mbyeeng alone replied in assent. This was where the king reported on wars, military expeditions, and travel. His attire included sword and war bell, and he sat on a stool that also was a martial emblem. If required, Kolm holding military titles also spoke. Nothing has been recorded concerning the origins or the evolution of this council. Given its martial character, its evolution must be closely tied to the military expansion of the kingdom. Given the place where it was held, one may speculate that it hived off from the original mbok ilaam, just as the ishyaaml split off.

In short, when Shyaam took over he found or organized a council of current affairs whose members were the already existing titleholders, heavily dominated by the mbaangt. It had been called ishyaaml, and it kept that name for some time. With the growth of royal power the main notables felt handicapped when they had to oppose the king's wishes, so they split off and kept the name ishyaaml. The king could not prevent this, but later was able to add other kolm, more favorable to his views, to this council. The old council then took the name mbok ilaam and continued as the central council. This explains why it handled questions involving the subordinate chiefdoms and why these matters were excluded from ishyaaml. Eagle-feather chiefs presented their cases to mbok ilaam and attended the meetings when they were called to the capital.[71] When they attended, the council could also act as a court, imposing fines on chiefdoms that had disobeyed royal commands. The iyoot may have split off from mbok ilaam, either before or after the ishyaaml did.

One former council continued as it existed before. This was the ibaanc, open to all, which had always been a court as much as a council. Its gradual loss of judiciary powers weakened the provincial governors, who are also known as the *kum mabaanc*, "chief [in a judicial sense] of the court." This happened gradually as more and more kolm offices were created, and the judicial system was accordingly transformed. All kolm were members of ibaanc, and all could and did speak there. The council came to be convened only for very weighty matters, and tried both to assess and sway public opinion in the capital. Decisions about peace and war came to be its most important business. It was convened by the king or by the kikaam, when the titleholders required the latter to do so, presumably after a meeting of ishyaaml. Its decisions were binding. They were summed up by the king, who always spoke last.[72]

A last type of meeting was the annual durbar, which took place toward the end of the dry season and could last as long as two weeks. All village headmen of the chiefdom came, accounted for their regular tribute, and gave a census report. In 1892 the occasion lasted two weeks and included constant merriment and dancing. Presumably the meetings were less formalized than those of other councils.[73] We can suppose that this type of meeting developed along with the territorial organization of the kingdom, perhaps being already formed by the end of the seventeenth century.

Within each dependent chiefdom the structure of councils was simpler. Eagle-feather chiefs had councils, ishyaaml, corresponding to the Bushoong mbok ilaam, and the public council still called malaang, which resembled the village councils. The kolm had no separate council, ishyaaml, on the one hand, and the king's crown council on the other. This modern situation seems to be quite old.[74]

In the Kete villages the kibanza council included all married men and all the kolm. Titleholders included the titles of most of the kolm matuk mabol and even kum ashin, although there were no "lands." Titles found in Bushoong villages were also found in the kibanza. But there were no mbaangt, and the council elected a village headman for life. Even when several headmen were chosen by a cluster of villages, each with his kolm, thus constituting one group of several villages, a single kibanza council might be retained. Even some Cwa villages took over a few titles, but they did so purely for prestige. It is quite plausible that some Kete titles were copied from the Bushoong or the Bieeng but that others were, at least in nomenclature, of Kete origin. They picked up the terms as they percolated through the whole Luba-speaking world from the southern savanna.

The judicial structure of the realm just after 1907 has been described in detail elsewhere.[75] A single court, ibaanc, existed at the capital, while malaang functioned as a moot court in the villages. Disputes between villages of the same county were settled by the county head. The court at the capital served as a court of appeal for all less important rural cases and as a first court for the capital or for cases involving different counties, as well as for all matters involving bloodshed or murder. A panel or jury of judges sat on the bench, and the judges were the kolm who had jurisdiction in the matter or over the litigants. Jurisdiction depended on the social status of the parties (e.g., a royal child, or a member of the royal lineage), on their residence ("land," residence in left or right part of capital), on the nature of the tort, misdemeanor, or crime (e.g., theft), and on the profession (e.g., woodworker or smith). A competent jury for each case was assembled separately, which meant that there were as many panels as there cases. This highly original development is repórted nowhere else in Africa. Historically it flows from the kolm system and the notion of representation by the revenue collectors and the administrators. The system may have developed only in the late eighteenth century or even later.

Appeals from the ibaanc went to a court where a single judge, the *baang*, decided. From him the case could go to the kikaam and then to the ibaam, from which there was no further appeal. The baang also judged cases of adultery in the first resort and kikaam cases of debt in first resort.[76] The system seems to have had a bias toward the preservation of property rights or perhaps rights over women (many cases of debt indirectly involved female pawns). The ibaam court was presided over by mbyeemy, and was composed of the nine "downstream" members of the ibaam council. The king was a member. Cases of rebellion, lese majesty, and murder were judged in first resort here because only the king could condemn to death.[77] As courts of appeal, each higher court inflicted heavier penalties. The only verdict ever rendered by ibaam as a court of appeal was to declare the whole matrilineage of the losing party enslaved to the king. Understandably, appeals to this level were quite rare.

The procedure was complex. Minor dignitaries called the parties to the court. Sanctions reduced the condemned to pawnship, to slavery, or even to death.[78] Jail existed only in the form of preventive detention. The jail was a shed in the kikaam's compound.

Cases involving bloodshed or murder were handled by a different court system. In these cases the iyol of the capital presided, using different symbols and formulas. When the ibaam tried the case in first resort the nyibit was assigned to guard the prisoner. Feuds were forbidden and no longer seemed to arise; during the whole Age of Kings there is no mention of a single feud. When the death penalty was pronounced the culprit either committed suicide, was executed, or was left alive until the king died, when he was sacrificed.[79] In civil cases, execution of the verdicts was left to the parties involved but could be enforced by the constabulary. Fines were payable to the kikaam and to the king, who could hand a certain amount back to the judges, although this was not necessary because the parties deposited a fixed sum (seven hundred cowries in 1907) with the court before trial as compensation for the judges. When appeal was contemplated, the party involved paid about one-sixth of the initial sum deposited with the court, in addition to the initial sum, to clear the right to appeal.

The unique features of the system—the panel of judges, the jurisdictional procedure—set it apart from the moot courts, which seem to have much older roots. Before a separate court system developed, most cases were settled by councils acting as courts. The separation of functions, the precision in procedure, and the hierarchy of the appeals are as much a product of the general political specialization of labor as is the jury system itself. The setting of precise fines antedates the colonial period, for a tradition concerning Mbo-Mboosh [3] mentioned specific fines for adultery. It also represents the first recorded instance of differential treatment according to status: its provision favored children of kings.[80]

The king stood outside the law. In 1892 it is evident that he had people arrested and tortured by his constabulary without recourse to the courts, and that he imposed the fine ishyeeng itaan when he fancied it.[81] He could not be sued or challenged directly. Plaintiffs could, however, appeal to ibaam on the grounds that the king was misinformed. The situation makes it clear that the most weighty matters never came to court. The struggles for the succession and the rivalry between great men were enacted by means of charms and whispered accusations of sorcery. At the other end of the spectrum, conflicts among members of the lower class, especially involving women as plaintiffs, never entered the court but were believed to be fought out with witchcraft.[82]

Below the level of the chiefdom there were no formal judicial institutions. The king could be asked to mediate between chiefdoms and was handsomely rewarded for it, since he set the amount of fines to be paid. In one case a whole village was given to him by each of two competing Ngeende chiefdoms.[83] Such arbitration was very rare and took the crudest forms. Bushoong military superiority was the sword on the scales of justice.

That fact serves as a reminder that a paradigmatic description and history of the administrative organization is a part of the political history. The real conflicts over power and the relationships between the factions or parties involved in competition over decision-making are the necessary complement of administrative history. The administrative organization set the stage and the rules, but did not involve the struggle for power, to which the following chapter is devoted.

Chapter 9

The Age of Kings: Power and Politics

Power is the ability to impose one's wishes on others, usually in order to gain a prize. The greatest prize in the Kuba kingdom was kingship itself; other prizes were goods and social prestige such as that accruing from titles. Politics is the process by which decisions are made that affect the existing distribution of prizes and spoils. Politics is always essentially segmentary, because one must vote yes or no to a decision regardless of how many competing persons or groups there may be in any arena.[1] There may be several factions, but they must join one of only two groups when a decision is to be made. In the Kuba kingdom decisions were frequent because competition among people for coveted prizes or spoils arose frequently. Conflict is inherent in society, and the Kuba had rules for conflict resolution and decision-making.[2]

An explicit set of rules was provided by the administrative framework. A less explicit but equally well-known set existed in the form of an unwritten constitution. In chiefdoms, chiefs could be deposed, but among the Bushoong, kings could not be deposed; the outright killing of an adversary was not condoned anywhere unless it was performed by a king. Killing an adversary by sorcery was, however, an expected gambit in this game. Only persons belonging to the royal line could claim kingship. Shyaam's accession was an exception to this rule. There had been other exceptions before, but after Shyaam, at least as far as the newly established kingship was concerned, the rule stood. (In other Kuba chiefdoms only members of the ruling line could claim chieftainship, but several exceptions had occurred there as well.)

The arenas in which persons competed were the village or the capital, the chiefdom, and the kingdom. Within a settlement, the issues at stake were resolved by the village moot or by the departure of one of the parties. Because the issues involved at this level were of minor importance and little about them has been recorded, they will be ignored in our discussion unless they arose at the capital. Issues in the chiefdom could be settled by its courts and councils, by migration, or by the splitting of the chiefdom in two parts. War was also a possibility. At the level of the kingdom, issues were settled by war or by decisions reached in the councils at the capital. In practice the capital was the most significant arena of all; its politics dominated the fate of the whole kingdom.

The prime competitors in the kingdom and in the Bushoong chiefdom were the king, his potential successors, and the mbaangt, or aristocrats. Kingship itself was the cynosure. The successors longed for it and the aristocrats tried to increase their collective power in relation to it. Within each chiefdom similar patterns no doubt existed. Each group of prime competitors was clearly divided within itself. Each successor wanted the big prize and each aristocratic clan section wanted to outdo the others.

Other competitors were after smaller prizes and provided support for the prime players in the game. Children and grandchildren supported their fathers and grandfathers, and clan members supported other clan members—at least those of the same lineage. These were the core supporters for each leader. More peripheral or mercurial supporters were the favorites of leaders and "the people." Between the core and the peripheral supporters were persons of servile status. Favorites or "the people" could change sides, but it was much harder for slaves or menials to switch their support. For direct descendants of a leader or members of his lineage, change was often impossible: the enemy would not easily accept their support. To build up support and reward faithful followers, the titled offices were a key institution. Naturally the prime competitors were those most eager to fill existing positions or to create new ones for their supporters. Not only did it give them more leverage—more power—in the councils; it also rewarded the faithful. For this reason the kolm can hardly be seen as a monolithic bloc in politics.

Because of the identity of the prime competitors, power alignments could arise only as confrontations between heir and king, king and aristocrat or heir and aristocrat. The first opposition provided the backbone for Bushoong politics over time; the second was expressed by the Bushoong in their sense of opposition between king and kolm (but we have just seen why the kolm as such were not even a corporate competitor), and the last seems to have been absent. At least there is no record of conflicts between heirs and aristocrats. In such clashes the king would have been involved of necessity, because the only conflict opposing all the aristocrats to all of the heirs concerns kingship: an attempted change in the whole ruling line. Such a goal would rally the king to the side of the heirs, which would give their alliance overwhelming power.

Similar alignments could arise between the prime competitors in the chiefdoms: chief, heirs, and aristocrats. As chiefs could be deposed by the aristocrats, the balance of power often tilted in favor of the latter, who, in certain cases, came to dominate the whole political arena.

The succession itself was regulated as follows. In principle the junior brothers of the same mother as the king were the first heirs. Since the king's father, like all husbands of women belonging to the royal lineage, had to be strictly monogamous, the king had no paternal half-brothers. His mother, like all women of his lineage, could take as many lovers as she wished, and the children of such unions were deemed to be those of her official husband.

Next in line were the children of the king's eldest sister. In theory, but not in practice, descendants from other sisters of the king were excluded, barring only the case where the eldest sister had no male issue. Then the next eldest sister's children were next in line.

Women could not succeed. It was also required that the heir and successor be the oldest (barring the king) among the men of the royal lineage. This rule could lead to a clash with the rules described above, and did so at least once. The younger person succeeded and the older committed suicide because in his lineage "no one can be older than the king."

Succession to high office was never automatic. The designation of a successor involves the legitimacy of rule, and in its function this process is identical to that of an election in a democratic republic. Dynastic strife, when it occurred, offered the opportunity for the kolm and the people to participate in the "election." It should therefore not be surprising that just as political parties arise when elections are part of the institutional process, political factions arise when questions of succession arise. Just as parties, once founded, continue to exist, so did Kuba factions, even though successions were much more infrequent than elections are in most cases.

King-heir confrontations formed the framework for the operations of permanent factions, which we will call parties, at the capital because that arena ultimately dominated all others in the realm. In the arena of the kingdom, itself, confrontations pitted chiefdom against chiefdom, the primary units involved. Resolution came through wars and demographic movement, which secured the ascendancy of the Bushoong chiefdom. Within the arena of each chiefdom the opposition was between court and village. It was resolved, among the Bushoong, by a permanent superiority of the capital over the other villages and the emergence within the chiefdom of a definite set of social strata which became much more pronounced than in other chiefdoms, where the court did not always succeed against the villages and where secession did take place from time to time. Using this overall approach and the available data (much of them drawn from the tales described in Chapter 4), I will describe the parties, the Bushoong ascendancy, and social stratification.[3]

The Parties

Most publications may well lead the reader to wonder if there ever was any serious political struggle within the Bushoong chiefdom, for they do not even consider the possibility of serious political struggle before the civil strife of

1886. A reexamination of the data leads to the startling conclusion that many successions were in fact disputed, thus giving substance to the Bushoong feeling that parties to most struggles were made up of the king and his followers on the one hand, and his heir apparent and his followers on the other. In almost every generation a struggle took place.

Mboongl a Shimy, a potential successor to Shyaam [1], tried to unseat him but was killed. Tradition may have confused Mboongl with Shyaam Mbweeky, who briefly succeeded Mboong aLeeng [2] but is not recorded as a king. Or the tradition may have made two men out of one. In the next generation, MboMboosh [3] murdered his elder brother under the pretense that he was a sorcerer or a witch. In the following generation, Mbakam Mbomancyeel [4] had to withstand an attempt by his successor and brother, Miingambeengl, whom he killed. He is said to have killed his mother as well because she supported Miingambeengl. Two generations later there may have been an irregular succession insofar as Mishe miShyaang maMbul [6] had an older brother, Ngol aShyaan; this brother may, however, have died before the succession occurred. Again two generations later, two contenders wanted to succeed Mbo Pelyeeng aNce [9] and both died. A woman, Mbulape, became regent for her son Kot aMbul [10]. One generation after that, Miko Mabiinc mamBul [13] and Kot aMbweeky II [14] contended for the throne, ultimately occupying it in succession (from about 1886 to about 1890). It is even possible that Kot aMbul removed his mother from the throne. And these are stories that have survived despite the desire to present the succession as "normal"![4]

The supporters for each party were the children and grandchildren of its members. Beyond this the king could count on the support of the heir to the heir apparent and his children; the heir apparent counted on the support of the children and grandchildren of the predecessor of the king, many of whom still held office. Both sides had their servile supporters and their favorites. Here the king could count on more support because he was in power and therefore had more offices to distribute than his opposition, although the opposition would hold more of the offices at the beginning of a reign. The king had more wealth to spend on gaining supporters than did the heir apparent.

The contests waxed and waned in phases. When a king grew old, the waiting heir apparent began to use his following to press his advantage and recruited favorites with promises. The supporters of the king, especially those who had been rewarded with office, were on the defensive and might try to keep a low profile in order to prepare for the transition. The establishment party began to ally itself more firmly with the heir to the heir apparent. This did not happen earlier because one never knew whether the heir apparent might not die and leave the ally of yesterday to become the major foe of today, but toward the end of a reign the chances that this might happen were much smaller and the alliance took effect. Once a new king was enthroned, he tried to eliminate the supporters of his predecessor, especially the predecessor's children, and first among them those who had been most active in the shaping of policies during the previous reign. Since offices were for life, he could not depose them, but as time went by more offices became vacant and were filled by the new king's own family and followers, and the establishment party grew strong. Crucial points in this process were the nomination of a new kikaam, the highest official, who had to be a son of a king and at the same time belong to an aristocratic clan. When the old kikaam died, the main obstacle in the bureaucracy to nominations by the ruling king was removed, for in the beginning the kikaam was the son of the previous king, and as kikaam he had an important role not only in councils but also with regard to nominations. Another stage in the process came when the mbeem, also usually a son of the preceding king, died.[5] The monarch could then appoint one of his favorite sons (regardless of clan) to this most important post in the capital. Once these posts were in the hands of sons of the ruling king, his party was at its zenith. At this point the opposition could find little to offer to its supporters, and its main weapon against the king was magic. Even then the ruling king, having more wealth and the services of special officials, could easily command the best magic.[6] The opposition had to wait until the reign was apparently drawing to its end before it could become very active again.

Because the parties linked support across the generations they achieved considerable permanence, despite the fluctuations of their fortunes. This was obviously a consequence of the rules for recruitment and succession to kingship and to the most important offices. It also presupposed that the women of the royal line would in general tend to remain neutral, although sisters may have discreetly plotted against each other because once a son of the eldest sister became ruler and her daughters had produced grandchildren, the other sisters were theoretically no longer a valid source for claims on the throne and could not become queen mothers. In 1885-86 the royal women remained neutral in the fight over succession and fled to Ntuun (the heir apparent's province) until the matter was settled. In earlier times we hear only of Mbakam's mother, who sided with his younger brother and was killed by him.[7] The aristocrats did not readily take sides in the ibaam. But representatives of the eighteen clans acted on their own councils. They would draw together when kingship was at stake, but not in conflicts between kings and would-be kings.

The pattern of conflict was real and is amply documented. It is said that Shyaam had no children except those begotten of his wives by other men. His son Kangoong Muleem was the first mbeem named under the rules of recruitment. Shyaam may have set the rule for the succession of the mbyeeng by naming his daughter's son Mishaamweel.[8] Shyaam clearly relied heavily on friends and supporters. The story of the origin of the nkolakol ritual is typical:

he invented it to prove his innocence of the death of his long-time backer Kaan aKambady, who is the ideal figure of the supporter.[9] That Shyaam should even have been suspected of causing his friend's death is revealing. Indeed, in later times when royal favorites accumulated too much influence and wealth, jealousy could erupt and "accidents" could happen to them.[10] We can imply from the nkolakol rite that Kaan was also the archetype of the kolm, the friend rewarded with an office, even though we do not know which one.

Support of the royal sons for their father appears even before Shyaam. The son of his predecessor was killed while saving his father during the coup that brought Shyaam to the throne. But such support was by no means automatic, as the following cases show. A son of Mboong aLeeng [2], Lambeengdy, committed adultery with one of the king's wives and fled to his mother's people, the ruling clan among the Ngongo. He sought support there but was defeated. One of the sons of MboMboosh [3] led an invading Nkucu force against MboMboosh. Whether his mother was Nkucu or not remains unknown. But as early as the reign of this king it is clear that the king could prevent the alienation of his children by granting them great favors and by trying to diminish the prestige of the successors in the eyes of his children. MboMboosh gave his children preferential legal treatment as a reward for the behavior of his daughter. The story of how the younger brother of Mbo-Mboosh convinced the majority of people at the capital to have MboMboosh killed by setting fire to his palace and how the king was saved by his daughter, who gave herself to the slave Bibokl because he had overheard the plot, is the paradigm in the traditions that establish relationships of king, heir apparent, and king's children. In the end MboMboosh was killed by his potential successors.[11]

Two reigns later, Kot aMbweeky ikoongl's son ruled over his mother's people, the Bieeng, but with his father's backing. The same king was able to take drastic action against the potential successors: he had them driven out of their village of Mweengt and forced them to live in the Ngel aMbiin quarter, next to the palace, surrounded by their servants, but all of them in turn surrounded by the royal slaves. The pattern of the royal son ruling over an ancillary chiefdom, now the Ngongo, reappears two reigns later. At that time, in the reign of Kot aNce [7], the power of the royal sons must have become very great, for when Mbo Pelyeeng aNce [9] succeeded he found it necessary to massacre seventy sons of Kot aNce. Perhaps the king had already come to rely on his sons for many of the practical tasks of enforcing the law and his will. This case is one where those killed should have been followers of the reigning king, but they were too many with too much power, and he distrusted them.[12]

In any case Mbo Pelyeeng's successor, Kot aMbul [10], used his own sons for collecting tribute among the dependent chiefdoms and to lead repressive forces. This was also the case under Mbop Mabiinc maMbul [12] in whose reign there are inferences of a conflict between the sons of the heir apparent and the sons of the king. But one of his predecessor's sons, Nyimiloong, was among the king's trusted favorites, which suggests that even by then the attribution of people to parties was not automatic. In the period after 1885 the pattern of kings in power backed by their sons and killing—or attempting to kill—the sons of their predecessors is quite clear and was without exception among the leading figures in these groups.[13]

The opposition of aristocrats to the king lasted throughout the era of the kingdom even though the aristocratic lineages as such lost power rather early in that period. The only allusion to this is the praise name recorded for Kot aNce's village, which may refer to awarding titles to the detriment of the aristocrats. But this was clearly what Shyaam had done when he regulated succession to the office of mbeem. In time the aristocratic lineages as a bloc represented the most influential kolm, whose offices were still ascribed to particular clans or sets of clans. In some circumstances these kolm could lead all the kolm in an opposition of king versus "the people." But this seems to have been rare. Most of the less important officeholders were, after all, protégés of the king.[14]

The opposition of king and aristocrats is the one that is reflected best in the careful composition of the councils, especially ishyaaml and mbok ilaam. Ishyaaml was dominated by the aristocratic clans, which had five members (four with veto power); only two positions were reserved for king's sons, and one of them, the kikaam, had to belong to an aristocratic clan. Two other positions were tied to specific clans and lineages: the mbyeemy was from the muyum's clan and the cikl belonged to a lineage from the royal clan, excluded from the succession. These would be expected to temper extreme attitudes adopted by the aristocratic clans, but could also be counted on to strengthen the bloc of hereditary (in the matrilineal line) positions among kolm in general. In the mbok ilaam, the aristocrats held as many as four more positions, but the king's descendants were the mbeem and mbyeeng and most of the additional kolm. In the ibaanc the "achieved" kolm outnumbered the "ascribed" kolm in great numbers, with the result that an aristocratic opposition could not gain points there. But it could in ibaam. On the other hand the king could not count on enough support to force every issue in which he wanted to increase his prerogatives or his income, because only his descendants could be expected to vote for him, and they often did not, at least in the twentieth century.[15] In the nineteenth century the active role of king's sons was much more visible and their power—derived from the king's—was real enough. They were probably listened to more then than later. Because of the open conflict between heir apparent and king it is likely that the kolm as such did not have the cohesion then that they were to gain during the colonial period.

The rules are clearly the outcome of a prolonged trial-and-error process by which aristocratic clans and the king tried to gain prerogatives at each other's expense. What is surprising is that the clans, which did not form a very coherent front, were able to hold a position of such strength and to embody the ideal of the titleholder to the extent that they did. This shows that force alone was not enough to explain the outcome of conflict; ideology was equally important. After all, those clans were the guarantors of legitimacy—that of the king, that of the kingdom, and that of the status of kolm as well. To most if not all of the Bushoong, legitimacy of the system was essential: it conditioned their support for the regime and their participation in it.

If the composition of the councils shows that aristocratic clans and royal core supporters were potentially in conflict (hence the need for balance), the traditions are silent about the evolution of this tension. This seems surprising until it becomes clear that the clans were the guarantors of the public order, a much more fundamental source of legitimacy than was the royal genealogy. Irregularities (that is, departures from the ideal) therefore did not matter so much in the genealogy (hence the traces of irregularity found in it) but would have been inexcusable with regard to the clans. But if the number of clans changed, and if the clans labeled aristocratic changed (as they probably did), where did their legitimacy spring from? If there were *abrupt* shifts in their relationship to the king (the only kind of shift that might be recorded in a tradition) how could kingship still be legitimate? Suppose that a change in the coronation and installation rituals was recorded that curtailed the initiation by the clans. Would later kings have the same aura of legitimacy as earlier ones? Conversely, if their role increased, would later kings not be more legitimate? But if the early kings had doubtful credentials, what was the basis of legitimacy for the later ones? Of course an argument from silence—the absence of information in traditions—is always weak, but it sounds convincing in this case. Even in the many tales about Shyaam no one utters a word of his relationship to the aristocratic clans, which presumably had approved his predecessor and later approved (and initiated?) Shyaam himself. The question was too pregnant with the possibility of setting precedent that would justify an overthrow to allow it to be recorded in the traditions.

The Bushoong Ascendancy

The kingdom as a whole grew through the increasing ascendancy of the Bushoong over all other chiefdoms. The basic opposition in this arena was, first, chiefdom versus chiefdom and, later, the Bushoong chiefdom versus any other chiefdom. As early as the reign of Mboong aLeeng [2], the second pattern predominated. The history of conflict resolution in this arena is mainly a history of wars. But the dominant motif was not necessarily coercion. Support by the ordinary people for one or another party in the confrontation could and did vary. People voted with their feet, and the population movements of the period corroborate the Bushoong ascendancy.

Shyaam is said to have been a peaceful king in contrast with his successor, who became typed as the warrior king.[16] Shyaam did, however, send at least one expedition north of the Sankuru to protect or avenge Bushoong traders, and one place name mentions "the wars of Shyaam." He may have expanded his area to the north of the Bushoong chiefdom, as indicated by the saying *Idiing iShyaam, Ngweemy Shyaam* which translates as "Idiing of Shyaam, the Ngoombe of Shyaam," listing the northernmost area (Idiing) of what is now the Bushoong chiefdom, and the neighboring area occupied by the Ngoombe.[17] It can also have meant "the slaves of Shyaam, the Ngoombe of Shyaam," meaning that he conquered the Ngoombe. But it is unlikely that, as one source has it, he conquered all the groups that later constituted the kingdom, barring only the Ngongo.[18] He may have fought in the north and even in the west, but he did not in one fell swoop incorporate all the other (sometimes later) chiefdoms in his kingdom. That he may have waged war in the west is indicated by a story telling of two famous warriors who, on the warpath near Ilebo, were killed because they would not stop smoking when battle had been joined.[19] But this tale, which tells how tobacco came to the Kuba, does not necessarily deal with a Bushoong army. On balance one can say that once Shyaam had achieved control of the whole Bushoong chiefdom he sought expansion, but achieving that control may have taken most of his career. In the tale that describes his efforts to succeed as ruler, the Kel are mentioned. The tale tells how traders reported to the king that Shyaam was living with the Kel, and the king summoned a Kel man to the court on charges of harboring Shyaam. The whole situation is perfect for the nineteenth century. It parallels that of Sheppard, whose presence in the realm in 1892 was reported by traders; a village headman harboring Sheppard was summoned to the court.[20] But were the Kel already part of the kingdom before Shyaam? The tale may be anachronistic; on the other hand, it could be true that the Kel had by that time been incorporated into the kingdom: there may have been a kingdom composed of the Bushoong chiefdom and one or two Kel chiefdoms. I doubt this, however. There is no support for it in any sources from the chiefdoms of the Kel or their neighbors.

Mboong aLeeng did wage war against many of the principal chiefdoms, including the Ngongo, far in the northeast. And he is alleged to have won all his wars, even the one in which he was killed. He is remembered for the war against the Bokila, a very small chiefdom, against one of the Ngongo chiefdoms (the one nearest the Bushoong), the Pyaang, and the Bieeng. The last two were the major campaigns.[21] The Bieeng war was won militarily but, since the king was killed, it ended in a stalemate. No Bushoong king ever held any territory south of the Lulua River for any length of time.

Another war may have been provoked by the Pyaang. Iloong (a Bushoong rendering of the common Luba name Ilunga) was said to be the chief of the Cwa. (The Cwa, however, have no chiefs.) He captured the capital and kidnapped a king's sister. The woman was later found in a Pyaang village. She fled to a Kete one, which harbored her and a rescuer. We find the familiar Kete-Pyaang-Cwa mix here, and one suspects that the Kete and Pyaang attacked first, perhaps to regain the chiefdom that had been lost to them by Shyaam's takeover. The Pyaang leader was Mashaal, and they lost because support at home crumbled. The Pyaang Ibaam tell how Mashaal handed over their chief to King Mboong aLeeng and how this chief made black magic, causing Mashaal to murder his mother and flee with part of the Pyaang to Lusambo. The Pyaang sources make it clear that they had quarreled among themselves and before the reign of Mboong aLeeng had split into at least two chiefdoms under their chief, Mboomiloong. They also were fighting the Cwa, who, according to at least one version, killed Mboomiloong, and Mashaal later was the chief of only the Pyaang aTyeen ("upstream"). Whatever the reconstruction given by each source, they all agree that a dislocation did take place. The Pyaang polity fell apart and they lost most of their Cwa and Kete supporters. With that dislocation, the main threat to the growing Kuba kingdom disappeared.[22]

Even after Shyaam's reign the Bushoong did not have automatic military superiority. Their weaponry remained the same.[23] Improvements in organization, such as amassing more men and perhaps doing so on shorter notice, were possibly made as the capital grew, but the capital could hardly have achieved what was later an impressive size relative to other settlements in a single reign. As for tactical organization or maneuvering or discipline, there is no evidence at all that the Bushoong were better than others. On balance, Mboong aLeeng's victories stemmed in part from the mobilization of more men because the chiefdom had become (or was) larger than the opposition, and in part from the internal breakdown of the major enemy, the Pyaang.

The campaigns against the Pyaang continued. MboMboosh [3] conclusively defeated one major chiefdom, the Pyaang Mbaanc. The Pyaang, however, tell that they fought some neighboring Ngeende chiefdom(s),[24] and they do not recall a campaign by MboMboosh. But could not the Ngeende have been the allies of the Bushoong? The Pyaang Mbaanc also fought King Mbakam [4]. The next Pyaang Mbaanc chief tried to expand toward the south and southwest, fighting the Caadi and the Bulaang near Kampungu. He died during this last campaign "somewhere among the Bushoong." This information comes from Pyaang sources, and it marks the end of any Pyaang attempt to overcome others. By the time of Kot aMbweeky ikoongl [5] they had ceased to be a menace to the Bushoong and were presumably incorporated into the kingdom. Bulaang tradition remembers a battle not far from Kampungu in which the Pyaang were completely defeated by a Bushoong king at the time that they immigrated into the country. The Bulaang are Bieeng who seceded from the main chiefdom. It is plausible that the Pyaang Mbaanc and Bulaang traditions about this area deal with the same war or the same set of wars.[25]

The most celebrated war of MboMboosh was his campaign against invading Nkucu. The head of the Shoowa Maloonc, the largest Shoowa group, advised the king how to overcome the enemy and probably joined forces with him. As a token of gratitude he was later called "the iyol of the eagle-feather chiefs" and was given seniority of rank among them. The Shoowa Maloonc had immigrated from across the Sankuru, but probably at a very slow rate. They met the Bushoong not long before this war. In most versions the first kum to arrive near the Bushoong went to the king and asked "for salt and land."[26] In later times there would be strife among Kel and Shoowa chiefdoms and perhaps also among different Shoowa chiefdoms. But they all acknowledged the authority of the king, perhaps as insurance against massive attacks by the Nkucu.

Bushoong expansion in the east and northeast is not well remembered. It took place under Mboong aLeeng, for the Ngongo are first mentioned at that time. By the reign of Kot aNce [7], in the mid-eighteenth century, the king was so powerful that he could at will remove eagle-feather chiefs, banish them, or have them murdered. He helped the Pyaang aTyeen fight off the Cishiba (Luba) near the iron deposits at the Mwabe River, almost on the border of the kingdom. It was a great victory, say the traditions, and one claims that it was won because the Kuba still used throwing knives and the Luba did not.[27] The same king also campaigned against the Ngongo settlement, which was the most distant on the Sankuru, and made it pay tribute. For a while he even controlled the Bieeng south of the Lulua, where his son ruled.

We can therefore conclude that by about a century after Shyaam's arrival, all the chiefdoms had been incorporated into one kingdom. This may have been true by the reign of Kot aMbweeky ikoongl [5]. The Bushoong ascendancy was not achieved through a few blitz campaigns. The 'conquest" was a process of gradual subordination that led to a situation in which the Bushoong clearly dominated the small chiefdoms on their borders and usually received tribute from those that were farther away. The kingdom consisted of a central core: the Bushoong chiefdom and all the incorporated Kete villages and satellite chiefdoms around it. Size of the chiefdom and distance from the

Bushoong were the variables explaining the degree of subjugation which ranged from almost total control over the Bulaang to intermittent control over the Ngongo chiefdom, farthest upstream on the Sankuru.

After Kot aNce, traditions refer to rebellions, usually by individual villages or small chiefdoms, and around 1800 to one last insurrection by the Pyaang Mbaanc—at least this is what one source claims to have happened under Kot aMbul [10], but by then the weaknesses of the kingdom had also become evident. The iron deposits of the Pyaang aTyeen had been lost. No Kuba tradition speaks of this occurrence, but the area is now Luba. By then, too, the Coofa had begun immigrating, and no concerted effort by Ngeende, Pyaang, or Bushoong was made to stop their immigration, or at least to force them to settle within the framework of the existing chiefdoms.[28] The lack of Bushoong military support for chiefdoms attacked from the outside was paralleled by their failure to establish an administrative framework for the whole kingdom that would permit unitary action. Even in the late 1890s, when the Zappo Zap attacked the Pyaang, the Bushoong did nothing to help them, and in 1900 the Zappo Zap came from the southeast and overran the capital.[29]

Bushoong ascendancy was due in large part to the continuing process of fission in the other chiefdoms. All the traditions of the other chiefdoms deal primarily with such splits. Within these chiefdoms the balance of power shifted more and more to the aristocratic clans, especially in the southeast among the Ngeende and the Pyaang, and ultimately the crown councils ruled there, the chief becoming only a figurehead. Moreover, chiefdoms shrank to the size of a single village.[30] In the chiefdoms the courts were unable to gain the upper hand in conflicts with other villages and the heirs to the chiefs were willing to push villages into rebellion. Conflicts within the arenas of the courts themselves and the arena of the chiefdoms spilled over from one arena into another, a process that must have increased their severity and their frequency. By contrast, the Bushoong success is due at least in part to the successful isolation of the capital arena from the chiefdom arena with its capital/village tensions.

The Bushoong success in establishing a large chiefdom that was generally peaceful contrasted with the insecurity that became more and more prevalent elsewhere, especially in the east and southeast. As a result people moved from unsafe areas to safer ones. This by itself strengthened the Bushoong chiefdom perhaps more than any single military campaign. The data that support this process are the clan-section histories. Granted that a certain imprecision is unavoidable because the base line for movements by clan sections is unknown—all we know is that a particular section moved from one ethnic group to another ethnic group. The total figures nevertheless reflect a trend for the whole time span from the onset of the Age of Chiefs to the nineteenth century, since those ethnic groups were in continual contact with each other.

Most movements seem to have happened during the Age of Kings. The Bushoong and Kete gained over one third of the migrant population at the expense of groups in the east and south. The data show the tendency of the population to move closer to the center of the kingdom, ultimately to the Bushoong capital.[31]

The population movements were not all toward the center. There were real losses too. The kingdom lost the Isambo, who were the Pyaang that followed Mashaal to Lusambo, which in the 1950s was the equivalent of two villages. A much larger number left under the reign of Mboong aLeeng [2].[32] This was the king who introduced initiation. The Binji, says the traditional account, found initiation too hard and fled. They now live east of the Kuba kingdom. Not all the present-day Binji are of Kuba origin, others having immigrated from the Bakwa Mputu. Those who came from the kingdom are mostly the Bakwa Kubale and the Babindi Bakusu, forming approximately eighteen villages in the 1950s. The initiation story may be a cliché adding motivation to an exodus that was probably fostered by Mboong aLeeng's wars. Most of the emigrants were likely to have been Kete. This exodus has been the only massive population movement on a scale comparable to the late-eighteenth-century Coofa immigration.[33]

Immigration from the outside, the Coofa excepted, was probably constant but on a very small scale and balanced emigration, except in the Sankuru area and the area north of the Lulua, where gains were probably made.[34]

Given all these data it is likely that a net balance of demographic gains from immigration developed in the center after the main wars of conquest by Mboong aLeeng and perhaps MboMboosh were over. The development was certainly gradual and must be attributed to the eighteenth and nineteenth centuries.

Social Stratification

Social stratification developed into social classes among the Bushoong as a result of the prevailing strength of the capital against the villages. In the arena of the chiefdom the capital was able to impose its wishes on the villages even from the time of Shyaam. Presumably it used its supremacy to further the interests of its own inhabitants and to raise their standards of living. The existing social strata became more pronounced, and the differences between the way of life of the menial class and that of the patricians increased. In the other chiefdoms the contrasts were much less noticeable because of the varying balance of power between their centers and their peripheral areas. The continual splits favored the prolongation of more egalitarian ways.

When Shyaam came to the throne there were two clearly distinguished social strata: slaves and freemen. It is possible that the Bushoong already considered the Kete as menials, not far removed from the condition of slaves.[35] By 1892 there was a class of patricians at the capital, a class of farmers, located primarily in the villages, and a class of menials, found in both capital and villages.

Menials bore the heaviest burdens. Their group included inhabitants of Kete villages and of matoon villages, pawn wives, and slaves, on a descending scale of prestige. The differences between Kete villages and Bushoong free villages were actually small. The Kete governed themselves but paid more tribute and were badgered by the paangl. They could not hope to rise in the system. Most of the extra fruits of their labor were siphoned off to the capital. Matoon villages were in virtually the same situation as Kete villages except that they enjoyed no administrative autonomy at all. Their headmen lived at the capital. In their origin they were in fact slave villages, whether they originally had been settled by prisoners of war or whether they had been declared matoon. But the inhabitants were free: they belonged to clans and clan sections and could hope for some modest aid from kinsmen in emergencies. More important, they could hope for an improvement in their situation when allowed by the king to move either to the capital or to another village. This was true in all matoon villages, including the bubaang, which had to provide more services than any of the others.

Why did the Kete and matoon villages not rebel? Why did they accept their position in society? They did in fact rebel from time to time, but each time were subdued. And repression was severe. In the case of Kopl, under Miko miMbul [11], thirty-one people in a village that had perhaps two hundred inhabitants (one hundred men) were killed.[36] In the nineteenth century Coofa villages were ravaged time and time again to reduce them to the status of Kete villages, and terror was used as instrument of policy. Atrocity stories circulated concerning men who were put in canoes and crushed to death as if they were maize, collective graves that were necessary for the executed, and pregnant women who were cut open.[37] The harshness of repressions explains why so few villages rebelled. A more positive incentive was also present in the matoon villages: there every man could hope to better his status by cooperation. The very severity of repressions also paradoxically limited the degree to which these villages were exploited by their "owners," who would try to avoid insubordination brought about by the despair of overtaxation because the destruction wrought by a punitive expedition lowered the productivity of the village and brought accusations of mismanagement at the capital. Thus the fear of uprising was balanced by the fear of retribution and set the level of exploitation.

Pawn wives, *ngady*, differed from slaves in that they could be redeemed, that some of their children often belonged to their own clans as free persons, and that the pawns continued to belong to their lineages and clans. Wholly arbitrary behavior by their masters and husbands was kept in check by these features. They differed from true wives in that they were usually the least considered by the husband—the head of the whole household—and were burdened with the most menial tasks, unless one of them happened to be his favorite. They worked harder than the other women in most situations and were at their beck and call, thus differing little from a slave. The question of their acquiescence in the social order did not arise because all women were considered wards by the Kuba and had very little to do with political affairs, except for the female titleholders and the women of the royal line. Dissenters among the women could only try using witchcraft against the persons they hated.[38] Any other action, such as appeals to the court or to kin, was limited to unusual cases. A very heavy schedule of work was not accepted as an unusual case by the men.

Slaves came to the Bushoong through war and trade. Most captured prisoners were settled in matoon villages; other slaves were bought. Most of the purchased slaves ended up as servants in a nuclear family, a few as members in a slave unit of the king's militia, or as servants of the leading patricians. Slaves lost their kinship connections with the groups they had been born into. Indeed, most of them were truly foreigners. They received new names, very often "man of x." They could be mistreated without redress but not killed.[39] Their lot was to do all the hard work or all the boring tasks. The main source of humiliation for male slaves was that they could be ordered to perform women's tasks such as fetching water or firewood or weeding the fields. But their children were free, whether they married slaves or free women, and so there was hope for improvement. Indeed, when they were not working for their masters or when they were, for example, trading on their master's account, they could accumulate wealth for themselves and even buy slaves. This obviously happened only to those who belonged to rich households where not all their time was taken up by chores.[40] In these cases they could buy their freedom, although the stigma of having been a slave would never be removed, just as, in the 1950s, a slave's child though free was always remembered as such. Only the grandchild was truly free.[41] From the time of Miko miMbul [11], female slaves could hope that their masters would marry them, which in effect freed them. This occasionally happened, if only because it allowed a man to consider his children as members of his own lineage and as his heirs. More often, women slaves were the concubines of their master and found themselves in daily life performing the same tasks as female pawns.

Why did slaves not run away or rise against their masters? First, the knowledge that their status was not hereditary must have acted as a brake. Second, the fact that they belonged to a household and were considered as junior children in it made their situation more tolerable. They were rarely brutalized. Their tendency was to see themselves as members of a particular household rather than as members of a class. It is important in this respect that slaves could not be sold. The worse that could happen was that they would be given as pawns when their household ran into difficult times. In the villages a slave's life was harder than that of his owner but not by much, and it seems that slaves were minorities in all villages at least until the 1850s. In short, the conditions for a slave uprising were not there.

Slaves in the capital had even less reason to rebel. The royal slaves led a life that was in many ways better than that of a villager—many of them were military men, messengers, and the like. All of them could hope for promotion to some titles and a part of the spoils; some could hope to buy their freedom. The slaves belonging to patricians were in the same situation except that they did not belong to a large group (the king's slaves numbered over five hundred and perhaps many more) and were more closely bound to their master's household. By 1892 even the most influential men had only a few slaves.[42] These slaves participated vicariously in the fortune of their masters, but they ran the highest risk of execution at their master's death. It seems that each of them assumed that such would not be his fate.

In sum, the lack of unity among slaves, their secure position within households, the possibility of upward social mobility, and the freedom of their offspring combined to explain why, despite their relatively large number (10 percent or more of the population), especially in the later nineteenth century, there was no trace of slave revolts in Kuba history.

Ordinary people (*ngwoong mbaang*) formed the large majority of the population. Most of them lived in villages and farmed. The slightly derogatory epithet *bakon*, "country yokels," was applied to them by certain people at the capital, but ordinary people also were found there: those who did not have a title, or were not married to kolm. Most were artisans. Ngwoong mbaang were taxed, although not as heavily as the menials, and they saw little of the profits. The men were eligible for titles, and each village had its administration and its own representative at court. Most of the ordinary people had at least one relative who was important. They watched the pageantry at the capital, or saw it when they went to the annual durbar to pay tribute and to participate in the dances, the mimes, and the merriment. They accepted the system and supported it actively in their individual quests for titles and favors. They did not perceive themselves as exploited, and they were not very much so. They imagined that court life was the hub of civilization, and they participated in it. They were civilized whereas non-Kuba were not, and even non-Bushoong were not really as civilized as Bushoong. To most bakon the capital was a dream come true, and the king in his court was the sun in whose glory they basked.[43] No other city existed within hundreds of miles of the capital, and no king with such glory ruled anywhere between the Kuba and the Lunda or the Kuba and the Luba Shankadi. It was an impressive achievement. Why should we suppose that it impressed only the visiting foreigners? Participation in political life and the very splendor of the capital help to explain why villagers accepted the polity. In the next chapter it will be argued that not only did the menials rather than the ordinary people, bear much of the burden for the kingdom's upkeep, but that the standard of living of the Bushoong farmer did in fact rise during the Age of Kings.

When was their support acquired? Certainly not when Shyaam overpowered Mishe miShyaang [F] because villages did help him, a foreigner, overthrow the ruler. The change in attitude came only gradually. Mboong aLeeng [2] still relied mostly on fear to earn the support of the villages. One story tells that Paam became a matoon village because it was accused of forging iron in secret while the famous smith Myeel was hiding the tiniest bell for the needle of a hat there. This tale, which is our only evidence for repression of villages, may not be true,[44] but its message contains truth: if you deviate you can become matoon. As the number of kolm grew, so did the city and so did its magnificence and power. By the eighteenth century the attitudes of the ordinary people may already have been fixed. They certainly were by the middle of that century, when Kot aNce's power reached its peak.

The patricians did not recognize themselves as such by the use of a single term, but their way of life, characterized by elegance and ease, bound them together, however much they might dissent among themselves. The very fact that they used the term bakon to designate the villagers betrays consciousness of their different ways of life and, implicitly at least, some consciousness of the ties a common way of life forges. To be a patrician was not only to be witty or elegant, it implied a certain wealth and a certain authority as well. The class consisted essentially of the king and his potential successors (sometimes called reverently "the ones with money"), royal descendants, and officeholders. Most traders and some artisans were kolm and can be included in this broad class. In the 1920s the total number was estimated at about two thousand. There were more in 1892, when the estimated population of the capital oscillated between five and ten thousand inhabitants.[45] The wealthier patricians lived within fenced compounds in lavishly decorated houses having several rooms and sometimes a separate kitchen, with slaves to serve them and perhaps a snake charmer or other performer for after-dinner entertainment. Their revenue stemmed from taxes and perhaps some trade. Much of their food came from impositions on matoon villages, and the rest was bought at one of the daily markets about town.[46] The men's interests among all the patricians revolved around the court, its intrigues and its ceremonies, while the women embroidered raffia cloth, did the shopping and kept house, freed from the hard chores of most other women, which included working in the fields, drawing water, and carrying wood, although by 1892 a large number of the women in the capital may have farmed and drawn water.

Most members of this class competed with one another as groups and as individuals within groups. Their appearance, their household possessions, their houses, their manners, their concern for acquiring a polished education in the oral literature and in the performing arts were all expressions of that competition. Each wanted to outshine the others and to do so within the approved style. Much conspicuous consumption was lavished on feasts and on funerals. High society contained the patron of the arts, and its tastes became the guide for the country folk to follow. The splendor of costumes, buildings, sculpture, and decorative work that resulted from this agonistic behavior made Kuba art, in its various forms, mark a high point in the art of all of Central Africa.[47]

This way of life and the privileges that accompanied it grew from the time that Mboong aLeeng [2] forbade the inhabitants of the capital to farm, and continued its growth when later kings protected their sons by creating more kolm. The emergence of this situation, characterized by pageantry and conspicuous consumption, was not inevitably correlated with the development of offices and the expansion of the bureaucracy. The seeds of its development were already present during the Age of Chiefs in the role of kum. The southern Mongo kum's significance derives partly from his conspicuous flaunting of wealth as expressed in clothing, ritual, and behavior. From the kum this habit spread in the end to the whole competitive patriciate. Out of the vanity of chiefs was born the spirit of *dyaash*: "personal independence, drive for individual expression coupled with restraint and respect for the hierarchy."[48] The spirit expressed itself in the specific forms of the prizes to be won by politics: prestige, wealth, and power.

In the dependent chiefdoms social stratification was not nearly so pronounced, mainly because the patriciate was not so large nor so wealthy or powerful and because there were far fewer slaves. The courts attempted to imitate the frills and fashions of the capital, although on a much more modest scale.

The social stratification that has been described was not the only social hierarchy. Just as real was the dominnance of men over women. Although their ways of life did not differ as much here as they did in the surrounding societies, differences existed: women performed the most tedious chores. The difference between the ways of life of men and women was perhaps most pronounced in the households of the patriciate. The royal wives did not enjoy a high status. They worked hard, even if they did not farm themselves, although some may have farmed in the nineteenth century and most did in the twentieth. Within every class women were inferior to men. The only women who led an easy life were the mother of the king and some of her polyandrous household—the king's sisters and sister's daughters and some of the king's daughters and son's wives—but in the household ease was limited to those who had achieved high position or whose spouses had. The position of women among the Kuba did change, however, during the Age of Kings, when monogamy and the fact that some men worked in the fields beside their wives brought spouses closer together and lessened the inequalities. But in the end it was the men who regulated social and political life and the women who endured it; it was for the men that palm wine was tapped and meat cooked first, while the dregs and leftover cuts were reserved for the women.

The patriciate could only have developed if there were means to sustain it. The economic means were not negligible by 1892, when this class constituted a few percent of the population as a whole, and when the capital constituted as much as 10 percent of the Bushoong chiefdom and the Kete villages put together. The wherewithal became available only as the result of a vigorous economic development that took place during the Age of Kings in a reciprocal relationship with the polity and its ideologies. Economic development is the subject of the next chapter.

Chapter 10

The Hoe and the Cowrie: Economics

In Kuba imagery the hoe, along with the ax, represents agricultural production, and the cowrie, which was their currency during most of the nineteenth century, represents wealth. This chapter concerns economic history and is divided into two sections: production and distribution. The hoe and the cowrie are apt images to describe each of these two aspects.

Production

One of the attractions of the country in which the Kuba settled was its diversified environment. Like the area they left it was heavily forested, and there were intercalary savannas not unlike those lying between the Sankuru and the Lokenye rivers. The landscape was different, however: the forests were more intertwined with the savannas than they were farther north, where one enormous intercalary savanna stretched along the whole length of the Lokenye-Sankuru interfluve. People wishing to use both ecological zones were forced to settle in a line running east to west along the Sankuru or on the edge of its gallery forest. Each village could then control parts of savanna, parts of forests, and a stretch of the mighty river itself. All could be fishing villages, and most were.

Along the Lokenye the situation was not similar because of the relative scarcity of savanna at convenient distances, although some intercalary savannas were to be found even north of that river and its valley. South of the Sankuru, almost all of what became the Kuba area was suitable for settlement by villages because woods, grasslands, and rivers (although usually smaller rivers) were available everywhere. In a way the environment was even more diversified than their previous one. In addition to the ecological zones of the dense gallery forests and the savanna, numerous hilltops were crowned with copses where the flora and especially the fauna tended to differ from that found in the dense forest. To the southeast of the territory a huge forest, Dibese, hindered communications with the upper Lubudi-Mwanzangoma area.[1]

The persistent movement of the southern Mongo from north of the Lokenye

172

to south of the Sankuru may have been motivated in part by this shift in environment from more uniform to more diversified and therefore better conditions. From a forest with only a few savannas north of the Lokenye, people were attracted by the main savanna north of the Sankuru, where they found three ecological zones within walking distance: the river itself with its half-mile-wide bed, the gallery forests, and the savanna. South of the Sankuru those conditions prevailed, with one difference: major fishing activities had to be reduced to more modest catches in the smaller bodies of water. Even so the Lubudi, Lacwaady, Lyeekdy, and Laangdy were navigable rivers, and in the south and west the Lulua and the Kasai were major rivers. Even in this century every Kuba village needed the three ecological zones, although in some cases the river might be a small stream or a small lake.[2] As far as we know, by the turn of this century villages were more spread out around the major rivers and just outside their gallery forests than they are now.

Among the aboriginal inhabitants, the Cwa had been primarily forest hunters and the Kete savanna dwellers. The northern immigrants, who were strongly devoted to fishing when they first entered the country,[3] were not at first a menace. Their settlements were partly complementary to those already existing. In their traditional accounts the three groups have preserved memories of the most important features in the landscape as their ancestors perceived it. The Kete tell of migrations from plain (savanna) to plain, the Cwa stress the forest, and the Kuba emphasize the dugout canoe and movement by water.

Soon the immigrants began to compete with the Kete for some of the grasslands and with the Cwa for use of forests. They also borrowed, especially from the Kete. They borrowed sheep, but never had much success with them: the animals did not thrive and later remained only as a status symbol of the Kuba king, who had two or three herds.[4] We do not know when hogs were introduced; they may have been of Kete origin. Those animals were welcomed by the Kuba, already partial to the venison of warthog. The raffia palm began to be cultivated assiduously, following the Kete example. The inter-digitated savanna-forest environment favors this tree, which does not thrive as well in dense forest. The Kuba knew how to weave from proto-Kuba days and used looms, although if their cloth was at all similar to that of the southern Mongo today, their loom was less efficient than the one later devised.[5] The Kuba visualize their ancestors as wearing bark cloth, as is still the custom during mourning periods and on special occasions. But the raffia palm meant more than just cloth. It was a new source of palm wine of good quality, an ideal source for building materials, and, after it had been cut down, a source of delightful grubs, which must be nearly 100 percent protein. The tree was an important acquisition. Just how important we cannot tell, for we lack quantitative data about raffia palms tended by Kuba before and during this period.

Despite the fact that plantains had been the staple food of the proto-Kuba, they borrowed a term for banana from the Kete, designating all the varieties which are smaller and are edible without cooking. They also, to judge from the fact that they borrowed the term for the plant, adopted sugarcane from the Kete.[6] The Kete also had an impact on agriculture. It may be their example that was gradually followed in relying less on plantains and more on sorghum and millet as staple foods, although this may have been simply the effect of easier access to grasslands.

A major Kete contribution was their method of extracting salt. They cultivated salty grasses in marshes, burned them, and filtered the ashes to obtain crystals after evaporation. The product was a salt of much higher quality than the former, proto-Kuba way of applying a similar process to the male inflorescence of the oil palm.[7] As a result the central Kuba gradually abandoned their production of salt and relied mostly on Kete salt.

The impact of these changes on nutrition and indirectly on demography was probably slight. In terms of animal protein, some Kuba lost fish but all gained palm grubs and some pork, and all continued to hunt and trap. No significant nutritional difference is apparent. Demographic change resulting from the alterations man introduced in the environment (clearing fields, planting bananas, which retain water that encourages nesting mosquitoes, etc.) was probably slight, although the new environment may have been somewhat more congenial to *Anopheles* and consequently the incidence of malaria may have risen. It is impossible even to guess at the incidence of the greatest killer of all: trypanosomiasis, transmitted by the tsetse fly. In the late nineteenth and early twentieth centuries, parts of Kuba country proved highly congenial to the spread of this disease.

The primary change in production was the change in management of the domestic producing unit. The patrilineal management unit in domestic production had been the extended family, in which the oldest man was perhaps a polygynist. The shift to matriliny implied that the unit of production became the elementary family, a much smaller unit. This probably resulted in a loss of productivity because a drop in the size of units meant that each unit, which was the basic unit of consumption, tended to be concerned with only its own needs. Moreover, less manpower was available for joint projects, although some of the functions of management that had been in the hands of localized lineages were now taken over by the villages. The most important one was land tenure. The matrilineage controlled only the fishing ponds it had dug through the labor of its own male members—or, if not dug, the ponds were at least made appropriate for raising fish—and these were rare, given the dispersal of the males, especially the younger males, of a lineage. We do not know to what effect the village put pressure on the producing units to increase output in order to attain self-sufficiency for the whole settlement, thus counteracting the tendency of each family to farm just enough to fulfill its own needs. There was probably some impact from the village, since this was one of the major attractions for inhabitants to live in villages.[8]

The Kete added a few products to the inventory of material culture. It is claimed that they "invented" hats—although the term for hats is related to the Ding term—and they introduced several new forms of baskets. The most important innovation was the heavy-duty farm basket, which is carried on top of the head, rather than the backpack type, which the Kuba had used before. The new basket was far better built and much more efficient.[9] A major Kete contribution was in sculpture. Their style was taken over by the Kuba, who developed it further. This was of minor importance during the Age of Chiefs, but became much more significant when fine platters, boxes, and knickknacks were in demand by the patriciate after the kingdom began to flourish. The Kuba knew how to carve before they met the Kete, as we would expect from any people living in the forest, and indeed any fishing people relying on dugouts.[10]

The most significant craft of all, iron smelting and working, was known to both groups before they met, at least according to the tradition of "the hammers and the anvils." The Kuba, however, may have used more efficient tools. Claims have been made that the proto-Kuba brought refined metallurgy to a region much wider than their own territory.[11] Certainly the Pyaang occupied the mines of the Mwabe stream near Kabuluanda. The Kete of nearby Kakenge were also famous for their blacksmiths, as indicated by their products and the praise names of the area. They probably learned improved smelting techniques from the Kuba. Another major Kuba contribution was in fishing techniques, since the Kete fished very little.

A starting point for economic development appears with the reign of Shyaam. With the onset of the last dynasty, technological innovations from the Kwilu-Kasai area, especially in agriculture, began to spread throughout the country. In the end the innovations amounted to an agricultural revolution because the staple crops were replaced by American crops, which had higher yields. The process was underway well before 1680.[12] The main innovation was the introduction of a double, and in some places even a triple, annual harvest of maize by each domestic producing unit. This change in the mode of production was not an import, but was developed in the realm itself, between c. 1620 and 1892. Taking crop rotation into account, this implies a double crop for beans[13] combined with peanuts, and a double crop of cassava. None of the neighbors of the Kuba took to double cropping at all.

The American food complex reached the Kuba over a period of several reigns. According to the tales about kings, chili pepper antedated even Shyaam, having been borrowed from the Leele.[14] Shyaam's reign saw the introduction of most staples except cassava and tobacco. All these crops presumably came from the Mbuun. Cassava, however, was introduced only under the reign of MboMboosh [3] (before 1680). It came from the Bieeng chiefdom, in the southwest, along the Kasai River. Since cassava is first mentioned on the coast only shortly after 1600[15] and maize was cultivated there perhaps half a century earlier, the lag in arrival in Kuba country sounds reasonable. The mention of tobacco is more surprising, given the scarcity of the plant at Malebo Pool as late as 1656 (and even 1698).[16] Yet a connection with Shyaam would bring it to the Kuba as early as 1650 or before. The diffusion of all these crops so far into the interior and so soon after their introduction on the coast is remarkable only if one assumes that no trade route existed from Kongo to the Mbuun area. If it followed a route, the diffusion does not seem so extraordinary.

Maize replaced sorghum and cassava replaced yams, but peanuts replaced *Voandzeia* only in part. The production of plantains and bananas diminished, and millet, a subsidiary crop, also lost importance. Double cropping does not necessarily imply that the acreage cultivated also doubled. Most banana plantations were abandoned except for groves near the small gardens behind the houses,[17] and tobacco, which is not a food crop, required at least a little land. In terms of labor tobacco was a very demanding crop, leaving much less time for other agricultural pursuits than a ratio of actual acreage used would indicate. Moreover, the acreage devoted to the crops that were double cropped was not exactly doubled. Even in the twentieth century there was one slightly bigger and one slightly smaller crop of maize per year. Nevertheless the introduction of double cropping must have required a large extension of cultivated lands.

On the other hand the yields of the new crops were much higher and less risky.[18] Maize is better adapted than sorghum to high humidity, weeds, pests, and insects. The birds took much less grain in the field than they did from a crop of millet or sorghum (in millet fields they sometimes steal half of the output). Cassava's ability to keep unspoiled in the ground for up to two years made it an insurance against the risk of bad harvests—and insurance was needed, for famines was apparently not wholly unknown. Cassava also yielded about ten times as much by weight per acre as yams, and peanuts yielded twice as much as *Voandzeia* by weight per plant. In sum, a much higher yield per acre resulted from the adoption of the American plants, and double cropping increased production even more. It is possible that the yield per banana tree planted near the small gardens rose as a result of better application of fertilizer. It seems not unreasonable to argue that the output per domestic producing unit doubled during the Age of Kings.[19]

This did not come about immediately. It is plausible to accept the general pattern provided by Rogers and Shoemaker,[20] since the process has been observed in many cases: the agricultural innovations were introduced by an influential group or person more "cosmopolitan" than the local people, one which could exert coercion. These are all factors that occur regularly in cases of agricultural innovation. Coercion among the Kuba is quite possible, considering that tribute could be required in maize and that each village was responsible for cultivating "the king's field" (shash anyim). In the beginning only a small percent of farmers tried the new crops. After a number of years and after having survived bad growing seasons, the crops proved themselves and began to be adopted rather fast, spreading over most of the population. But a small portion was probably reluctant to abandon the old staples and the rate of acceptance per year lagged again before the old plants were completely abandoned.[21]

It was not just a matter of replacing one crop with another. The whole agricultural calendar had to be reorganized, including the division of labor by sex. Yams, for example do not grow in the savanna, where the women have their main fields. Cassava does, and it became the last crop in this crop rotation sequence, as it was in the sequence of the main fields in the forest. This made the women's fields more important than before, especially as the next crop in the sequence shifted from *Voandzeia* to peanuts plus eggplants and *Voandzeia*. Cassava requires elaborate treatment before being cooked: it must be soaked for days, then cut up and ground. This may have been true as well of the varieties of yams used, but they had not been a major staple. Bananas and plantains required much less work. The work load of women therefore increased. The farming units in general had to make complex adjustments to their calendar of activities by day and by season to meet the requirements of the American food complex. The process was further complicated by the requirement that consumers switch staples. They had to acquire new tastes, and since the consumers were themselves the producers, this may have helped to slow the conversion process even more. I would not be surprised if general acceptance of the new way of farming was gained only in the nineteenth century, having taken more than a century to oust the previous system.

The record indicates that the change was not swift. In a tale about Mbo-Mboosh [3], the seeds that the king put into the basket were millet or sorghum, not maize. If sorghum had been quickly abandoned as a staple, the chances are that the grains would have been maize. The praise name for sorghum is "Sorghum comes from the Pende, maize from the Mbuun, the seeds are everywhere." This praise name is an ascending anachronism, in Delivré's terminology,[22] for in Shyaam's day there were as yet no Pende near the Kasai River. When they later settled there, they became known for their sorghum plantations, and by the nineteenth century they were contrasted to the Mbuun, who were famous for their fields of maize. The difference between the two neighboring groups is described in the praise name, but perhaps the difference was remarkable only to a society that had not yet adopted maize as it main staple. The slogan seems to imply that both sorghum *and* maize were Kuba staples. Unfortunately, we cannot date the praise name. At the latest it is nineteenth century, at the earliest late seventeenth century.

To oppose this interpretation one can cite the tale that describes Shyaam as eating maize and the attribution of the "invention" of maize to his reign.[23] But one source even attributes the introduction of sorghum to his reign, which is false. The Shyaam tales are anachronistic and can be dismissed as such.

One of the last crops introduced, perhaps with the American complex, was the sweet potato.[24] Like tobacco it was planted in the small gardens but it did not spread and become a major crop; eggplants, for example, remained more important than the sweet potato. The same applies to chili pepper, whose introduction into the small gardens did not require a major shift in agricultural practice.

Another undated technical change, unrelated to introduction of the American crops, was the new practice of tapping palm wine. The Kuba claim to have known about palm wine since the time of Woot.[25] But the praise name for the raffia palm calls it "the raffia palm sent by the Ding," and the technique of tapping wine is ascribed by some sources to Shyaam. This may seem surprising, but the linguistic evidence bolsters the claim for a western origin: the term for palm wine, *maan,* is definitely a term from beyond the Loange, used in the Kwilu and lower Kasai areas. The claim may well be correct if it is restricted to a new way of tapping wine, for the Kuba use a technique unknown to their nearest neighbors, including most of the Leele, although the Leele also use the term maan for palm wine. Rather than cut the tree down to tap the wine, the Kuba make an incision at the base of the male inflorescence. Once a tree was tapped in this way (in its fifth or sixth year), it yielded wine for two to four months rather than for a few days, and then it died. The Kuba and Leele add different roots for flavor when fermenting the wine but otherwise the eastern Leele and Kuba use the same technique of fermentation. The western Leele and other Kuba neighbors did not use this technique of tapping, or else they may have adopted and then abandoned it. The western Leele were unwilling to invest more labor (implied in the Kuba technique) to make a resource last longer. The matter is not trivial because of the implication of this labor aspect. The Leele were always short on labor, whereas the Kuba were not, a fact that is accounted for by their respective sociopolitical organizations, as Mary Douglas has so brilliantly demonstrated in her seminal article.[26]

In order to expand their output the Kuba had to alter the combination of factors of production. They could and did improve technology, where their achievement is not to be underestimated. Sheppard, an American who knew maize well, said that he was told by farmers that the yield was fifty to sixty bushels an acre.[27] The figure certainly is incorrect: what Kuba could cite figures in bushels per acre? Sheppard obviously incorrectly converted their quantitative answer. After 1945, and before any improvements in corn strains were introduced, Kuba yields were around twenty to twenty-five bushels per acre.[28] This explains Sheppard's enthusiasm: these yields were as high or higher than any he had seen in his native Virginia.

The most remarkable part of Sheppard's statement is that the Kuba were evidently accustomed to calculating yield per surface unit and were indeed dedicated farmers.[29] The very presence of small fields around the springs of brooks, where a harvest can be obtained up to a maximum of five weeks ahead of the main harvest, testifies to that. Once again it also shows that there had been experimentation that resulted in technological innovation. Technological improvement is further attested by the fact that the Kuba found it worthy of remembrance that an eighteenth-century king improved the razor blade, which earned him the nickname that in Luba became Lukengu (razor blade), the generic Luba title for Kuba kings.[30]

Land and resources were not a problem because the population density throughout Kuba country certainly lay below eight people per square kilometer.[31] The bottleneck among factors of production was the relative scarcity of labor. More than the introduction of a new crop or a particular technique, increased labor was responsible for increased production. The organization of labor was altered to apply more work to producing food. By 1892 the Kuba men not only cleared the fields, as men did in all the surrounding societies, but also assisted with the harvest and built granaries in the field to store the crop quickly and safely or else built granaries in the village. Nowhere else did men perform that much field work.

The techniques for trapping were ingenious and efficient, although the ones for warthogs required the building of stout palisades across whole valleys for miles and miles. Ponds were dug for raising fish, and in the bigger rivers, especially in the Sankuru, long dams jutted out into the water, pierced at intervals by openings to allow the water and the fish to pass through. In the openings weirs were set, some with pulleys, and above them guardhouses were built so that the traps could be hauled in day and night.[32] This technique certainly permitted more fish to be caught in a more reliable fashion than did other techniques, just as more game was caught more regularly within the palisade fences, but the labor requirements were enormous. Even the powerful royal sons had to work, to judge from the tradition that the seventy sons of Kot aNce [7] were killed while they were weaving cloth at the palace.[33]

During the Age of Kings the allocation of labor was totally reorganized and led to a different product mix. Doubling productivity could not have been accomplished simply by utilizing the "underproductivity" of the previous agricultural system. If Chayanov's rule had prevailed before, as it did in so many cases, the available vent for surplus was still not high enough to explain the results. In any case the Kuba farmers probably did not adhere strictly to the rule because of intravillage cooperation, and the lack of productivity that is predicted by the rule would have been reduced.[34]

The first step in raising productivity was for the men to work more in the fields. This did not quite double the labor force per producing unit, but added some 50 percent to it at least. Second, the age of marriage was lowered, bringing young and vigorous men into the agricultural labor force. Young men did not work in the fields at all before marriage, except perhaps when they worked a single year in the fields of their future mothers-in-law.[35] Under Mboong aLeeng [2] the boys' initiation was either introduced or was reorganized under royal control at the capital, and it came to be expected that they would marry soon after the conclusion of the rituals. By 1892 the king conferred the hat, the emblem of adulthood, on all young men (of his capital?) and personally and strongly urged them to marry. Monogamy was introduced at the latest in the seventeenth century, marriage partners were not lacking, and by 1892 bridewealth was fairly low. It may have become lower as a concomitant to early marriage and monogamy, itself the consequence of reserving polygyny to eagle-feather chiefs and kings. But data about the amount of bridewealth before 1892 must remain mostly speculative.[36] By the nineteenth century the result was that boys married young, at less than twenty years of age rather than at twenty-five or even, as among the Leele, thirty-five, thus adding a sizable portion to the labor available for agriculture, and a portion that included the strongest laborers.

Mboong aLeeng also created settlements for prisoners of war. They did not add very much to domestic production per unit, but slaves, who began to be imported under the first kings,[37] did. They came from outside the realm and they were incorporated into the producing units. Their children were free, adding to the number of subjects. The number of slaves acquired as imports in the seventeenth century was probably rather small. Later their number grew to the point that in the early nineteenth century King Miko miMbul [11] allowed the Bushoong to marry slave girls and married one himself.[38] At that time slaves were available, and the new marriage rule spurred the desire of many men to buy them because children of such a union belonged to the matrilineage of their father, thereby combining the attractions of gaining children and nephews. During the nineteenth century the number of slaves grew as a result of imports via the Luso-African trade. There were so many by 1892 that each household at the capital had at least one slave. In 1953–54 it was estimated from genealogical material that 6 percent of the population at that time consisted of descendants of slaves imported in the last years (1890–99?) of the trade. This estimate is based on a small sample and is almost certainly lower than actual figures.[39]

If labor was so valuable, why then was it wasted as, for example, in human sacrifice? Slaves were sacrificed as a form of conspicuous consumption at funerals. In 1892 the number of those sacrificed varied in the capital from one or two for the head of a family to "a thousand" for the king's mother.[40] Such destruction of labor was only possible because of an ample supply, which grew to a flood after 1880, when the Luso-African trade became well organized.[41] The action in part is conspicuous waste: the Kete sacrificed goats, the Bushoong, people, said the king to Sheppard. But the major reason was religious: to provide dependents for the deceased. These sacrifices may have been much less spectacular before 1880. Archaeological excavation of royal graves would certainly contribute to our knowledge of the practice.

The Kuba kings were fully aware of their need for labor. In the 1950s the ruling king explained that he ruled over people, not land. To know the exact boundaries of the realm made no sense; to know who paid tribute and who could be commanded did. This attitude also existed earlier, and it explains the existence of a census, which was taken annually when the headmen of the Bushoong villages came to pay tribute. They reported the number of deaths and births. Similarly, a kernel was kept for each boy who had been initiated at the capital with one of the king's sons. Since all of these boys were inhabitants of matoon villages or of the capital, a tally of the labor force in the matoon villages and the capital was provided by these means.[42] Legalizing marriages with slave women may indicate a concern for spurring the growth of labor. Certainly the king's urging that young men should marry early suggests a policy of increasing labor. It is true that existence of a census does not mean that kings were concerned with agricultural labor; it shows that this concern was a part of the general interest in tribute. The connection between tribute and labor presumably was perceived, and the need to increase labor followed from that.

We can only guess at the demographic effects of changes in the agricultural production and of the population policies that were followed. True, some royal praises refer to multitudes, as in the song for the ngesh composed in honor of Mishe miShyaang maMbul [6], in the eighteenth century:

> The king of the people who are numerous,
> The king of the people who are a thousand,
> The king of the flies and the bees.[43]

Texts such as these may evoke an increase in the overall population, but as worded they merely indicate an increase in population at the capital. The capital is clearly intended by the designation "the great crowd," the title of one of the capitals of Mbop Mabiinc maMbul [12]. In general, natural population increase is due to a lowering of mortality (probably by a reduction of infant mortality) or an increased birthrate, presumably as a result of early marriages and perhaps an increase in fertility. The nutritional advantages of the crops in the American complex are not self-evident. Only in case of bad harvests would they help to preserve the existing population from starvation, and thus might indirectly lead to a population increase. But shortages of crops because of bad weather, although not very frequent, were not totally unheard of, at least not in the case of maize and cassava. Kuba tales mention only one famine, in Shyaam's day. They differ strikingly from those of Luba groups, where famine is a recurring theme of major importance.[44] If bad harvests were rare with the old crops, the demographic impact of the new crops is not definite.

If the reduced risk of famine caused perhaps a slight increase in the population, an earlier marriage age for the boys probably did not alter the previous population pattern: girls had always married rather young. Furthermore, the population at the center of the realm increased by immigration from outlying areas.[45] Whether the Age of Kings also brought a higher rate of increase of the population can only be surmised from the above. I believe that a moderate increase in that rate did occur. Unfortunately, precolonial population densities of the kingdom and the surrounding areas cannot even be estimated because no adequate population data can be construed.[46] The most that can be said is that the probable density was higher in the realm than anywhere around it, except perhaps south of it. One therefore cannot link this conclusively to double cropping and the introduction of American crops, unless it could be shown that the density in the kingdom was higher than that of the population along the Lulua, where American crops were introduced but where double cropping was not practiced and a state organization did not exist.

Craft production must also have risen during the Age of Kings, but, unlike the agricultural situation, no estimates of increases can be made. Still, we can conclude that the increase in agricultural yield freed more labor for artisanal work. And the number of craftsmen, many of them kolm, increased.

The Bushoong pay special attention to metal work. Traditions mention Myeel, a member of the royal house, a foundry master and a smith, who was portrayed as a stern and demanding taskmaster but also as a virtuoso who achieved the impossible. He forged models of a complete iron house of natural size, of a boat and its occupants, and of statuettes. But he did not become king because he was so harsh. Once, when he had put some ore out to dry in the bush, a man inadvertently started a bush fire and ruined the ore. Myeel imposed a fine so great that the Bushoong feared to choose him as a successor to Mboong aLeeng [2].[47] Whether there ever was a Myeel or not, the preservation by tradition of these details and his link with royalty indicates the high prestige of the craft. It was even said that, ever since the early days of the kingdom, all men of the royal lineage had to know the art of smithing.[48] Its production was controlled and had to be reported. Because the inhabitants had forged metal without letting the king know, the village of Paam is said to have been reduced to matoon status by Mboong aLeeng.[49] Where a smithy existed, the villagers—even in the twentieth century—were loath to sell the implements that belonged to it because they felt strongly about the need for iron tools.[50] The major wars with the Luba in the nineteenth century were fought over possession of excellent ores in the southeast.[51]

From the state of crafts in the late nineteenth century it is evident that a specialization of labor among craftsmen had grown up in the preceding centuries, which resulted in genuine technical innovations or improvements and a superior mastery in each craft by at least some artisans. Thus every Bushoong man can carve, just as most children learn to write in our own culture, but specialists produced far better carvings. The specialization became so advanced that there were special carvers of pipe bowls and others who worked only on pipe stems, which were not fashioned out of wood. In precolonial days such specialists may have worked at their craft full time, at least in the capital. The needs of the patricians in part explain the development of such specialists as the jewelers who use rotating firing drills to pierce tiny holes in shells. Technical innovations such as the inlay of copper wire and later tin, and encrusting copper into iron, welding, and wiredrawing were not found outside the kingdom. In textiles, the manufacture of a velvet type of cloth and the invention of several dyeing techniques that presumably began in the seventeenth century as imitations of imported specimens from the Mbuun, or perhaps later from the Pende, are noteworthy.[52] Whether craftswomen from the Mbuun or the Pende settled in Kuba country we do not know. New techniques were acquired, copied, or invented for embroidery, and among others the specialization of hatters arose. These events provide evidence that the division of labor was symbiotically accompanied by technical innovation.

The division of labor also developed on an areal basis, no doubt fortified by the specific requirements for tribute. Thus "raw" cloth and "raw" iron flowed from the periphery to the capital, where the products were transformed. This probably increased the efficiency of the total output by concentrating skills and causing enough basic resources to be produced to keep the artisans at the capital employed full time. Some of the resources originated in the capital itself. The thousands of palm trees Sheppard saw at the capital were raffia palms.[53] Palm wine was prized. The rolling and waving of thread was a major occupation, as we are again reminded by the image of the seventy sons of Kot aNce weaving at the palace. At least half of the women in the harem embroidered cloth.

There can be little doubt that the production of craft objects increased over time, but by how much cannot be determined. The volume was also directly influenced by the demands of trade.

Why did the Kuba push for increases in productivity? Mary Douglas has written: "Somehow, somewhere, the Bushoong took decisions . . . ."[54] Was

the surplus something natural that led to the elaboration of the political structure because manpower could be spared? But who would work to produce a
needless surplus? Could a surplus somehow have been due to sheer accident?
No, at least not to build up a reliable surplus that could be tapped from year to
year. The "natural surplus" that results from accidental overproduction when
a year has been better than foreseen is a fluctuating and transient form of
surplus. Nothing stable can be built on it.[55] It takes a conscious effort to raise
a surplus. Could that have been due to some impulse linked to the value
system? In 1892 most Kuba worked from six in the morning to eight at night.
A work ethic definitely existed. Kuba mythology as taught to boys in initiation equated laziness with the supreme evil: witchcraft.[56] But was this the
moving force behind production and subsequent economic development, or
was it a consequence?[57] The data point to other causes. Shyaam and his
successors can be considered responsible for the first agricultural innovations
and thus made surplus possible.

Could it be that the interest in technology brought with it a will to produce
more? This also probably puts the cart before the horse. The call for a surplus
came from above, from the political authorities. It was imposed on the people.
The farmers were coerced into higher production. The creation of many titles
for kolm in charge of the collection of taxes on special goods and services and
the reorganization of the tribute system in basic foodstuffs, the existence of
inspectors (the kol mat)—all created demand. Even when these titles multiplied far beyond the requirement of an efficient revenue-collection system
they did so because such officials could collect goods and keep part for themselves. Taxes and tribute were spoils, and the spoils had to be produced
mostly by the farmer. With the growth of the city came a demand for its daily
food supply that was met largely by creating the bubaang villages. The spiral
that led to greater development was fed by the expansion of the patricians.
Their number grew because they could be sustained, and the more they were
sustained the larger the number of patricians grew to be. Here a theory about
surplus must start with the creation of a bureaucracy leading to the creation of
surplus, rather than the reverse.[58] Once the process was set in motion, however, the relation between economics and political development became reciprocal: after all, nothing succeeds like success. The decisions which the
Bushoong took "somewhere, somehow" were political decisions.

Why did the kolm and the patricians in general need wealth? First, for the
maintenance of those who were no longer producing foodstuffs: the political
elite, traders, and artisans. A second bloc of surplus was needed in goods
other than food, and these were produced by the artisans, the group that the
kolm bukwemy taxed. These were prestige, conspicuous commodities also
used for export against imported luxuries, which in turn became sumptuary
expenditures for the elite as well.

Wealth was an essential part of power. The king himself, and to a much lesser extent the men of his lineage, needed treasures.[59] The members of the royal lineage were collectively called "the moneyed ones." Even in 1953 the Kuba still believed that the king was fabulously rich. He owned a number of storehouses containing treasures, located within the inner palace. There the income from tribute was piled up: heaps of textiles of all types, pottery, hoes, ivory, and so on. He could use these goods or money (cowries) to favor his supporters and sons. The mere fact that he was reputed to be so wealthy attracted supporters and was one of the mainstays of his power. Subjects were advised to give the king preserved foodstuffs,[60] and there was also a drive to collect goods that were not food, for the proper ingredients of a king's treasure should not spoil over time. They should, if possible, be prestige items. If goods spoiled easily they *had* to be given away, which lessened the flexibility of the king in their disposition. He had to be able to give or to retain, and to give when it suited him. As the song for the ngesh in honor of MboMboosh [3] puts it:

> MboMboosh, food in the hand; he does not give it to you.
> MboMboosh, the raffia square, the raffia square, he gives nothing.[61]

This text lists the two types of commodities by paradigm—food and currency, which in his day was raffia squares. The power to withhold is significant, and the possession of storehouses of wealth that can be given away attracts permanent followers and produces power. Others possessed such treasures on a much more modest scale and their power to attract supporters was proportionally more modest. In 1892 the entire treasure of perhaps the most powerful and wealthiest among the king's sons was stored in his bedroom. Compared to the treasure in the storehouses of the king, his was little indeed.[62]

The competition at the court made the display of prestige goods important because it indicated each person's status. It was the barometer of success and influence. The goods that counted most were those of every affluent society: rare items which came from afar, or those representing considerable labor. For example, cooking-pot lids were made with exquisite care and were decorated all over, yet after a few weeks they were so begrimed with soot that not a single pattern remained visible. Their value derived from the labor they represented. Labor was the bottleneck of production, yet these people were so well off that they could afford to squander it. A more direct display was the habit of showering cowries into graves. The many pounds of shells thrown into the graves of kings amounted to fortunes for others. Throwing the money away strengthened both kingship and those who participated in the act. The nature of prestige goods thus tied them to the economy in both its productive and its distributive (foreign luxury goods, currency) aspects.

Prestige goods had to be flaunted, for they were the indicator of political success. Hence the feasts, and there were many. They were the occasion to measure the relative status of groups within the patriciate: king's sons versus kolm, the women of the royal lineage versus the king's daughters, etc. And within each of these groups each individual tried to do better than the others. To preserve power or to augment it, one always had to have better clothes, better jewelry, better housing, better furniture, and certainly one had to give more and better feasts.[63] Those feasts were the occasions which kept the ordinary people entertained and happy and left them with a feeling of participation. By their very existence the sumptuary laws recognized the political potential inherent in conspicuous consumption. Hence they were meant to restrict such commodities and services (the feasts) to certain categories in the hierarchy.[64] Their aim was not at all to limit the display, but merely to regulate it.

The court therefore needed more and more surplus to convert into prestige items. But in the end coercion was not the only factor that made the Kuba work harder, adhere to a work ethic, and remain interested in collective labor and advances in technology. There were rewards to the producers as well. The general standard of living rose in the Bushoong chiefdom, probably also among the Kete, and to a lesser degree elsewhere. The common man had more, better, and more varied goods than before. He also had a few luxury articles: a jewelbox, a pipe, a piece of fine velvety cloth or an embroidered textile, all of which he had bought from the artisans with cowries.[65] The common man had cowries in the nineteenth century because by then the effects of trade had reached every village. The basic tribute was paid in cowries, and bridewealth was calculated and often paid in cowries. Trade had developed because the elite demanded exotic goods, and once long-distance trade in these goods had been established the commercial network offered an outlet for other products as well. Thus the surplus of goods helped bring about the expansion of trade, which led in the end to a rise in the standard of living of the same farmer who was exploited by the elite. The economy as a whole had developed far beyond what it had been two and a half centuries before.

Distribution

Narrative traditions cannot be accepted at face value when they mention the existence of such items as cowries at very early dates; anachronisms should be suspected in every case. These tales consist of anecdotes that can be presented as the performer wants to present them, and usually detail is added to give a touch of reality to them. But the material touches of reality derive from "traditional trade" as the teller knows it—i.e., trade in the nineteenth century. Other evidence should be used to confirm oral data. Such information can be derived from songs or poems, which are memorized, but usually the confirming data is linguistic.

In view of the danger of anachronism, very little can be said with certainty about trade in early times. That it existed is axiomatic. Most terms relating to it, however, are innovations in the language and cannot be dated or are connected with later periods. The term for price ("salt-cake") may date from the Age of Chiefs, whereas "to buy" is earlier. The word for market is found only among the Kuba, Ndengese, eastern Ding, and the river people between the Ding and the Kuba, a distribution which could suggest a Kuba origin for the term just as easily as an origin in the north or west.[66] We do not know whether or not markets existed in the Age of Chiefs. The traditions about the coming of Shyaam suggest that there were markets and a flourishing trade, but they so faithfully conform to nineteenth-century practices that they leave us with grave doubts when a date in the seventeenth century is suggested. It is wise to posit no more than a local trade among the Kete, different Kuba groups, and the riparians of the Sankuru, Kasai, and Lulua rivers before Shyaam's arrival.

Perhaps Shyaam was a trader—traders, hunters, and fugitives were then the only foreigners, and of them traders might have enjoyed the most protection. The Kuba attribute his success to magic, but that success becomes more understandable if he was wealthy and came with even a relatively small following. The attribution to Shyaam of all innovations from the Kwilu area makes better sense in this interpretation. Even if he was not a trader, trade with those regions seems to have begun during his reign because contacts with the Mbuun are so strongly attested. The traditions stress aspects of trade in Shyaam's career more than in that of any other king. Even if they do this in anachronistic terms, they intend to convey the notion that trade was important in his reign, as when they mention that he waged war near the Lokenye to protect traders.

The strongest argument for accepting the notion that trade developed during his reign and that he was perhaps a trader is that a free foreigner could only be a merchant or a kind of prophet, for a mere refugee risked prompt servitude. And it is evident that he did not arrive alone: Kwilu features in Bushoong speech spread from the capital and presumably the court.[67] To attribute these changes to an innovation of speech brought by one man alone, even one who became a king, is not nearly as reasonable as to attribute it to a group that set the pattern of speech at court. An even stronger explanation is provided by assuming that the changes in speech were reinforced by caravans arriving later on trading missions to the capital. This explanation also fits in better with the overall picture in the southern savanna. Maps 6 and 7 show the major markets around 1900 and the trade routes over the centuries.

Probably as early as c. 1619 the Mbuun were in contact with Okanga, a

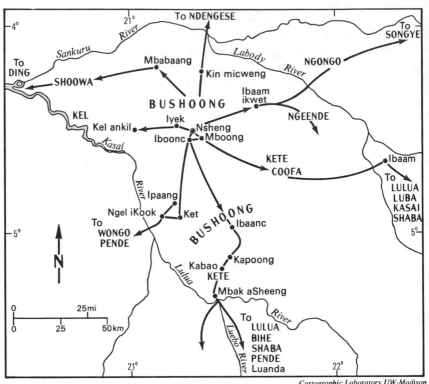

Map 6. Major Markets around 1900 (Based on map in Jan Vansina, *Le royaume kuba*, Musée royal de l'Afrique centrale [Tervuren, 1964], p. 21)

territory on the Kwango River where a major marketplace, the Pumbo of Okanga, was actively trading with Kongo. Before 1640 it was one of the two major marketplaces between Kongo and the interior. About 1619 a certain Rafael de Castro made a journey eastward from Okanga and traveled for two hundred miles before he turned back because Kikongo was no longer understood in those parts. Other calculations of distances are correct in the source that reports this, but they are based on the testimony of many people. If the calculations of two hundred miles is correct, the traveler would have reached the middle Kasai. He apparently did not: the figure is too high, as shown by the fact that he does not mention the crossing of larger rivers, but presumably it is not out of all proportion to other distances mentioned, and he may well have gone beyond the Kwilu area into the land of the Mbuun. He mentions their western neighbors, the Tsong, by name.[68] It is not surprising that Kikongo was understood that far east because variants of this language were spoken by the populations as far as Tsong territory. In the nineteenth century Kikongo was the trading language of the whole Kwilu area.[69] It is also more than likely that Castro, starting as he did from a major market, traveled along the existing routes rather than striking out into the unknown. Moreover, the Mbuun remember the Okanga market, calling it Poom aNdzoom, the Pumbo of the Zombo.[70] After the collapse of the Kongo kingdom in 1665, the Zombo took over trade in this sector; they may in fact have been trading there from the beginning. Further evidence of a trade route can be found in the Mbuun practice of naming the four days of the week by terms that are demonstrably Kongo in origin, in their use of the same currency that was tender in the Kongo kingdom, and in a similar designation for "market."[71]

Granted, all of this establishes only that a trade route existed between Mbuun and Kongo in precolonial days and does not allow us to date it. In conjunction with the journey of Castro, however, the connection of the route with the Tsong becomes certain, and one with the Mbuun seems at least plausible. The existence of such a trade route best explains the rapid diffusion of American crops. It also explains how a Kongo term for a sort of cloth became the Kuba word for woman's dress, and how the *mancala* game came to be adopted so quickly by the Kuba when in 1652 its introduction was still so recent in Kongo that a dictionary there listed it as *warri*, its West African name.[72] This game is strongly associated with Shyaam; it appears as his emblem at the base of his dynastic statue. The final significant linguistic distribution associated with the trade route is the new term *mbey*, a loan from the Kwilu languages meaning "comrade" or "age mate," and also found among the Leele, where *bumbai*, "age friendship," was extended to trading partners, *mbai*.[73] Historically, however, the extension may have gone the other way: from "trading friend" to "age mate." If so, it occurred earlier than the seventeenth century, when Leele society was completely organized on the basis of age-grades.

How long had a trade route existed between Kongo and the Kwilu? The evidence suggests that it was a main trade route by 1620 and had been in existence at least since the late sixteenth century, when Okanga begins to be mentioned in texts.[74] It clearly flourished as an extension of the new overseas trading relationships, which gathered much strength during the sixteenth century. We can surmise that "inventions" of Shyaam are not the work of a single individual but the side effects of trade with the Kwilu area and ultimately the effects of the new pattern in transoceanic trade.

Even so, the link between the Mbuun and the Kuba was weak. The route that reached the Kuba was a slender tendril at the end of the network of routes feeding the Atlantic trade. The Kuba did not accept the common currency used on the Mbuun-Kongo route, the *Olivancillaria nana* shell, or *nzimbu*. The only ones found in Kuba country are isolated specimens embedded in the handle of war swords. Perhaps they once were an item with magical properties, but they were never used as currency. The specimens found can only

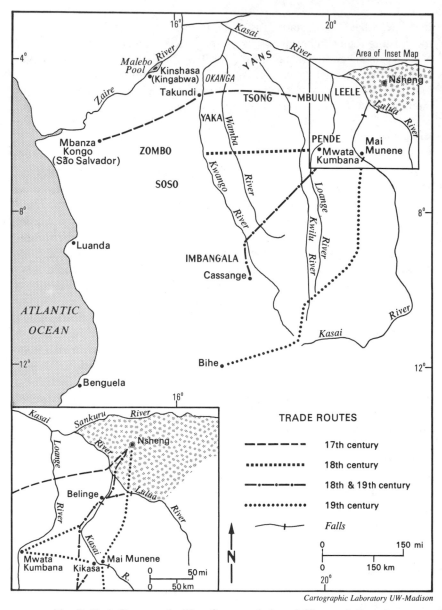

Map 7. Trade Routes to the West, Seventeenth through Nineteenth Centuries

have come from the Luanda area, as do the Kongo nzimbu, and the Kuba name
for them derives from the Kongo; in short, they were once traded. One of the
names for the four days of the week was adopted by the Kuba as the name for

market day and to designate the notion of week itself, but they borrowed no term for the other days and no other market terms.[75] All of this evidence seems to indicate that the contacts were not frequent and that the Kuba were not overwhelmed by an influx of merchants. Trade became influential enough, however, to spur the Kuba economy. Kuba products were neither unique nor vital to the long-distance trading network. The Kuba probably did not export slaves, although they adopted a Kwilu word for "slave" to supplement the indigenous term. In later times they imported them. The Kuba bought slaves, and I believe they had already begun to do so in the seventeenth century. They may have exported some ivory, but in the seventeenth-century Kongo trade this was not a product of major importance and could be obtained from areas much closer to the coast.

The Kuba used raffia squares *(mbal)* as a local currency, in common with the Mbuun markets. Such cloth was traded farther west, and the term occurs over a large part of the western half of the southern savanna.[76] Since an alternative name for the Bushoong is Bambal, which can be understood as "people of the cloth," it is tempting to speculate: it *could* be a nickname given by outsiders and accepted by the people themselves, but in the praise poem associated with it, it is presented as a name going back to the time of creation.[77] I believe that the traffic between Mbuun and Kuba was slight and involved the import of a few luxury items, such as the expensive types of raffia cloth that the Kuba imitated later, some nzimbu, and perhaps a very few items of European cloth and brass. A tale about Mboong aLeeng [2] tells that the war between this king and the Bokila was prompted by the fact that the chief of the Bokila wore brass, a royal prerogative. Again one suspects that this is an anachronism, as the Kuba king in 1892 was punctilious about wearing brass,[78] and the motive for the war may actually have been quite different. Brass merely symbolizes the refusal to be or become a subject. Exports from the Kuba probably included camwood and perhaps ivory. Raffia squares served as the standard of value and may even have been used as currency.

Once the trading link was in place it never disappeared. Okanga declined, but in the eighteenth century the Yaka capital farther south took its place. From there a trade route supervised by political authorities, all belonging to the Lunda system, ran to Mwata Kumbana among the Pende and then to Mai Munene, Kikasa, or Belinge on the middle Kasai. The more distant link between Mai Munene and the Lunda imperial capital seems to be attested by 1755.[79] By then it is quite possible that Kuba traders went via the Bieeng chiefdom as far as Mai Munene or Kikasa, south of the Bieeng. They certainly traveled in small caravans along this road in the later nineteenth century, for von Wissmann met a group of them in 1881. References to "Pende pottery," the name for a type of pottery among the Kuba but ironically not a type of

pottery used by the Pende, imported from the middle Kasai, and the insistence
that velvety cloth "came" from the Pende are more than straws in the wind:
Pende was a name used for traders and trading places to the southwest.[80] The
route was well known, and went either from the confluence of the Kasai and
the Lulua to Belinge, near the falls of the Kasai, where Pende lived and
traded, overland to the area of Kikasa or overland to the Bieeng capital and
from there to Kikasa. The Bieeng chiefdom controlled both approaches, and
in 1896 it was claimed that the chief of the Bieeng and the title Mai Munene
were in the same lineage. The claim may be false, but it indicates the
privileged position of the Bieeng.[81]

In the eighteenth century, long-distance trade brought the first cowries and
the first Angolan beads; the first imports of copper from Shaba also appeared,
perhaps a few decades later. The evidence for this is a ncok song for the son of
Kot aNce [7] as well as certain objects in the royal treasury. The song states:

> Complete do I dance
> with the *bwoom* mask,
> made out of ordinary hide
> without cowries or beads.[82]

The dynastic statues, the earliest of which date from the later eighteenth
century, show carvings of cowries as decorations on the throne, belts, and
headgear. The dynastic drums, kept at the capital, are decorated with copper,
beads, and cowries. The earliest specimens, ascribed to the eighteenth century, have only a small but massive copper ornament; on the later specimens
copper wire figures prominently.

In the eighteenth century imports were still luxury products. Kuba raffia
cloth may have been exported in larger quantities along with camwood and
ivory, but the trade became truly voluminous only in the nineteenth century.
Using internal evidence, the rule that slave women could be married, introduced before 1835, implies that slave imports from the south were increasing.
By 1854 the name Mai Munene is mentioned as a terminus on a direct route to
Luanda, and when in 1880 Silva Porto arrived in Kuba country he found that
caravans of Imbangala and Ovimbundu had preceded him. Indeed, his decision the year before to go to Kuba country at the head of what was then the
largest caravan ever fitted out implies that he knew that the trade was large
and very profitable. We can conclude that by 1750 perhaps the Kuba were
drawn into the Luso-African trading zone and by the 1870s they were becoming an important link in the export of ivory.[83] Ivory was certainly the export
that grew most during this century. It went either to the Imbangala and from
there to the coast north of Luanda, or more directly to the Yaka and then via
the Zombo to the same harbors. Only after about 1836, when the ivory tax
was repealed in Luanda, would Kuba ivory have found its way to Luanda itself.

In return for it came salt and copper from Shaba and beads and cowries from Angola. Beads and cowries were reexported in part to the territory between the Sankuru and the Lokenye and even farther north, but not in raw form: they were sewn onto clothes, hats, or jewels at the capital, and these finished products were the main export, along with some copper, salt, and ordinary raffia cloth. Because of its position, the Kuba realm blocked any access from the south to the rich hunting grounds for elephants to the north.

The importation of "Pende" pottery from the south continued; by the 1880s the Kuba did not make any more pottery, if they ever had done so. The clays in Kuba country are not abundant and it was easier to import from the Sankuru-Lokenye area, from the Lulua, and from the area south of that river. How this trade developed could eventually be clarified if archaeological digging uncovers a number of sites. Trade in mats, baskets, foodstuffs, and other perishable products will probably never be properly documented.

Another trade route may be quite old as well. This ran from the Bushoong via the Shoowa to Ilebo, near the junction of the Kasai and the Sankuru, and from there along the lower Kasai to the Ding and their neighbors. Kuba tradition recalls only that the very special red cosmetic earth came from the Ding. But the use of a common word for "market" indicates that this was an artery of trade as well. It is even possible that in earlier centuries some of the copper products from the mines below the Malebo Pool trickled through as far as Kuba country. Again only archaeological work, and perhaps chemical analysis of the copper found or of copper objects in museums, will provide an answer. In any case, the lower Kasai below Ding country was no longer a continuous trade artery by 1865, if it ever had been one. In the other direction, upstream, the Sankuru was a highway of trade leading to Songye country. From the Ngongo villages Colobus monkey skins, lidded baskets, and even ducks were exported to the Songye or at least as far as the Isambo of Lusambo, who traded these farther and also raided almost to the confluence of the Mbujimai and the Lubilash. But the evidence for this route is also of a very late date.[84]

Trade with the Leele was much more varied. The Kuba exported copper, carved objects, costly cloth, razors, and ikul knives in return for very tightly woven cloth, drums, and carved objects.[85] Dugout canoes probably came from the riparians of the lower Kasai or the Sankuru. The Leele trade is an example not of direct long-distance trade in the nineteenth century but of the older regional networks, which flourished even more when long-distance trade increased. This is shown for instance in the export of copper by the Kuba to the Leele. Much of the Kuba trade with the Luba (Lulua) must be seen as a strengthened regional trade. Luba exports of amulets, pottery, and slaves were balanced by the imports of camwood, ivory, embroidered cloth, other cloth, mats, and perhaps smoked meat and smoked fish. Before the nineteenth century the volume of trade was perhaps not so remarkable, but trade did exist and was spurred on when long-distance commerce expanded. The modest regional and even local trade had prepared the ground for later expansion by establishing a network of exhange, a system of markets, and a form of currency. The trade maps reflect this.[86]

Without ivory, long-distance trade would not have flourished as much as it did. It is therefore not surprising to find a Kuba association, Itwiimy, formed by the elephant hunters, most of whom were specialists. Anyone who appreciates the risks involved in hunting elephants with spears can also appreciate the complex elaboration of protective charms and rituals that grew up around this enterprise. By the 1950s Itwiimy was a semi-secret association (if only because hunting elephants had been forbidden by the government) and had to some extent taken on the character of a classical religious movement. We do not know whether these characteristics were already developed in the nineteenth century. All we know is that toward the end of the century the association existed among the Kuba and their northern neighbors.[87] It is certainly not a coincidence that the organization developed at a time when the affluence of these societies was intimately linked with the export of ivory. Another effect of that demand could have been improvement in the position of the Cwa, professional hunters par excellence, but we have no evidence concerning this.

Just as ivory was crucial to long-distance trade, an analysis of products traded in regional or local networks shows that Bushoong luxury products—embroidered cloth, velvet cloth, jewelry, carvings, clothing stitched with cowries and beads—were the most important items traded.[88] Other groups within the realm exported mostly raw materials, salt, and pottery to the Bushoong capital and imported Bushoong luxuries. The luxury products were produced from these raw materials, brought to the capital as tribute or trade. The court provided the dynamics in the development of the whole system. Once the products existed they attracted traders, who brought new goods to be used as raw materials or to satisfy the needs of the general public for such items as pottery and salt.

The political leadership also played a dominant role in the creation and upkeep of marketplaces by providing the required peace and protection. In time some tribute collectors became "the king's traders," several hundred of whom went on annual expeditions to the Lokenye as late as 1893.[89] Not all of them were kolm; apparently a group of semi-professional or professional traders had developed as well. The sources clearly mention two sorts of ivory: one type that could only be sold by the king's traders, the other by private individuals. Presumably some officials (two were mentioned) and free traders also traveled south of the Lulua, where von Wissmann and Saturnino

Machado met them at Muketeba and at Kapuku.[90] There they traveled in small parties. A full caravan was reserved for trade around the Lokenye, probably because the security of traders was much less assured in the north. In the south no excessive risks were run by small parties: earlier in the nineteenth century, and perhaps even before, small groups went as far south as Mai Munene.

By 1880 the general affluence of the Kuba was built on their position as obligatory middlemen, a position that could only be held by military power. Even Silva Porto's caravan did not dare march toward the Sankuru to find cheap ivory. After the Kuba military collapse in 1899 this barrier was breached from time to time by Cokwe and Ovimbundu traders, thus proving the obvious: without a Kuba state and its deterrent force, the long-distance traders could have marched at least to the Sankuru, and the Kuba would not have been middlemen.[91]

Because of the peace that reigned in the country, the security of the markets, and the caravans sponsored by the "king's traders" for northern expeditions, individuals could also "target trade," usually for bridewealth, as different sources report.[92] This petty trade raised the income of the young villagers who practiced it and brought wealth to the villages, as indicated by the fact that in 1892 the annual basic tribute and bridewealth were both paid in cowries, a currency that had made the long journey from Angola.[93] Enough wealth was by then percolating down so that in the villages cowries ousted articles of longer standing. This fact shows that the income of the rural population and its standard of living, at least in the core areas, was rising. Considering the widespread impact that trade exerted and its importance by 1892, it is unfortunate to designate this type of economy a "peripheral market,"[94] even if it satisfied most criteria which theorists have attached to that label. For most of the Kuba market was no longer peripheral, and at the capital it had become a major source of income along with the proceeds from the collection of tribute.

The Kuba case shows clearly that surplus was triggered by political demand. Once the initial step was taken, a continuous interplay between both spheres obtained. It would be too extreme, however, to attribute even the details of the objects in demand to the political structure. If Kuba household goods were artistic, if their cups were carved, it was not because the elite willed it in a vacuum. Why then would the Leele, who did not have chiefs, exhibit a similar art? It is true that among the Leele, objects owned by the village, such as the dancing drums, were the best decorated, and the village was the sovereign political unit. But pipes and cups still belonged to individual elders. The difference is mainly that among the Kuba more classes of objects were carved or produced from more materials and that more families owned such objects. To that extent, and that extent only, the demand of the political elite can be cited as a cause. A comparison between Ngongo chiefly courts and the capital shows that while there was a difference in the number of types of objects, there was none in the quality of objects. The elite at the capital created a demand for more luxury objects and provided an incentive to diversify the production of those objects. In the same way the elite stimulated the growth of trade, but local and even regional trade antedated the rise of the elite.

Kuba history clearly is characterized by economic development. Agricultural potential increased dramatically, the social and technological division of labor became more and more pronounced, trade at all levels intensified, and at least one city, the capital, developed. A demographic increase, whether it resulted only from migration or also from a natural increase in the population, accompanied this growth. These are the factors that Michal Tymowski lists as criteria of genuine economic development. The Kuba economy was booming in the 1880s, and its development was not recent. Its dynamics extend well back into the seventeenth century.[95]

Chapter 11

White Porcelain Clay: Religion

To the Kuba white porcelain clay, kaolin, is the epitome of sacredness and of religion. The symbol must be very old, for it is shared by all the peoples of equatorial Africa. But how old? And how did its multiplex connotations change over time? We do not know. The problem posed by white porcelain clay is the paradigm of problems encountered by the student of the history of Kuba religion.

A full history of Kuba thought and emotion as expressed by the changes in their religion cannot be written now, and perhaps never will be.[1] Despite the pervasive role of religion in society, only scraps of data exist. Although there were religious specialists, collective representations (beliefs) and ritual practices are not remembered in the traditions except for the few cases that were institutionalized within the political system. Religious practice was so tied up with other institutions that it lacked sufficient autonomy and visibility to develop systematic traditions of its own. It is diffused throughout the society.[2] Furthermore, change in the representations and in the practice of ritual was so slow as often to be unconscious and hence could not be remembered. Where change was not so slow, the need to adhere to the new consensus effectively prevented development of traditions that would indicate what previous representations of ultimate reality might have been. Oral traditions are therefore sources that are not promising for intellectual history in general and religious history in particular except when they touch on the ideology of kingship. The data must be found in other sources or can only be deduced from archaic features embedded in traditions learned by rote.

Much of what we know is derived from interpretations gathered since 1892, especially by Sheppard, Torday, the Brown Edmiston dictionary of the 1920s, and my own research in the 1950s. We can sketch a picture of what Kuba religion was in the nineteenth century, and much of what follows necessarily applies only to that period. It would be tempting to argue that most of the religious attitudes and practices remained unaltered for many centuries. Religion would then belong to the realm of the "long term" described by Braudel. As a "system," religion would be one of the "deep structures." But we are not certain that Kuba religion formed a single "system" in the usual sense of the term.[3] We can state with some certainty that constellations of thought and collective attitudes toward ultimate reality did indeed exhibit great continuity over time,[4] judging from the facts that these constellations altered very little during the whole of the colonial period despite many extrinsic changes,[5] and that the "commissions" related to religious status and roles are still similar over large parts of Zaire.[6] Nevertheless, it is evident that changes did take place. Perhaps an analogy with Christianity can clarify this: although the fundamental attitudes toward ultimate reality manifested in Christianity did not change for many centuries, the history of Christianity both as a history of changing churches (autonomous institutions) and of changing thoughts and emotions (intellectual history) indicates change in almost every generation. In short, much of what follows is restricted to the nineteenth century, and this chapter is more descriptive than historical. I am convinced that a much fuller history of change in religion may never be written. The following discussion concerns the preternatural entities: divinations and oracles, charms and sacrifice, life-cycle rituals, religious movements, and rituals of state. The diachronic scraps of data that are available have been added to each of these.

During the Age of Chiefs proto-Kuba convictions underwent major changes. The cult of ancestors was lost when lineages became less important and genealogical recollection correspondingly less deep. It came to be held that peoples' ghosts, *mween,* lived another life after death, similar to life on earth, then died again to be reborn as human babies, *nshaang.*[7] This notion of metempsychosis took some time to be adopted. The term for reborn person, nshaang, stemmed from the Kete, as did the term used for ghost. It fitted well with the new kinship structure. Every alternating—i.e., second—generation saw the rebirth of a person who had lived some two generations before the baby was born. But a conviction carried over from earlier times that ghosts could harm the living by sending illness or death to avenge their own demise. Such calamities could only be countered by running naked through the village. This, at least it is said, was the remedy a famous magician had found to cope with such occurrences when the Kuba were still at Iyool.[8] After a while that ritual was lost and people lost their power to control ghosts. Nevertheless, in recent times Ngeende women still occasionally ran around naked after the death of their husbands to avert harm to themselves. No doubt the ritual fell into disuse because the representations of ghosts altered. In more recent times, mween could come to the living in dreams but to help rather than threaten. At some point the notion also developed that after mween had died in their extraterrestrial life they first were reborn as an animal, or could be reborn as an animal; the informants are not certain. If reborn as an animal, a person would become a leopard or a crocodile; only when the animals died would they be reborn as people. This may have been an elaboration linked to the local conviction that sorcerers could transform themselves into leopards or crocodiles. An old notion was that the deceased went to live in *ilweemy*, the extraterrestrial world. The term may be identical with the one used for the ritual specialist in war, which during the Age of Chiefs probably was still used for the ritual specialist in charge of defending the village.

In the 1920s and perhaps later the Kuba also kept the notion of *nkady*, glossed by Brown Edmiston as "magical charm supposed to cause death, an apparition or being or ghost that can appear at will or at any time or place." This was the last trace of the southern Mongo conviction that certain spirits, the *bokali*, especially those of witches, roamed the world searching to harm people. The Leele as well as the Mbuun also retained this conviction.[9] To the Leele their *nkadi* was the familiar sorcerer who had withdrawn his victims from the cycle of reincarnation to make them his familiars in the form of carnivorous animals. This fits in with the rather inchoate Kuba statements of the 1950s about some people being reborn as animals.

The forebears of the Kuba were convinced that these were spirits, and some of these may have been nature spirits. During the Age of Chiefs, Mboom and Ngaan were considered the two creators. Possibly Mboom was historically older, because in later times his name was the equivalent of supreme deity among the other Mongo. Ngaan was master of the waters, and a cult was established for him by the mbyeemy, who was the ritualist of the chieftainship of the Bushoong at that time. The mbyeemy's duty was to offer the hallowed white, yellow, and red substances to Ngaan in order to avert calamity.[10] The beings Kop aNgaan and Nyony aNgaan—the Siamese twins without articulations—were seen as responsible for fate. Kop aNgaan was a nature spirit who lived in the sun and was identified first as the Bushoong ethnic spirit and later with the king himself.

During the Age of Kings the Kuba accepted the name Ncyeem apoong for the creator, a term derived directly from the Kikongo name Nzambi Mpungu. Given its distribution this development presumably occurred only after the trade route with Okanga had been opened, and the spread of the name may be linked to the presence of a mission station at Okanga.[11] The name appears in various praise names or songs linked to the kings. We cannot state exactly when the concept was introduced or what the term specifically referred to. What changes did occur in the collective representations of Mboom, Ncyeem, or Ngaan? Even in 1953 it was not possible to make out whether Mboom and Ncyeem were synonyms or not. In daily usage Ncyeem prevailed, but missionary activity had since 1892 used this term. The only certainty is that an evolution in the concepts must have taken place, since the connotations of Ncyeem overlapped with those of Mboom. It is therefore not possible to pursue the hypothesis that with the consolidation of the kingdom a corresponding strengthening of the notion of creator and supreme deity occurred, and that other spirits became subordinated to it.[12] The dedication to Ncyeem of a ritual site, the *nkiin,* on each village plaza is, however, clearly a sign that in this ritual at least the local nature spirits were displaced by the supreme deity. We cannot tell when this happened. It was precolonial and may date from the eighteenth century, when the regional spirit cults were abolished by Mbop Pelyeeng aNce [9].

When the forebears of the Kuba arrived in Kete country they found that some springs, rivers, and even gallery forests were said to be the abode of ngesh, nature spirits, whom the autochthonous Kete revered. The notion was probably not foreign to the newcomers, since throughout the Mongo world such nature spirits are recognized. The newcomers accepted the Kete views and began to worship the ngesh. Soon dances and even a mask of Kete origin were linked to this cult. Some Kuba women became priestesses of the ngesh. In later times the pattern of vocation was clear: a young women fell ill, ran away in the forest, behaved erratically for a while, and eventually emerged as both the medium of the ngesh and its priestess.[13] Whether or not the first priestesses were drawn into their vocation in the same way is unknown. In time almost every village found that it possessed a ngesh on its domain and in most villages there was a priestess to serve it. Concepts about nature spirits had merged with concepts about the territory of village domains. Such ngesh had to be propitiated because they could visit calamities on the village. The priestesses could learn in trance why the spirit was angry and how to please it by ordering new dances or new songs to be performed for it. As they were for other Kuba religious practitioners, dreams were very important in this regard.

Most, but not all, villages had ngesh priestesses in the 1950s. Every village had one or more ngesh spirits, which were thought to control all fertility, and the villagers were anxious to know where they stood in relationship to their spirit at all times. The village ritual gardens may have been dedicated to them before they were claimed for Ncyeem. A good way of knowing how the ngesh related to the village was provided by the success of the communal hunt. This technique is so widespread among the southern Mongo, Leele, and others that it may be presumed to be old—older perhaps than the appearance of ngesh priestesses.[14] If the ngesh was satisfied with the behavior of the villagers the hunt would be excellent, especially if warthogs were captured; if not, the hunt would be fruitless. In the latter case the ngesh priestess was supposed to find out why, and where there was no priestess divination was conducted. For as the nature spirits came to occupy a more central place in the perception of the preternatural, and as the ancestor cult declined and disappeared, divination came under the spirits' aegis. The rubbing oracle, described below, was carved in the shape of the ngesh itself (ngesh were male or female and had names) or in the shape of its animal, the warthog, in the shape of a crocodile, an incarnation of ngesh, or in the shape of a dog, who can perceive what humans cannot because of his sense of smell.[15]

At one time it was held that there were spirits ruling over larger areas; these were the spirits of whole ethnic groups. They were "killed" by King Mbop Pelyeeng aNce,[16] and by the colonial period no ritual was offered to them nor do the Kuba seem to have preserved them as spirits. Such "national" spirits were supposed to have lived in the sun—some were in the sun when it rose, others in the sun at high noon, and still others in the sun at dusk. Apparently by 1892 this was no longer maintained.[17] Perhaps the spirits of ethnic groups had been so tied to the sun that when the spirits disappeared in the late eighteenth century the conviction waned that there were any spirits at all in the sun. At some time even the old name for the sun was dropped and the present name was adopted from Kikongo. Since the term also refers to the notion of time, perhaps the conception of time altered during the Age of Kings and brought this change with it.

Divination and the use of oracles go back to the time when the forebears of the Kuba lived north of the Sankuru. No doubt the Kete also used both these techniques, since the rubbing oracle was of Kete origin. During the Age of Chiefs, the ilweemy continued to be the village religious specialist whose task was to ward off all outside natural or preternatural attacks on the village. How these specialists viewed the rise of the ngesh priestesses, who were after all competing with them for the obedience of the villagers, remains unknown. All we know is that a division of specialties arose and that ilweemy specialized in the defense of the village against outside attack and perhaps played a role in the detection of witches. During the Age of Kings the term came to be reserved for war magicians at the court, the most famous of whom have been remembered.[18] A new term, *ngwoom,* originally from the Kwilu area, replaced ilweemy as "general diviner."

The need for diviners arose from the belief that most calamities that befell individuals, as opposed to groups, stemmed from the actions of witches or sorcerers. The conviction that some persons could bewitch others without any material means is very old; indeed, the term used for witches is Common Bantu. Sorcerers used material means to harm their victims, who had no kinship relation to them. In the nineteenth century sorcery was practiced most often among political competitors, whereas witches harmed either close kin or at least coresidents. The term for witch later included sorcerers, but earlier, especially during the Age of Chiefs, a special term may have been used for sorcery. The fact that it was lost is historical change that implies more than just the loss of a word: it implies a rearrangement of categories. Witches and sorcerers came to be almost identified, and the oracles could uncover either by using the same techniques.

The forebears of the Kuba used divination, as the term bukaang (oracle) indicates. But at some later time the techniques changed so much that a new term, *apoom,* meaning "to divine," appeared. At least one major new oracle, the rubbing oracle, *itoom,* was taken from the Kete. A small piece of wood was rubbed on the flat back of a statuette while questions were asked, and when the wood stuck to the back of the statuette, a diagnosis of the preternatural situation could be made. The oracle was used for finding witches and later also for many questions where witchcraft was not involved, such as theft or adultery.[19]

The main test to detect witches was the poison ordeal. We know that it is older than the Age of Kings, since *ipweemy,* the main term connected with it, has a connection with the Mongo area. The preliminary test preceding the ordeal was to cut a piece of bark from the ipweemy tree and determine by the way it fell a yes-or-no answer to the question of whether the suspect might be a witch. The ordeal itself consisted in giving poison extracted from the tree to the suspected witch. The ritual involved was quite complex, and in some ways the accused witch was treated almost as a sacrificial offering.[20] If the accused survived, she or he was innocent and compensation had to be paid. Death was the sign of guilt and the body was burned to prevent rebirth. By 1892 the poison ordeal was frequently used and most of the accused were women. In theory a court official, the nyim sheky, supervised the ordeal, but probably he only did so at the capital, since cases were settled in villages as well. Or perhaps any diviner who prepared the poison was known by this title.[21] It is noteworthy that sorcerers were not subjected to this kind of test. Sorcery was instead fought by countersorcery and the use of charms. The frequency of the poison ordeals certainly varied over time from the Age of Chiefs, but there are no data relating to this, just as there are no data telling us what changing views were held about the sorts of calamities to attribute to witchcraft, to the anger of ngesh, and, if any, to other causes. Even data about the internal evolution of the ritual surrounding the ordeal are lacking. The elaboration indicates that invocations, songs, and ritual episodes were certainly added during the last centuries, but no one knows exactly what, or when, or in what order.

The notion of charm, *nnyeeng,* is also basic to Kuba religion. Yet the term is an innovation that does not go back before the Age of Chiefs. It means charm or medicine and could be linked to a verb, **aneengy,* "to strengthen, to encourage."[22] In 1892 charms and amulets to protect against other charms were ubiquitous among the Kuba, but we know nothing about their history, or what the main types of charms were, or about the trade in charms, the fashions in charms, the ideas and feelings associated with them, etc. Probably a connection exists between the notion of charm and the specific notion of pollution, *nyec.* This term is also an innovation. Charms were always associated

*Indicates not attested.

with some ritual, and many were communal.[23] The village ritual site, the *nkiin*, with its tiny garden for Ncyeem, also contained communal charms for the village and this term, and probably the practice as well, went back to the proto-Kuba. The medicine men who made these charms were also diviners and healers. The old Mongo term for such persons *(kaang)* disappeared completely, as did the Kete equivalent. Ngwoom ousted all other terms. This implies that during the Age of Kings charms brought from the Kwilu proved so effective that they replaced most of the previous types, since, as we have seen, the divination practices are probably older than this period. But most individual charms and amulets had disappeared from public view by the time I did my fieldwork, and some of the techniques used by medicine men were then clearly linked to Zappo Zap magic introduced after 1892 or to Cokwe practices, which may not be very old. Consequently we lack even enough data to make comparison with areas around the Kuba.

The situation is even worse with regard to sacrifice. We know from sources of 1892 and before 1930 that sacrifices were made in the royal compound and that they involved goats, lambs, and fowl. But no one recorded any ritual connected with these and no special vocabulary seems to have existed; at least none was recorded.[24] This leaves out an important dimension of Kuba religious practice, and it does not console us much to hear in the 1950s that sacrifice was not remembered as a Kuba custom: it was then considered a foreign practice. Yet the tale in which the diviner sacrificed a fowl to help Shyaam,[25] even if anachronistic, shows that it was not foreign in the nineteenth century, since by then the tale was current.

The same difficulty arises when we come to a discussion of religious reform movements. All we know is that they did exist before 1892 in an area that had not yet been touched by the colonial situation.[26] They can be presumed to be older than the colonial period, but no evidence from that time has survived. We know that in the colonial era they included the teachings of a prophet, who was inspired during an initial retreat or in dreams, and that they involved rituals of joining the community, communing with each other, accepting a charm together, and cleansing the community of all witchcraft and sorcery. Religious movements restored harmony to disturbed villages without the need of resorting to massive poison ordeals. They were spread from settlement to settlement by people from villages which were not yet initiated who came to ask for the central charm, the songs, and the ritual. Not all villages in an area would accept a new movement; those that did might adhere to one for long periods of time, perhaps longer than half a century. The charm was put into the nkiin garden with other charms, and no traditions have preserved information about this activity. The absence of information is probably due to the fact that most villages accepted new movements during the colonial period and that in such a case the collective memory concerning earlier movements, now displaced and even outlawed by the new movement, rapidly faded. None were recorded before 1909, perhaps because the Presbyterian and Catholic missionaries were themselves introducing a new religious movement: Christianity.

All that can be said about these movements in the precolonial period is that they did not lead to major clashes between political authorities and prophets. Perhaps the names of famous magicians such as Tooml aKwey, usually considered an ilweemy or war magician of Kot aNce [7], were those of important prophets coopted by the dynastic traditions. Perhaps even Shyaam attracted support at first by being a prophet. There is no way to check these conjectures.

When one turns to an examination of the rituals for crisis situations, such as healing, or the rituals applied to recurrent situations, such as rites of passage, especially puberty rites and funerals, where we know that some ritual complexity existed, there is little the historian can say. Yes, Mboong aLeeng [2] is said to have introduced the boys' initiation,[27] but this probably constitutes in part a descending anachronism, since some form of initiation may have been older than this king, who merely reformed parts of the ritual. Some ascending anachronisms are certainly involved: the ritual as recorded in 1908 and 1953 includes accretions of a date later than this king. The term for initiation itself, *nkaan,* is of Lunda or Pende origin, and some of the masks, as well as a number of expressions and songs, are Kete. Prototypes must be sought south of Kuba country, in the Kete area near the Pende, in the general vicinity of Mai Munene. Some elements there were of Lunda origin. This explains such masks as *kaloongaloong,* which is Pende or Lunda Kalunga, and such expressions as *katuum aLeesh,* which corresponds to the Kete word *Katumbaleza* and perhaps to the Lunda *Katuumba Leza,* "the glory of the creator."

These borrowings do not necessarily mean that the entire initiation was borrowed from the Kete, who received it from the Lunda or the Pende, nor that this all occurred during the reign of Mboong aLeeng. It simply shows that by 1908 initiation in the southern parts of the kingdom was strongly influenced and that this influence may or may not have originated in one wave at some time in the past. It is more likely to have seeped through over a long period. Perhaps the innovations followed the trade route from the Pende from the eighteenth century. I believe that Mboong aLeeng's innovation consisted simply in requiring the youths of matoon villages to be initiated at the capital and to remain there for about a year afterward. This may be the source of the story about the hardships of initiation that drove some of the Binji out of the kingdom.[28] It is not at all clear that the boys' initiation as practiced in the northeast and east of the kingdom was similar to that of the Bushoong.

The myth explaining why the initiation exists tells us that when Woot once lay drunk, naked, and helpless on the ground, his sons mocked him but his daughter, walking backward came and covered him. He decided to punish his sons by having them undergo initiation and by instituting matrilinearity. Parts of this story are acted out in the ritual. The tale clearly is the Noah myth or, as de Heusch labeled it, the myth of the drunken king. It could be of Lunda origin, but on balance it is more likely to be of Western origin. Travelers from the kingdom of Kongo via Okanga may have told the Noah story, having learned it themselves from Christians or missionaries.[29] The interesting point is that the Kuba adopted it when they had not yet forgotten that once they had been patrilineal and thus presumably they learned this myth not long after the Age of Kings had begun, probably still in the seventeenth century. One could claim that the Luba practice of patrilinearity could account for the myth after the Kuba had forgotten that they too had once been matrilineal. But the latter line of reasoning seems to me less convincing than the former.

It is quite likely that, despite the great interest of the historian in learning the *sequence* of changes in the initiation rituals, songs, and practices, they will never be known. It may never be possible to reconstruct the ritual as it occurred even in the late nineteenth century. Significant differences exist between the account of 1908 (which probably went back to an initiation in 1898 or before) and the 1953 account, and not all of these can confidently be ascribed to faulty memory or fabrication. Some represent genuine differences in the manners of initiating boys at the capital and in the villages, but a few represent actual changes which occurred between 1898 at the capital and 1953 in the villages. Within a ritual sequence such as initiation, innovation was not discouraged, and except for the major sequence of ritual "episodes," changes would occur almost imperceptibly. Even when change was perceptible, no traditions chose to single it out and commit it to memory.[30]

Even less well documented are the funeral ceremonies, and marriage ceremonies are known in only the barest of outlines in 1892, when they were apparently more important than in 1953.[31] For all of these rites of passage, just as for the crisis rituals, no history can be recorded. The reinforcement of collective representations, the exposition of moral norms, the teachings about cosmology, and the value system which were involved in these rituals are all gone. We cannot trace any of their histories. All we know about Bushoong funerals is that human sacrifice connected with them increased sometime before 1893. The Kete sacrificed only goats; this may have been the former Bushoong practice as well.[32] The hope of finding out very much concerning the intellectual history of the Kuba is also forlorn.

Insofar as charms and rituals and representations touched on kingship, some data have been saved. The ideology of chieftainship and later kingship was inevitably tied up with the dominant ideology, which was that of religion. During the Age of Chiefs, the power of chiefs was attributed both to charms and to a choice made by the nature spirits. The charms were stored in a special house, a practice abandoned at the court perhaps only after 1892.[33] Objects that were important for kingship were also kept in a separate house, in which the dynastic drum—dating at the latest from the eighteenth century—and the dynastic statues were kept.[34] In other special houses in or near the palace, other emblems were kept, including the round drum called *kwey abol* or the drum named *pel ambish*. The oldest royal charm according to tradition was Inam, connected with crocodiles, Lake But aPoong, and Woot. It was also linked with powerful ngesh who, it was thought, ruled over the whole territory of the Bushoong. Similar spirits held sway over the lands of the Pyaang, the Ngeende, the Kel, and the Leele of the Ibo region, in Bushoong territory.[35]

The most important hoard of charms was kept by the muyum in the forest near But aPoong. His shrine included the skull attributed to Lashyaang [E], a kaolin egg which could kill any tyrant king and was attributed to the reign of Mboong aLeeng [2], the remnants of a huge iron double bell—the bell of Woot—and a paddle on which the ethnic markings of all ethnic groups within the kingdom were carved. The engravings on the paddle presumably are not older than the constitution of the kingdom and thus do not antedate the Age of Kings, but the bell of Woot and the lump of kaolin probably do. Both are similar to the objects kept by the Yajima in the shrine called Itoci.[36] They may have been the first objects, resembling those kept in many other shrines for many other chiefs, whereas the skull, the egg, and the paddle came later. Perhaps some elements of the original shrine of the muyum during the Age of Chiefs have been lost. He was at that time very likely considered the "lord of the land," whose blessing was necessary for its fruitfulness. None of the charms preserved by him indicates this, unless it is the skull, to which prayers were addressed.

The ritual involving mbyeemy's offering of colored substances to the river of Ngaan has been mentioned. This was abandoned at an unknown later time. Why? We do not know. Ngaan became relatively unimportant, even though the kings in their praise names identified with Kop aNgaan, the Siamese twin of fate and the spirit that "represented" the Bushoong, and even though Buloom aNgaan, "the wisdom of Ngaan," was the collective name for their capitals.[37] The connection between Ngaan and the Bushoong chiefs may have been close, but during the Age of Kings it was lost, probably to be replaced by the connection between Ncyeem and the king. During the same period mbyeemy was assisted by a new colleague, pok ibaan, "their pot," who made, or perhaps bought, charms to protect the king and kingship, charms which were apparently no longer linked to any ngesh. By the time his office was created, the notion of charms that had no relation to spirits had apparently been well developed. By the late nineteenth century no charms except those in the village shrines were linked with any ngesh.

Kingship and before it chieftainship was tied not only to charms. The true legitimation of the first Bushoong chief came at Iyool, *after* his hammer had floated, the water had become colored, and the trees had bent when the crocodile appeared with Mboong [C] on his back, riding out to the middle of the lake to show that he was the chosen one. These "miracles" are in the tradition of the southwestern Mongo means for legitimizing a newly elected kum.[38] In the tale of the hammers and the anvils the miracles refer to Mongo values. They imply that a chief rules because a nature spirit for a whole area has accepted him. This spirit for the Bushoong was Kop aNgaan.

Shyaam altered this ideology. According to tradition he was a medicine man or a diviner who won the kingdom by clever use of magic. Like a ngesh priestess he was ill, "insane," for some time, and while in this state invented the songs for the ngesh and claimed to be a ngesh. Once he climbed a palm tree (the oil palm bears his name, *Shyaam*) feet first and exclaimed: "Why, if I am not a ngesh would I [thus] climb a palm tree?" He had to be cured by magic, but he remained ngesh. And because he was such a great shaman he remained sterile.[39] The reader is aware that these traditions represent the ideal medicine man–king and have been probably much embellished, altered, and streamlined since his lifetime, but the major point remains: the tradition attributes behavior to him as if he was a medium, a ngesh priest. Because of the confusion inherent in the term ngesh, which can mean a spirit or its servant, we do not know what the early traditions told. Perhaps they only implied that the king was the medium of the spirit of the Bushoong. But as the power of kings grew, they came to be seen as spirits themselves. Their legitimation no longer came from a ngesh but from God, now called Ncyeem, as in the poem

> My eagle is the eagle of the ngesh of the forest,
> My kingship stems from Nyony aMboom.
> It is Ncyeem who gave this kingship into my hands.[40]

The kings were called *Ncyeem nkwoonc*, "God on earth." The title dates from the Age of Kings because it includes the term Ncyeem. Nkwoonc, now translated as "riverbank, hill, earth," is perhaps the old term for leader, *bokonzi*.[41] The expression may have once meant "the God of the leaders."

As early as Mbakam Mbomancyeel [4] the king claimed to be identical with Kop aNgaan,[42] and the praise name of Kot aNce [7] refers to this identification with the "national" spirit of the Bushoong:

> Kop aNgaan, the circles of Kop,
> Nyony aNgaan, the circles of Nyony,
> They and the members of their clan speak the same word.[43]

The identification is perhaps not yet complete in this praise name, for it claims only that the king is "related" to the spirits and that his word has the power of fate behind it. A generation later Mbo Pelyeeng aNce [9] exclaimed

"I am not a spirit, yet I dug a pond,"[44] perhaps implying that he was one, perhaps stressing that he was not. In any case it is this king who abolished the cult of the ethnic spirits, including the Bushoong spirits, perhaps by performing a ritual that annihilated them. After him there is no doubt that the kings were considered to be nature spirits or ngesh. A century later it was clear to all that kings were no longer reborn but after death became spirits. With Mbo Pelyeeng a new ancestor cult may have begun, one restricted to the ancestors of kings, who had been kings themselves and then became spirits. The invention of dynastic statues, which express this notion and this cult, may go back to his reign; it certainly went back at least to the beginning of the nineteenth century.[45] In the end, then, a king was legitimized because he had been chosen by Ncyeem and because he became a spirit when assuming office. For this reason we can speculate that the notion of Ncyeem itself as the creator and supreme deity developed along with the notion of kingship. We will never be able to prove it, but the argument is rather plausible.

Apart from the royal funerals and enthronements, by 1892 the main rituals of kingship (described by Sheppard) occurred monthly, at the time of the new moon. The king offered a sacrifice of a goat or a lamb and sprinkled the blood on a large idol kept in his own charm house, in the presence of his "councillors," perhaps meaning the senior members of ishyaaml. A secret rite performed by the ngwoom incyaam also took place. The sacrifice was made for the well-being of the king's country.[46] The large idol has so far not been found, but this does not invalidate Sheppard's testimony. If one of the ngwoom incyaam died during the period of the new moon (three days) he was buried like a chief.[47] The king's "sister" kept certain charms associate with the moon (perhaps the idol?) and could not go out during the period of the new moon without covering her head.[48] Other prohibitions were probably enforced.

The moon was undoubtedly associated with the fertility of the earth. I was told in 1953 that during a new moon "a woman cannot bear a child nor can a man die." King and moon possessed the same powers, and the cemetery for the members of the royal lineage was called "the repose of the moon." The association between moon and fertility is in fact widespread in Central Africa, and I take it to be quite old.[49] The myth that explained the ritual of the new moon may not have been as old as the association of fertility with the moon: Woot, it is said, lost his way for nine days, when there was a new moon; when he returned the moon rose in the sky.

Whether it was because of his charms or because of his being a spirit, the king was credited with extranatural powers. He could send storms or tornadoes and could ward off attacks by witches against his capital, as is shown by his mastery over lightning, thought to be an animal. He protected the fertility of villages by throwing white porcelain clay in the air and reciting a formula, but he could also withdraw his protection.[50] A whole set of avoidances—negative ritual—was linked to his powers. These were acts to preserve the fertility of the land. A king could not walk for long, sit on the bare ground, cross a field, eat in front of his wives, cross the Kasai River, or look at tombs, corpses, or wounds.[51] A transgression of any of these, and of certain other prohibitions, made the people think that "the ground would be burned." By the same token the king's saliva was blessed. Hence Shyaam in the dynastic tales needed to be spat upon by the king to succeed to the throne. He was addressed as the "head and the fingernails," because hair and nails continue to grow after death. When he sneezed he was applauded. All of this expressed the vitality of the king and thereby of the country. The exact avoidances, images, and even rituals certainly varied over the centuries, but we can conclude that some element of sacredness was attached to kingship and even to chieftainship before Shyaam. As to the different interpretations about the reason for the sacred nature of kingship, there is a dispute which may be quite old. The Kuba skeptics claimed that it stemmed from the fact that the king as the richest person commanded the best charms, while the more mystically inclined attributed it to a quality inherent in kingship.[52] Both of these, it has been seen, were present in the makeup of kingship.

Over and above this, one can speculate about the relationship of the king to the creator. Was he a divine king? The most that the ruling king claimed in 1953 was that he was the lieutenant of God, implied in the title "God on earth." But there was more: the king also claimed to be polluted, and the Bushoong took him to be an archsorcerer.[53] These convictions were not new; they added to the power of the monarch. A ritual performed at the burial of important kolm testifies to the relative antiquity of these representations. This ritual, the nkolakol, aims at showing that the king was not to be held responsible for the death of the kolm. As has been described earlier, its origin is ascribed to Shyaam.[54] In some of its implements—such as the signal drum used—the ritual shows Nkucu elements that may not be as old as Shyaam, and it certainly underwent an evolution in the course of time. Even if it does not reach back to the days of Shyaam, its presence in the cycle of tales attributed to him indicates a certain antiquity. It was certainly practiced in the nineteenth century, and I believe also in the previous century, and therefore the connection between royal power and the power of a sorcerer is equally old.

As this chapter shows, little can be retrieved concerning religious history and indeed the whole intellectual history of the Kuba. The historian must face the implications of this. We can only guess at the kind of motives that drove Kuba leaders and followers to action, and we must realize that we are groping for shadowy patterns in the absence of evidence about personalities. Our reconstructions present use with a stage and the sets for the play, but the actors remain invisible. Now and then objects on the stage move and we infer that something like the force of gravity or magnetic attraction propels them, because the actors and their motives remain hidden. We give labels to those forces, but most expressions of past thought and custom which would lead to a genuine understanding are lacking.

The situation is not peculiar to the Kuba: it is the state of much of the precolonial history of Africa. And I must draw attention to this debility of our reconstructions. I have arrayed the little we have to go on, in the case of the subject of this chapter. Perhaps no one will be able to go much further, although analysis of a large corpus of oral literature does at least allow us to approximate the thoughts and feelings of the actors in the later nineteenth century. But in the end this particular lack of knowledge will remain a weakness in early African history. And we need to be reminded of that whenever we contemplate trends that are the product of ignorance about both a multitude of events and the motives behind the actions.

Chapter 12

Shapes in the Past:
The Visual Arts

No introduction to the visual arts of Africa omits the Kuba, for theirs is no doubt one of the great artistic traditions on the continent. The reputation of Kuba sculpture derives both from the aesthetic qualities of a set of master-pieces, the dynastic statues, *ndop,* carved for kings, and from the fact that the Kuba lavished their creative talents on nearly all objects used in their culture. The versatility in treatment of volumes, the skeuomorphic tendencies, and the quality of the patina are the characteristics most cited. In the decorative arts the Kuba position is unique: their art exhibits the greatest variety of decorative patterns found south of the Sahara. Over two hundred such patterns have been distinguished and named. The general public best knows the patterns from their presence on raffia textiles, where they are either embroidered or exe-cuted as a pile cloth not unlike velvet, a technique which at the end of the nineteenth century was found only among the Kuba.

A comprehensive art history cannot yet be written. Thousands of Kuba art objects have found their way into museums or private collections since the early years of this century. The three great early collections are those of Sheppard (1892), Frobenius (1905), and Torday (1908). It is astonishing to note that, despite its reputation, so few scholarly studies have been devoted to this art. Catalogs of the three major collections mentioned have not been published, nor has a systematic examination of the printed or photographic record been made, nor have archival materials, which would allow us more accurately to locate the origin of the objects in time and space, been investi-gated. Not even the unraveling of the different ateliers of carving has yet been undertaken. An analysis of the woods used for carving dates only from recent years, and no further attempts have been made to examine the physical prop-erties of the objects. There are no studies concerning the exact composition of metals employed. Some objects are still labeled as zinc although this is highly unlikely, given the complex metallurgy of that metal, which is recovered in a gaseous form. In short, despite an abundance of data and of interest in the objects, they have not been thoroughly studied.[1]

It is therefore not surprising that none of the possible physical clues as to the antiquity of certain objects has been examined. Certainly a large part of the objects in the early collections dates from the last century and testifies to the situation and the traditions of that entire century. But some objects should be and can be older. The notion that tropical wood decays quickly even when the object is well cared for has not been substantiated. In the collections there may be early objects, especially among those that came from the royal court. Sheppard claimed that one ikul knife dated "seven generations" back.[2] If this is true it would go back to the seventeenth century, and in any case it could easily be eighteenth-century work. At least one royal statue is claimed to go back to the seventeenth century, and in a set of royal drums kept until 1969 at the capital two are claimed to be of the eighteenth century.[3] There are enough indications to allow us at least to sketch an outline of Kuba history in the visual arts.

In the southern part of the country, during the nineteenth century, the Kete carved anthropomorphic poles with single or with Janus-like heads as charms to protect their villages.[4] The Janus-like features were connected to Kalunga, a spirit also found among their southern neighbors. A forerunner of such pole statues was first reported by Desmond Clark during excavations in northern Angola and dates from the first millennium. Despite erosion, it clearly is stylistically related to the Kete objects, as it is to some Pende objects of the middle Kasai, between Angola and the Kete. It can therefore be assumed that this style existed during the entire period covered by this book.[5] The working hypothesis best supported by the present data is that the proto-Kuba did not carve statues or masks but that the Kete did. The large statues used in the late nineteenth century by the central Kuba were mainly female figures employed during the boys' initiation, and these, like many of their features, could be of Kete origin. One "large idol" reported by Sheppard from the capital[6] has unfortunately been lost and remains undescribed.

In the southern part of the country little figurines, the *nnoon*, which have a pointed end permitting them to be stuck in the soil, were fairly common. The details of their style make them akin to the better-known dynastic statues, but they did not play similar roles nor is the overall treatment of volumes at all similar. In some ways they resemble the Lulua carvings of ancestral figurines of the same size. The area where nnoon were found borders on Lulua country, where similar statuettes were regarded as ancestral figurines. The Kuba pieces I saw *in situ*, however, were not perceived as such nor given any real function. They may even have been imported from the Lulua along with the "amulets" sold to the Kuba by the Lulua.

These data therefore support a conclusion drawn from the name *iping*, "statue," which is a borrowing from Kete or Luba. Yet there were other statues in different styles. One, a rough functional style, included not only girls' dolls but statuettes linked with religious movements of the twentieth century, though these could be older since their name, *ishak ndweemy*, is of

Mongo derivation. This suggests that the forebears of the Kuba might have carved charms in human form. There were larger statues connected with chieftainship, very few of which are known. In the southeast they were usually fashioned in the general shape of the dynastic statues of kings, whereas in the northwest, among the Shoowa, the style, while unmistakenly Kuba, was different, being closer to the style of drinking cups than to that of statues. The Shoọwa had one such statue, called *mwana,* in each chiefdom, where it may have represented a nature spirit of the chiefdom. Frobenius brought back from the northeast at least one statue that perhaps fulfilled a similar role and which is carved in the same tradition.[7] But this one could possibly be linked with the initiation practices of the northeast, practices which are still not described today.

Sheppard reported that he saw four statues of kings, all of which we know are now in museums.[8] One had a board game as its emblem and represented Shyaam [1], another had an anvil before it and is linked to Mbop Pelyeeng aNce [9]. Of the four others that are in museums, we do not know which are the two he saw. They probably were the ones with drums standing before them, which found their way into museums before 1913.[9] Such statues were considered to be the doubles of the kings they represented and as such were revered if not actually regarded as sacred. In theory only one was carved for each king, and when Torday collected four of them he gathered the name of the king with the statue. He does not mention the name attached to the fifth statue. That may have been the one given soon afterwards to the visiting Belgian minister, Jules Renkin, and which is the MboMboosh [3] statue now in the Brooklyn Museum. These five statues and that of Mbop Kyeen [16] all form one set within the general style. Were traditions taken literally, the statues of Shyaam and MboMboosh belong to the seventeenth century and three belong to the latter part of the eighteenth century and the beginning of the last century. Why Sheppard saw only four and not the five that Torday later encountered, or the seven which are known to have come from the capital between 1908 and 1913, and why many kings are not credited with a statue, including for instance Mbop Mabiinc maMbul [12], who died in 1885 or 1886 after a long reign, remains unexplained if we accept the traditional attributions and chronology. The dynastic statues have been the subject of much speculation. Like most other Kuba objects except masks, they are carved out of *Crossopterix febrifuga* (iloonc) wood, the most suitable for carving in this environment.[10] Only one has been tested to verify this, however, and it could be that some of the others were not carved in this medium. Opinions about them have varied from taking the traditions at their face value to the suggestion that one artist carved all of them—and, as one art historian jokingly (but only in part) told me, out of one block of wood. A recent study by Jean Rosenwald[11] suggests that the ndop were not created until the reign of

Mbo Pelyeeng aNce [9], who killed the ethnic ngesh. The one for Shyaam would then have been carved by the same artist who created one for Mbo Pelyeeng. The only problem here is that MishaaPelyeeng aNce [8] ruled *before* his brother and yet a statue is ascribed to him. The idea of carving the statues belongs to the same inspiration that promoted the sacredness of kings and demoted ethnic ngesh. And the statue for MishaaPelyeeng aNce [8] was certainly made either by the same hand or at least in the same atelier. On stylistic grounds Rosenwald proposes that the four statues collected by Torday and the one of MboMboosh [3] were by the same hand, and that of Miko miMbul[11] and a statue of Mbop Kyeen [16], who ruled in 1900, belong to another master; these seven are more closely related to each other than to later works. A close examination of the sculptures with regard to hairline, eyebrows, nostrils, lips, ears, nipples, eyes, collarbones, thighs, navels, and decorations substantiates her account in my view, and the distinctions between two carvers seem apparent, although the overall similarities among the seven do indeed outweigh the differences.

The main problems deal with the attribution to kings of two of the statues whose emblems are drums: the one to Mbop Kyeen, who ruled for perhaps only three months,[12] and the one assigned to MboMboosh. Given the stylistic affinity, the first one could be seen as a statue of Mbop Mabiinc maMbul [12], who succeeded Miko miMbul, to whose statue this one is most closely related. The statue ascribed to MboMboosh is linked so closely to the main group that it would be much more satisfactory to postulate that it was carved during the same period. It therefore could be one carved for Kot aNce [7]. In that case the practice of carving ndop would have begun two reigns earlier than the proposal of Rosenwald and can be estimated as beginning in the mid-eighteenth century. The differences observed in the statue ascribed to Shyaam are related to insignia of rank, which is to be expected from the founder of a dynasty. The first king of the line *should* be differentiated by the greater number of rows of cowries of his bandolier and should have an additional set of arm rings, especially if the statue was made long after his death to justify the practice of carving ndop. I believe then that we have one statue per king from the mid-eighteenth century to 1886. The civil war and subsequent turmoil could explain why no statues were made subsequently, although one would expect one for Kot aMbweeky II [14], who died in 1896. If the MboMboosh statue had stylistic characteristics aligning it with the set of Miko miMbul [11], this would probably have been the king to associate it with.[13]

So we are left with two ateliers, or perhaps, if the reasoning about individuality of style is pushed to its extreme, only two pairs of hands. Later statues are attributed to kings after 1904 and are obviously carved by different hands. From the comments of Sheppard about the emblems of the four statues he saw in 1892, the one of Miko miMbul [11] was not on display, because his emblem is not a drum but a little person. Admittedly this leaves the field open for speculation that the set of two (Miko miMbul and Mbop Kyeen) had not yet been carved and that Miko miMbul really represented Miko miKyeen [17], who ruled from 1901 to the spring of 1902. This would in fact retard the onset of the tradition by only one reign, granting that one, and one only, of the statues was made for each succeeding king.

It is useless to speculate any further. The tradition dates from the middle or the later eighteenth century and is linked with the developing cult of kings as ngesh, whether or not it was started by the king who "killed" the ethnic ngesh.

Where did the model come from? More than once it has been suggested that it stems from the Kongo *mintadi* tradition, which also represents seated chiefs, although they are in very different poses. I cannot accept the suggestion that a mintadi statue was carried by a trader directly to Kuba country. The idea of representation may have reached the Kuba from Kongo, although the mid-eighteenth century is a late date for this to occur, since by that time there was little direct trade with Kongo.[14] It may be that there was no simple model and that a great sculptor invented the type, basing his conception perhaps on the appearance of the drinking cups in the shapes of heads, if they existed at the time, and on details borrowed from the tiny nnoon figures.

The statues eloquently testify to the concept of kingship in the eighteenth century. They also tell us something about ornaments and regalia. The kings are presented in martial costume, seated on a square stool—not their most formal throne, but a seat equivalent, although better ornamented, to those of the eagle-feather chiefs. Their war swords are those of present-day form. Cowries were freely used for belts and for special bracelets. The traditions linking Shyaam to the board game called lyeel were already current, and if the item described by Sheppard and the later collector as an anvil with the statue of Mbop Pelyeeng aNce [9] was in fact an anvil, then the tradition about this statue would be nearly contemporary with the reign of this monarch. Details about the hats, the seats, the arm rings (probably a representation of copper rings) and some ornaments can also be derived from this iconographic record.

Above all the statues testify to the artistic taste then prevalent: essential symmetry of volume, flowing lines that avoid angular effects except at the base, a serene expression of the faces. The patina and the gloss of the finish (which should be analyzed), and the varieties of geometric and other decorations, expecially on the drums, evoke the sumptuous quality of Kuba art in general, which clearly was already well developed by the late eighteenth century.

No extant masks are known to be of the antiquity of the ndop. Of the earliest masks collected, those that can now be identified are probably the ones in the Frobenius collection of 1905, although it would not surprise me if a few earlier ones, from 1897 and later, should turn up in small collections. The traditions quite often mention masks. The oldest are supposed to be the helmet mask, *bwoom,* and a mask of wood, elephant hide, and raffia, the *mwaash aMbooy.* The latter supposedly represented the king. A less widespread type of helmet mask, the nyeeng, is linked to the boys' initiation and is said to have been worn by Shyaam, but that may be an anachronism, as is the tale that Shyaam's wife invented the mask called *mukyeeng,* which resembled the mwaash aMbooy. My best informant on this subject, the shesh, claimed that all of these were much older and dated them in the reign of the legendary Queen Labaam, whose very name and praises suggest carving.[15]

The central traditions indicate that these masks hark back at least to the Age of Chiefs. The ncok song for a son of King Kot aNce [7] mentions a bwoom mask. If its attribution is correct, this type of mask dates back to approximately the middle of the eighteenth century. This ncok song alludes to the beginning of the practice of adorning bwoom masks with cowries and beads. It is said that the earlier Kuba objects were less lavishly ornamented, and in this instance the song, if ascribed to the correct person, substantiates this tradition.[16] The bwoom mask represented ngesh and may well be the oldest. Its style is comparable to a type widespread along the middle Kasai[17] and, given the total distribution of these types of masks, they could indeed be older than the Age of Kings and even go back to the time when the Kete lived alone, before the Age of Chiefs.[18] Other masks, with the exception of the mwaash aMbooy, are linked to the bwoom type. These include the buffalo mask, the ram mask, and the initiation masks *nnup, kalyengl,* and *ishyeen imaalul,* all from the northeast, as well as the *ngady mwaash aMbooy,* "woman of the mwaash aMbooy."[19] The nyeeng helmet mask also belongs to this set, of which it is perhaps the most deviant. All of these are very different from other initiation masks, some of which are primarily made out of raffia fibers, such as the *minyiing,* or are carved heads set on poles. The latter are very similar if not identical with the Kete masks of the middle Kasai, which were used for the same purposes.

The bwoom masks do not form an undifferentiated group. Regional differences in style are clear, especially between the eastern varieties and the central varieties. How these differences evolved from what once may have been a single prototype of mask in this class can no longer be documented. All the different types existed in the nineteenth century, and we do not know how long it took to evolve these types. Certainly the eighteenth century must have witnessed an evolution within many ateliers, and part of this evolution can perhaps still be recovered. These helmet masks were mostly carved of *Ricinodendron heudelotii africanum,* a light and easily carved wood. The diameter of sections cut from the trunks can exceed one meter, allowing for construction of helmet masks.[20] Its lightness and size partly explain the popularity of this wood, but not completely: in addition to its availability in different environments there may be a cultural element involved in this choice. Some ateliers may have copied others; the different substyles and, if possible, the ateliers should be sorted out. The fact that so many of them are carved out of one sort of wood may help one day to date them through analysis of the properties of that wood.

Kuba art for conspicuous consumption or display is often expressed in carving, and also in pottery, in the modeling of pastes made out of camwood ground fine and mixed with palm oil, in mats, and in textiles. All sorts of objects were carved, even the hooks on which to hang other objects. Some hooks were carved in the shape of little men. The volumes of boxes offered full play to the talents of inspired artists. Boxes for razor blades or jewels acquired all manner of shapes, some of them demonstrating a play of volumes in space, some resembling human forms, some in the shape of utensils. A wooden box might be shaped to resemble a calabash or a basket of some type, and a pot might be shaped to look like a wooden object. Some dishes are so well made that one cannot immediately perceive whether they are pottery or wood. The originality of each artist found room for expression, even though there were restrictions exerted by types of objects. Yet cups, platters, and pipes allowed artistic fancy and virtuosity to be displayed. Many unique pieces were thus created; they pleased the patriciate as conversation pieces and the artist as opportunities to show off his skill. We have, for example, a plate supported by the lower half of a kneeling human body and decorated with little figurines on the rim, a drinking cup carved in the shape of a human head, another in the shape of a person holding a miniature cup in his hands, and an oil pot with a human foot as its base. Many of these pieces are commentaries on cultural and social life, and some are even puns.

The ages of different pieces should be established, if possible, before we can perceive how this art and its experimentation of form developed, and how this occurred at different ateliers in different parts of the kingdom. It is my impression that the older collections show greater diversity than the twentieth-century products, which came to be more and more standardized, in part as a response to the tourist trade—the new patrons—and in part also for the former patrons.

Is this an "aristocratic art"? Frans Olbrechts believed that a distinctive court style evolved,[21] but this is easily refuted. Apart from style, did the influence of the court lead to the flowering of this art? Did it all develop after Shyaam? This is doubtful, since excellent works of art have been found everywhere. Ngongo work and indeed Mbeengi sculpture were apparently as technically proficient as the products of the Bushoong. Yet not until inventories of precise origin have been made will it be possible to establish whether the best artists of the realm were attracted to the court or not, and whether the whole range of items found at the capital was also found elsewhere. Meanwhile one can only suppose that the court was arbiter while one retains the contradictory impression that excellent ateliers were spread through the realm. It is tempting to believe that Kuba style developed in response to the demand of the patriciate at the capital and that the workshops in other chiefdoms or in Bushoong villages arose as imitations of the fashions at the capital. Not only is this implausible on the grounds that regional styles do in fact differ, but it does not explain why the Leele and even the distant Wongo (Njeembe) sculpted drinking cups and pipes. Certainly the superb communal drums of the Leele show that tendencies toward an ornamental art were not limited to the Kuba of the kingdom. On the other hand it is true that among the Leele and the Wongo the range of carved objects was much more limited. They lacked, for instance, the richly decorated jewel boxes. On the other hand, in the 1950s the Mbeengi settlements had a profusion of artistic objects that was greater than any left elsewhere. Mbeengi villages are far away, and the great collections were gathered mostly from the core area, which explains its impoverished look. But to go further and claim that the capital had been richer than any other settlement remains implausible.

Part of this art probably antedates the kingdom, and some of its manifestations outside the capital can be attributed to imitation or emulation. Only painstaking comparisons will establish this. I suspect that such an examination will show that drums, palm wine cups, and a few of the common decorative patterns derived in part from pottery or basketry will be found to have existed before the kingdom. Much of the remainder, especially the fancy jewel boxes, carved posts, pipes, and boxes for razor blades may well have been developed first at the capital.

One subclass of objects found only within the realm is the complex metalwork with inlaid or chased copper or brass displayed in ceremonial knives and in the few sculptures known, such as the human figurines at the Antwerp Museum.[22] These are the only objects to survive from what the Kuba term a class of objects made by the famous smiths Myeel and Pyeekol, and which they ascribe to the seventeenth century. Like the ikul knife given to Sheppard and now at Hampton, Virginia, they were virtuoso pieces. These can be tested by physical means to establish their date. This would tell us when Kuba artists began to delight in creating works of virtuosity.

Most of these metal pieces were restricted to the Bushoong.[23] So are the camwood-paste sculptures made by women at the capital. These were given away at funerals; some were broken up and used as an ointment to rub a mourner's body. The most remarkable were treasured and were again given away at a later funeral. This art was linked to the patriciate, and the destruction of the objects after a short or long period was directly related to prestige. A sculpted art created by women most of the objects were slabs ornamented with decorative patterns. Some were sculptures in the round, showing little heads, lizards, knives, animals, and even a canoe containing women and their boxes. Clearly some of the talented women expressed their aesthetic impulses by this means.

Another class of wooden objects, the rubbing oracles, have been studied by Thérèse Thomas.[24] Carved in the shape of a person, a warthog, a dog, a crocodile, or perhaps a lizard, these objects are older than the Age of Kings. Thomas believed that the inspiration for the oracle came from the zoomorphic sculpture of the upper Kasai. A link is not impossible, for zoomorphic sculpture from that area has recently been discovered and has been claimed to be the oldest carving in Central Africa.[25] The discovery, however, merely establishes the existence of zoomorphic motifs. Given the delight of the Kuba in skeuomorphic experiments and the presence of all sorts of plant and animal motifs and evocations, the shapes could have developed independently, again most likely during the Age of Kings. And only those animals that evoked the ngesh would be fitting in this context. Indeed, no others have been found. It is of interest to note that such items have also been found among some of the Leele. Was the practice borrowed from the Kuba? Or does their presence mean that they antedate the establishment of the kingdom? The oracle itself certainly antedates the Age of Kings.

At the occasion of each king a new drum (the drum of reign) was made. The drums of reign ascribed to MishaaPelyeeng aNce [8] and subsequent rulers were kept at the capital until 1969. These drums of reign are called pel ambish. On the earliest specimens, copper and beads were sparsely used for decoration, but by the end of the nineteenth century the whole surface of the drums was covered by these two materials. A superficial examination of the drums, which I saw only once, revealed no great alteration at all in the size of the drums nor in the patterns with which they were decorated. A closer study of the set, if it still exists, may establish a more precise sequence and help date the items. The presence of two late-eighteenth-century drums should not be overlooked by art historians.

Costumes and textiles were not only decorated with intricate patterns, but the variety of the embroidery, the suppleness of the cloth, and the quality of the finish, especially that of the velvety cloth, was remarkable. Kuba cloth is not as tightly woven as that of the Leele, who have developed perhaps the tightest-woven textiles in Central Africa[26] through use of a superior carding device, but Kuba cloth is more supple and can be made to look more shiny. New cloth was soaked and beaten to give it a silk-like finish.[27] The technical development may have been entirely local, but the creation of velvety cloth, characterized by raised and dyed geometrical patterns, is not. True, dyeing by staining thread or the whole cloth with red camwood and black, yellow, and later also a bluish color is clearly due to the local invention of a number of elaborate techniques for that purpose. The technique for producing the pile, some techniques of embroidery, and at least the idea for polychrome textiles came from the Kwilu area, as tradition asserts by ascribing these innovations to Shyaam's wife.[28]

Similar textiles were exported to Europe from the kingdom of Kongo in the seventeenth century. A raffia piece at the museum in Ulm is perhaps the oldest extant specimen: it is mentioned in the catalog of 1659.[29] Within Kongo such textiles were mentioned as early as 1508, which in effect means that they existed when the Portuguese arrived there. By 1583 Duarte Lopes tells us that they were made in the lower Wamba-Kwango area and that one of the names given for a variety of these was *enzaka*.

This area of early production corresponds the region of Okanga. The name enzaka is probably the origin of the Bushoong *ncak,* "women's dress," and specimens of the cloth may have reached the Kuba from the days of Shyaam. By the nineteenth century this type of cloth had disappeared except among the Mpiin, Pende, and Kuba.[30] The Mpiin were the southern neighbors of the Tsong and were therefore very close to the trade route presumably traveled by Rafael de Castro from Okanga in 1619–20. The Pende lived south of the Mbuun and east of the Mpiin. They reached the area of the Kwango and Kasai rivers at the earliest in the mid-seventeenth century.[31] It is plausible that the technique involved in these textiles moved from the Wamba River area to the Mpiin and then, but not before 1650, to the Pende, then to the Kuba, bypassing the Leele-Wongo area. A more direct introduction to the Kuba from the Mpiin should not be excluded: it better explains the transmission of the Kongo name, which is not found among the Pende. In any case the technique clearly came from the Wamba-Kwango area and reached the Kuba in the seventeenth or perhaps the eighteenth century.

An examination of available photographs shows that seventeenth-century cloth items now in museums at Ulm, Copenhagen, and London and originating in the Wamba-Kwango area or the Kongo area are similar to Kuba velvet cloth in patterns of decoration, and Angelika Stritzl's study of Kongo cloth shows that the techniques used were almost identical.[32] This supports the general argument for a diffusion whose direction is indicated by the available chronological data.

Torday found embroidered cloth only among the Bushoong.[33] Some of the Kuba's embroidered textiles are a jour work reflecting a technique called Richelieu embroidery, a great favorite of the Italian clergy in the seventeenth century. The Italian missionaries very likely had such vestments in Kongo, and the similarity of technique suggests that the Kuba ultimately borrowed the technique from there, although it is possible that they developed it independently. The linguistic evidence also favors borrowing because we know that the term ncak is a loanword from Kikongo.[34]

Luxury objects of all sorts, including textiles, pottery, woodcarvings, carved ivory and buffalo horn, and indeed even the human body itself were ornamented with decorative patterns. Two classes of motifs exist. The first, which was used for scarification on women, on drinking horns, and on certain types of cloth, consisted of isolated motifs more or less juxtaposed according to the fancy of the artist. The second, which was used for decorating all other objects, consisted of geometric motifs of angular or flowing lines. Close to two hundred patterns can be reorganized. This second category was much more dynamic than the first, and it was considered an achievement to invent a new pattern. Every king had to create a pattern at the onset of his reign; his pattern was displayed on his drum of reign and, in the case of some kings, on the dynastic statue. Some patterns were known by the name of their inventor, among whom we find women. The liveliness of the spirit of invention is illustrated in an anecdote told by Conway Wharton: when missionaries displayed the first motorcycle to the king in the late 1920s the machine aroused little curiosity on his part, but he was enthralled by the novel pattern the tire treds made in the sand, had it copied, and gave it his name.[35] Not only did each pattern have a name, it often had more than one, usually because patterns had different names in different parts of the country. Variant names referred to natural objects, such as "the folds of the python," more often than to an inventor's name. The evidence thus suggests considerable dynamics among embroidery patterns. This has been substantiated by Donald Crowe's study of artistic geometry, which showed that the Kuba achieved a very high number of the possible permutations of simple patterns.[36]

Crowe, like Torday, thought that most patterns of the second type originated from weaving and perhaps from plaiting, as in basketry or mat-making.[37] No doubt decorations on the rims of pottery were also a source of inspiration. Among the patterns of the first set, many are stylized human, animal, plant, and object shapes. I found one object on which such patterns were used as a kind of rebus, the beginning of a pictographic script,[38] but this was almost unique. I believe that the patterns were not intended to be so used, or "read," in previous centuries, although some meaning may have been attached to the juxtaposition of such patterns as "moon," "knot," "knife," which we find on drinking horns. To establish the exact evolution, at least in some outline, it will be necessary to seriate objects and to recover archaeological specimens, especially of pottery. The similarities of Kuba cloth with the old Kongo cloth and of Kuba patterns with some of the patterns on Kingabwa (Kinshasa) pottery, which dates back to the seventeenth century or slightly earlier, suggest that the main differentiation between the two types of decoration was old.[39]

There is almost no doubt that fancy textiles were related to the differentiation of social status and class. The first such cloths may well have figured among the luxury imports from beyond the Kwilu in the seventeenth century. The appreciation shown for innovation in artistic matters is also best explained by linking it to social prestige. True, insofar as we know today, special patterns were not reserved for certain ranks, but rank was measured by the novelty of pattern, the skill in execution, and the labor expended on the object, especially cloth, so that unusual, new fashions that required considerable expenditure of labor made these textiles favored objects among the patricians.

The *horror vacui* of Kuba art is well known.[40] Every inch of the available surface on wooden cups and on the lids and sides of boxes was carved. A few objects of pottery and wood were not, however, decorated over the entire surface, and Torday believed that the trend toward complete decoration may have reached its conclusion only in the nineteenth century. The drums allegedly from the eighteenth century that I saw showed a general background of finely carved geometrical motifs rather like Leele motifs in shape but not in execution. They served as a background for one or two superimposed decorative patterns, executed in greater relief and covering a smaller area of the drum. Later dynastic drums were entirely covered by a bold pattern executed in cowries and beads of different colors. Similar situations can be found on other classes of objects, including textiles. It is also of interest to note that, unlike the Leele drums, most ordinary Kuba drums, especially of the *bulup* (dancing drum) variety, were not covered with decorative patterns. Only a few motifs carved in low or high relief sufficed for their decoration. Once again these observation suggest that we see here the effects of the drive for affluence and prestige. To the Leele the drum was always a village drum and its decoration reflected the independence of the village. To the Kuba these communal drums occupied no particular place of pride at all. The village was not a sovereign entity; it was nothing to boast about. The carving was therefore simpler. It is evident that future study concerning the amount of decoration on different kinds of objects perhaps can tell us something more about the growth of political prestige, rank, and affluence.

Kuba sculpture and decoration, although praised for their technical perfection, have been rated by some art historians as less creative than those of many other cultures because they demonstrate too much adherence to basic canons, too much respect for the grammar of form and pattern, too much repetition from object to object.[41] In short, although the evidence of a drive toward individual creativity is abundant, there is still too much overall conformity. These judgments apply primarily to nineteenth-century art and exclude the creation of new types, such as the dynastic statues and the unique Kuba objects that are not so widely known. But there is something to this criticism. It tallies with the Bushoong's own vision of their ideals: to be independent and individual, yet to show proper respect for the hierarchy at the same time.[42] Within the culture, people were struck less by the aspect of conformism and more by the departures from the expected norm. Individual variations stood out much more sharply, even in such apparent trifles as slight variations in decorative patterns. The objects themselves, which were made as master-pieces of virtuosity and were so intended by their creators, seemed to the Kuba to be extreme departures from the norm. A cup in the shape of a man riding an antelope was not only very difficult to carve, it was highly original as well in comparison to other cups, even if the art historian from another culture fails to fully perceive that originality. Had this not been so, the piece would not have been as appreciated by the public as it was. The situation resembles that of the pipe bowls that the Kuba recognize immediately as caricatures of definite persons but which to Western eyes do not even give a hint of caricature.

The meager historical evidence marshaled thus far indicates a lively, crea-tive movement in Kuba culture which led to a diversification of shapes, volumes, and ornamentation as great as the diversification in symbols or political titles. Clearly this art "belongs" to this type of complex society.

Like sculpture and decorative art, Kuba architecture was characterized by an overall sense of proportion to which other details were subordinated. The horizontal line dominated in the proportions of the houses as well as in the layout of the city of Nsheng. Houses were really basketry work fixed to poles and decorated like mats. The decorations were not random, however: they were framed by oblong rectangles of bamboo strips that accentuated the horizontal lines of the whole. In the city, the walls and other devices achieved a similar effect. Other characteristics of the architecture were the use of open, walled spaces as the main principle of monumental architecture and the notion that perspective should not be evaluated from a stationary vantage point but from walking down the thoroughfares. Hence the main avenues of the capital were blocked off by public buildings of various heights and widths to mask the approach to the main plazas. I was told that trees were also consciously used as elements of the architecture both to set off the horizontal line and perspective or to reduce the monotony of views that would be too long without them. The principles from which this art developed were those of the simple rectangular house with a saddle roof and a courtyard. The development of the capital allowed the architecture to become more sophisticated, just as the development of the house, though aimed at comfort, allowed its design to become more intricate. By 1892 some houses boasted as many as three rooms, separated by well-made partitions running from ceiling to floor. The walls had become very elaborate to build, or, more accurately, to plait, stitch, and sew together. The doorposts were carved, as were the frames of the bed, and the doorway itself had become wider. Sliding doors had been invented as an improvement over the mats that unrolled to perform the same function in simpler buildings elsewhere.[43]

Although there is no hope of uncovering the details of such improvements as those made in doors, excavation might uncover floor plans and even, perhaps, the layout of part of a capital. By and large the history of Kuba architecture will remain a comparison between the simplest forms of rural houses and villages and the most intricate arrangements recorded in the twentieth-century capital.

This chapter has presented only an outline of the problems involved in a historical study of the visual arts. It has used a working hypothesis that maintains that there did exist a meaningful relationship between these arts and society: the increased artistic sophistication, as well as the respect for rules and the creativity within that framework, coincided with the virtues expected from an analysis of the political and economic sectors. The ordering of decorative art, geometric or not, the balancing of square and rounded volumes in sculpture, even the short elegiac poems betray the same spirit that created trial by a panel of judges or that balanced councils one against the other. And yet an undercurrent betrays enthusiasm for competition. This working hypothesis must remain vague until the necessary task of cataloging and dating the extant corpus of art objects is undertaken. This is the task of a museum. The study of Kuba art has in fact barely begun.

The performing arts, which include oral literature, are still largely unknown. Except for samples of literature (sayings, songs, praise names, tales) the data have not even been collected. For dance and mime it may already be too late. Massive collections of music and literature should be undertaken in and around the area. The effects of twentieth-century influences arising from all sorts of situations, beginning with the school primers, must be assessed. Only then will there be hope for a comparative ethnography that may yield a few historical inferences. We know so little today that we cannot even say whether there will eventually be enough information available for a general historical outline.

Future research is likely to lead to a much more complete history of the visual arts, especially in sculpture and decoration. Objects will be excavated and dated. Collections in the museums are extensive; they can be classified and studied. Parts of them can perhaps be dated. In time we may hope for a history of Kuba art that will add to what has been recovered to date in the area of political and economic history.

Part IV

Coda

Chapter 13

Reflections

The conclusions of this book are presented in this chapter, which deals first with the questions of why and how the Kuba have selected their own perceptions of the past, and to what extent the effects of this selection can be overcome when their history is reconstructed. A presentation and discussion of the results obtained follows.

The Kuba Select Their Past

To the Kuba, history is the remembrance of *some* things past. The main process of building oral history involves not so much a passive, haphazard loss of memory as an active choice of items to remember, and that choice is dictated by their perception of history. History must explain and thereby justify the world, mankind, and the Kuba way of doing things. It involves a selection guided by ontological speculation cast within a structured form of exposition. Dynastic history in particular must consist of reflections about kingship and the state, both being to a very large extent identical in Kuba thought.

I started out in Chapter Two by discussing the Kuba concepts in relation to the limits within which this idea of history could be worked out. History is the product of a consensus in the community of which it is a record. It is relative to the community that elaborates it, whether that community is a clan section, a village, a chiefdom, or the kingdom. But dynastic history encapsulates all other communities, and hence its history provides the framework for an overall assessment of the past. Absolute truth matters as little as does exact chronology. Myths and anecdotes become true by common agreement and can be altered by common agreement. What is selected becomes true ipso facto. What was held to be true in the first half of this century has been told in Chapters Three and Four. This gives us the substance of the Kuba perception of their past.

The structured exposition within which ontological explanation is cast should be analyzed somewhat more in the style of Edmund Leach than in the style of Claude Lévi-Strauss.[1] In presenting Kuba genesis, only the raw material has been given in order to show what the historian can use and why most of the data are ontological speculation divorced from real events and processes in a real past. An adequate analysis of these data would require a separate monograph.

Structuring occurs in the tales about kings. Anecdotes about them are not haphazardly remembered: the figure of Woot [A], progenitor of mankind, is complemented by Shyaam [1], creator of the Kuba way. It is normal that Woot should invent fire and Shyaam the typical Kuba hat, although even here some informants are confused.[2] Woot, Mboong [C], and Shyaam are all founders, and there is a tendency to confuse the achievements attributed to them.

In the dynastic traditions a strong contrast exists between the king as the source of fertility and the king as sorcerer. The ideal king was a life giver— but also a destroyer. The traditions often separate both aspects of this paradox by attributing typical traits to pairs of succeeding kings. As opposed to Mboong aLeeng [2], Shyaam is the creative innovator, the peace-loving medicine man as opposed to the warrior. This particular opposition recurs in the paired rulers MishaaPelyeeng aNce [8] and Mbo Pelyeeng aNce [9], and Kot aMbul [10] and Miko miMbul [11]. Yet in none of these cases is this feature sufficient to explain all the anecdotes told about these kings, nor have all destructive and life-giving features been totally separated. Without fully analyzing the dynastic tradition here, we must be aware of the force that structural considerations may exert in selecting anecdotes to be included and in identifying those that must be excluded.

The process of selection takes time and is continuous. Certain items are never considered for inclusion in the record because they are not perceived as community affairs, or because change was so slow that it was not consciously perceived, or because to remember the events would be to deny the correctness of present behavior or views. Structural amnesia of this last kind must have helped to erase memories about religious history, especially about religious movements, while unconscious change explains the omission of detailed accounts about social, economic, religious, and artistic evolutions. Moreover, dynastic history dealt with the history of kings, which meant that most events to be remembered had to be recast as the actions of kings. Consequently many unrelated matters were excluded, but not all of them, since major changes which happened during a reign might be remembered as items king x did—e.g., king x brought cassava.

But one should not conclude too readily that nothing was ever recorded that did not tie in with ontological positions or reflections about the nature of kingship. Most anecdotes about kings deal with war and magic. Yet some anecdotes are not explained by this or any other general principles. Kot aNce [7] was small and invented a long hat to appear tall; his successor improved the design of the razor blade. These tales seem to have little if any bearing on the concept of kingship. And the tale about Mbo Pelyeeng aNce that praises him for being a sound farmer conflicts with the express rule that kings were not supposed to farm. One can attempt to explain the last two anecdotes by linking the razor blade to the title the Luba used for Kuba kings and by stressing that "farming" is an image of peace and belongs in the cluster that casts Mbo Pelyeeng aNce as a life-bringing king. But the hat story cannot easily be fitted into any scheme. Kot aNce's hat shows that not everything in the traditions is rigidly structured or rigidly selected. Structural amnesia does not operate as the inexorable reaper of all irrelevancy.

The greatest selection occurs soon after the events have taken place. At this first stage most events are actively excluded. One case allows us to show that selection aimed primarily at preserving the extranatural features associated with kingship. Kot aPe [18] led the Kuba in their insurrection of 1904 against the Congo Independent State, and veterans were still around in the 1950s. But the dominant story that emerged from that event was the miracle the pok ibaan—medicine man for the king—wrought by killing his killers when, despite his powerful magic, he was executed at the behest of the king. Such miracles never happened, but they presumably existed in the fictional oral literature, and from there they gravitated into the record because of incidents that vaguely resembled them. And they did help preserve memory of some major events.

Obvious selection by the Kuba can be seen when Frobenius in 1905 lists Mbop aMbweeky [19] as regent "after" the reign of Kot aPe [18], but in 1908, when Kot aPe was king again, Mbop's regency was not mentioned to Torday. Indeed, Mbop became king in 1916 and in Torday's time was the designated heir to the throne, but he was not even mentioned as such to Torday.

A fascinating case deals with King Mbop Kyeen [16], who ruled for about three months in 1900. Frobenius was told by his informant, Mishaamilyeeng, that this king liked the Europeans and sent his people to work for a commercial company. For that reason he was murdered by poisoning. Actually, it is almost certain that the king, like his predecessor and successor, died as the victim of an epidemic. In 1900 the poisoning was already a current explanation, for the European who was establishing a trading post at the capital recorded it, albeit from memory in 1908.[3] Mishaamilyeeng did not tell Frobenius that he himself had contested the right of Mbop Kyeen to rule and that the government of the Congo Independent State had arbitrated the matter and decided in favor of the king. Nor did he tell Frobenius the version about the death that was current in 1905: as early as 1902 King Kot aPe accused Mishaamilyeeng of having made a medicine that had eliminated all the kings who had ruled since 1896, including Mbop Kyeen and his successor, Miko miKyeen.[4] Indeed, Kot aPe secured the services of a foreign medicine man to undo the effects of Mishaamilyeeng's murderous medicine. By 1906, as in the 1950s, this account of the death was a firm part of the tradition. Mishaamilyeeng lost the power struggle and with it his version of the events was discarded. The one glorifying Kot aPe survived.

Even the fact that Mbop Kyeen had encouraged Kuba to work for the company was forgotten. This also may not have been an accident, for Kot aPe collaborated fully with the Compagnie de Kasai after 1905, sanctioning their methods for obtaining rubber and accepting compensation in return. No one in 1953 had forgotten the forced labor imposed to collect rubber and the resulting hardships and atrocities, which were the main cause of the 1904 insurrection and which culminated in the years 1906–8. Family traditions and even personal memories were still rich, but no account of those events appeared in the dynastic traditions. The rulers who had benefited from the system were not about to commit this to official memory. Political success, then, dictated what would become history.

Other processes also intervene to reduce the complexity of events to the simplicity of the anecdotal traditions. Some informants clearly remembered changes in the system of imposing fines in court, the virtual abolition of the crown council, the abolition of the boys' initiation and age-grades, as well as the creation of a new kolm title to represent the successors, all of which are attributed to Kot aPe's reign (1902–16) and most of which had been accomplished before late 1908. Those who cited these changes were kolm who had lived through the whole period; younger Bushoong knew next to nothing about them. It is quite likely that when these kolm died, the memories also died out or became grossly transformed, just as the memories of fighting against the Congo State troops in 1900 and 1904 died out when the veterans passed away. Of that warfare, only the anecdotes about the miracles of pok ibaan and the capture of the king survive. Most other reminiscences about Kot aPe's reign, such as the social and administrative changes or the descriptions of the confusion of the battles, will not survive because they lack the intrinsic quality required to develop into anecdotes. Of the two that survived one appeals to miracles, a common theme in many earlier anecdotes of the corpus, and the other centers around a pithy paradox called "the snake on the calabash,"[5] an attractive literary device.

Moreover, many reminiscences conflicted with the basic notion of causality. A cause is a beginning and a beginning is always full-blown. Under king x or y an institution is founded, and after that it does not change. This applies to the system of titles or fines in court, initiation, age-grades, and the crown council. The Kuba notion of cause blots out continuous change. It becomes impossible to record that initiations at the capital were not held from perhaps the 1880s or the 1890s, but continued in an altered setting within the matoon villages until the 1930s, when they were suppressed, to begin again only in

1953. When initiation appears anywhere in the traditions, it is attributed to Mboong aLeeng [2] and that is all. This procedure leads of course to anachronism both ascending and descending. The system of fines introduced by Kot aPe is linked to the court system and hence is assigned to Shyaam [1] or perhaps to MboMboosh [3],[6] both cases being ascending anachronisms. The kolm who in 1953 remembered the abolition of initiation attributed it to Kot aPe, a descending anachronism. If consciousness of change in the tribunals had become strongly attached to Kot aPe he might have been credited with their invention, a descending anachronism. This, we suspect, happened to the elaboration of initiation rites under Mboong aLeeng.

And so the process of selection begins to operate almost simultaneously with the occurrence of the events themselves. It is conditioned by the extant body of tradition, by the political situation, and by the notion of cause as an absolute "beginning." In practice only some political events survive the first round of winnowing, especially if they are colored by supernatural explanations and are also remembered by other means, such as village traditions, traditions of office, or songs, poems, and sayings.

But the process does not stop there. A second round may eliminate many among them to bring the remainder more closely in line with the rest of the corpus. This is structural selection of a sort, and as a corpus grows, this force continues to operate not merely by eliminating anecdotes but also by reassigning them to the "proper" kings. The process is not absolutely perfect, as shown by the case of Kot aNce's hat. It represents a tendency rather than an absolute rule.

Thus we can readily show how pairs of succeeding kings fit the paradigm of peaceful king followed by destructive king, as with MishaaPelyeeng aNce [8] and Mbo Pelyeeng aNce [9], Shyaam [1] and Mboong aLeeng [2], and even Ngup aShyaang and Mishe miShyaang Matuun [F], for Ngup was so peace-loving or "lazy" that he never became king. It applies also to Kot aMbul [10] and Miko miMbul [11]. But here, as in the case of MishaaPelyeeng aNce and Mbo Pelyeeng aNce, the pattern is not perfect. The peaceful kings show some destructive traits, and vice versa. The pattern is only a tendency. And as the reader checks Chapter Four, he will sense that the closer we come to our time the more mixed the pattern is. For the eighteenth and nineteenth centuries this history has not yet been completely worked out on structural grounds. Whereas MishaaPelyeeng aNce improved the razor blade (an iron implement), it is Mbo Pelyeeng aNce who was the excellent smith. Taking their reigns together and dividing up the known anecdotes according to the peaceful-destructive paradigm would yield an image in which *A* was a good smith, improved the razor blade, was a sturdy farmer, and disliked dancing, implying that he disliked the conspicuous fetes at court where competition was expressed. He was unimaginative and ruled for a long time. His praise name was "the eye of the bird, which does not neglect the hunter," indicating caution. *B,* his brother, lived in a capital whose praise name was "the lair of the male leopard; the town has found its master." He killed the seventy sons of their uncle. Later on he was overcome by nightmares, then by guilt, and he died quickly. He was too imaginative and too warlike. It was also *B* who killed the ethnic ngesh and magically dug a valley by mistake. This would be the perfect arrangement of the known anecdotes, but the point is that they are not so divided between the two brothers. In practice all of this is usually attributed to a single king, and the brother is credited only with the razor blade and the motto "the eye of the bird." It seems as if tradition was on its way toward eliminating one of the two and building the same contrast peaceful-warlike, between the pairs MishaaPelyeeng aNce and Mbo Pelyeeng aNce, and Kot aMbul and Miko miMbul. The whole pattern would be simplified and of four kings only two would survive.

In these cases anecdotes were selected but the assemblage of anecdotes was not yet perfected. Perhaps the process had not gone further because village and even family traditions still existed about the last son of Mbul, the mother of Kot aMbul and Miko miMbul, and could be collected by bulaam as they were by me. It should also be remembered that each anecdote was told separately. No immediately perceived need existed to streamline the corpus, even though it is true that one anecdote tended to evoke another. In part this explains why all the kings are not neatly classified as units in sets of contrasts and repetition, expressing Kuba thought about kingship. When other contrasts are tried out as paradigms, similar irregularities or inconsistencies appear.

At a deeper, third level of selection structural amnesia does appear. The founders of dynasties are remembered, but only in the last dynasty do we have a record of all—or most of—the kings. Even here the paucity of data about Mishe miShyaang maMbul [6] and Kot aMbweeky [5] shows that a new hiatus was in the making. On the one hand, Kot aNce [7] and the later kings were linked, if only by their matronyms. On the other, kings Lashyaang [E], Mishe miShyaang Matuun [F], and Shyaam [1] are linked because events in one reign impinge on events in the preceding one, producing a concatenation which helps to remember all of them. I confess that I cannot find a truly compelling argument to explain why Mboong aLeeng [2], MboMboosh [3], and Mbakam [4] have been spared by the process of structural amnesia, an event which suggests that this process was not as inexorable during the course of the last dynasty as it was before. From the data one acquires the feeling that the warlike qualities of Mboong aLeeng assured the survival of his memory as a contrast with the character of Shyaam, whereas MboMboosh has been remembered mostly because of his age and Mbakam because of the wonderful things that happened during his reign. This feeling falls far short of constituting proof, however.

I have argued that the processes of selection operate in three different stages: one soon after the events, when a selection of reminiscences is transformed into anecdotes; one when those anecdotes are rearranged (and some eliminated) to express general tendencies in the whole body of tradition; and one, structural amnesia, when traditions about all preceding dynasties are eliminated and the remainder tends to gravitate around the period of foundation of the present dynasty and "recent history." I have also argued that these processes are not inexorable and that exceptions occur. They may occur for all sorts of reasons. Certainly one reason may simply be the importance of certain reigns for the internal and external politics of the state.

Nevertheless the processes of selection constitute a severe challenge to the historian. To reconstruct Kuba history one must constantly remember that the available data are the product of selection and constitute a tiny part of the events that actually happened. Therefore it is extremely important to attempt to locate other sources that may help to overcome the lack of data and the bias of selection. It is *not* true that the most momentous events are the ones that are remembered. Is a tall hat momentous? One should therefore not stick too closely to the patterns outlined by the sources used to discover the Kuba view of history. It is imperative to attempt, if at all possible, to find other kinds of sources.

On the other hand, the fact of selection itself does not mean that the anecdotes told are fictitious. Oral data should not be rejected out of hand except when they deal with periods or events that could not have been witnessed—e.g., creation. One will remember, however, that oral data freely borrow existing themes or even episodes from oral literature, as in the case of the saying that concerns the snake and the calabash. This must be kept in mind when specific traditions are assessed. But oral tradition can and indeed must be used in historical reconstruction. It is the essential source for Kuba history.

The chronological problems can be severe. Here it is important to recall that the structural rearrangements and structural amnesia have not led to complete streamlining, and the chronology is not hopelessly lost. As for anachronisms, an understanding of the Kuba notion of cause as "beginnings" helps to pinpoint where a chronological argument could be weak. An appreciation of the art of reciting a vivid tale also helps to prevent overhasty acceptance of some implied chronologies, such as the attribution of cowries to the reign of Shyaam.

Despite all efforts, including the search for other sources, it is clear that the processes of selection have effectively prevented the recovery of whole sectors of the past. The chapter about religious history testifies to this. It is unlikely that an intellectual history of the Kuba can ever be written because to them history never was individual, and collective representations were altered by consensus, erasing previous collective representations by branding them as "lies," which then were not remembered much longer. So only traces of former situations have survived. The lack of detail in all the chapters reminds us of the severe restrictions imposed by the process of selection. Nevertheless I think that I have overcome some of the limitations inherent in the situation. I would argue that a general reconstruction of Kuba history is possible, that the reconstruction presented is fundamentally correct, and that it adds to our knowledge.

The methodology used here is not new. What is perhaps novel is the use of linguistic data in conjunction with the chronology derived from oral tradition. Items that go back to an original language have been distinguished from loanwords having a different source—all, however, from Bantu languages. This kind of search for precolonial loanwords tied to a chronology of loans has been attempted before within the Bantu area, but very sparingly. The results seem promising. The linguistic evidence yielded rich returns for technological and economic history, and the data for kinship terminology led to more results than were expected at the outset. Many items, however, relating to social, political, and religious history are so closely linked to the basic vocabulary that no conclusions could be reached. When a definite institution is dubbed an "assembly," deriving from the verb "to assemble," which is related to other such verbs with a similar meaning in other languages, no conclusions are possible with regard to the institution. Yet on balance it is evident that linguistic data can contribute much more to historical reconstruction in Central Africa than has been achieved so far.

It is equally clear that comparative ethnography has not yet yielded all the data that could be useful. Here one must wait in particular for studies to be conducted among the southern Mongo. It would be wrong, however, to be overly sanguine about this. Arguments from ethnography are usually very difficult to use because so many possibilities for explaining the extant situation exist. The greatest increase in data can be expected from archaeological work, which would enrich the data concerning technology, economy, and art and possibly would also contribute to a better knowledge of nutrition, demography, some aspects of settlement, and social stratification. But the soils are acid, no spectacular sites have been reported so far, and the kinds of excavations required are rather expensive to conduct. Moreover, the later Iron Age has not yet attracted interest sufficient to initiate large-scale work in these areas.

A considerable amount might also be learned from a thorough study of Kuba art, where, amazing as it sounds, almost nothing has been done sys-

tematically. The gathering and study of oral fictional literature is also potentially of importance. Last but not least, the search for early documents from
the colonial period should not be abandoned. There certainly exists more
iconographic and archival material than has so far been exploited. In the main
I limited research to printed sources.

The strategy used to identify change in Kuba society has essentially consisted of comparing the situation in about 1892 with the proto-Kuba reconstruction as set forth in Chapter Six. The differences that show up in the
comparison must be due to change. This means that I made a reconstruction of
the situation existing in 1892 (even though this is not set forth in a single place
in this book), which was not accomplished by a guesswork subtraction of the
situation that existed in 1953. It uses the work of Sheppard as a base and takes
Kuba colonial history into account.[7] The traditions led me to use three broad
periods: proto-Kuba, the Age of Chiefs, and the Age of Kings. The approach
worked well.

When the results were assessed in terms of the assumptions of Fernand
Braudel and the *Annales* school concerning duration, it appears that while
portions of the history of events *(histoire événementielle)* were recovered, no
trends *(conjonctures)* were discerned, but some long-term change *(longue
durée)* stood out. This is not simply the result of my approach. I could have
tried to specify trends more clearly, but with the lack of knowledge about
events, the trends perceived can very well be merely the product of chance,
the Kuba's vision of history, and my own interpretation. This, however, is
clearly not so for the long-term changes, which correspond to the three
periods mentioned. Fundamental changes, and not just political ones, flowed
from migration and the adaptation to a new human and natural environment,
resulting in the second period. Deep economic changes along with political
innovation ushered in the third period, which lasted for close to three centuries. The recovery of such long-term changes is important because the
historical time units become comparable to those used by contemporary mul-
tilineal evolutionary theorists. Both the Braudel view of the past and the
evolutionary perspective can be combined, and in his perspective the Kuba
"case" is relevant to the latter theory.

Kuba History in Perspective?

The reconstruction of the Kuba past has unfolded the story of how a simple
agricultural society, relatively isolated from the world outside central Zaire,
evolved into the "neolithic success" acclaimed by de Heusch. This involved
first the merging of two cultural traditions, that of the southern Mongo with
that of the early Kete. During this period the most dramatic adaptation was the
change by the Kuba immigrants from a patrilineal to a matrilineal mode of

descent while keeping the virilocal mode of residence, at least to a large extent. The adaptations involved a fundamental change in the political system composed of small chiefdoms, which were brought with them from north of the Sankuru and now came to be exclusively territorially based. Some of them grew to a much larger size than the others, while some were affected by fission. The situation remained unstable. The fusion of different economic systems was less dramatic because they were already rather similar and the change in environment was small. The new culture mostly took over the artistic traditions of the Kete, but compromised with regard to religion. A major change consisted in abandoning the ancestor cult and a corresponding increase in the importance attached to nature spirits. We do not know how long this period lasted. But such fusion of two different ways of life into a new tradition seems to me to have required at least a century and probably much longer. The process of immigration itself may also have taken well over a century. This projects the date for our reconstruction of proto-Kuba life, north of the Sankuru, at least back to the first half of our millennium.

The early seventeenth century saw the onset of a second transformation, brought about by contact with peoples to the west (especially the Mbuun), and through them with the Atlantic coast. The first changes occurred in the political system; a genuine kingdom emerged and incorporated the extant chiefdoms. Along with this came increased centralization and an expanded bureaucracy. At the same time new crops with potentially higher yields were introduced from the west, and a tenuous long-distance trade began to appear. The demands of the political system prompted the conversion of the basic agricultural mode of production, resulting, in the end, in at least a doubling of output per farming family. As more surplus became available the bureaucracy expanded and the further specialization of labor occurred in the form of greater numbers of specialized artisans and even traders. Groups of artisans and traders concentrated at the capital, which became an economic center as well as the political node of the kingdom. Gradually the long-distance trade network expanded in response to the demand by the new patriciate for prestige goods. By the middle of the eighteenth century the Kuba were on the fringes of the large Atlantic trading area of Central Africa. They remained in a marginal position within this system until well after 1850, when their supply of ivory became more and more important to it. With this new development wealth, mostly in the form of slaves and cowries, poured into the country, especially after about 1875. During this second period the domestic and kinship institutions may not have changed very much, although monogamy for all but the ranking chiefs came to be the imposed rule. Clans and lineage groups became rather unimportant, and a clear and fairly complex social stratification occurred in connection with both the production of surplus and political development.

During this period the population of the realm, especially within the core of the kingdom, increased as a result of an excess of immigration over emigration. Given the increase in agricultural production per farming family and the relief from potential famine due to cassava plantations, there may also have been a larger natural increase than in earlier days. By the time the kingdom was overwhelmed by foreign forces it was reaching a peak of prosperity while holding onto almost all the territory it had controlled in the eighteenth century.

The vigorous development of the decorative arts, artistic textiles, and sculpture is related to the prosperity of the patriciate, but the styles themselves and their evolution do not seem to have any discernible connection with the general evolution, except perhaps for the increasing profusion of decorative patterns on all available surfaces of luxury objects.

Changes in religious representations were only partly linked with the growth of the kingdom. The king became a more sacred figure than chiefs had ever been before: gradually he was seen as a nature spirit, and a form of worship, functionally equivalent to ancestor worship, arose with the creation of dynastic statues. Other religious changes, such as those concerning ritual, are much harder to document precisely. Some, such as the change in concepts of the creator, may bear a relation to the expanding scale of society during this period whereas others—in divination, for instance—may not have any direct connection with the general evolution.

This summary of the results of our inquiry constitutes a simple process model. In this view the arrival of Shyaam [1] initiated a political transformation, which, for reasons unknown, was compatible with the existing situation. The political transformation was the driving engine that triggered changes in the other areas, especially in economics. Surplus grew out of political demand and not vice versa. To view political organization as central is fairly consonant with the Kuba view of their past. This does not mean that it therefore must be wrong. It probably is not.

A major feature of the kingdom since Shyaam has been a surprising territorial and organizational stability. It is not enough to point out that there was no outside power strong enough to challenge the kingdom, and leave that as the sole explanation. The processes of development and stability are related. Three political processes must be considered here: the manner of centralization, the handling of legitimacy, and the balancing of competing aspirations at the capital.

The state developed a strong capital, but one that moved within a limited radius. This averted problem of provisioning this center, the kind of problem that is invoked to explain the downfall of Great Zimbabwe.[8] Although the Kuba did move, unlike the Kongo at Mbanza Kongo or the Bini at Great Benin, their solution stabilized the general location of the capital. In the end the capital comprised about 10 percent of the population of the core of the kingdom, which included about half of the total population and territory. The rest of the territory consisted of satellite chiefdoms, too weak to be a challenge. This solution is not dissimilar to that of other states in Africa, such as Kazembe on the Luapula. But the strength of the core compared to that of the surrounding areas was greater in this case than in many others. Comparisons with the Lozi, Bini, and Asante states are instructive. Furthermore, the delegation of power was neither simple nor total within the core, and it did not go to hereditary officials. Multiple channels were also used for the supply of taxes, corvée labor, orders, and information. The system looks more complex than that of the Lozi or even of the Rwanda (before the nineteenth century). The institutionalization of the balance of power within the capital, and the sharing of power between different interest groups as indicated by the sets of councils, may well have been the most complex in Africa.

Problems of legitimacy were tackled in two ways. First, by gradually raising the ideological status of the king vis à vis other chiefs or subjects: kings alone came to be seen as nature spirits. Second, the rules of succession became more precise over time. Before the Age of Kings, succession among the Bushoong had already been limited to the offspring of the king's sisters, and the principle that the "oldest" was to succeed had been established. From the time of Shyaam or his successor, Mboong aLeeng, an heir apparent was designated, and even an heir to the heir apparent was named. Still, confrontations over the succession did arise, even though by the nineteenth century it had been made clear that seniority referred to genealogical position and not age. A desultory civil war was waged from 1886 to about 1891, but the effect of these rules was to dissociate the bulk of the population, and even of the royal lineage, from the fight. Only candidates and their immediate supporters were involved. The struggles for succession had been channeled and delimited. In this the state was more successful than the Kongo state ever was, if only because Kongo succession rules allowed too many challengers, and they often had autonomous bases of power.

Social stratification developed to a fairly high degree among the Kuba. Why then did it not create uncontrollable tensions? The stratification was further developed than anywhere else in Central Africa, and the creation of panels of judges, in which the notions of representation and social status were paramount, attests to it. The fact that most status was achieved rather than ascribed helped alleviate tensions between the segments of the population, because it implied a high mobility. The attainment of an important political position by one person did not mean that other persons had to give up hope forever. The position was also retained for life, which meant that continual infighting at court did not occur, unlike Rwanda, for example, where the all-important position of the king's favorite was not guaranteed for any length of time. Furthermore, there were many positions. And, finally, rivalry between the ambitious was channeled by the king and the senior kolm, who were prevented by the council system from creating insoluble tensions between king and kolm. In this way the Kuba state avoided tension of the sort which, it has been argued, led to a devastating civil war in Benin around 1700.[9]

A detailed reexamination of the points made here shows that stability was not static at all but dynamic, and that it grew over time. Whether or not the arrangements affecting centralization, legitimacy, and social mobility could have withstood a massive increase in trade, especially one involving firearms, cannot be known. Still, even during the period of intensive trade from 1886 to 1897, and even though there was a civil war for part of that period, the mechanisms worked well enough to prevent any outside African or European power from interfering.

The process model leaves us with the impression that it constitutes a functional-structural analysis, so that when change occurs in one institution, it leads to change in the others. The impression is the one conveyed by the data. There existed a general structural system and within it a core of tightly interlocked institutions and structures. Outside of this core, change could and did occur, as in the evolution of styles and perhaps in religious ritual, without affecting many other institutions. Too few data are extant about religion, oral literature, and changes in values or ideas to document clear change in those areas and its eventual impact, or lack of impact, on the core. In what can be reconstructed, most change is still linked to the institutional core. This may be an effect of selective bias in Kuba historiography. Nevertheless it is clear that a large, interconnecting set of institutions and structures had come about within which change bred further change and then, by backfeeding, returned to alter the original area of change. Political, social, and economic institutions, as well as part of the value system and the world of ideas, were all tied together in this fashion. And while changing, the core kept expanding throughout the Age of Kings.

During the Age of Chiefs institutions and structures were more autonomous. The interplay primarily affected social and political structures, and economic institutions were less affected by changes in the social and political system. Even a major innovation such as the shift from patriliny to matriliny and the corresponding emphasis on territoriality in the political organization may have had little or no effect on agricultural technology and output. It is not clear at all whether the innovation brought with it any serious increase in the availability of more labor for communal projects. The main transformation brought by the shift resulted from the confrontation of differing social and cultural traditions, which affected every aspect of the way of life but did not integrate the resulting society internally any more than either of the preexisting traditions had been. The interlocked institutions were limited to society and politics, with a certain ideological influence. This was not impressive on the whole, but it was enough to allow the arrival of Shyaam to have repercussions that would in the end alter everything and eventually create the Kuba way of life.

It is tempting to examine the position of the Kuba compared to other societies. But any comparison must remain crude, if only because an analysis cannot be more precise than the data allow it to be. The data are too scarce to allow for anything more than the scanty process model that has been presented. For example, we know next to nothing about the impact of personalities, changing ideas and values, or even about most of the specific events. The fine texture of the past escapes us and so comparision must remain impressionistic.

Any historical reconstruction is in fact a process model. And any historical comparison is of necessity, then, a comparison between process models. The main body of theory that deals with such comparisons is the evolutionary theory in cultural anthropology. It has developed a number of "forces," "mechanisms," and "criteria," which approximates the list of "causal factors" that conventional historians are wont to invoke. These causal factors include natural ecology and change therein, change in the use of energy (technological change), change in the mode of subsistence, change in patterns of redistribution, gradual emancipation of natural constraints (through technology or alteration in management), change in the rate of social rivalry or in patterns of stratification, social pressure, problems of security, alterations in the mode of communications and symbols, changes in ideology, ambivalence in value systems, increase in social or geographical scale, population changes, growth of complexity, and effects of personality.[10] Complexity per se is so arbitrary a category that it must be rejected. And to the factors cited any historian adds external forces: a consideration of the impact of the surrounding area, and through it the rest of the world, on the society studied.

During the Age of Kings the natural environment did not change, although there probably was a growth in the area of cleared or fallow land; and changes in the value system remain unknown. Apart from that the Kuba case registers change for all the other factors. Redistribution in particular became a complex pattern of tribute, and reciprocity was in effect reduced to a mere gesture as the royal treasuries developed. By this the Kuba state overcame the dilemma of the kingdom of Hawaii.[11] The mode of susbsistence changed with the introduction of new crops such as cassava, which as a famine food represented a slight gain in the emancipation from nature. Double cropping was very rare in Central and East Africa, though not in West Africa. Triple cropping was unique. The yields became higher per unit and may indeed have represented some savings in energy.

The preexisting social rivalry among chiefdoms may have helped their acceptance of subordination to a kingdom, and the population movements to the center are best explained as a search for security. Social rivalry also decreased as achieved positions became more numerous and more important than ascribed positions and as the search for position was regulated by rules for the proper expression of competition. Social stratification grew, perhaps apace with the growth of surplus. Here, to cite other Central African kingdoms, the Kuba went further than the Bemba or the kingdom of Kazembe and as far as the Kongo. The very growth of the state produced changes in social pressure and problems of security.

The mode of communications was not greatly altered. Perhaps the Kuba's intensive use of the drum telegraph is a by-product of centralization. Wolf reported that he had seen such intensive communication only in the Cameroons.[12] But he had not been to Tetela country, where an equally intensive signaling system exists. The Kuba did not invent any form of writing, which perhaps remains the crucial difference between their state and such states as Axum or that of the lowland Maya in the Classic period, which are comparable to it in other respects, such as size, population of the capital, degree of centralization, and, among the Maya, economic base, which was more sophisticated among the Kuba.[13]

There was growth in public display of symbols, perhaps greater than in other Central African cases, although sound data for comparison are lacking from other courts. And there clearly was a growth in ideology, evidenced by equating kings with nature spirits and by the growth of ritual to ensure the transmission of preternatural power and hence legitimacy.

The social and geographical scales increased, but not nearly to the degree achieved by the kingdoms of the savanna, to the south. Population increased, and the density per square mile may have been equal to that of the kingdom of Kongo. It certainly was higher than in the other kingdoms of the savanna, except at the center of the Lozi state and in the Luapula valley, the center of the Kazembe state. Here exact comparison is a fallacy because of the vagueness of the data.[14] The effects of personality are epitomized in the figure of Shyaam.

Such comparisons are stimulating but ought not to be taken too seriously. They merely suggest that the Kuba achievement deserves perhaps more attention that it has received heretofore. The external influences must also be stressed: the arrival of a foreigner, Shyaam, and the development of trade. The latter line of reflection leads one to note the unique geographical situation of the Kuba—on the margins of the tropical forest and the wooded savanna, at once remote enough from the Atlantic to be shielded from the most disruptive effects of the growing trade, yet close enough to benefit from these same stimuli. However weak it may be, there is a link between the growth of the Kuba kingdom and the commercial expansion of Europe.

One difficulty that historians encounter when assessing evolutionary theory is neatly exemplified by the Kuba case. The transition from a kinship-based type of society to territorial chiefdoms and then, rather abruptly, to a kingdom, seems to be a perfect illustration of the theory.[15] But, on closer examination, the case points to a major weakness in the theory. The onset of the Age of Kings is an almost paradigmatic mutation from "tribe" to "state." But the previous transformation from proto-Kuba to Kuba has to be dismissed as an accident of differential mutation.[16] It is the theory that does not fit. It fails because evolutionary theory does not cope with the massive intrusion of factors stemming from the outside, such as the blending of cultures through immigration. Because of this, the theory cannot account for the Kuba "miracle." The Kuba developed their civilization as much as a result of outside influences—immigration, the acceptance of foreign leaders, and the development of trade—as by the operation of dynamics inherent in the society and the culture itself.

The Kuba achievement has been underrated in the history of Africa. At best it receives a few lines in general texts dealing with equatorial Africa. And yet the achievement was not minor. In many ways it was comparable to that of the kingdom of Benin from about 1500 onward. The similarities suggest that, like the Bini past, the Kuba past consisted of more than events concerning a few people in a corner of the tropical woods.

The Kuba past is important for the Kuba today and for other Zairians. It belongs to their national history. The Kuba case also happens to present a fortunate opportunity for examining and illustrating the use and validity of oral traditions. The traditions are the obligatory starting point, but their interpretation brings into play many other ways of recovering the past. At the same time Kuba history reveals the limitations of history studied in a verbal society. Kuba civilization, like any other, deserves to be better known as a human experience, unique yet comparable to others. It is therefore of interest to anthropologists. On reflection the case shows that genuine comparison can only be a comparison between process models. At present we lack the tools and the insights to accomplish this. Yet how else can we put the Kuba past in perspective? That task is for the future.

Appendixes

Notes

Reference List

Glossary

Index

List of Kuba Rulers

This list must be regarded as containing the minimum number of Kuba rulers. I am certain that all persons listed in it ruled, and the number of generations for the Matoon dynasty is definite. It is possible, however, that even in that dynasty—the most recent one—other kings ruled for some months or even a few years. For example, Mbɔ́lyɛɛng áMboom is sometimes mentioned as a ruler before Kɔt áNcé, but there is no other evidence to substantiate this: no names for his capitals, no mention of his mother in the list of queen mothers that is a part of the song for the spirits, no praise names or songs in his honor; and many informants knew nothing of him. As reconstructed here, the list tallies with that of Frobenius, who took down his information from a king's son in 1905, although I saw his list only in 1974.

It is certain that many names have been lost from the first two dynasties, a loss that has created the hiatuses shown in the list.

To reconstruct the chronology of Kuba rulers, one must rely on a count of regnal generations: that is, the interval of time between the onset of one king's reign and the onset of the reign of the first king born in the next generation. The average length of each regnal generation from 1835 to 1969 was 33.5 years. If this figure is projected backward for the known generations (in the sense that we know which kings were of the same generation and which were of successive generations), it becomes evident that the solar eclipse mentioned as occurring in the reign of King Mbákám Mbɔman-cyeel [4] must be the one of 1680. The time span 1680–1835 therefore yields as average regnal generation of 31 years. The average regnal generation in the overall time span of 1680 to 1969 is thus 32.1 years, a length which accords with David Henige's large sample of generation lengths given in *The Chronology of Oral Tradition: Quest for a Chimera* (Oxford, 1974), pages 123 and 126. Projecting that figure backward for two generations from 1680 would produce a date of 1616 for the onset of the regnal generation of Shyáám [1]. Since a ruler of the same generation preceded him, we can roughly date his accession as 1625.

Lengths of reign are extremely variable, as a glance at the dates of reign since 1885 shows. In addition, the reader should keep in mind that even generation lengths are only statistical averages. Over four to five generations reality comes closer to the average, but it would still be unrealistic to date the regnal generations 32 years apart. This list of rulers does not, therefore, carry time indications such as "eighteenth century," "nineteenth century," or "c. 1625."

For more detail concerning the list and related points of discussion, see my article "Kuba Chronology Revisited," *Paideuma* 21 (1975):134–50.

The bracketed numbers and letters are used on occasion in the text for convenience of reference. Numbers are used for kings of the Matoon dynasty because we have genealogical information about them. Letters designate the preceding rulers, for whom we lack trustworthy genealogical information.

List of Kuba Rulers

Ruler	Regnal Generation
Archaic Period: Genesis	

[A] Wóót
hiatus
[B] Diambaan and the brothers of Mbɔɔng

Archaic Period: Mbɔɔng Dynasty	

[C] Mbɔɔng (alias Mancu maShyaang)
hiatus
[D] perhaps a woman, Ngɔkády
hiatus
[E] Lashyááng

Archaic Period: Penultimate Dynasty	

hiatus
[F] Mishé miShyááng Mátúún   Generation I

The Rise of the Kingdom: Matoon Dynasty	

[1] Shyáám áMbúl áNgoong   Generation I
[2] Mboong áLɛɛng
[3] MbɔMbóósh   Generation II

Classical Period: Matoon Dynasty	

[4] Mbákám Mbɔmancyeel (ruling in 1680)   Generation III
[5] Kɔt áMbwééky íkoongl
[6] Mishé míShyááng máMbúl   Generation IV
[7] Kɔt áNće   Generation V
[8] MishááPelyeeng áNće   Generation VI
[9] Mbɔ Pelyeeng áNće
    Mbúlápe (a woman), regent
[10] Kɔt áMbúl   Generation VII
[11] Mikɔ miMbúl
[12] Mbɔp Mábíínc máMbúl (ruled c. 1835 to late 1885 or 1886)

List of Kuba Rulers (continued)

Colonial Period to the Present: Matoon Dynasty

[13] Mikɔ́ Mabíínc máMbúl (ruled 1885 or 1886 to before 1892) Generation VIII
[14] Kɔt áMbwééky II (ruled from before 1892 to 1896) Generation IX
[15] Misháápe (ruled 1896–1900) Generation X
[16] Mbɔ́p Kyeen (ruled c. three months, 1900)
[17] Mikɔ́ miKyeen (ruled 1901–1902)
[18] Kɔt áPe (ruled 1902–1916) Generation XI
[19] Mbɔ́p áMbwééky (ruled 1916–1919)
[20] Kot Mábíínc (ruled 1919–1939)
[21] Mbɔ́p Mábíínc maMbéky (ruled 1939–1969)
[22] Kɔt áMbwééky III (ruled 1969–) Generation XII

Lexical Comparisons

In this appendix, a selection of Bushɔɔ́ng terms is compared with the lexicon of neighboring Bantu languages. The list includes only items that can be shown to be proto-Kuba in origin, loanwords, and internal innovations. The items that I chose for my comparisons, not all of which appear in this list, include the specific vocabularies of religious, social, political, economic, artistic, and technological terms encountered during my fieldwork and in Bushɔɔ́ng texts; they also include the terms in the list of one hundred words compiled by Morris Swadesh, which was designed for statistical use and is the standard used in lexicostatistics.

Languages with which Bushɔɔ́ng was compared were chosen from all around the area if vocabularies or dictionaries existed. To the north this includes Mongo, Lia, Ntomba (Tumba), and Tetela. A few Nkucu, Ndengese, and Ooli terms were culled from the general literature, and I used Ngombe when I wanted to establish whether a term was only Mongo or could be attributed to Guthrie's zone C. To the west, the Kongo dictionary of Roboredo or Van Geel (c. 1652; ed. Van Wing and Penders, 1928) was checked, as were published Mbala, Tio, Pende, Dzing, and Sakata word lists and unpublished Mbuun and Yans dictionaries or word lists. Some items from other languages could also be gathered from the general literature. To the south, Luba Kasai, Songye, and Luba Shaba were regularly used, and Lunda was used occasionally. I am grateful to Jeffrey Hoover for sharing with me his comparative word list covering all the languages of zones K and L. To the east, Songye was regularly used. Unfortunately, no Binji word list exists. The comparative lexicons and studies of Common Bantu, including those of Harry Johnston, Malcolm Guthrie, and Albert Meeussen, and a comparative vocabulary from the 1920s for the former district of Kasai, compiled by Joseph Maes, were also used. Bibliographical information for these works and others cited in the list of comparisons can be found in the Reference List of this book.

The main weaknesses of the appendix stem from the facts that dictionaries are not available for Binji and that the word list extant for Mbuun is meager. Moreover, we have almost no data for the neighbors immediately north of the Kuba. The effect of this is to obscure eventual loans from the east and to hinder establishment of a vocabulary common only to southern Mongo languages, resulting either from loans or from a common origin. Another type of weakness could result from the fact that Gustaaf Hulstaert's dictionary of Mongo is so complete and outstanding compared to all others that it could skew the results in favor of Mongo. It has so many more entries than any other dictionary that it is conceivable that links with Mongo and not with other languages were established merely because the corresponding entries were not listed in other dictionaries. I do not believe, however, that a serious distortion has resulted from this because few esoteric items were included and because the specialized technological vocabulary that could be found in Hulstaert but not in other vocabularies was omitted.

Bushɔɔ́ng is related to the Mongo group within zone C of Guthrie's classification. The affinities are so evident that, for example, Bushɔɔ́ng has nouns derived from verbs known only in Mongo and vice versa, and the meaning of some Bushɔɔ́ng items is listed as "archaic" in Mongo and vice versa. An overwhelming number of basic items corresponds in both languages. This cannot be attributed to proximity, for the Mongo speech recorded by Hulstaert near Mbandaka is hundreds of miles farther away than Ding, Mbuun, and Luba Kasai.

Correspondences have been fully accepted when there are no exceptions to the phonemic and morphophonemic correspondences of form, which must be regular: for instance, tone in the L languages is inversed. The L languages have only five vowel systems, whereas Bushɔɔ́ng has seven. Luba u always corresponds to Bushɔɔ́ng o and never to u; therefore any term with a Bushɔɔ́ng u cannot be a loan from Luba. Rules for correspondence are easily found for the languages involved, the main difficulties being the occasional absence of k, b, or f in the initial position in the languages of zone C. In this group it will be noted that Tetela u also corresponds to Bushɔɔ́ng o. Correspondences conform in general to the expected, the reflexes from Common Bantu being known for most languages (see Guthrie, *Comparative Bantu*, 2:28–64, esp. p. 41 for Bushɔɔ́ng). Guthrie's data are neither complete nor always exact. For the languages other than Bushɔɔ́ng, Mongo, and Luba, I used Guthrie; when the language was not represented there, internal consistency—i.e., consistency among all the comparisons made—was the rule.

The rules for correspondence have not always been strictly adhered to, especially when shifts in noun classes occur and sometimes when tone or vowel aperture changes. This is indicated in the comment for the item. I have allowed one deviation, but never two. I feel that differences in tone often are due either to wrong notation at some point or to a genuine irregular shift. Erroneous notation is also a possibility in some cases involving vowel aperture.

Many lists have no tone notations and have reduced seven-vowel systems to five. It is clear that in such circumstances correspondences are actually inferred rather than shown, for lack of better data.

High tone is indicated by an acute accent (´), nominal classes by the Common Bantu numbering (e.g., 5, 6), and third-degree vowels by the symbols in the alphabet of the International African Institute, ɔ and ɛ. Common Bantu spelling does not follow this convention for the third-degree vowels, which can lead to confusion. Its seven vowels are $i̧$, i, e, a, o, u, $u̧$; its i and u therefore correspond to e and o of the International African Institute alphabet.

I have divided the material into eleven groups: I. Conceptual Categories; II. Environment; III. Farming; IV. Hunting, Gathering, and Fishing; V. Crafts; VI. Trade and Markets; VII. Kinship Terminology; VIII. Social Organization; IX. Political Organization; X. Religion; and XI. Visual Arts. Within each group items going back to proto-Kuba are given first, followed by innovations, followed by loanwords from the south, followed by loanwords from the west or southwest, followed by others.

An item that is Common Bantu or has a very wide distribution is described as proto-Kuba, and its Comparative Series (CS) number of Guthrie is given in the comment; ps indicates a partial series number.

Entries include the concept and its Bushɔɔng form in the first column, comparable forms in the second column, and comments on the Bushɔɔng form in the third column. Not all comparable forms are given, especially when the item is listed in a CS or exists in several Mongo languages. In such cases I give the Mongo form and add the names of the other languages in parentheses. Occasionally I give a form other than Mongo—e.g., Luba Shaba.

The language name means that the word occurs in the standard dictionary used for that language. "Kongo 1652" means that the word is in Van Wing and Penders; "Kongo" means that it is in Laman; "Dzing" means it is in Mertens, "Ding" that it is in Maes, who is also the source for languages of the Kasai area, for which no dictionaries are available. "Ndengese" refers to my own word list; "Luba" refers to Luba Kasai; "Luba Shaba" means just that; and "Ntomba" refers to the Ntomba of Lake Tumba. The sources for the most common languages can thus be checked by the general reader. Linguists will find all the linguistic sources listed in Bastin, *Bibliographie bantoue selective* (1975). Terms found in an ethnographic account rather than in a word list or dictionary are accompanied by a reference to the source.

Only a minority of the sources gives tonal indications; absence of tone in the comparable forms therefore does not necessarily mean low tone.

List of Lexical Comparisons

I. Conceptual Categories		
Bushɔ́ɔ́ng	*Comparable Forms*	*Comment*
1. word: *dweéy, moóy,* 5, 6.	Mongo: *jói,* 5, 6 (also Lia, Ntomba, Tetela, Bobangi).	CS 954. Proto-Bantu.
2. important word: *ikaam,* 7, 6. Intensive: *ikakaam,* true.	Mongo: *likambo,* 5, 6 (also Lia, Ntomba, Tetela, Bobangi, Lingala, Ngombe).	Proto-Kuba, probably proto-C. The Bushɔ́ɔ́ng class 7 often corresponds to class 5 elsewhere when the plural is class 6.
3. a long time ago: *wal.* invariable intensive: *awalawal.*	Mongo: *kala;* invariable: *kalakala* (also Ntomba). Dzing: *kɛl* (adj.); intensive: *kela kɛl.* Luba: *kálá,* formerly. Songye: *kalakala.* Ruund: *kál.*	CS 983 ("old times") or CS 979½. Proto-Bantu; initial *k* disappears.
4. day: *lashú,* 10, 11.	Mongo: *loswo,* 10, 11 (also Lia, Ntomba, Ngombe).	CS 434 and 437. Proto-Bantu.
5. night: *butú,* 14, 6 (also means a period of 24 hours).	Mongo: *botsó,* 3, 4 (also Lia, Ntomba, Ngombe).	CS 434 and CS 437; CS 1863 and 1864. Proto-Bantu.
6. month: *ngwɔ́ɔ́n,* 9, 10 (also means moon).	Tetela: *ngɔndɔ,* 9, 10. Luba: *ngondo,* 9, 10. Kongo 1652: *ngonde,* 9, 10.	Proto-Kuba; most Mongo languages lack the term. It is widespread enough (CS 855 and 856), especially in northwest Bantu, to be quite old.
7. season: *kyeek,* 9, 10.	Mongo: *ekeké,* 5, 6, time.	Proto-Kuba, perhaps then meaning "time."
8. space (an area): *itaan,* 7, 8.	Mongo: *etando,* 7, 8 (also Lia, Ntomba, Ngombe). Luba Shaba: *ntándá* 5, 6: region, territory, bush. Luba: *ntándá,* region of origin, village (9, 10).	Proto-Kuba. The noun is derived from a verb still existing in Mongo and other languages, which may be proto-Bantu. Cf. CS 1663.

I. Conceptual Categories (continued)

Bushɔ́ɔ́ng	Comparable Forms	Comment
9. place: *idi*, 7, 6.	Mongo: *njié*, 9, 10. Lia: *ndié*, 9, 10. Ntomba: *ndie*, 9, 10. Sakata: *njii*, 9, 10.	Proto-Kuba. The shift in classes to 7, 6 encompasses other concepts of space.
10. place: *imbét*, 7, 6. Cf. *bétm*, to sleep; *bét*, to stay flat.	Mongo: *béti*, to be flat (also Lia, Ntomba).	The verb is proto-Kuba. The noun is an innovation similar to Mongo "bed."
11. time: *itááng*, 7, 6 (also means sun). world: *matááng máNce* (in which *matááng*, 6, means expanse, distance).	Kongo 1652: *ntangwa*, hour; . . . and then. Kongo modern: *ntangwa*, 9, 10, sun. Sakata Tere: *ntangu*, 9, 10, moment in time. Pende: *tangua*, 9, 10, times. Pende: *lutangua*, 11, 10, moment of day. Mbuun: *ɛtáng*, 5, 6, sun. Mbuun: *ntang*, 9, 10, time, hour. Mongo: *itangó*, 5, 6, distance. Ntomba: *itangó*, 5, 6, distance.	CS 1679 and 1680, with the meaning "sun." Johnston adds Yaka, Hungana, Boma. This is claimed to be an early western Bantu term. Note all the low tones except in Bushɔ́ɔ́ng and Mbuun. A loan from Kongo with the meaning "sun" and "time," but before that the term was used with the meaning: "distance"; hence the classes.
12. year: *nci*, 3, 4 (perhaps also with the general meaning "season").	Mbuun: *ɛshyi*, 7, 8.	Possibly from Mbuun, with the meaning "year."
13. week: see section VI, Trade and Markets, item *4*.		
14. cause: see section IX, Political Organization, item *9*.		

II. Environment

Bushóóng	Comparable Forms	Comment
1. plain: *bushépy*, 14, 6 (also means outside).	Mongo: *esóbé*, 5, 6. Lia: *bohóbe* 3, 4.	Proto-Kuba: intercalary savanna. Note that the old class 3 became class 14.
2. ravine: *ibɛky*, 7, 6.	Mongo: *mbɛki*, escarpment, 9, 10; high bank of the river.	Proto-Kuba. Note the tonal difference.
3. hill: *nkwoonc*, 3, 4 (also means world).	Mongo: *bokonjî*, 3, 4, anthill.	There are no hills in northwest Mongo country. Proto-Kuba: hill.

Note: In the expression *ncyéém nkwoonc*, "God on earth," the term *nkwoonc* could be linked to *mokonji*, wealthy person, leader, as in Bobangi. Mongo: *bokonjisa*, 1, 2, wealthy person; Ntomba: *mokonji*, 1, 2, chief; and Mongo: *konja*, to become wealthy. This term is also proto-Mongo and hence proto-Kuba.

4. (sandy) island: *ishaang*, 7, 6 (sandy).	Mongo: *esanga*, 7, 8 (also Lia, Ntomba, Tetela). Mbala: *saangi*, 7, 8. Ding (south): *isange*. Songye: *kisanga*, 7, 8. Luba: *tshísángá*, 7, 8.	CS 289. Widespread but by itself not proto-Bantu. Proto-Kuba. The Luba word is not derived from Kuba.
5. island: *itól*, 7, 6.	Lia: *itóló*, 7, 6, spiny waterplant (also Ntomba, Konda).	Related to western Mongo. The Kuba term could refer to floating islands.
6. downstream: *ngɛl*, 9, 10.	Mongo: *ngɛlé* (also Lia, Tetela, Ngengele).	Cf. CS 798 ("to flow"), CS 799 ("stream"), of which the first is proto-Bantu. Proto-Kuba: downstream.
7. small river: *loósh*, 11, 10.	Mongo: *lŏse*, 11, 10 (also Tetela). Bobangi: *loásá*, 11, 10, side of a marshy river that stands dry at low water.	Proto-Kuba.
8. stream: *nkɔ́k*, 9, 10 (also means head of stream).	Mongo: *inkɔ́kɔ*, 5, 6, spring, upper part of stream.	Mongo- or Luba-related. Hulstaert gives it as a derivation of CS 1204,

II. Environment (continued)

Bushɔɔ́ng	*Comparable Forms*	*Comment*
8 (continued)	Luba: *nkoka,* 9, 10, water gully. Tetela: *kɔ́kɔ́* 9, 10, upstream.	ps 309, *nkɔ́kɔ,* Mongo: lineage elder. Can be proto-Kuba.
9. brook: *nkɛdy,* 3, 4. *1*	Mongo: *bokɛli,* 3, 4 (also Lia, Tetela).	CS 801, derived from CS 798. Proto-Kuba.
10. lake: *idíp,* 7, 6.	Mongo: *elia,* 7, 8. Bobangi: *eliba,* 5, 6. Lia: *eliba,* 5, 6. Ntomba: *eliba,* 5, 6, artificial pond. Luba: *díjíbá,* 5, 6. Songye: *oshiba,* 5, 6.	Cf. CS 603 and 605. Tone agrees with 605 (''water''). Cf. also CS 2022. Northwest Bantu. Proto-Kuba. Note tonal uncertainty also in the CS. Kuba is related to Lia and Ntomba; Mongo lost the *-b-;* Bobangi and Luba have opposed tones. A direct loan from Luba is to be excluded because of tone.
11. sandbank: *shyɛéngy,* 9, 10; back-formation from *lashyɛɛngy,* 11, 10, grain of sand.	Lia: *ihɛngɛ,* 5, 6, sand beach. Tetela: *sɛnga,* 5, 6. Luba: *lúsééngé,* 11, 10. Songye: *lúsééngga,* 11, 10, island.	Cf. CS 325, ps 94. Lia has the most regular correspondence in form, Luba and Tetela in meaning (but note tone!). Could be proto-Kuba with this meaning.
12. harbor: *mbóóng,* 9, 10.	Lia and Ntomba: *ibóngo,* 5, 6. Mongo: *ióngo, baongo,* 5, 6. Pende: *mbungu,* 9, 10. Luba: *dibungu,* 5, 6, bank.	CS 205. Proto-Kuba. Initial *b* dropped in Mongo. The spread of the term is not yet fully determined.
13. small wood: *yook,* 7, 8.	Tetela: *dihuka,* 5, 6. Mongo: *efoka,* 7, 8, wood (dialect).	Proto-Kuba, meaning a small wood in intercalary savanna.

II. Environment (continued)

Bushɔɔ́ng	Comparable Forms	Comment
14. dry season: *isho,* 7, 6.	Mongo: *isoa,* 5, 6, period of first rains after low water. Dzing: *ishüüw,* 7, 8. Mbuun: *sonyi,* 9, 10. Songye: *eshifu,* 5, 6. Songye: *eshipu,* 5, 6. Luba: *múshípú,* 3, 4.	Proto-Kuba. Connection with Dzing possible, not with Mbuun, Songye, or Luba.
15. small stream: *nshaancy,* 9, 10, or 3, 4. These contain iron deposits. Cf. *incaancy,* 7, 8, barge (metal). Cf. many toponyms.	Mongo: *injanja,* 5, 6, tin object, loanword perhaps from Swahili. Ntomba: *inzanza,* 5, 6, tin. Lia: *injanja,* 5, 6, tin. Many toponyms for small rivers in the southern Mongo area are *nshaanci.*	Could be Proto-Kuba, because of the toponyms. In this case the "loanword" in the Mongo languages is not a loan but a new formation, as in Bushɔɔ́ng "barge."
16. bank: *nkol,* 3, 4.	Luba: *ńkoló,* 9, 10, fence put in a river. Sakata: *ngkall*(e). Dzing: *ngkil,* 9, 10.	The most comparable form is northwest Sakata (Bampey). The Luba tone is wrong and the meaning diverges too much. No Mongo connection. Origin unknown.

Note: Ding: *ngkil andzaal,* bank of the river, corresponds to the Kuba toponym Kil aNcal, a village located near the Sankuru River. This suggests that Dzing *ngkil* became Bushɔɔ́ng *Kil.*

17. upstream: *tyeen,* 13.	Luba: *tendé,* straight.	Tones do not correspond. Connection by borrowing from Luba barely possible.
18. gentle valley: *labaan,* 11, 10.	Luba: *tshíbándá,* 7, 8. Songye: *ebanda,* 5, 6.	CS 52. Loan from Luba.
19. ocean: *mbúp,* 9, 10.	Kongo 1652: *muwu.* Luba: *mbu,* 9, 10. Mongo, *mbú,* 9, 10 (loanword).	Kongo origin. Luba cannot be the origin because its *u* would become *o* in Bushɔɔ́ng.

II. Environment (continued)

Bushᴐᴐng	Comparable Forms	Comment
20. (big) river: *ncál*, 9, 10.	Mongo *njále*, 9, 10 (one term among several). Lia: *njale*, 9, 10, big river, lake. Tetela: *ndjalé*, 9, 10. Kongo: *nzadi*, 9, 10.	Full distribution given in Johnston and summarized in Vansina, *Geschiedenis*, p. 100, n. 104. Besides Mongo, the term is used by the riparians of the Kasai, Sankuru, and middle Zaire rivers and those of their major affluents. It spread along Kasai and Zaire, but the origin is unclear. Perhaps Kongo.

Note: Zaire, the name of the country and of the river, is this term. *Ndjare* or *nzali* also used as a name for fishermen on the lower Kasai.

21. ground, earth: *maán*, 6.	Luba: *manda*, 6, valley, downstream. Hungaan: *man* (Johnston). Buma: *man* (Hochegger). Yans: *mmen* (Johnston).	A loan from lower Kwilu area.
22. forest: *bwaány*, 14, 6.	Nzali: *bwanyi* (Maes). Binji: *bwanî* (Maes). Luba: *díaaní*, 5, 6, leaf. Luba: *lúaanyí*, 11, 10, tall grass. Luba Shaba: *díaanyí*, 5, 6, leaf. Luba Shaba: *byaanyí*, 8, tall grass.	CS 1928, 926 ("leaf", "grass"). The Nzali are fishermen of Ding and Sakata connections; the Binji are Mbagani. Luba loan. If the term was proto-Kuba, it should survive in southern Mongo, but there is no evidence of this. The term is derived from leaf, CS 14, making the abstraction.

Note: It is remarkable that perhaps the major feature of the landscape cannot be traced to proto-Kuba, and is instead presumably a loan from Luba.

III. Farming

Bushɔɔ́ng	Comparable Forms	Comment
1. field: *ngwoon,* 9, 6.	Nkengo: *ngona,* 9, 10. Mongo: *ngonda,* 9, 10, forest on dry land. Tetela: *okunda,* 3, 4.	CS 897. Common Bantu. Proto-Kuba.
2. plant: *woón.*	Mongo: *-óna.* Luba: *-kuná.* Tetela: *nkuná.* Mbuun: *kakôn.* Songye: *-kuna.*	CS 1217. Supposed western Bantu. Proto- Kuba.
3. harvest: *akún.* work: *ngun,* 3, 4.	Mongo: *kunda,* to stash, to heal up. Songye: *-kula,* to harvest maize.	CS 911 ("to help"). Both the noun and the verb can be derived from this form. See also CS 231 (to harvest). Homburger reconstructed the form as in CS 911 and mean- ing "to harvest." Dis- tribution eastern Bantu, except for Tetela. Proto-Kuba: to harvest, to help; work.

Note: The difference between CS 911 and 231 lies in the reconstruction of initial *b* or *g.* The Kuba would have *g.* No form closer than Ila (barring Tetela) is reported. I take the Mongo meaning to be derived.

4. woman's field (in the savanna): *iyoot,* 7, 6.	Mongo: *joto,* 5, 6, the first cut to fell a tree.	Could be proto-Kuba, with a later shift in meaning.
5. fallow *iyoot:* *iyóiyoot,* 7, 6.	Mongo: *jó* plus root for woman, as in *jómoto,* woman.	Either a reduplication of the previous (but why the tone?) or as in Mongo; but the latter is barely possible.
6. abandoned village site: *iyoom,* 5, 6.	Mongo: *jombo,* 5, 6, cemetery. Tetela: *lukumbu,* 11, 10, cemetery. Dzing: *iyum,* 5, 6. Suku: *mayumbu,* 6 (pl.) (Lamal, p. 88). Mbuun: *aalóóm,* 6 (pl.).	Proto-Kuba: cemetery, abandoned village site. The Kuba bury their dead in such sites. The distribution (Mbuun is doubtful) is not limited to Mongo, but extends far southwards.

III. Farming (continued)

Bushóóng	Comparable Forms	Comment
6 (continued)	Ntomba: *liombo*, 5, 6, cemetery. Lia: *liombo*, 5, 6, cemetery.	
7. plantain: *ikwɔɔn*, 7, 6.	Mongo: *lingkɔndɔ*, 5, 6 (also Lia, Ntomba, Tetela Ngombe).	CS 1090, 1144, 1146. Proto-Kuba. Expected reflexes in Luba, Songye, Mbuun, Pende also occur.
8. millet: *mashááng*, 6. cereal seed: *lash(y)ááng*, 11, 10.	Mongo: *basángú*, 6, maize. Kongo: *masaa*, 6, maize. Kongo 1652: *masa*, a cereal in the expression *masa matrigu*, "wheat." Tio: *asáá*, 6, maize. Tio: *sáálinsáá*, millet ("the true *-sáá*"). Kete south: *mesangu*, 6, maize. Sala Mpasu: *masangwa*, 6, maize. Lwalwa: *masa*, 6, maize. Pende: *disangu*, 5, 6, millet. Pende: *disaa*, 5, 6 maize. Mpiin: *masa*, 6, maize. Mpiin: *masangu*, 6, millet. Yans: *asaa*, 6, maize. Buma: *máshia*, 6, millet. Lwer: 6, maize bread. Mbuun: *sáng*, 6, millet. Cokwe: *masangu*, 6, millet. Lunda: *massangw*, 6, kind of millet.	CS 288, 293½, 294. Common Bantu: cereal. Proto-Kuba: millet. Numerous forms from other languages with the same meanings, or with the meaning "cereal beer," confirm this.

(continued)

III. Farming (continued)

Bushɔ́ɔ́ng	Comparable Forms	Comment
8 (continued)	Lwena: *masangu*, 6, millet. Luba: *lusánga*, 11, 10, cereal seed. Luna Inkongo: *lusangu*, 11, 10, cereal seed. Mongo: *lisangu*, maize (also Lia, Ntomba). Tiv: *ishange, ashange*, grain of seed.	
9. yam *sp.* (domestic): *ikup*, 7, 6.	Mongo: *ekufɛ*, 7, 8. Fumu: *nkubi*, 9, 6.	Proto-Kuba.
10. yam *sp.* (wild yellow): *yéém*, 7, 8.	Mongo: *iémbé*, 7, 6, *sp.* banana. Tetela: *lɔpɛma*, 11, 10.	Proto-Kuba.
11. bean: *lakwɔ́ɔ́n*, 11, 10.	Mongo: *ngɔndé*, 11, 10. Tetela: *lɔkɔ́ndɛ́*, 11, 10, pea. Luba: *lúkunde*, 11, 10. Songye: *lukunde*, 11, 10. Dzing: *nkwɛn*, 9, 10. Pende: *kunde*, 5, 6.	CS 1222. Proto-Bantu (edible bean). Proto-Kuba. Vowel aperture precludes loan from Luba, Dzing, Songye, or Pende.
12. eggplant: *lashól*, 11, 10.	Mongo: *losóló*, 11, 10 (also Lia, Tetela).	Proto-Kuba.
13. pineapple: *ikam*, 7, 6.	Mongo: *ekamú*, 7, 8, dialect for *bɔnkɔ́n*, 3, 4, whose fruit is *ɛnkɔ́n*, 7, 8; *ɛnkɔmbéla*, pineapple, 7, 8, is derived from *ɛnkɔ́n*. See Hulstaert, *Notes de botanique mongo*, No. 656. Ntomba: *ekamú*, 7, 8; *ikamú*, 5, 6, fruit from *bokamú*, 3, 4, tree. Tetela: *ɛkɔmi*, 7, 8.	The noun is derived from the name of a tree, probably *bukam*, 14. This was probably the Mongo *bɔnkɔm* (*Myrianthus arboreus* Beauv) cultivated for its fruits. Later the name was transferred to pineapple. This may have happened independently among the Kuba.
14. oil palm fruit: *lambá*, 11, 10.	Mongo: *lombá*, 11, 10. Tetela: *lombá*, 11, 10. Mbuun: *labá*, 9, 10.	CS 1. Common Bantu for the oil palm tree. Proto-Kuba.

III. Farming (continued)

Bushɔ́ɔ́ng	Comparable Forms	Comment
15. palm frond: *diááng,* 5, 6.	Mongo: *janga,* 5, 6 (also Ntomba, Tetela). Dzing: *maanga,* 6. Mbuun: *láang, máang,* 11, 6.	Proto-Kuba.
16. marsh palm: *diaan,* 5, 6.	Ooli: *mayanda* (De Langhe, p. 210). Buma: *mayánda,* 6. Buma: *mazian,* 6.	Could be proto-Kuba; more data needed.
17. small palm *sp.* (wild and spiny): *ikady,* 7, 6.	Mongo: *likali,* 5, 6, raffia palm (also Tetela, Ntomba). Songye: *ekadi,* 5, 6.	CS 767 (a CS for oil palm). Proto-Kuba, with the meaning "raffia palm."
18. dwarf palm *sp.* (in marsh, prob. *Eremospatha cabrae*): *mapet,* 6.	Mongo: *lofete,* 11, 10. Several Mongo dialects: *ifete,* 5, 6 (several plants).	Proto-Kuba. For Mongo, see Hulstaert, *Notes de botanique Mongo,* Nos. 170, 289a, 363. The Kuba plant is probably No. 430. The semantic displacements can be accounted for by similar functions.
19. dog: *mbɔ́shoong,* 9, 10; this is *mbɔ* + *bushoong,* 14 (hunt).	Mongo: *mbwá,* 9, 10.	CS 174 and 220. *bóà:* Common Bantu and very widespread. The Bushɔ́ɔ́ng compound may be proto-Kuba.
20. goat: *káámdý,* 9, 10; archaic: *mbódy,* 9, 10.	Bobangi: *mbóli,* 9, 10. Tetela: *mbúdi,* 9, 10. Luba: *mbuji,* 9, 10. Songye: *mbuji,* 9, 10. Dzing: *mbut,* 9, 10. 2. Dzing: *nkyaam,* 9, 10; 1, 2. Mbagani: *kambiji* (Maes). Nzali: *n'kaame* (Maes).	CS 185. The archaic form is widespread but not universal. The recent form is an innovation adding prefix class 12 (*ka*) and reducing the whole. Dzing and Nzali share the innovation. Proto-Kuba, despite lack of Mongo forms (which follow CS 1635, except Bobangi), is proto-Bantu, like CS 185.

III. Farming (continued)

Bushɔ́ɔ́ng	Comparable Forms	Comment
21. pigeon: *imbyeengy*, 7, 8.	Mongo: *embengá*, 7, 8. Tetela: *evenga* or *eengá*, 7, 8.	The Mongo pigeon is *Treron calva* Temm. *Columbidae*. CS 131, probably varying *sp.* of wild pigeons. Proto-Kuba: wild pigeon. Domesticated pigeons date from the colonial period.
22. fowl: *kɔ́k*, 9, 10.	Mongo: *nkɔ́kɔ́*, 9, 10. Mongo: *nśośo*, 9, 10. Tetela: *nkɔ́kɔ́*, 9, 10.	CS 1126. Proto-Kuba and related to the first Mongo form.
23. banana: *imbɔt*, 7, 6.	Luba: *díbóte*, 5, 6. Lwalwa: *dibote*, 5, 6. Tetela: *dibɔté*, 5, 6.	Borrowed from Luba. Tetela may also have borrowed from an L language.
24. cassava: *mpwɛɛp*, 9, 10.	Luba: *mpópò*, 10, grass ears. Lwalwa: *lupempu*, 11, 10.	The closest form is Luba, the Kuba vowel being ɔ. Probably the form is borrowed from Luba (plant is American and was borrowed from the west).
25. food mush: *bishim*, 8.	Luba: *ńshimá*, 9, 10. Luba Shaba: *nshimá*, 9, 10. Tetela: *nshimá*, 9, 10. Nzali: *bisima* (Maes).	In Luba, only the mush made from cassava; for the Kuba, made from cassava or maize. A loan from Luba, but the tone as indicated by Bushɔ́ɔ́ng does not fit. Cf. also Tetela tone. Distribution very similar to item *23*.
26. sugarcane: *mwɛɛng*, 3, 4.	Luba: *múéngé*, 3, 4. Songye: *muenge*, 3, 4. Pende: *muenge*, 3, 4, sugary stem of cereals; palm flower. Tetela: *wɛɛngé*, 3, 4.	A loan from Luba or the east. Distribution similar to items *25* and *23*, except for Pende. The Pende meaning may have existed before the sugarcane was introduced.

III. Farming (continued)

Bushṍṍng	Comparable Forms	Comment
27. raffia palm: *ibwɔɔn*, 7, 6.	Lia: *ibɔndɔ*, 5, 6. Luba: *díbóndó*, 5, 6. Songye: *ebondo*, 5, 6. Luba Shaba: *díbóndó*, 5, 6 (resembles raffia palm; used for weaving). Cokwe: *mabondo* (Maes). Lunda: *diwonda* (Maes).	A loan from Luba. The Lia form is unexpected. Luba is supported by forms in Maes for Kete north, Kete south, and Sala Mpasu. For the previous Kuba term, see item *17*.
28. sheep: *paang*, 9, 10.	Luba: *mpangá*, 9, 10, ram. Songye: *kimpanga*, 7, 8, ram. Tetela: *pángá*, 9, 10, curved horn of the ram. Mongo: *mpangá*, 9, 10, antelope (*Boocercus eurycerus* Ogilby). Nkucu: *panga* (Maes), sheep.	CS 1443. The distribution includes all of zone L and parts of K. Form probably Mongo and proto-Kuba for the antelope. Transfer of meaning under Luba influence; this accounts for tonal irregularity in the loan.
29. fallow: *iyuung*, 7, 6.	Dzing: *iyɔng*, 5, 6, field.	Possible connection, but note vowel aperture.
30. gourd (calabash): *mbyéén*, 9, 10.	Bobangi: *mbénda*, 9, 10. Kongo: *mbinda*, 9, 10. Tio: *mbíína*, 9, 10. Mbala: *mbíínda*, 9, 6/10. Dzing: *mbiin*, 9, 10. Mbuun: *mbeen*, 9, 10. Pende: *mbinda*, 9, 10. Mpiin: *mbinda*, 9, 10? Lwalwa: *binda*, 9, 10? Songye: *fondo*, millet.	CS 128. André Coupez points out that with the meaning "container" this form is proto-Bantu. Not proto-Kuba. From Kwilu. Former name for calabash was dropped; perhaps a new species was introduced from Kwilu?
31. maize: *mambwoon*, 6; *imboon*, 7, ear of maize; *mpwoon*, 3, 4, tassel of maize (envelope of the ear).	Luba: *mupóndó*, 3, 4, raw cassava. Luba: *mpónda*, 9, 10, millet (also Mbagani, Kete north, Lwalwa, Lunda, Ding, Dzing). Mbuun: *wṍng*, 5, 6, millet.	Except for Kongo 1652 and Yombe, no comparable form fits because of vowel aperture. But the tones of Kongo and Yombe are unknown. Kongo 1652 corresponds well. The

(continued)

III. Farming (continued)

Bushɔ́ɔ́ng	Comparable Forms	Comment
31 (continued)	Pende: *ponda,* 9, 10, spice. Kongo 1652: *mfundi,* bread. Yombe: *mbundi,* 9, 10, loose tissue under leaves of palm trees.	plant is American in origin. Word origin is either Kongo or, with an unexplained shift of vowel, Kwilu.
32. yam *sp.* (wild yellow): *ishɔɔng,* 7, 8.	Dzing: *musɔng,* 3, 4, sugarcane. Dzing: *idzung,* 7, 6/7, 8, yam (dark-colored).	Possible link between second Dzing and Bushɔ́ɔ́ng, but note vowel aperture.
33. flour: *puup,* 9, 10.	Kongo 1652: *mfumfu,* flour. Kongo: *mfumfu,* 9, 10, cassava meal (*fufu*).	Of Kongo origin. Often thought to be a recent loan, but 1652 evidence shows that it may be old.
34. peanut: *lanco,* 11, 10.	Tio: *liyuu, ndzuu,* 11, 10. Dzing: *ndzuu,* 10. Mbuun: *ládzu,* 11, 10. Ngwi: *edzoku.* Mpiin: *inzu.* Nzali: *edzuwo.*	CS 961. Origin from west, perhaps from Tio. Spread via Kwilu.
35. tobacco: *makɛy,* 6.	Kongo: *lukaya,* 11, 6, leaf. Pende: *kanya,* 5, 6. Mbuun: *ekanya,* 5, 6. Dzing: *ikiya,* 5, 6. Mpiin: *makaya,* 6. Lwer: *kie* (class?). Nzali: *ikia,* 5, 6. Buma: *ikáy,* 5, 6. Tio: *kɛɛ, ākɛɛ,* 5, 6. Luba: *makanya,* 6. Kongo 1612: *magkay* (Brun, p. 27).	CS 1019, 1021. Kongo origin, spread via Kwilu. Luba borrowed independently from Bushɔ́ɔ́ng. Bushɔ́ɔ́ng *ɛ* is often the combination of *a* + C + *i,* or *aya.*
36. pepper: *ishyééngy,* 7, 6.	Dzing: *isung,* 7, 8. Dzing: *isɔng,* 7, 8, to redden (fruit). Buma: *kesíé,* 7, 8, tasty.	Possibly related to Dzing, but vowel aperture and meaning (in the second form) irregular. The plant is American. The

III. Farming (continued)

Bushɔɔ́ng	Comparable Forms	Comment
36 (continued)		Mbuun form differs completely, as does Pende. Buma corresponds best. Loan from Buma probable.
37. oil palm: *shyáám,* 9, 10.	Dzing: *ntsaam,* 9, 10. Mpiin: *samba,* 9, 10. Nzali: *samba,* 9, 10. Buma: *nsíám,* 9, 10. Mbala: *mbáámbu sáámba,* 9a (part of palm leaf; *sáámba* designates the palm tree). Pende: *samba,* 9, 10.	A loan from Kwilu. Proto-Kuba probably used *dibá,* 5, 6. The meaning of this loan remains unclear.
38. palm nut: *nkɛny,* 3, 4.	Luba: *lungaji,* 11, 10. Pende: *mukanji,* 3, 4. Songye: *luashi,* 11, 10, nut. Songye: *kiaji,* 7, 8, fruit.	CS 768. The Kuba reflex is not regular. Possible loan from Pende.
39. palm oil: *shɛdy,* 9, 10.	Pende: *ishieta,* 8, deposit of palm oil. Njabi: *syɛdi,* 7, 8, palm nut.	In the Njabi form, *sy* is a prefix. Too far away for direct loan. Despite irregularities, possible loan from Pende.
40. palm wine: *maan,* 6.	Tetela: *wǎnú,* 6. Mbuun: *man,* 6. Ding, *maan,* 6. Buma: *maan,* 6. Luba: *máni,* 6, palm oil.	A loan from Kwilu. Mbuun, Dzing, Ngul, Nzali, Lwer, Tsong also report it.
41. pig: *ngul,* 9, 10.	Kongo 1652: *ngulu.* Mongo: *ngúlu,* 9, 10, derived from Kongo. Mbuun: *ngúl,* 1, 2. Pende: *ngulu,* 9, 10. Luba: *ngúlúbé,* 9, 10. Songye: *ngulube,* 9, 10.	CS 887. Western Bantu. The Kuba reflex is irregular for vowel aperture and tone. The Luba form differs, being CS 888. Loan from Kwilu or southwest, indicated by total distribution.
42. duck (domestic): *mbat,* 9, 10.	Tetela: *diwata,* 5, 6. Mongo: *ibata,* 5, 6, loanword.	A loan from the southwest, ultimately Portuguese, probably

(continued)

III. Farming (continued)

Bushɔɔ́ng	Comparable Forms	Comment
42 (continued)	Dzing: *ibat*, 5, 6. Songye: *ebata*, 5, 6. Mbuun: *bát*, 5, 6. Buma: *ibár*, 5, 6. Cokwe: *phado*, 9, 10. Lwena: *patu*, 5, 6. Portuguese: *pato*.	(note classes) via Cokwe.
43. hemp: *kabɛɛ́ngy*, 12, 13.	Mongo: *bangi*, 9, 10. Songye: *kabangi*, 12, 13. Swahili: *bangi*.	A loan from Songye. Indian origin (*bhang*). The Kuba did not intro- duce hemp from the Luba or the Luso- Africans.

IV. Hunting, Gathering, and Fishing

A comparison, even a partial one, of terms relating to game and plants gathered is beyond the scope of the appendix. Such a comparison strengthens the impression that most terms are of northern origin and proto-Kuba.

Bushɔɔ́ng	Comparable Forms	Comment
1. mushroom: *bɔ*, 14, 6.	Mongo: *bobwo*, 3, 4. Ntomba: *bobú*, 7, 8 (*sp.*). Lia: *boiwo*, 3, 4. Luba: *boowa*, 14. Songye: *bowa*.	CS 2102, 2108. Proto- Bantu. Proto-Kuba.
2. to hunt: *-byeeng*.	Mongo: (*b*)*enga* (also Ntomba, Tetela). Mbuun: *-beng*.	CS 129. Proto-Bantu. Proto-Kuba. A col- lective hunt is implied in the meaning.
3. hunting: *bushóóng*, 14.	Tetela: *cóngi*, 1, 2, hunter. Pende: *sunga*, hunt. Mbuun: *ɔsóng*, 14, hunter.	Either proto-Kuba or a loan from the south- west.
4. poison for hunt: *lalyɛɛng*, 11, 10.	Nkucu: *lulengo*, 11 (Van Laere). Luba: *lulengu*, 11, 10, poison. Songye: *elengu*, 5, 6.	Proto-Kuba. Origin south- ern Mongo, derived from verb cited.

IV. Hunting, Gathering, and Fishing (continued)

Bushɔ́ɔ́ng	Comparable Forms	Comment
4 (continued)	Mongo: -lɛnga, tremble, vibrate. Tetela: lɔlɛngɔ, 11, 10.	
5. wooden poisoned arrow: labaancy, 11, 10.	Dzing: lubaa, 11, 10, arrow. Mongo: loási, 11, 10, poisoned arrow. Lia: lobáhí, small arrow (also Ntomba, Bobangi, Poto, Tetela). Mbuun: labaanci, arrow, 5/11, 9/10.	CS 57. CS 56, denoting the same shape, means "rib." The two may be related. Found in zones B, C, H, K, L. The Kuba form has an aberrant tone, but is still proto-Kuba.
6. spear: ikwoong, 5, 6.	Mongo: likɔngá, 5, 6. Tetela: dikɔngá, 5, 6 (also Lia, Ntomba).	CS 857. Widespread northwest Bantu. Vowel aperture of the Bushɔ́ɔ́ng does not correspond. Proto-Kuba, despite this.
7. trap (hunting and fishing): ilóóng, 7, 6.	Mongo: ilóngá, 5, 6. Tetela: djungá, 9, 10 (also Ntomba, Lia).	Proto-Kuba.
8. bow (also net): bɔt, mat, 14, 6.	Mongo: botá, 3, 4. Lia: bontá, 3, 4. Ntomba: motâ, 3, 4. Luba: bútá, 14, 6. Songye: buta, 14, 6. Kongo 1652: uta, 14, 6. Pende: uta, 14, 6. Mbuun: bot, 14, 6.	CS 1630, 1631, 1632, 1633, 1634. Proto-Kuba, with the meaning "net."
	Mongo: botái, 3, 4, dialect for "net." Lia: bɔtéyi, 3, 4, hunting net. Ntomba: bɔtéyi, 3, 4, hunting net.	Proto-Kuba: hunting net. The ending then distinguished it from "bow."
9. to hunt: kinc (Brown Edmiston).	Mongo: -kínda, to drive fish into weirs.	The reversive intransitive is -kiñjwa in Mongo.

(continued)

IV. Hunting, Gathering, and Fishing (continued)

Bushɔ́ɔ́ng	Comparable Forms	Comment
9 (continued)	Ntomba: -kindola.	Possibly proto-Kuba, applied to fishing, but the Mongo form would be -kínjwa.
10. Sarcophrynium leaves: kwoong, 9, 10.	Mongo: lokongo, 11, 10 (also Lia, Ntomba).	Proto-Kuba. The Cwa use these for roofing. They are also used for packaging.
11. fish: shwéy, 9, 10.	Mongo: nsé, 9, 10. Ntomba: nśi, 9, 10. Lia: nśi, 9, 10. Tetela: losé, 11, 10, 9, 10.	CS 429, 427. Proto-Kuba. Note instability of final vowel.
12. fishhook: ilɔ́p, 7, 8.	Mongo: ilɔ́fa, 7, 8. Lia: ilɔ́pɔ, 7, 8. Ntomba: ilɔ́pɔ, 7, 8. Luba: ndobó, 9, 10. Kongo 1652: loa, to fish. Songye: bulobo, 14, 6.	CS 640, derived from CS 638. Proto-Bantu. Proto-Kuba.
13. dugout canoe: bwaát, 14, 6.	Mongo: wáto, 3, 4 (also Lia, Ntomba, Tetela, Ngombe, Lebeo). Luba: búatu, 14, 6. Songye: buatu, 14, 6. Mbuun: bwáat, 14, 6.	CS 1949. Proto-Bantu. Proto-Kuba.
14. paddle: kéy, 9, 10.	Mongo: nkáí, 9, 10. Lia: nkápi, 9, 10 (also Ntomba). Tetela: lokáhi, 11, 10. Luba: nkaaya, 9, 10. Luba: nkapi, 9, 10. Songye: nkafi, 9, 10.	CS 1014. Proto-Bantu. Proto-Kuba.
15. to paddle: -lú.	Mongo: -lúka (also: Lia, Ntomba). Luba: -lúká.	CS 735. Note irregularity of Luba tone. Proto-Bantu. Proto-Kuba.
16. fishing dam and weir: ngal, 9, 10.	Buma: ngal, 9, 10.	Incomplete distribution. The term may be spread along the Sankuru-Kasai area.

IV. Hunting, Gathering, and Fishing (continued)

Bushɔ́ɔ́ng	Comparable Forms	Comment
17. harbor: *mbóóng,* 9, 10. See section II, Environment, item *12.*		
18. To bathe: *-ɔk* (also means "to swim").	Mongo: *ɔ́ka.* Ntomba: *ɔ́kɔ.*	CS 2107. Proto-Bantu. Proto-Kuba.
19. elephant: *ncɔk,* 9, 10.	Mongo: *njɔku,* 9, 10. Tetela: *ndjɔvu,* 9, 10. Luba: *nzovu,* 9, 10. Kongo 1652: *nzau,* 9, 10.	CS 951. Proto-Bantu. Proto-Kuba.
20. tusk: *mwɔɔng,* 3, 4. In *lambil* (Johnston) the form is *bonjo*— i.e., the Mongo form.	Mongo: *bɔnjɔ,* 3, 4. Lia: *bɔɔ́njɔ,* 3, 4; also a trumpet (also Nkucu, Yela, Soko, Poto, Lingala, Bobangi, Ntomba).	Proto-Kuba. Well established for zone C.
21. warthog: *shoom,* 9, 10.	Mongo: *nsombo,* 9, 10, *Potamochoerus porcus* (also Lia, Ntomba, Tetela). Mbala: *suumbu,* 2. Mbundu: *kiombo,* 7, 8 (Johnston). Ovimbundu: *ociombo,* 7, 8, pig (Johnston). Pende: *sumbu,* 5, 6. Lwena: *combu,* 9, 10. Tiv: *i-soam(s), we-soam* (pl.), pig.	No CS, although the term occurs in zones C, H, B, K, R. For zone C, Johnston adds Sengele Nkusu, Nkucu, Yela, Genia, Buja, Bwela Mpama. Proto-Bantu. Proto-Kuba.
22. dog's bell, for hunting: *ilep,* 7. 8.	Mongo: *elefó,* 7, 8. Tetela: *eluhú,* 7, 8. Luba: *ludíbu,* 11, 10. Kongo: *dibu,* 5, 6. Ntomba: *elepó,* 7, 8. Lia: *elepó,* 7, 8.	CS 560x, 560y. In the CS, as reconstructed, the tone of the last syllable is low. Proto-Kuba. Note aberrant vowels of Tetela.
23. to fish with a hook: *shosh* (Brown Edmiston).	Tetela: *ncɔ́.* Kongo: *-sos-,* to search for.	CS 364, ps 115. CS 365 is a lesser possibility.

(continued)

IV. Hunting, Gathering, and Fishing (continued)

Bushɔɔ́ng	Comparable Forms	Comment
23 (continued)	Kongo 1652: -sosola, to find. Tio: soo, to search for. Bobangi: -sɔsɔl, to pick out.	The exact Bushɔɔ́ng form is not known. Perhaps of Kongo or Kwilu origin.
24. arrow (with an iron point): pwoonc, 9, 10.	Kongo 1652: lubunza, 11, 10, dart, throwing javelin. Suku: punza, 9, 10 (Laman, p. 89; he adds Yaka, Kongo). Lwalwa: punsa, 9, 10. Mongo: mpóngó, 9, 10, spear.	A borrowing from Kongo, but no tones are given for any form there. The proto-Kuba term for this was ikul (see section V, Crafts, item 12). The Mongo form may ultimately be related, but the distribution makes it unlikely. The Kongo form derives from -bunda, to hit.

V. Crafts

Bushɔɔ́ng	Comparable Forms	Comment
1. artisan: mwiin, biin, 1, 2. drawing, pattern: bwiin, 14.	Luba: búíná, 14, similar to. Yombe: buinu, 14, 6, drawing. Luba Shaba: bwínó, 14, skill.	A loan from Luba.
Metallurgy		
2. to forge: -túl. smith: ntúdy, 1, 2.	Mongo: -tula. Luba: -túla. Tetela: -culá.	CS 1861. Proto-Kuba. The derived nominal botúli, in Mongo, also corresponds, whereas Luba múfúdí, 1, 2, does not.
3. iron ore: butády, 14 (pl., 6, means rust).	Kongo 1652: utari, 14, iron.	CS 1643 ("iron ore"), 1642 ("stone"), 1644 ("iron"). Proto-Kuba.

V. Crafts (continued)

Bushɔ́ɔ́ng	Comparable Forms	Comment
	Kongo: *tadi,* 7 or 14, pig iron.	
	Luba Shaba: *bútàlé,* 14, pig iron.	The meaning may have been stone, then was transferred, and *mbɔk*
	Pende: *utadi,* 14.	took on the meaning
	Mbuun: *tali,* 14.	stone, whereas it had
	Ntomba: *itale,* 5, 6, stone;	meant iron. Note the
cf. *mbɔk,* 9, 10, stone.	*ibɔkɔ,* 5, 6, stone.	Ntomba forms.
	Mongo: *liɔkɔ,* 5, 6, iron ore.	
	Ntomba: *mbɔkɔ,* 9, 10, iron ore.	
	Lia: *ibɔkɔ,* stone, 5, 6.	
4. wrought iron: *labol,* 11, 10.	Mongo: *loolo,* 11, 10.	Proto-Kuba. Kongo *mbodi* has the wrong vowel
	Tetela: *luwulu,* 11, 10, pl. *mbulu,* 10, metal.	opening.
	Kongo: *mbodi,* 9, 10, heated lead, metal.	
5. metal: *buml,* 14.	Mongo: *bomele,* 3, 4, thick, solid liquid (such as grease solidifying).	Proto-Kuba, with the meaning "raw metal."
6. pig iron: *latɔ́l,* 11, 10; pl., lump of pig iron.	Bobangi: *bɔlu,* 14, lead.	CS 1775 ("metallic lead"). Tone of
	Lingala: *mondɔlu,* 3, 4, lead.	Bushɔ́ɔ́ng is reversed.
	Ngombe: *mɔndɔlu,* 3, 4, metal.	Probably proto-Kuba. Note Ngombe.
7. hammer: *ncoon,* 9, 10 (anvil: *iloon,* 7, 6, is a back-formation of hammer).	Mongo: *njondo,* 7, 8, hammer (also Lia, Ntomba, Bobangi, Tetela).	CS 965, 965½. The southern Mongo have classes 9, 10 for hammer. Proto-Kuba, with
	Luba: *nyíndú,* 9, 10, hammer, anvil.	the meaning "hammer," and derived
	Songye: *nyindu,* 9, 10, hammer.	"anvil."
	Pende: *nzundo,* 9, 10, hammer.	
	Kongo 1652: *nzundu,* 9, 10, hammer.	

V. Crafts (continued)

Bushɔ́ɔ́ng	Comparable Forms	Comment
8. hammer (a type lighter than item 7): *nsháák*, 3, 4.	Mongo: *bosákẃa*, 3, 4 (also Ntomba, Lia).	Proto-Kuba.
9. to hammer: -*kɔk*.	Mongo: *kɔk*, sound of knocking, -*kɔkɔmeja*, to hammer in a nail. Pende: *kokula*, to knock at the door. Luba: -*kókólá*, to knock at the door. Ruund: -*kóókál*, to knock at the door (Hoover).	Proto-Kuba. The verb is derived from the ono- matopoeia.
10. bellows: *kuuk*, 9, 10.	Mongo: *nkuka*, 9, 10 (also Lia, Ntomba, Tetela).	Proto-Kuba.
11. adze: *kwɛɛt*, 9, 10, from -*kwɛɛt*, to make a hole in an object; also *lakɔtl*, 11, 10, a needle to pierce walls.	Ntomba: *nkɔ́tɔ́*, 9, 10. Luba: *kota*, split wood. Mongo: *kɔta*, to cut trees. Dzing: *ngkɔt*, 9, 10. Yans: *nkwɛr*, 9, 10. Tsong: *nkwɛt*, 9, 10. Buma: *nkwɛr*, 9, 10. Sengele: *ngkweti* (Johns- ton). Tio: *likwero*, 5, 6.	The verb is proto-Kuba; the noun may be, with the meaning ''ax.'' Ntomba and Buma tones are aberrant. The term is widespread in zone B. The meaning ''adze'' may come from the Kwilu, re- placing ''ax.''
12. knife (largely cere- monial): *ikul*, 7, 6.	Mongo: *lokulá*, 11, 10 (dialect and archaic), knife. Mongo: *likulá*, 5, 6, iron arrow point. Lalia: *lokula*, 11, 10 (De Rijck). Nkucu: *dikfula*, 5, 6, arrow; and *lukfuła*, 11, 10, knife (Johnston, who has the same general forms and dis- tinctions in his south and north Songo Meno).	Proto-Kuba. The noun is derived from Mongo *kula* (3), to hit.

V. Crafts (continued)

Bushɔɔ́ng	Comparable Forms	Comment
13. machete: *mbaam*, 3, 4.	Mongo: *boambo*, 3, 4, stick, knobkerry. Luba: *múbámbó*, 3, 4, oar, yoke. Ngombe: *mubambo*, *mbambo* (pl.), broom.	Proto-Kuba? Meanings are not very close; cf. CS 44, CS 38 ("peg" and "to peg out").
14. machete for work in field: *nshál*, 3, 4.	Mongo: *bosála*, 3, 4, work (also Lingala, Bobangi); a loanword from Lingala. Mongo: *sála*, cut, hoe (old meaning). The Lingala forms for "work" and "to work" have spread over a large part of Zaire, obscuring older occurrences and meaning.	CS 247 ("to work," "to cultivate"), ps 60 ("garden"), CS 250 ("work"), ps 61, CS 254. The verb is widespread in northwest Bantu. The noun is derived from it. Proto-Kuba.
15. charcoal: *iyál*, 5, 6.	Mongo: *jála*, 5, 6. Mongo: *likála*, 5, 6. Mongo: *wála*, 3, 4, place where charcoal is prepared (similar forms for charcoal in Ntomba, Lia, Tetela). Luba: *díkàlá*, 5, 6. Songye: *makala*, 6. Kongo 1652: *ekala*, 5, 6.	CS 980, related to CS 982. Proto-Bantu. Proto-Kuba. The relationship between charcoal and metallurgy is quite close. Since another meaning is "ember," it cannot be used to argue that metal smelting was proto-Bantu.
16. adze (only for dignitaries): *ikéɛ́ng*, 7, 6.	Tetela: *kɛ́ngɛ́*, 9, 10, ax. Nkucu: *ikenge*, 7, 13, ax (Johnston; he adds Nkucu, Yela). Luba: *cikenge*, 7, 8, adze (Johnston; he adds Kanyok).	Not found in Luba dictionaries. The meaning corresponds better to the Luba entries from Johnston than to southern and southeastern Mongo. Either proto-Kuba or a loan from Luba.

V. Crafts (continued)

Bushɔ́ɔ́ng	Comparable Forms	Comment
17. razor: *lakyɛɛng,* 11, 10.	Mongo: *lɔkɛngɔ,* 11, 10 (also Ntomba, Lia, Tetela). Luba Shaba: *dííkéngo,* 5, 6. Songye: *lukengu,* 11, 10, tool for scarification.	Proto-Kuba. The closeness of item *16* in both form and meaning is puzzling. Without the tonal difference, both would form a single entry.
18. hoe: *ishú,* 7, 6.	Luba: *lúkasú,* 11, 10. Songye: *lukasu,* 11, 10. Tetela: *sɔ́,* 9, 10, ax. Nkucu: *coo,* 5, 6, and *acooa,* 6 (Johnston).	CS 436 and 973½. Probably a loan from Luba, with *-ka-* dropping out, but note its tone and change of class.
19. sword: *ilɔɔn,* 7, 6.	Luba: *cílonda,* 7, 8, emblem, ax of headman. Luba Shaba: *kílóndá,* 7, 8, iron weapon.	Probably a loan from Luba. Closest to Luba Shaba, however. Songye form (if any) is unattested. Typologically the Kuba sword is closer to some of the Mongo types.
20. lead: *latyɛ́ɛ́n,* 11, 10.	Luba: *lúténdé,* 11, 10, bullet, lead. Luba Shaba: *mútende,* 3, 4, metal tube, including barrel of gun. Dzing: *ntsɛɛn,* 10, lead for bullet, filings. Lingala: *tende,* 10, cannon. Tio: *tiene,* 5, 6, cannon. Ndembu: *lutenda,* 11, 10, bullet. Kongo 1652: *-tenda,* to wound.	The meanings of all these terms may be connected. In shape the tone of Luba is not congruent, nor are the classes of Luba Shaba and Tio. The Kuba probably borrowed it from the west. The source would be Kongo, applied first to barrel of gun, then to the filings with which it was loaded, and finally to the metal lead, most often used for filings.
21. foreign metal: *ndél,* 3, 4, esp. tin, zinc, aluminum, but also means foreign cloth.	Kongo: *mundele,* 3, 4, European.	New meaning extended from "foreign cloth." Kongo origin.

V. Crafts (continued)

Bushɔ́ɔ́ng	Comparable Forms	Comment
22. ax: *ngyeem*, 9, 10.	Imbangala: *ngimbo*, 9, 10 (Johnston, who adds Lwena, Luchazi, Kisama, Umbundu, varying between *ngembo* and *ngimbo*).	CS 803, 933 (hoe, ax). Even though not found near the Kuba, the term is old, and can be added to CS 803 or 933. But probably an Imbangala import, given the distribution.
23. copper: *mwɛ́ɛ́pdy*, 3, 4; or *mwɛ́ɛ́dipy*, 3, 4. Note: -*ɛɛp* means to look back.	Mongo: -*kɛ́fɔla:* to attract the eye. Mongo: -*kɛ́fɛla:* to glance at.	Mongo origin of the verb from which the Kuba noun is derived; perhaps related to Kuba verb. Innovation suggested by the brightness of the metal. See also item 24 for a similar etymology.
24. brass: *kyɛ́ɛ́ngl*, 9, 10.	Dzing: *kyɛɛng*, 7, 8. Luba: *kengela, kengele*, luminous. Mongo: *kɛ́ŋgɛ́lí*, ray, flash. Lwena: *kengeleji*, brass, copper (Hoover). Cokwe: *kengelia*, brass, brazen ware (Hoover).	Of Cokwe origin. The Cokwe derived it from a verb meaning "to be luminous." A loan, first applied to rods or lumps imported from Europe. The root is *kangi*. The loan fitted in well and acquired its present form (final *l*) by contamination with notions of luminosity, which can be of Luba or Mongo origins. Origin of the root -*kangi* remains unclear. It must be in the lower Kwilu area or further west. Dzing borrowed from Kuba.

Salt

25. local salt: *ngɛl*, 3, 4.	Luba: *múkele*, 3, 4. Luba: -*keléká*, to strain	CS 1031, 1030 ("strain," "filter"). Possibly

(continued)

V. Crafts (continued)

Bushɔɔ́ng	Comparable Forms	Comment
25 (continued)	plant ash during salt-making. Mbuun: ɔ́kyɛ́l, 3, 4. Mbala: gédi, 3, 4. Tetela: ŋɡɛlɛ́, 3, 4.	Proto-Bantu. Probably here a Luba loan, but possibly proto-Kuba, derived from a verb preceding item 27.
26. imported salt: nshɛ́y, 3, 4.	No comparable forms nearby. Yans: moo-se, 3, 4 (Johnston). Tio: musio, 3, 4, fine salt. Fumu: musege, 3, 4, fine salt.	Could be related to CS 311, 313, or 314 (all meaning "grain of sand"). Loan from Malebo Pool, despite the fact that by 1896 salt was coming from Luanda and Kisama.
27. to precipitate salt: -lɛ́k.	Mongo: -lɛ́ka. Tetela: -dɛ́ka. Tetela: lɔlɛ́kɔ, 11, 10. Lia: -kɛ́lɛ. Ntomba: iálaka, 5, 6, filter.	Proto-Kuba. The Lia form is an inversion, corresponding to CS 1030 and probably older than this verb.

Pottery

Bushɔɔ́ng	Comparable Forms	Comment
28. to mold clay: -bóóm. adobe: labwóóm, 11, 10.	Mongo: bomba. Lia: ibómba, 5, 6, pottery clay (Lia, Ntomba, Tetela, also to mold pots). Luba: -bumb-. Luba: díbumbá, 5, 6, pottery clay. Mongo: liómbo, 5, 6, adobe floor. Songye: -bumba, to make pots.	CS 199. Proto-Bantu. Proto-Kuba. In the Mongo languages the initial b often drops: e.g., Mongo word for floor.
29. pot: pweky, 9, 10.	Mongo: mpoké, 9, 10 (also Lia, Ntomba, Tetela). Dzing: mfwe, 9, 10.	CS 1594, ps 405. This lists Yans, Ntomba, Tetela. Add at least Ngwi, Nzali, and perhaps Mbagani (Maes).
30. pitcher: iboong, 7, 6. cup: mboong, 9, 10.	Luba: dibungu, 5, 6, pitcher.	Proto-Kuba. The tonal evidence suggests a

V. Crafts (continued)

Bushɔ́ɔ́ng	Comparable Forms	Comment
30 (continued)	Luba: *mbungu,* 9, 10, cup.	loan *by* the Luba from Bushɔ́ɔ́ng.
	Lia: *mbongo,* 9, 10, cup.	
	Mongo: *mbongo,* 9, 10, cup, pipe.	
	Ntomba: *mbongo,* 9, 10, pottery pipe bowl.	
	Mbuun: *ɛbong,* 5, 6, pottery; *mbong,* 9, 10, cup, glass.	
	Pende: *dibungu,* 5, 6, pitcher.	

Note: Pottery came from the Lulua, the Kasai, the Labody, and the Sankuru. The shapes involved came from the Sankuru. Pots from the middle Kasai were called *pok áPyɛɛn,* "pot of the Pende."

31. potsherd: *ikyeeng,* 7, 8.	Tetela: *lokenga,* 11, 10. Songye: *kiinga,* 7, 8. Songye: *luyinga,* 11, *kiyinga,* 10, rubbish.	A Songye loan from Tetela, and perhaps a Kuba loan from Songye.
32. plate: *ilɔɔng,* 7, 6.	Ntomba: *ilɔng,* 5, 6. Lia: *ilonga,* 5, 6. Tetela: *dɔnga,* 5, 6. Kongo 1652: *elonga,* 5, 6. Dzing: *ilɔɔng,* 5, 6. Mbuun: *ɛlɔng,* 5, 6, basin. Pende: *longa,* 5, 6. Lwena: *lilonga,* 5, 6 (Hoover). Sala Mpasu: *ilonga,* 5, 6 (Hoover). Ruund: *díílóóng,* 5, 6, (Hoover). Luba: *dílonga,* 5, 6. Songye: *elonga,* 5, 6. Luba Shaba: *diloongo,* 5, 6, pottery clay. Luba Shaba: *díínóóngo,* 5, 6.	CS 662½ lists Yans, Bobangi, Kongo, Lwena. A loan from Kongo. This holds also for other languages except the Luba group, which may have borrowed from Kuba, Ruund, or both. The distribution is perfect for imported plates, but the term applies to others also. Kuba plates were made on the Sankuru or came from the Lokenye and have the same shape as imported plates.
33. cooking pot: *ncoon,* 9, 10.	Luba: *nyúngu,* 9, 10. Pende: *nzungu,* 9, 10.	CS 965½ and ps 267. See comment, CS 2173

(continued)

V. Crafts (continued)

Bushɔɔ́ng	Comparable Forms	Comment
33 (continued)		and 2173a. Proto-Bantu, yet this form is probably a loan from Pende.
34. dish: *ipwa,* 7, 6.	Dzing: *mfwɔ,* 9, 10. Luba: *lúpú,* 11, 10, piece of a plate. Luba: *cípú,* 7, 8, piece of a plate. Tetela: *ehase,* 7, 8.	Connection with Dzing. No connection with Luba or Tetela. Origin unknown.
35. demijohn: *ishaangl,* 7, 8.	Luba: *cíśangálá,* 7, 8. Kongo 1652: *esanga,* 5, 6, bottle. Tetela: *kisangála,* 9, 10. Songye: *kisangala,* 7, 8.	A loan from Kongo. Demijohns are fairly recent. The term may have applied to other bottles earlier.
36. flat pottery: *ibáy,* 7, 8.	Songye: *kiba,* 7, 8, wooden plate for food.	Connection with Songye.

Woodcarving

37. box: *ikuuk,* 7, 6 (also means basket, plate, neckrest, pillow).	Mongo: *bonkukú,* 3, 4, box. Ntomba: *monkuku,* 3, 4, box; *nkuuk,* 3, 4.	Proto-Kuba term for box. Perhaps also for neckrest, but that object is absent from the central Mongo area.
38. backpack: *kwíky,* 9, 10 (also means basket with lid).	Mongo: *yúka,* 5, 13.	Proto-Kuba possible, but class changes and final palatalization lead to doubt.
39. backrest: *iyék,* 7, 6. Brown Edmiston, *eka:* to lean against.	Tetela: *yĕkɔ́,* 5, 6. Mongo: *yékɔ,* 1, 13.	In Mongo, derived from -*ɛkama,* to lean against.
40. backrest: *ishuk,* 7, 6. to hold: *shuk.* knot: *nshúk,* 3, 4.	Mongo: *suka,* to hold. Mongo: *nsókó,* 9, 10, knot.	Verb is proto-Kuba; noun may also be.
41. to carve: *-shɔɔng.* carver: *nshwɛɛngy,* 1, 2. tool to drill and scrape: *nshɔɔng,* 3, 4.	Mongo: *-sɛnga.* Mongo: *bosɛngi,* 1, 2. Luba: *-soṅgá.* Tetela: *-sɔng.* Lia: *-hɛnge.* Songye: *-se.*	CS 385, 386, 387, 388, 384. Proto-Bantu. Luba origin. Note *wɛ* = ɔ in Bushɔɔ́ng.

V. Crafts (continued)

Bushɔ́ɔ́ng	Comparable Forms	Comment
42. cup, glass: *ikɔ́p*, 7, 6.	Luba: *dikópó*, 5, 6, cup. Pende: *giopo*, 7, 8, cup. Dzing: *lukɔp*, 11, 10, cup. Tetela: *dikɔhɔ́*, 5, 6, cup. Lia: *ikɔ́pɔ*, 5, 6, cup. Lingala: *kɔ́pɔ*, 5, 6, glass, tin can. Ruund: *diikoopw*, 5, 6 (Hoover). Lwena: *kopo*, 5, 6 (Hoover). Songye: *ekopo*, 5, 6. Ndembu: *cikopu*, 5, 6 (Hoover).	Loan perhaps from Portuguese *copo* or English *cup*. It could be from the early colonial period.
43. chest, box: *ikwέpy*, 5, 6.	Mongo: *nkofo*, 9, 10, box, casing. Kongo: *lukobe*, 11, 10, box. Tio: *nkobi*, 9, 10, box. Suku: *mukobi*, 3, 4, or *lukobi*, 11, 10 (Lamal, p. 103).	CS 1097½ lists Bobangi and Duala, along with Kongo and a Teke form. Mboshi can be added, and all Teke groups, as well as Suku and Yaka. The tone of this form is low. Either Bushɔ́ɔ́ng has an error in tone, or it took high tone under the influence of item *42*. A similar influence would explain the final vowel in Mongo. In sum, I think the Kuba form, with low tone first, was borrowed from the Kwilu area, ultimately from Kongo.

Note: Lukobi in Kongo was a basket used as an emblem of power. The first mention dates from 1620 (Cuvelier and Jadin, p. 135). Baskets similar in shape are called by this form among the Kuba and are used as emblems.

44. water pot (of wood): *nyiing*, 9, 10.	Luba: *nyíingu*, 9, 10. Pende, *nyingu*, 9, 10, calabash plant.	CS 2084. A loan from either Luba or Pende. The shape is related to item *33*.

V. Crafts (continued)

Bushóóng	Comparable Forms	Comment
45. plank: *ibéy,* 7, 6.	Kongo (1652): *ebaya,* 5, 6. Songye: *ebaya,* 5, 6. Luba: *díbáyá,* 5, 6. Mongo: *libaya,* 5, 6 (loanword). Mbala: *-baayá,* 5, 6. Mbuun: *ɛbáy,* 7, 8, wall. Dzing: *ibay* (*libay*), 5, 6, plank, potsherd. Tetela: *dibaya,* 5, 6.	A loan from Kongo; not from Luba. The term is old, and the loan may be, but it could also date from the colonial period.
46. water pot (of wood or pottery): *nnɔɔn,* 3, 4.	Luba: *múlóndó,* 3, 4. Pende: *londo,* 5, 6, pitcher. Ruund: *múloond,* 3, 4 (Hoover). Ndembu: *mulondu,* 3, 4 (Hoover). Eastern Lunda: *murondo,* 3, 4 bottle, pitcher (Hoover). Songye: *mulondo,* 3, 4. Songye: *elondo,* 5, 6, pitcher.	A loan from Luba rather than Pende, because of the classes.

Basketry

Only two out of nineteen types of baskets are indicated. The other names have not been traced or distribution data are insufficient.

47. to plait: *-tóóng.*	Mongo: *-tónga,* to plait, to build. Mongo: *litónga,* 5, 6, basketry. Lia: *-toṅga,* to plait. Luba: *-tunga,* to sew. Dzing: *-tsung,* to sew. Dzing: *-tung,* to plait.	CS 1846 and 1849 have the correct shape, but mean "to sew" and "to thread on string." CS 1848 means "to build," and CS 1849 means "basket" (related notions), but the tone is wrong. Proto-Kuba: to plait, to build.
48. vine: *lakɔdy,* 11, 10.	Mongo: *bɔkɔli,* 3, 4. Tetela: *ɔkɔdi,* 3, 4.	CS 839 and 839a. Proto-Bantu. Proto-Kuba.

V. Crafts (continued)

Bushɔɔ́ng	Comparable Forms	Comment
48 (continued)	Lia: *lokɔlí*, 11, 10 (*sp.*). Ntomba: *lɔkɔli*, 11, 10 (*sp.*).	
49. rope: *mwaan*, 3, 4. to fasten: -*kaan*.	Dzing: *mukaan*, 3, 4. Luba Shaba: *múkanda*, 3, 4. Luba: *múkanda*, 3, 4. Mongo: -*kanda*, catch. Mongo: *bokandampambi*, 3, 4 (in which *mpambi* = vine). Ruund: *múkand*, 3, 4, leather strap.	CS 1004 ("strap") but with high tone. Proto-Kuba probable, derived from verb. Luba seems derived from Ruund.
50. big vine: *nnaam*, 3, 4. to creep: -*laam*.	Mongo: -*lamba*, to creep. Luba: -*laḿbá*, to creep. Tetela: -*damba*, to creep.	Verb is proto-Kuba; noun may also be, or was derived later. Cf. CS 483, 483a ("sprawl").
51. door: *ikwiky*, 7, 6.	Mongo: *ekukɛ*, 3, 4 (also Ntomba, Tetela).	Proto-Kuba.
52. sieve (fine): *ikál*, 7, 6.	Mongo: *ekálá*, 7, 8, flat basket, cup. Ntomba: *ekaláli*, 7, 8, sieve for fishing. Ntomba: *ekála*, 7, 8, cup, vase.	Probably proto-Kuba.
53. box (of wood or basketry): *nguum*, 9, 10.	Mongo: *bongumba*, 3, 4, heavy package. Dzing: *ngwǫm*, 9, 10, pocket. Tetela: *dikumbɛ*, 5, 6.	Probably proto-Kuba: "large-sized container."
54. broom: *yɔɔ́m*, 7, 8. to sweep: -*ɔɔ́m*.	Mongo: *lɔkɔ́mbɔ*, 11, 10. Mongo: -*ɔmba* (also Lia, Ntomba, Tetela). Luba: *tshíkombó*, 7, 8. Songye: *lukombo*, 11, 10. Songye: *kikombo*, 7, 8.	CS 1137, 1141. Proto-Kuba. Classes are influenced by Luba.

V. Crafts (continued)

Bushɔ́ɔ́ng	Comparable Forms	Comment
55. mat (for sleeping): *itɔ́k*, 5, 6.	Mongo: *itɔkɔ́*, 5, 6 (also Lia, Ntomba).	Proto-Kuba. In recent time such mats were Luba imports. Earlier the Kuba probably made them themselves. Note tone.
56. big mat: *ikaangl*, 5, 6 (for officeholders, wooden slats used in making it). hamper, basket carried on head: *nkaangl*, 3, 4.	Luba: *cîkáángá*, 7, 8. Cokwe: *cikanga*, 7, 8 (also Ndembu, Lwena, Lunda Kahemba) (Hoover). Ruund: *cikááng*, 7, 8 (Hoover). Kanyok: *cikaang*, 7, 8. Kanincin: *cîkááng*, 7, 8 (Hoover). Eastern Lunda: *cikanga*, 7, 8, mat, now a royal symbol (Hoover).	Kuba loan from Luba possible, despite the added *l*, which could indicate a location in Luba. No Luba form *cikangala* is known, however. The eastern Lunda usage comes close to the Kuba. Ultimate origin seems to be the Lunda group, so that a loan from Cokwe, or perhaps Pende (not attested, however), is also possible.
57. *shap:* 9, 10, purse.	Luba: *nsapó*, 9, 10. Ruund: *ńsapw*, 9, 10 (Hoover). Kanincin: *yinsap*, 10, small basket worn by certain titleholders (Hoover). Kanyok: *nsaha*, 9, 10, type of basket. Cokwe: *sapa*, 9, 10, jar, vessel.	A loan from Luba. Ultimately may be of Ruund or Cokwe origin.
58. fish trap: *nnɛ́k*, 3, 4.	Mongo: *bolɛ́ka*, 3, 4 (also Lia, Ntomba, Tetela, Ngombe).	Proto-Kuba. Possibly proto-C.
59. shield in basketry: *ngup*, 9, 10. hippopotamus: *ngup*, 9, 10.	Mongo: *nguá*, 9, 10, shield. Mongo: *nkufó*, 9, 10, hippopotamus. Lia: *nguba*, 9, 10, shield. Lia: *ngubú*, 9, 10, hippopotamus.	Proto-Kuba "shield" and proto-Kuba "hippopotamus" differed in final vowel and perhaps tone. CS 906 ("shield"), CS 908, 875 ("hippopotamus").

V. Crafts (continued)

Bushↄↄng	Comparable Forms	Comment
59 (continued)	Tetela: *nguwú,* 9, 10, hippopotamus. Dzing: *ngup,* 9, 10, hippopotamus. Buma: *ngub,* 9, 10, hippopotamus. Luba: *ngabu,* 9, 10, shield. Luba: *ngubu,* 9, 10, hippopotamus. Songye: *ngabo,* 9, 10, shield.	Both proto-Bantu.

Note: Shields covered with the skin of hippopotamus are not recorded among the Kuba, but are recorded elsewhere.

60. reed or bamboo for plaiting: *ntɛtl,* 3, 4.	Pende: *mutetele,* 3, 4, reed. Mbuun: *ↄtɛt.* Luba: *mutete,* bamboo vine. Songye: *ntete,* 9, 10, firewood.	A loan from Pende. The loan could be from Luba, but the final *l* makes it clear it must be Pende.

Weaving and Textiles

61. thread: *nshiing,* 9, 10. to thread: *-shiing.*	Mongo: *bosinga,* 3, 4, rope. Mongo: *-singa,* to thread (both also in Lia). Ntomba: *nsinga,* 9, 10, rope. Tetela: *oshinga,* 3, 4, rope. Mbuun: *ↄshing,* 3, 4, thread. Mbuun: *-shing,* to make thread. Dzing: *musing,* 3, 4, rope. Buma: *mushia,* 3, 4, thread, rope. Luba: *múshínǵa,* 3, 4, plaited rope.	CS 359. Western Bantu, Proto-Kuba, both verb and noun.

V. Crafts (continued)

Bushɔ́ɔ́ng	Comparable Forms	Comment
62. raffia fiber: *kííng,* 9, 10 (a tough black thread used for sewing).	Mongo: *wiínga,* 3, 4 (dialect form 11, 10). Ngombe: *likíŋga,* 5, 6, raffia tree. Dzing: *luking,* 11, 10. Mbuun: *laciŋg,* 11, 10.	Proto-Kuba.
63. raffia: *lapyɔk,* 11, 10.	Mongo: *lɔfɛkwá,* 11, 10 (also Lia, Ntomba, Tetela). Ngombe: *lipeké,* 5, 6. Luba: *lúpéku,* 11, 10. Luba Shaba: *lúpéko,* 11, 10. Songye: *lupeko,* 11, 10, raffia thread.	Proto-Kuba. The term has a wide distribution, but no CS. Probably proto-C.
64. to sew: *-túm.*	Mongo: *-túma,* to plait bunches of leaves together. Lia: *-túma,* to pierce, to stick a needle into. Ntomba: *-túma,* to plait.	CS 1865, 1866. Proto-Bantu. Proto-Kuba. Despite the general spread, only Luba has the same meaning in the area and it is a synonym for another term, "to sew." Luba loan from Kuba.
65. to wear clothes: *-díing.* circle: *idíingl,* 5, 6.	Mongo: *-líínga,* to wrap around, to encircle; not used for clothes. Luba: *-jingá,* to wrap around. Tetela: *-diinga,* to wrap around. Dzing: *dzinga,* to wrap around, to encircle.	CS 625 and 625½, "to wrap around." Said to be Proto-Bantu. Bushɔ́ɔ́ng has an innovation in meaning.
66. to wear clothes: *-láát.*	Mongo: *-lɔta.* Lia: *-lɔtia, lɔtɔ,* to put on clothes. Ntomba: *-lɔtɔ.* Mbala: *-váád,* to dress. Songye: *kilamba,* 7, 8.	Bushɔ́ɔ́ng vowels do not correspond at all to Mongo. Origin unknown. Mbala is closest.

V. Crafts (continued)

Bushɔ́ɔng	Comparable Forms	Comment
67. clothes: *ilaam*, 7, 8 (imported clothes and others).	Luba: *cílamba*, 7, 8. Mbala: *dilambu*, 5, 6, rag. Ngwii: *elamba*, 5, 6 (Maes). Kongo: *lamba*. Bobangi: *elambá*, 7, 8. Dzing: *mulaam*, 3, 4, rag.	CS 487. Could be proto-Kuba, but unlikely. Probably a loan from Kongo. Not a loan from Luba (cf. tones).
68. bag made of raffia: *ipoosh*, 7, 8.	Kongo (Ekeleve): *kipusu*, 7, 8, handbag. Pende: *lupusu*, 11, 10, raffia. Mbala: *luhúsu*, 11, 10, raffia. Kongo 1652: *kifunzu*, 7, 8, handbag, moneybag. Kongo: *phusu*, 9, 10, raffia fiber (Plancquaert, p. 54).	Loan from Kongo, perhaps via Pende.
69. rag: *ishyaan*, 7, 8.	Dzing: *isyaan*, 7, 8. Sakata: *keshaa*, 7, 8. Sakata: *keshyaa*, 7, 8. Buma: *máshyan*, 6.	A connection between the forms is certain. Origin unknown.
70. raffia cloth: *mbal*, 9, 10.	Mbuun: *mbal*, 9, 10. Pende: *mbala*, 9, 10. Tsong: *mbal*, 9, 10 (De Beaucorps, p. 57). Yaka: *mbaari*, 9, 10 (Plancquaert, p. 54). Kongo: *mbaadi*, 9, 10 (Bentley). Yombe: *mbala*, 3, 4, merchandise. Yombe: *mbalu*, 9, 10, profit, trade. Luba: *lubalé*, 11, 10, midrib of a frond.	A loan from Kongo. These raffia squares were used as currency from the Kuba to the Kongo area. The name of both the Bushɔ́ɔng and the Mbala of Kwilu could be derived from this term.
71. European cloth: *ndél*, 3, 4. See also item 21.	Kongo 1652: *mulele*, 3, 4, cloth.	Kongo origin. The form of 1652 appears also in

(continued)

V. Crafts (continued)

Bushɔ́ɔ́ng	Comparable Forms	Comment
71 (continued)	Pende: *mulele,* 3, 4, cloth. Mpiin: *mulele,* 3, 4, wrapper (Maes). Mbuun: *ɔ̂ndɛl,* 3, 4, Europeans. Kongo: *mundele,* 3, 4, European.	CS 516. Despite Guthrie's reluctance, CS 516 and 517 must be linked.
72. shuttle for a loom: *ngwoonc,* 9, 10.	Mongo: *lokóango,* 11, 10. Pende: *ngunza,* 9, 10.	Pende origin. Mongo may be distantly connected. Distribution data inadequate.
73. warp of a loom: *shíím,* 9, 10.	Dzing: *indzim,* 5, 6.	Distribution data inadequate. Connections with the Kwilu area.
74. man's dress: *mapel,* 6.	Nzali: *mapele,* 6 (Maes). Luba: *mapela,* 6, fiber or fabric (no tone). Ruund: *mápil,* 6, elephant grass (Hoover). Lwena: *cihela,* 7, cloth, woman's headband. Ndembu: *cibeli,* 7, short cloth.	Nzali is from Bushɔ́ɔ́ng. It could be a loan from Luba, although the vowel aperture does not fit. More likely Luba is also a loan from Kuba. Innovation? More data needed.
75. woman's dress: *ncák,* 9, 10.	Kongo 1591: *enzaka,* embroidered raffia cloth (Bal, p. 3). Luba Shaba: *nsáka,* 9, 10, raffia cloth.	Of Kongo origin. Luba borrowed from the west or even from Kuba (but note tone).
Other		
76. pipe calabash: *ntɔ́p,* 3, 4. to pierce: *-tɔ́p.*	Dzing: *muntɔp,* 3, 4. Tetela: *ɔtɔpa,* 3, 4. Pende: *mutopa,* 3, 4 (Hoover) (also Lwena). Ndembu: *mutompa,* 3, 4, pipe. Ruund: *mutóómp,* 3, 4, pipe (Hoover). Luba Shaba: *mútóómpó,* 3, 4, pipe calabash.	Kuba form is a loan from Pende, and Luba forms are from Ruund (Hoover). Dzing is from Pende or Kuba. Tetela is from Kuba. The Luba and Songye forms for a calabash spoon differ. Formally, the Kuba term could

V. Crafts (continued)

Bushɔɔ́ng	Comparable Forms	Comment
76 (continued)	Luba Shaba: *kítóómpó*, 7, 8, pipe calabash. Luba: *lútobó*, 11, 10, half of a calabash. Songye: *lutobo*, 11, 10, half of a calabash, serving as spoon.	derive from them, but the meaning of the Pende makes it the more likely source.
77. camwood: *toŏl*, 13 (also means red cosmetic powder).	Mongo: *ngola*, 9, 10 (also Lia, Ntomba). Tetela: *diŭlá*, 5, cosmetic. Luba: *ńkulá*, 9, 10, red earth. Kongo 1652: *ngula*, 9, 10, red powder. Kongo 1652: *lukula*, 11, 10, camwood tree. Kongo 1652: *tukula*, 13. Tio: *tsuula*, 9, 10. Sakata: *ngula*, 9, 10. Sakata: *nguaa*, 9, 10. Pende: *lukula*, 9, 10, red cosmetics. Buma: *nkúla*, 9, 10, red earth, red cosmetics. Songye: *nkula*, 9, 10, red earth.	CS 877. Western Bantu. Bushɔɔ́ng lost the initial *k*, presumably after taking class 13. The term was proto-Kuba (like Mongo), but altered under influence of trade, i.e., Kongo influence.

VI. Trade and Markets

Bushɔɔ́ng	Comparable Forms	Comment
1. to buy: *-shwoom*. gift: *shoom*, 9, 10. polyandric spouse: *nshweshweemy*, 1, 2.	Mongo: *-sómba* (also Lia, Ntomba, Ngombe, Tetela). Mbuun: *-sóóm*. Dzing: *-suum*. Pende: *-sumba*. Luba: *-sumba*. Kongo 1652: *sumba*.	CS 414. Widespread in western Bantu. Proto-Kuba.

VI. Trade and Markets (continued)

Bushɔ́ɔ́ng	*Comparable Forms*	*Comment*
2. market (periodic): *imboom,* 5, 6.	Nzali: *imbumu,* 7, 6, (Maes). Ding: *mbum,* market day (Mertens, 1:305). Ndengese: *imbombo,* 7, 6.	The connection between the items, Ding excepted, is certain. The distribution remains very narrow. Origin on the Sankuru or Kasai.
3. market (daily): *mwaak,* 3, 4. street: *mwaak,* 3, 4 (Brown Edmiston). *-mwaak:* to live or or dwell (Brown Edmiston).		Origin unknown. Meaning derived from those given by Brown Edmiston. CS 34½ ("to build") and CS 1903 ("to build") conflict on tone. CS 1323 corresponds better to the verb in shape but means "to scatter, to sprinkle."
4. market day: *nkǐl,* 3, 4.	Vansina, "Probing the Past," pp. 351–53.	Origin in Nsundi, north of Malebo Pool.
5. commerce: *ngaang,* 9, 10. trader: *muna ngaang,* 1, 2.	Kongo 1652: *mukangala,* 3, 4, traveler. Kongo 1652: *-kangala,* travel. Kongo 1652: *mukangari,* 1, 2, travelers.	The resemblance among these forms may be chance, esp. because the meaning does not correspond. But *ngaang* is rarely used, apart from the compound expression, trader. Probable connection between these terms. Specific origin of *ngaang* is unknown.
6. trade: *iyɛ́pdy,* 7, 6, plus *ató:* "to go out for." to look around: *-ɛ́ɛ́p.*	Mongo: *-ɛfa,* to glance.	The noun is derived from a verb. The whole may mean "to travel to look around" (for opportunities). The verb is proto-Bantu, if it corresponds to Mongo. The vowel quantity of the verb in Bushɔ́ɔ́ng may be in error.

VI. Trade and Markets (continued)

Bushɔ́ɔ́ng	Comparable Forms	Comment
7. price: *mbaan*, 3, 4.	Luba: *-bandá:* to go up, to climb (prices). Luba: *mbandá*, 9, 10, a loaf of local salt, often sold. Pende: *mubando*, 3, 4, price.	A loan from Pende; not from Luba because of tone. Note for Luba that the name came to be applied to the commercial loaves of salt, an important and standardized export (a currency?).
8. *Olivancillaria nana* (shell): *ncim*, 9, 10 (not used as currency).	Kongo 1652: *nzimbu*, 9, 10, money. Pende: *njimbo*, 9, 10, wealth, money.	The distribution includes the whole of Kwango and Kwilu. Of Kongo origin, as are the shells, which come from near Luanda.
9. cowrie shells: *lapash*, 11, 10 (also means currency, money).	Mbuun: *lapash*, 11, 10. Pende: *pashi*, 9, 10. Luba: *mpashi*, 9, 10 (Denolf, pp. 130–31). Tsong: *mpias* (Dartevelle, p. 109). Lunda: *pasi* (Dartevelle, p. 187). Lwena: *mpashi*, 9, 10.	Pende, Mbuun, ultimately originally from Luanda.
10. money: *pish*, 9, 10.	Lunda: *mpíc*, 1, 2, wealthy person (Hoover). Lwena: *wupici*, 14 (Hoover) (also Ndembu). Luba Shaba: *búpécí*, 14, wealth. Songye: *mpeta*, 1, 2, wealthy person.	From Lunda or perhaps from nonattested Cokwe. Lunda, Lwena, Ndembu may derive it from a local verb, also attested in Cokwe, Sala Mpasu, and Pende (Hoover). Kuba does not derive from Luba or Songye.
11. wealth: *budi*, 14. wealthy person: *nnyi*, 1, *badi*, 2.	Luba: *múdi*, 1, 2, eater, devourer.	Tone and vowel aperture make a connection unlikely. Not likely to be derived from Kuba *-dyá*, to eat. Loan suspected; origin unknown.

VI. Trade and Markets (continued)

Bushɔɔ́ng	Comparable Forms	Comment
12. bracelet of cowries: *ibiim,* 7, usually *mabiim,* 6; plural also means a monetary unit.		Innovation from the same form and classes, with the meaning "bunch of palm fruit."
13. beads: *diísh, miísh,* 5, 6.	Angola: *misanga.* Kongo: *misanga.*	A loan shortened. The *misanga* served as a unit. See Vellut, "Notes sur Lunda," pp. 85–86, for 18th and 19th centuries. The similarity with the term meaning "eye" is fortuitous.
14. beads (a specific type): *tungoombi,* 13.	Luba: *Tungombe,* 13, Ovimbundu.	Beads named after the Ovimbundu traders who brought them.
15. foreigner, immigrant: *Imbaangl,* 7, 8.		Also the name of the Imbangala nicknamed *imbaangl ipash,* "the Imbangala with the cowrie."
16. debt: *mbát,* 9, 10 (also means credit).	Mongo: *mátá,* 9, 10. Lia: *mátá,* 9, 10. Luba: *mbata,* 9, 10. Ngombe: -*máta,* to be involved in a trial.	Proto-Kuba, most probably. On the evidence available, it can also be a loan from Luba, but the term is not widespread in zone L. It could be proto-C, derived from the verb given in Ngombe.

VII. Kinship Terminology

Kinship terminology forms a coherent system. Parts of a foreign system can be borrowed and incorporated intact, or foreign terms can be borrowed but made to fit the original system. The origin of terms is examined in this section. From all the evidence it becomes clear that the proto-Kuba system was much like Mongo, except that it diversified categories (e.g., affines) and adopted some Luba and Kwilu features.

VII. Kinship Terminology (continued)

In this section the usual order is not followed: items are first presented by generations, from that of the grandparents to that of the furthermost descendants, with affines following consanguines. This order makes changes in categories easier to spot.

Bushɔɔ́ng	Comparable Forms	Comment
1. *maam*, 1, 2: grandparents and all relatives in their generation; plural means ancestors.	Luba: *máámu*, 1, 2, my mother. Mbuun: *maám*, 1, 2, mother. Pende: *maama*, 1a, 2, mother.	CS 1282, usually meaning "my mother." A loan from Luba or Pende; Luba more likely, given context.
2. *mɛ́ɛy*, 1: my mother.	Sakata: *mé, ma, maama* (Bylin, p. 260).	CS 1288½, 1289. Bushɔɔ́ng would be derived from **mááyí*, but none of the languages cited is close. The only parallel would be Sakata. Note that the term is not Mongo. Innovation. Back-formation from item *1* possible.
3. *nyɔ:* your mother. *-n-:* his mother. *-y-:* mother (pl.).	Mongo: *nyɔngɔ́*, your mother (sing. and pl.); *ngóya*, my (our) mother (sing. and pl.); *nyangó*, his (their) mother (sing. and pl.). (Also Lia, Ntomba, Tetela.)	CS 537, ps 536, for the plurals. CS data for "mother" (Guthrie, *Comparative Bantu*, 2:152) show great variability. Proto-Kuba related to Mongo. *nyangó* survives as interjection.
4. *taat*, 1a, 2: my father.	Lulua: *táátú*, 1a, 2. Luba Shaba: *táátá*, 1a, 2. Pende: *tata*, 1a, 2. Mbuun: *taat*, 1a, 2. Buma: *taa; tata*, 1a, 2. Songye: *tata*, 1a, 2.	CS 1686, 1687. A loan from Luba most likely; from Pende possibly, but Dzing, Tsong, Yans, Sakata, Tio, Buma, Songye, Kongo all have related forms.
5. *ish-́*, 7, 8 (root-*sh-́*): father (yours, his, and plurals).	Mongo: *is-́*, 1a, 2. Luba: *-sh-*, 1a, 2; cf. *sha*, the father of.	See Guthrie, *Comparative Bantu*, 2:149, "father"; the variants *-ce* and *-ci*

(continued)

VII. Kinship Terminology (continued)

Bushɔ́ɔ́ng	*Comparable Forms*	*Comment*
5 (continued)	Pende: *-sh-, sha.*	are closest. CS 2027 (Guthrie's discussion). Proto-Kuba. Luba and other *-sh-* should yield Bushɔ́ɔ́ng: *-c-.*
6. *ngol,* 1, 2: elder sibling or cousin of same sex; plural means ancestors, but not in a genealogical sense.	Eso: *bongole,* 1, 2. Lalia: *ngolo,* 1, 2, elder. Ngandu: *ngolo,* 1, 2. Tetela: *wolo,* 1a, 2. Luba: *múkulu,* 1, 2, elder. Songye: *-kulu,* elder.	CS 1198, itself a specialization of CS 1195, 1196, and 1197. Proto-Kuba, but note related forms all in eastern Mongo. Luba is not related.
7. *mɔɔkdy,* 1, 2: younger sibling or cousin of same sex.	Luba: *múákuni,* 1, 2.	A loan from Luba. The ending *ny* becomes *dy* in Bushɔ́ɔ́ng.
8. *pééngy,* 1, 2: sibling or cousin of opposite sex. Cf. *mwaan apééngy,* 1a, 2: sister's son.	Kongo 1652: *mpangi,* 1, 2, sibling. Mbala: *paangi,* 1, 2, sibling. Pende: *pangi,* 5, 6 or 9, 10, sibling, clan member, compatriot. Dzing: *mpang,* 1, 2, cousin? Dzing: *mwa apaang,* 1, 2, clan member (Mertens, 1:217). Ding: *mpang,* brother of the same clan (Ndaywell, p. 444). Mbuun: *mpang,* 1, 2, sibling of same sex. Yans: *mpɛɛ* (class?), kin on mother's side (De Plaen, p. 321). Yans: *mwaan ampeng,* 1, 2 (Swartenbroeckx, 2:75). Ruund: *ḿpany,* sibling of opposite sex (Hoover).	No CS. Origin Kwilu. In all the comparable forms the meaning includes members of the clan and the ingroup. The Ruund meaning comes closest to Bushɔ́ɔ́ng.

VII. Kinship Terminology (continued)

Bushɔ́ɔ́ng	Comparable Forms	Comment
9. *Mwaán*, 1, 2: child; all of that generation.	Mongo: *bɔ́na*, 1, 2. Tetela: *ɔ́ná*, 1, 2. Luba: *mẃana*, 1, 2. Songye: *mwana*, 1, 2.	CS 1922. Proto-Kuba. Note that the term is not restricted to kinship only.
10. *nkaan*, 1, 2: grandchild; all of that generation. *nkaanl*, 1, 2: great-grandchild; all of that generation. *ncɔ́nkaanl*, 1, 2: great-great grandchild; all of that generation.	Mongo: *bokáná*, 1, 2. Mongo: *bonkánola*, 1, 2. Mongo: *bonkánoola*, 1, 2. Luba: *munkáná*, 1, 2, grandchild or great-grandchild.	Because of tone it is clear that Bushɔ́ɔ́ng *nkaan* is a loan from Luba. Its categories and the ending *-l* are proto-Kuba (Mongo). The *nc-* prefix could be related to *ish*, "your father," esp. because I also heard *shɔ́nkaanl*. No CS.
11. *nǔm*, 1, 2: husband (also male, for animals); pl. *balüm* or *balwimy*.	Songye: *mulume*, 1, 2. Luba: *múlúmé*, 1, 2, male. Mongo: *bóme*, 1, 2. Ntomba: *boóme*, 1, 2. Tetela: *ómí*, 1, 2. Mbala. *lúmi*, 1, 2. Pende: *mulumi*, 1, 2 (De Sousberghe, "Forgerons," p. 36). Tio: *olū,́* 1, 2. Buma: *mulúm*, 1, 2.	CS 697. The Bushɔ́ɔ́ng form presupposes form **dụ́mi*. Because of tone, it cannot be a loan from Luba. Not related to Mongo. From Kwilu; Pende, Mbala and Tio correspond.
12. *mwaamsh*, 1, 2: wife. *-am:* to give. *-amsh:* to cause to give.	Mongo: *-amba:* accept, receive.	Causative of the verb *-am* as a noun. Innovation from a proto-Kuba verb. A wife is the cause of bridewealth gifts.
13. *bɔ*, *mɔ*, 14, 6: in-law of parents' and odd higher generations.	Songye: *muko, 1, 2*, in-laws. Luba: *búko*, 14, in-laws. Luba Shaba: *múko*, 1, 2, any in-law. Dzing: *bukɔ*, 14, any in-law.	CS 1092 ("relative by marriage"). Mbala has aberrant vowel. Proto-Bantu. The Mongo forms are all related to CS 826 and 822. Therefore Bushɔ́ɔ́ng is a loan

(continued)

VII. Kinship Terminology (continued)

Bushɔ́ɔ́ng	Comparable Forms	Comment
13 (continued)	Mbuun: ɔ́kɔ́, 1, 2, in-law. Pende: *uko,* 14, 6, in-law of other generation (De Sousberghe, "Forgerons," pp. 35, 36). Tsong: *buko,* mother-in-law. Yans: *bóko,* in-law (De Plaen, p. 55). Mbala: *magu,* 6, in-law. Tio: *uko,* 14, in-law.	from Luba or from Kwilu. The shape is derived from a verb, "to give bridewealth to" (Meeussen, 1969). Given tone, it is most likely a loan from Kwilu.
14. nshaam, 1, 2: in-law of same generation, same sex. *-shaam:* to overtake, to pass.	Mbuun: ɔsaam, 1, 2, friend. Mbala: *saamba,* 3, 4, sibling-in-law. Pende: *zamba,* 9, 10, brother-in-law, companion; term for alliance with parents of a wife. Pende: *dizamba,* 5, gift to nephew-in-law, when his wife bears a child (De Sousberghe, "Forgerons," p. 35, n. 1). Songye: *kisamba,* 7, 8, tribe. Songye: *kisambo,* 7, 8, race. Luba: *císamba,* 7, 8, clan, tribe, family. Luba Shaba: *-sámbá,* to spread, to jump from branch to branch; to become allies or friends.	Because of tone, it cannot be derived from Luba. Loan from Kwilu, perhaps from Pende. The verb of Luba Shaba corresponds to a similar verb in Mongo and Pende and Luba, but not in Bushɔ́ɔ́ng.
15. ishón, 7, 8: husbands toward husbands entering in group reciprocally.	Pende: *gisoni,* 7, 8, cross-cousins. Mbala: *-sóni,* 7, 8, cousin (probably cross-cousin). Luba: *císuná,* 7, 8, vagina.	The Mbala form cannot be related because the vowel aperture should be -ɔ-. Hence, the Pende is probably not related either. Luba fits.

VII. Kinship Terminology (continued)

Bushɔɔ́ng	Comparable Forms	Comment
15 (continued)		Loan from Luba. See item *16*.
16. mbápdy, 1, 2: co-wife; all women entering a group reciprocally.	Luba: *mbafúla,* 10, groin. Tio: *mbaa,* 1, 2, co-wife.	Loan from Luba, parallel to item *15*. These categories do not exist in either Luba or Mongo.
17. nkidy, 1, 2: friend.	Mongo: *bokiló,* 1, 2, in-law (also Lia, Ntomba, Tetela).	CS 822, 826. This is a noun derived from a verb meaning "to avoid, to taboo." Proto-Kuba, with the Mongo meaning. It later shifted to the opposite.

VIII. Social Organization

Bushɔɔ́ng	Comparable Forms	Comment
1. clan: *ilooncy,* 5, 6. canes of office: *malooncy,* 6.	Mongo: *ilɔngɔ,* 5, 6; 5, 12, kin. Mongo: *bɔlɔngɔ,* 3, 4, kin. Luba: *cílóngó,* 7, 8, kin. Luna Inkongo: *bulungu,* 14, 6. Keté: *bulungu,* 14, matri-lineage. Ndengese: *donji,* 5, 6 (Ndjond'a 'Ngele, pers. comm.). Pende: *ilwang,* 5, 6, chief's cane (De Sous-berghe, 1958, pp. 12, 18). Mbuun: *lwang,* 11, 10 "kin."	CS 665 corresponds to the Mongo and Luba forms cited and is reputedly proto-Bantu, but its vowel aperture does not agree with the Bushɔɔ́ng, Kete, and Luna Inkongo forms. The latter two correspond to CS 714. The Bushɔɔ́ng form shows yet another irregularity: final *-ng* is *ncy.* Only the Ndengese (and Leele) forms fit well. Origin unknown, perhaps proto-Kuba, but at least with changes in shape.

VIII. Social Organization (continued)

Bushɔ́ɔ́ng	Comparable Forms	Comment
2. lineage: *ikuun*, 5, 6 (also means belly).	Mongo: *likundu*, 5, 6, family lineage, belly (also Lia, Ntomba, Tetela).	Proto-Kuba. The meanings "belly" and "substance of witchcraft" are widespread in the whole forest. No CS.
3. people: *nshí* + noun, 1, 2 (also means member of a group).	Mongo: *bosí*, 1, 2. Lia: *bohí*, 1, 2. Tetela: *osé*, 1, 2.	CS 330, 331. Proto-Kuba.
4. homonym: *ndwey*, 1, 2.	Mongo: *ndoí*, 1a, 2 (also Lia, Tetela, Ntomba, Ngombe). Kongo: *ndoyi*, 1, 2. Tio: *ndui*, 1a, 2. Mbala: *-dóyi*, 1, 2. Leele: *ndwi*, 1, 2, warrior.	CS 694 ("to name"). Proto-Kuba.
5. age-grade: *loong*, 11, 10.	Mongo: *inɔngɔ*, 5, 6/7, 8. Mongo: *bɔlɔngɔ*, 3, 4, line, set (also Lia, Ntomba). Tetela: *ɔnɔngɔ*, 3, 4, line, set, order. Luba: *múlóngo*, 3, 4, line, set. Songye: *-longa*, classify. Songye: *mulongo*, 3, 4, line, row. Pende: *mulongo*, 3, 4, line, row. Mbuun: *ɔlɔng*, 3?, 4, line, row. Yans: *ōlwang*, 3, 4 (Guthrie).	CS 664. Tentatively Guthrie adds Bushɔ́ɔ́ng, despite difference in vowel aperture, which parallels items *1* and *12* (as well as other cases: e.g., *4, 6*). The class differs from the Mongo forms. Probably proto-Kuba in class 3, 5, meaning "line, set."
6. twins: *yǝ́sh*, 7, 6.	Mongo: *jǎsa*, 5, 6 (also all western Mongo, Tetela). Luba: *dipásá*, 5, 6. Songye: *mafasa*, 6. Songye: *mpasa*, 6.	CS 1407. Proto-Kuba. The Mongo forms and Bushɔ́ɔ́ng correspond to *-baca*, not CS 1407 *-paca*.
7. eldest twin: *mbóóy*, 1.	Mongo: *mbóyo*, 1. Ntomba: *mbóyó*, 1.	Proto-Kuba.

VIII. Social Organization (continued)

Bushɔɔ́ng	Comparable Forms	Comment
7 (continued)	Ngwi: *mbo* (Ndaywell, p. 443). Mbuun: *mbo*. Buma: *mbo*. Kete south: *ambuye*, 1, 2, twins (Maes). Lwalwa: *bambui*, twins (Maes) (also Mbagani). Sala Mpasu: *mbueye*, 1, twin. Ndembu: *mbuj*, 1, twin.	
8. youngest twin: *ishák*. to be surprised: *-shak*.	Tetela: *osako*, 1, 2. Tetela: *shako*, 9, 10.	Proto-Kuba or more probably an early innovation. The noun is probably derived from the verb.
9. slave child: *mbótl*, 1, 2. Cf. *-bót*, to give birth; *mabótl*, 6, birth.	Mongo: *mbotela*, 1, 2 (also Lia, Ntomba, Ooli, Ikolombe, Yela, Munju).	Proto-Kuba. See data in De Jonghe, pp. 59–75.
10. marriage: *bulaancy*, 14, 6. spouse living in the other's village: *nnaancy*, 1, 2.	Mongo: *-langa*, to love (also Ntomba, Tetela). Mongo: *lolanga*, 11, 10, lover. Mongo: *elangyá*, 7, 8, friendliness.	Proto-Kuba verb. Innovation from it for the nouns.
11. Pawn woman: *ngady*, 1, 2; cf. woman: *ngaat*, 1, 2.	Mongo: *wálí*, 1, 2, wife (also Lia, Ntomba, Tetela, Ngombe). Tetela: *wăto*, 1, 2, woman. Mongo: *jómoto*, 1, 2, woman.	CS 986. Proto-Bantu ("wife," "woman"). The Mongo group differentiated in various ways. This form proto-Kuba ("wife").
12. harem: *dwééngy*, 5 (only for chiefs).	Mongo: *ndɔngɔ́*, 9, 10.	Mongo vowel aperture does not fit, as in items *1* and *5*. Tone also differs. Origin unknown.

VIII. Social Organization (continued)

Bushóóng	Comparable Forms	Comment
13. initiation: *nkaano,* (for boys without circumcision).	Keté: *mukándá,* 3, 4 (also Luba, Luba Shaba, Yaka). Pende: *mukanda,* 3, 4, circumcision camp, foreskin. Cokwe: *mukanda,* 3, 4, circumcision. Ndembu: *mukanda,* 3, 4, circumcision camp. Ruund: *mukáánd,* 3, 4, circumcision. Eastern Lunda: *mukanda,* 3, 4, circumcision hut. Mbuun: *ɔkáán,* 3, 4, initiation, circumcision.	Loan from Keté, who borrowed it from Pende. Ultimately perhaps from Ruund. The meaning "foreskin" is the original one. See CS 1002 ("skin"), hence CS 1003 ("letter").
14. initiand: *mbyeen,* 1, 2.	Luba: *múbindi,* 1, 2, savage, uncivilized person. Keté: *múbindi,* 1, 2, initiand.	Loan from Kete.
15. adultery: *shaash,* 9, 10.	Luba: *músasa,* 1, 2, adulterer.	The Luba term probably originates from Kuba.
16. mark (of ownership): *yiingt,* 7, 8. to examine: *-ingt.*	Dzing: *iyiit,* 7, 8, mark. Luba: *-ińángílá,* to look into.	Innovation derived from verb. Connection with Luba barely possible.
17. comrade: *mbéy,* 1, 2 (also means age-mate).	Mongo: *mbáki,* 9, 10, witness. Luba: *mbakani,* 1, 2. Pende: *mbai,* 1, 2, cross-cousin of same sex, comrade (De Sousberghe, "Forgerons," pp. 36, 39). Mbala: *-báyi,* 1n, 2n. Leele: *mbai,* 1, 2, age-mate, trading partner (Douglas, *Lele,* pp. 73, 75). Ruund: *ḿbay,* 1, 2, friend, colleague.	Loan from Kwilu, perhaps Pende. Mongo possible, Luba barely so. The term is connected with trade.

VIII. Social Organization (continued)

Bushɔ́ɔ́ng	Comparable Forms	Comment
18. slave: ngɛ́t, 1, 2. Keté: ngɛt, 1, 2.	Pende: Keté, 1, 2, artisan (De Sousberghe, Art Pende, p. 5).	Innovation of term "slave." Meaning probably derived from Keté, despite opposite tones. The term for slave took the high tone on the second syllable of Keté. Comparable cases are Leele: ninga, 1, badinga, 2, slave or a Ding person; and Yaka: musuku, 1, 2, a slave, a Suku person. The Pende form may correspond to Keté, or be derived from it, or provide an etymology for it.
19. slave: nshɔ́, 1, 2.	Dzing: musoo, 1, 2, another person's slave. Mbuun: ɔsɔ́ɔ, 1, 2. Tsong: muswo, 1, 2. Yans: wusuu, 1, 2. Hum: kitsu, 7, 8. Kete south: mutsuke, 1, 2. Ikolombi: baiso, 2 (De Jonghe, pp. 70–71).	A loan from Kwilu.
20. founding clan: mbáángt, 3, 4. to create: -áng.	Mongo: ánga, to invent, to create. Luba: -bángá, to begin, to prepare. Songye: -banga, to begin, to prepare.	CS 59 ("to open up"), 59a. Innovation from a proto-Kuba verb. The Luba verb cannot be the origin, given the tones.
21. hostage: ibwoon, 7, 8 (also a title).	Nzali: ebundu, 7, 8 (Maes), slave. Leele: ibundu, 7, 8, a bought slave (De Jonghe, p. 74).	Innovation. Note Leele vowel probably is -oo-, as in Bushɔ́ɔ́ng. The innovation comes later for the title, whereas the meaning "hostage" spread earlier and can

(continued)

VIII. Social Organization (continued)

Bushɔ́ɔ́ng	Comparable Forms	Comment
21 (continued)		be close to proto-Kuba. There is no evidence, however, that it was proto-Kuba.
22. concubine: *yéékl*, 1, 2. to get used to: *-éékl*.	Mongo: *éka*, to learn; applicative *ékela*.	Innovation from the verb in the applicative, which is proto-Kuba.

IX. Political Organization

Bushɔ́ɔ́ng	Comparable Forms	Comment
1. village: *bol*, 14, *mal*, 6.	Mongo: *bolá*, 3, 4, village to which one belongs. Ntomba: *bolá*, 3, 4. Mbuun: *bol,́* 14. Dzing: *bwal*, 14, village, house. Tsong: *bwal* (De Beaucorps, p. 164). Sakata: *boi, bol, bula*, 14. Yans: *bola, bul*, 14. Luba: *búla*, 14, interior of village. Buma: *bulá*, 14.	CS 447. Proto-Kuba. Western Bantu.
2. camp, village: *ngaan*, 9, 6.	Mongo: *nganda*, 9, 10. Ntomba: *ngando*, 9, 10. Lia: *ngandi*, 9, 10. Mbala: *ngaandá*, 9, 10, main village. Luba: *ngánda*, 9, 10, interior court. Mbuun: *ngaan*, 9, 10, little hut. Pende: *nganda*, 9, 10, small, sacred hut. Pende: *ngando*, 9, 10, small hut in woods.	CS 780, 781 ("house"), and 779 ("clan") are related. Proto-Bantu. Proto-Kuba. Note variations in final vowel.

IX. Political Organization (continued)

Bushɔɔ́ng	Comparable Forms	Comment
3. house: *mbul,* 9, 6.	Sakata: *lɛbulú,* 11, 10.	Despite close form of Sakata, probably an innovation: back-formation from item *1*.
4. house, shed: *ncúúm,* 9, 6.	Mongo: *botúmbá,* 3, 4, shed, house (also Lia, Ntomba).	No CS fits. Proto-Kuba. The term has a very restricted distribution. It may have meant only "shed."
5. capital: *nshɛɛng,* 3, 4.	Mongo: *bɔsɛngɛ,* 3, 4, central authority, capital. Dzing: *musɛng,* 3, 4. Sakata: *mushiɛ, moshɛngɛ,* 3, 4. Buma: *mushie,* 3, 4, the villagers. Songye: *musengye,* great agglomeration (Wauters, pp. 120, 242).	Proto-Kuba, meaning "the chief's residence."
6. ground: *shín,* 9, 10 (also means province, on the ground). shoot of a plant: *ishín,* 7, 6. horizon: *mashín,* 6. cause, foundation: *ishín,* 7, 8.	Mongo: *ntsína,* 9, 10, base, foundation, cause, beginning. Ntomba: *itína,* 5, 6, base of tree, cause (also Lia, Tetela). Nkucu: *ecindu,* 7, 8(?), territory. Ngombe: *litína,* 5, heart of the matter. Kongo: *sina,* 5, 6, base of tree. Mbala: *shína,* 7, 8, origin. Mbala: *shína,* 6, base, foundation. Dzing: *ntsi,* 9, 10, land, region.	CS 1756 ("base of tree, root"). Proto-Kuba, also with the meaning "territory," which is restricted to the southern Mongo on the available evidence. (The Dzing form is not necessarily related.)

IX. Political Organization (continued)

Bushɔɔ́ng	Comparable Forms	Comment
7. border, limit: *nnel*, 3, 4.	Mongo: *bolelo*, 3, 4 (also, Lia, Ntomba, Tetela). Dzing: *mulil*, 3, 4. Kongo: *ndilu*, 9, 10.	CS 566. Western Bantu. Proto-Kuba.
8. dependent chiefdom: *mabil*, 6. old language: *lambil*, 11. subject clans: *mumbimbil*, 3, 4.	Mongo: *bobila*, 3, 4, village, group of people. Mongo: *mbila*, 9, 10, kinship. Lia: *mbila*, 9, 10, degree of kinship. Ntomba: *mbila*, 9, 10, kinship. Sakata: *bubil*, 14, 6, clan territory (Van Everbroeck, *Religie*, p. 8). Dzing: *mbil*, 9, 10, clan. Mbuun: *mbil*, 9, 10, clan. Ngwi: *mbil*, 9, 10, clan (Ndaywell, p. 443). Yans: *mwel*, 1, 2, ruling clan (De Plaen, p. 322). Tsong: *muwil*, 1, 2, chief of the land (De Beaucorps, p. 90).	Proto-Kuba, meaning kinship. Present meaning and shape also in Sakata. Total distribution among Kwilu and part of the Mongo group. The original verb could have been CS 139, ps 32 ("to follow"): *-bįd-*.
9. villager (a rustic, an uncouth person): *nkon*, 1, 2.	Luba: *múkundí*, 1, 2, important person. Luba Shaba: *nkúndwé*, 1, 2, a clean, orderly, foreseeing person.	A loan from Luba Shaba with reversal of meaning is unlikely, given the tones of Luba (Kasai).
10. chief: *kúm*, 1a, 2. chiefdom: *búm*, 14. chiefly office: *bukúm*, 14.	Mongo: *nkúm*, 9, 10 (also 1a, 2 for Lia, Ntomba, Tetela, Ngwii, Ngengele). Dzing: *ngkum*, 1a, 2.	CS 1265. Proto-Bantu. Proto-Kuba.
11. head of first half of the village: *mbɛ́ɛ́m*, 1a, 2.	Ngwi: *mbeam*, 1a, 2, second village headman (Ndaywell, p. 443).	Link between Bushɔɔ́ng and Ngwi. The distribution may be greater. See item *12*.

IX. Political Organization (continued)

Bushɔ́ɔ́ng	Comparable Forms	Comment
12. head of second half of the village: *mbyeeng,* 1a, 2.	Ngwi: *mbeang,* 1a, 2a, power, and a title (Ndaywell, p. 443). Ooli: *mbengi,* 1a, 2, one of the two village headmen.	See item *11.* The distribution seems to include groups along the Kasai, north of the Kuba. Can be early Kuba or even proto-Kuba.
13. king: *nyim,* 1a, 2.	Mongo: *elímo,* 7, 8, patriarch, jurist, chief, king. Ngengele: *nimi* (class?), a special title (Moeller, p. 438). Ngwi: *nyim Vwii,* a special title (Ndaywell, pp. 179, 445). Sakata (Bobai): *nnem,* 1, 2, king (Simon, p. 6).	The Mongo form does not correspond in tone. Other tones unknown. Innovation, but Sakata and Ngwi forms may be related. If so, the form could be proto-Kuba, meaning a title.
14. to succeed: *-kit* (also means to inherit).	Tetela: *-kitá.* Mongo: *-kita,* to become, to arrive. Mongo: *-kitana,* to succeed (also Lia, Ntomba). Dzing: *-kit.* Yans: *-kit; -kii.* Mbuun: *-tshit.* Tio: *-kira.*	Proto-Kuba.
15. to install, to give an office: *-béky.* to be given an office: *-békm.* town crier: *mbéky,* 1, 2.	Mongo: *-békya:* to proclaim. Mongo: *-békyama,* to be proclaimed. Kongo 1652: *bikila,* to claim. Luba Shaba: *biká,* to predict, to announce.	CS 121 ("to announce publicly"). Possibly Proto-Bantu. Kuba and Mongo meanings more closely related. Kongo unrelated. Proto-Kuba.
16. king's title: *ncyéém nkwoonc.*	See section II, Environment, item *3,* note; section X, Religion, item *19.*	

IX. Political Organization (continued)

Bushɔ́ɔ́ng	Comparable Forms	Comment
17. titleholder: *kɔ́lm,* 1a, 2.	Tetela: *nkɔlɔ́mɔ,* 1, 2, elder. Yela: *kolomo,* 1, 2, elder, notable (Empain, pp. 252, 255). Ohindu: *okolomba,* 1, 2, elder, notable (Torday and Joyce, p. 265). Luba: *nkolomo,* 1, 2, an old, used man.	May be related to CS 1104 ("to become strong"). Possible loan from Luba. More likely proto-Kuba, given distribution among southern and southeastern Mongo.
18. a sort of court: *ishyaaml,* 7, 6. to judge: *shaaml.* to overcome: *shaam.*	Mongo: *nsámbi,* 1, 2, judge. Mongo: *-sámba,* to judge. Mongo: *-sámbela,* to rule in favor of. Lia: *-hámba,* to plead a cause. Ngombe: *-sámba,* to judge. Ntomba: *-hamba,* to plead a cause. Tetela: *-sambúlá,* to judge. Tetela: *losambo,* 11, 10, judgment. Songye: *nsambo,* 9, 10, judge. Luba: *nsámbo,* 9, 10, *nsámbu,* 9, 10, favorable judgment. Ruund: *-sáamb,* to settle a suit. Ngengele: *esambo,* 7, 8, association (Moeller, pp. 294, 436–43). Kamba and Luamba: *kisambo,* 7, 8, association (Moeller, pp. 443–46).	Proto-Kuba. The form is widespread in zone C, but with opposite tone in Mongo. Ntomba, Tetela, and Luba have tones corresponding to the Kuba form. For forms given by Moeller the tone is unknown. The form is also widespread in Shaba and may be old in zone L, but Luba Kasai does not report it.
19. assembly: *ikweeky,* 7, 6.	Ntomba: *ikoká,* 5, 6, assembly.	Proto-Kuba. Last Mongo item, assembly, is not

IX. Political Organization (continued)

Bushóóng	Comparable Forms	Comment
19 (continued)		
to assemble: *-kweeky.* to meet: *-kookm.*	Ntomba: *-kokana,* to assemble. Lia: *-ikoká,* 5, 6, to assemble. Lia: *-kɔkía,* to assemble. Mongo: *-koka,* to suffice in numbers (also Ngombe). Mongo: *nkúko,* 9, 10, assembly. Songye: *lukuku,* 11, 10, council.	related. Affinities with Lia, Ntomba, and Songye.
20. council: *ibááncy,* 7, 6 (also means a courtyard).	Mongo: *loańjá,* 11, 10, courtyard. Luba: *lúbanza,* 11, 10, courtyard. Luba: *cíbanza,* 7, 8, place of assembly. Kongo 1652: *mbanza,* court and city. Lia: *lobańjá,* 11, 10, courtyard, branch of the family.	CS 55. Proto-Bantu. Proto-Kuba.
21. crown council: *ibaam,* 7.	Mongo: *liamba,* 5, 6, participation. Mongo: *-bamba,* to ally, to unite, to add, to join. Bobangi: *-bamban-,* to meet.	Proto-Kuba.
22. council: *makaam,* 6.	See section I, Conceptual Categories, item 2.	
23. justice: *loók,* 11, 10. to listen: *-óók.*	Mongo: *loóko,* 11, 10, clan authority. Mongo: *-óka,* to hear, to listen (also Lia, Ntomba, Ngombe).	Proto-Kuba. The verb is CS 2152.

IX. Political Organization (continued)

Bushɔ́ɔ́ng	Comparable Forms	Comment
24. decree: *lashaang*, 11, 10 (also means order, message, business).	Mongo: *losango*, 11, 10, news (also Lia, Ntomba). Mbuun: *losaang, ntsang,* 9, 10, news.	CS 292. Either western Bantu or proto-Bantu ("news"). Proto-Kuba.
25. war: *bit*, 8.	Mbuun: *bit,́* 8. Mongo: *litá*, 8 (only in dialect). Luba: *mvíta*, 9, 10. Kongo 1652: *vita*.	CS 151. Proto-Bantu (probably). Proto-Kuba. Most Mongo forms recorded for this meaning are different. The meaning cannot have derived from Luba either, nor Kongo (note classes and initial consonant).
26. prisoners of war: *matwíngy*, 6. to become untied: *-tuńg*. to untie: *-túngl*.	Mongo: *-tuńgola*, to liberate from prison. Mongo: *-túngi*, to be put in jail. Lia: *-túngia*, to tie. Lia: *-túngola*, to liberate (both also Ntomba).	Verb CS 1877. Proto-Bantu ("to tie"). The verb in Bushɔ́ɔ́ng is a back-formation from *-túngl*. The noun stems from the simple verb, but probably with its first meaning. Hence the noun is old, perhaps proto-Kuba.
27. title (specific): *iyol*, 1, 2.	Mongo: *yolo*, 12, 13, bailiff, ext. warrior. Mbuun: *yul*, 1, 2, warrior (De Decker, *Clans Ambuun*, p. 95).	Proto-Kuba. In ethnographic sources the form *yulu* occurs in Ndengese, Ooli, Nkucu.
28. title (specific): *kól mát*, 1a, 2. bow: *bɔ́t, mát*, 14, 6.	Mongo: *nkóló*, 1a, 2, master, lord (also Ntomba, Lia). For "bow," see section IV, Hunting, Gathering, and Fishing, item 8.	Innovation from two proto-Kuba terms.
29. title (specific): *kíkaam;* = *kiníkaam*, as in *kín mímbáángt*.	Mongo: *-kínda*, to satiate, to be satiated (also Lia, Ntomba). For *ikaam*, see section I,	Innovation from two proto-Kuba parts probable. The Luba form for the Kuba title

IX. Political Organization (continued)

Bushɔ́ɔng	Comparable Forms	Comment
29 (continued)	Conceptual Categories, item 3.	Kímíkambú is a back-formation from kíkaam.
30. title (specific): nyaang, 1, 2.	Mongo: -nyanga, to prevail, to win. Mongo: lonyanga, 11, 10, hegemony. Ntomba: -nyanga, to receive monyango. Ntomba: monyango, 3, 4, tribute in fish to the owner of the fishing ground.	Innovation from a verb similar to Mongo, or Ntomba.
31. tribute collector (specific): meshɔɔsh, 1a, 2.	Mongo: nsɔsɔ, 9, 10, escort, attendants, crew.	Proto-Kuba is possible, as these collectors were in charge of obtaining food from the Cwa. CS 364, ps 116 ("to search for") is also possible.
32. crown prince: bwéémy, 14, 6.	Mongo: boémbi, 1, 2, overseer. Mongo: -bémba, to go somewhere with an aim, to inspect. Mongo: -kéma, to be strong, strengthened.	Innovation from a verbal stem -éém. CS 814½, ps 222 *gimb ("become strong") (Duala Bobangi) is possible. The innovation may be proto-Kuba; indeed, a bo prefix was fossilized in class 14, but then the term probably did not have the present meaning. Origin of verb unknown, as is the precise form of the verb.
33. title (specific): iyéli, 5 (tone uncertain), the chiefly title of the Ngongo.	Ntomba (Mayi Ndombe): iyɛli, royal title. Ntomba: iyɛli, royal title. Ekolombi: yeli, fifth title of nobility (De Jonghe, p. 65). Ooli: yeli, title (Motte).	Presumably also Yajima. Proto-Kuba title. Probably the distribution is continuous along the Lokenye to Mayi Ndombe.

IX. Political Organization (continued)

Bushɔɔng	Comparable Forms	Comment
34. chiefly title (specific): *mpécy,* 1a, 2, in use along the Sankuru.	Sengele: *mpeti,* war leader, heir to office (Le Bussy). Ngwi: *peci* (Ndaywell, pp. 395, 448). Onga: *mpeci,* noble family (De Heusch, "Système"). Tetela: *epétá.* Luba Shaba: *mpéci,* 1, 2, title; replaces chief during interregnum. Songye: *mpeta,* 1a, 2, wealthy person.	The noun is derived from a verb. The distribution seems wide and may also reflect more than one original verb (tones and vowel aperture are not known). Proto-Kuba. Distribution at least equal to item *33.*
35. throne (a stool or chair): *mbát,* 9, 10.	Mongo: *mbátá,* 9, 10, chair. Ntomba: *mbátá,* 9, 10, chair. Komo: *mbátá,* 9, 10, stool. Pende: *mbáta,* 9, 10, stool. Ngombe: *mbátá,* 9, 10, stool.	CS 63 ("to lie flat") is related. At least proto-C. Proto-Kuba with the meaning "stool."
36. throne: *ipon,* 7.	Songye: *luhuna,* 11, 10 (also Luba Hemba, Zimba, some Tetela; see Moeller, pp. 508– 39).	Songye or Luba Hemba origin.
37. mat for officeholder: *ikaangl,* 7, 6.	See section III, Crafts, item *56.*	
38. eagle feather: *póóng,* 9, 10 (also eagle; also means subject chief, in expression *kúm apóóng*).	Mongo: *mpóngó,* 9, 10 (also Lia, Ntomba). Mbuun: *kapong,* 12, vassal. Pende: *kapungu,* 12, "minister" (De Sousberghe, "Pende," pp. 56, 63).	CS 1603. Proto-Bantu ("eagle"). Proto-Kuba with meaning "eagle." The Pende and Mbuun meanings may be in this case derived from Bushɔɔng.

IX. Political Organization (continued)

Bushɔɔ́ng	Comparable Forms	Comment
39. aristocratic clan: *mbáángt*, 3, 4 (also means founding clan).	Mongo: *-baṅgola,* to open by force. Bobangi: *-bángola,* to open up. Luba: *-bangúlá,* to open up.	CS 59 ("open up"), 59a (same meaning). Perhaps proto-Bantu verb. The noun is derived from a verb, which can be CS 59 and extension. Innovation.
40. compound (in the capital): *laan*, 10, 11 (also means enclosure).	Luba: *luaanu,* 11, 10, mat.	Loan from Luba. The name is applied to enclosures formed by weaving leaves around sticks or poles.
41. tribute: *nnáám*, 3, 4. to cook: *-láám.* council (specific): *mbók iláám*, "the way of the kitchen" (refers to tribute).	Tetela: *olámbo,* 3, 4. Luba: *múlambu,* 3, 4. Songye: *mulambo,* 3, 4. Luba Shaba: *múlambu,* 3, 4. Ruund: *mulambu,* 3, 4.	CS 486 (high tone), "to cook"; CS 484 (low tone), "to pay tribute"; CS 489, "tribute." "Tribute" is a loan from Luba (Kasai).
42. council: *malaang,* 6.	Luba: *-laṅgá,* to exhort, to instruct. Luba Shaba: *-laṅgá,* to think, to argue. Songye: *-langidisha,* to instruct. Luba Shaba: *dílángó,* 5, 6, thought, advice.	CS 500 ("to show, teach, reprove, announce"). Mostly eastern Bantu. Loan from Luba.
43. Keté village headman: *shanshenge,* 1a.	Luba: *Sha,* 1a, father. Songye: *Sha,* 1a, father.	Composite of Luba *sha* + *nshɛɛng,* capital, item 5.
44. Cwa leader: *nyimmwaan*, 1a, 2.	Ruund: *mwáant,* 1a, chief. Ndembu: *mwanta,* 1a, chief. Luba: *mwáta,* 1a, chief. Cokwe: *mwata,* 1a, chief (also Lwena, Pende, eastern Luba).	Composite form of *nyim* + *mwaan.* Borrowed from Ruund and not via Pende, Cokwe, or Luba. Clearly widespread in zone K. The borrowing could be very old.

IX. Political Organization (continued)

Bushɔ́ɔ́ng	Comparable Forms	Comment
45. title (specific): *shɛ́sh*, 1a, 2, a warrior title.	Songye: *shashe,* authority. Songye: *shesha,* 1a, 2 (Merriam, p. 7), a title. Luba Shaba: *-sesa,* to notch. Luba Shaba: *nseso,* 1, (*-ban*), 2, adze. Luba Shaba: *másesó,* 6, adze. Luba: *nsésú,* 9, 10, adze. Mongo: *-sésa,* to salute (also Lia, Ntomba).	A loan, probably from Songye or eastern Luba Kasai; ultimately from Luba Shaba. The adze is a major emblem. Tones of Luba Kasai do not fit. The Mongo group's meaning does not fit.
46. title (specific): *cíkí,* 1a, 2, regent during inter-regnum. Term derives from *-cik,* to put, and **-cíkl,* to remain.	Luba Shaba: *nsikálá,* 1a, 2. Also *shikála* or *cikála;* while *bucikála,* 14, is regency. Luba: *cikála,* 1a, 2 (Weydert, pp. 3–4). Songye: *bamacikala,* 2 messengers (Wauters, p. 358). Ruund: *ncakal,* 1a, second to a chief (also Kanincin). Kanyok: *cikala,* 1a, regent, lieutenant. Eastern Lunda: *ntikala,* 1a, subchief of king. Lia: *botíkélá,* 1, 2. Ntomba: *ntíkélá,* 1a, 2, adoptive father. Ntomba: *botíkélá,* 1, 2. Ohindu: *Cikala,* 1a, 2 (Torday and Joyce, p. 265). Ooli: *cikela,* 1a, 2 (Motte). Ndengese: *cikala,* 1a, 2 (Van der Kerken, p. 669).	A loan from Luba. The southernmost Mongo may have had it from the Kuba. Where meaning is not given, "regency during interregnum" is implied. The Lia forms are derived from *-tíka,* to put, and *-tíkala,* to remain, which are parallel to the Bushɔ́ɔ́ng forms. Note, however, that the Bushɔ́ɔ́ng tones are not the reverse, nor do they correspond to the Luba tone. This may be due to the influence of the Kuba verbs. The Luba word was understood as "remaining person, replacement."

IX. Political Organization (continued)

Bushɔ́ɔ́ng	Comparable Forms	Comment
47. Title (specific): *ipaancl*, 7, 8.	Luba Hemba: *kihanzula*, 7, 8 (Colle, 10:175). Eastern Luba Kasai: *cipanshula*, 7, 8 (Weydert, pp. 3, 4). Luba: *cipanzula*, 7, 8, in charge of strangers (Kanyinda Lusanga, p. 40). Ohindu: *epanchula*, 7, 8 (Torday and Joyce, p. 265).	A probable loan from eastern Luba Kasai or Songye. Ohindu had it from the same source or from the Kuba. Distribution less wide than item *45*. Note that not a single form with tones is well attested, nor is the verbal base for this noun certain.
48. female title (specific): *mbaan*, 1a, 2.	Kongo: *mumbanda*, 1, 2, assistant of medicine man. Luba Shaba: *kíbándá*, 7, 8, lost ghost haunting a medium.	CS 50, 51 ("medicineman"). A possible loan from Luba Shaba, probably not as a title, but as medium.
49. female title (specific): *katyɛ́ɛ́ng*, 12, 13.	Luba Shaba: *kátenga*, 12, 13, first months of pregnancy. Luba: *-tengá*, to put in order (esp. village).	Loan from Luba with meaning "mothers of potential chiefs." Functionally the equivalent of Luba Shaba *kyabuta*.
50. county: *nnung*, 3, 4 (also means country, land).	Dzing: *mukung*, 3, 4, meeting. Dzing: *ikung*, 7, 8, assembly. Luba Shaba: *dílúnǵu*, 5, 6, large grassy plain. Luba Shaba: *-lúnga*, to request tribute for chief.	Loan from Luba Shaba, perhaps through the eastern Luba Kasai. Link with Dzing possible.
51. tribute collector (specific): *paangl*.	Luba: *-pańgúlá*, to tear from, to force to come out, to extort. Mongo: *fanga*, to annoy someone.	The Luba verb is the base for the noun.
52. secret meeting of a council: *kuum*, 9, 10.	Dzing: *ngkuu*, 9, 10, discretion. Yaka: *kuum*, 5, 6, judicial	Loan from Kwilu. Link with Yaka seems best, but we have no tone;

(continued)

IX. Political Organization (continued)

Bushɔɔ́ng	Comparable Forms	Comment
52 (continued)	council (Devisch, p. 285). Mongo: *nkúmbo*, 9, 10, plot. Lia: *nkúmbo*, 9, 10, hospitality.	just possibly related.
53. title (specific): *mbaang*, 1a, 2, judge for adultery cases; also, judge in appeal.	Yaka: *mbaangu*, 1, 2, diviner, healer (Devisch, p. 292). Kongo, end of 16th cent.: *Bangu bangu*, main judge of king of Kongo (Randles, p. 60).	Probable loan from Kongo. Links from Kwilu are missing.
54. highest notables: *ngwɔɔm incyáám*.	Kongo 1652: *ngombo*, 1a, 2, diviner. Kongo 1652: *nsambu*, 9, 10, basket.	Of Kongo origin.
55. staff of office: *pááng*, 9, 10.	Mbala: -*haangu*, 3, 4. Mongo: *mpangi*, 9, 10, influential person. Mongo: *mpángá*, 9, 10, handcuffs.	Only Mbala is connected with Bushɔɔ́ng. The Mongo form that has a correct shape (*mpángá*) is too different in meaning.

Note: A great number of minor titles, emblems, and other items of the political vocabulary have not been included. Most of these are innovations based on terms of everyday life.

X. Religion

Bushɔɔ́ng	Comparable Forms	Comment
1. creator god: *Mboom*, *Mboomyeec*.	Mongo: *Mbombiańdá*, 9, 10. Mongo: *Iańdá*, 5, 6. Lia: *Mbomb ibańdá* (also Ntomba).	Proto-Kuba: *Mboom* meant a superior spirit. The term is also attested among the Nsengele and Ntomba of Mayi Ndombe.

X. Religion (continued)

Bushɔ́ɔ́ng	Comparable Forms	Comment
2. ghost, deadly charm: *nkal*, 3, 4 (tone unknown).	Mongo: *bokáli*, 3, 4, soul of deceased, shade, ghost (also Ntomba, Ngombi). Lia: *bokáli*, 3, 4, jinn, monster in stories.	Proto-Kuba, meaning ancestor.
3. witch: *nnwɛky*, 1, 2.	Mongo: *-lɔka*, to bewitch. Mongo: *bɔlɔki*, 1, 2 (also verb and noun in Lia, Ntomba, Tetela, and noun in Ngombe).	CS 644, 647. Proto-Bantu. Proto-Kuba. Mongo still has the verb.
4. war magician: *ilweemy*, 7, 8. netherworld: *ilweemy*, 7. Presents itself as derivative of a verb, but comparable forms show that it is not.	Leele: *ilumbi*, 7, 8, official diviner. Mongo: *elombé*, 7, 8, intrepid person, judge. Ngombe: *elombé*, 7, 8, leader. Lia: *elombé*, 7, 8, notable, patriarch. Ntomba: *elombé*, 7, 8, elder, notable. Ooli: *elome*, 7, 8, diviner, warrior leader (Van der Kerken, p. 654). Luba: *cílúmbu*, 7, 8, a cause to judge. Luba Shaba: *kílumbu*, 7, 8, diviner.	Proto-Kuba with meaning "official diviner, medicine man, for the village," especially for defense. No CS. Kuba Shaba has the wrong tones.
5. custodian of the poison ordeal: *nyim shɛky*, 1, 2.	Mongo: *-saka*, to bless. Mongo: *bosaki*, 1, 2, who blesses. Ngombe: *-saka*, to invoke, to bless. Bobangi: *-sak-*, to search for. Luba Shaba: *-saka*, to search for, to want, to be about to.	CS 257 ("to search for"). Proto-Bantu. Proto-Kuba with meaning "to invoke." Construction with *nyim*, 1a, 2, king.

X. Religion (continued)

Bushɔ́ɔ́ng	Comparable Forms	Comment
6. poison oracle: *ipweemy*, 7, 6 (also the tree).	Mongo: *efomi*, 7, 8, tree whose bark is used for the poison. Mbuun: *epomi*. Pende: *epumi*. Yela: *ephumi*.	Proto-Kuba.
7. main village charm: *kíín*, 9, 10. (Consists of a tiny garden with a banana tree and other plants.)	Mongo: *nkiṅdá*, 9, 10. Ntomba: *nkiṅdá*, 9, 10. Ooli/Yajima: *nkina* (De Langhe). Dzing: *lukiin*, 11, 10. Tio: *nkííní*, 9, 10. Sakata: *nkina*, 9, 10 (Van Everbroeck, *Religie*, p. 11). Yaka: *nkiindzi*, 9, 10, ritual defense (Devisch, p. 392).	Proto-Kuba. The term (except among the Yaka) has the same content everywhere. The region of Mayi Ndombe is included in the distribution.
8. oracle for testing a witch: *bukaang*, 14, 6.	Mongo: *nkanga*, 9, 10, diviner, magician. Tetela: *okanga*, 3, 4, charm. Tetela: *nkanga*, 1, 2, diviner, healer.	CS 786, 787. Proto-Bantu. Proto-Kuba. It is likely that proto-Kuba also had *kaang*, 1a, 2, medicine man.
9. taboo: *ikin*, 7, 8, avoidance. to abstain: *-kin*.	Mongo: *ekila*, 7, 8 (also Lia, Ntomba). Ngombe: *ekia*, 7, 8. Luba: *cíjíla*, 7, 8. Mbuun: *tshin*, 7, 8. Mbuun: *-tshyin*, to forbid.	CS 822, 823, 826. Verb is proto-Bantu; noun is western Bantu. Proto-Kuba.
10. spirit of deceased: *mwɛɛn*, 3, 4 (*ɛɛn* = to go).	Keté: *mwendwa*, 3, 4. Luba: *mwéní, bééní*, 1, 2. Leele: *mwendo*, 3, 4. aMbundu: *mwenho*, ?	CS 806/807, 1975/1976. Innovation from proto-Bantu and proto-Kuba verb. Could be loan from Luba.
11. symbol: *yiingt*, 7, 8. to disturb: *-iing*. to unravel: *-iingl*. to look at intently: *-iingt*.	See section VIII, Social Organization, item 16.	

X. Religion (continued)

Bushɔɔ́ng	Comparable Forms	Comment
12. to bewitch: -kut. -kutl: to clean, to purify (but Brown Edmiston: -kut, to be washed also).	Dzing: kur, to lie, to fake.	Dzing belongs to CS 1275, but the meaning is still too far from Bushɔɔ́ng for it to be truly comparable. Innovation?
13. to divine: -póóm (also means to detect, recognize, perceive).	Mongo: -óma, to breathe. Mongo: -mpóma, 9, 10, breathing, blowing with breath.	CS 1600. Proto-Bantu ("to breathe"). Innovation of meaning: one main form of divining was by blowing on a bag.
14. rubbing oracle: itóóm, 5, 6. to throw on the ground: -tóóm. to breathe: -tóóm.	Dzing: -tɔ́m, to throw from up to down (also -toem). Mbala: -omb-, to throw.	Innovation from the verb. Note correspondence between the meaning of the second verb with Mongo in item 13. A correspondence between divination and blowing was noted there. The noun can best be derived from the second verb and in turn, can be the source of the first verb.
15. charm: nnyeeng, 3, 4. to become strong: -nyeeng.	Luba Shaba: nyíngá, to be or become strong.	Derivation from verb. The verb may be derived from Luba Kasai.
16. nature spirit: ngésh, 3, 4.	Luba: múkishí, 3, 4, spirit of the dead (also Luba Shaba, Keté, Lwena, Songye). Songye: nkishi, 9, 10, statue for ancestral spirit. Songye: bukishi, 14, ritual cult. Ruund: múkish, 3, 4, charm, "fetish."	CS 1072 ("charm"), 1073 ("spirit"). Western Bantu. A loan from Luba. The Bushɔɔ́ng form is not derived from Kete or Luba mungici; these forms seem derived from Bushɔɔ́ng. Otherwise Bushɔɔ́ng would have a final c and a low

(continued)

X. Religion (continued)

Bushɔɔ́ng	Comparable Forms	Comment
16 (continued)	Ruund: *nkishi,* 9, 10, statue for ancestral spirit. Kanyok: *mukisha,* 3, 4, spirit of the dead. Kanincin: *mukish,* 3, 4, spirit, "fetish." Cokwe: *mukishi,* 3, 4, staff with figures carved on it. Kongo 1652: *mukisi,* 3, 4, witchcraft, charm for poisoning. Yombe: *nkisi,* 3, 4, spirit, charm (Bittremieux, pp. 501–4). Tetela: *okíshi,* 3, 4, imaginary being, spirit, statue. Tetela: *weécí,* 1, 2, medicine man. Southern Mongo: *weécí,* 3, 4, medicine man. Mongo: *wĕtsí,* 1, 2, medium, possessed woman. Keté: *mungicí,* 3, 4, nature spirit. Luba: *mungicí,* 3, 4, masked and costumed person (also Luba).	tone. Before the Luba loan, the term for nature spirit in Bushɔɔ́ng probably was *weécí,* 3, 4 or 1, 2, ultimately derived from Mongo *-éta,* to call, to name.
17. reborn spirit: *nshaang,* 3, 4.	Keté: *múshángi,* 1, 2. Luba: *músángu,* 1, 2, born with the defect of a deceased member of his family. Luba Shaba: *músángu,* reborn spirit.	CS 294, ps 78 ("inherit") could be linked to this form. A loan from Luba.
18. cult statue: *ishak ndweemy,* 7, 6	Mongo: *bosako,* 3, 4, incantation, wish.	For the first term, see item *5.* For the second there

X. Religion (continued)

Bushɔ́ɔ́ng	Comparable Forms	Comment
18 (continued)		
(used during rites for initiation, but also in other cults).	Kongo 1652: *ndombe,* to blacken. Kongo 1652: *ndombe,* black. Luba Shaba: *ńdúmba,* 9, 10, statue for boys' initiation rites.	is a link with Luba Shaba, which may be the origin. This could also be item *4.* I suspect a loan from Luba.
19. creator god: *Ncyéém poong.*	Kongo 1751: *Nzambi mpungu.* Mbala: *Záámbi puungu maweesu.* Tsong: *Nzem ampung.* Yans: *Nziam, Ngul Mpwo.* Mbuun: *Ozaaḿi, mpung.* Luba: *Nzambi.*	Loan from Kongo. For *Nzambi* alone: CS 925, 1917. The title has been attested since 1491.

Note: This distribution has often been traced. I have included only the mentions of the full expression, not the name alone.

20. diviner: *ngwɔɔ́m,* 1a, 2.	Kongo 1652: *ngombo,* 1a, 2. Yaka: *ngoombu,* 1a, 2 (Devisch). Tsong: *ngwoom,* 1a, 2 (De Beaucorps, p. 146). Mbala: *ngoombu,* 9, 6. Yans: *ngwòm,* 1a, 2. Buma: *ngwom,* 9, 10, divination object used by women diviners. Pende: *ngombo,* 9, 10, magic object for divination. Ndembu: *ngombu,* 9, 10, diviner's kit. Ndembu: *-honga,* to divine.	Origin from Kwilu, perhaps from Pende, since most other languages, unlike Pende and Kuba, precede *ngombu* by *nganga.* The Bushɔ́ɔ́ng meaning may, however, be closer to Kongo, Yaka.

XI. Visual Arts

Bushɔ́ɔ́ng	Comparable Forms	Comment
1. to carve: *-shɔɔng.* carver: *nshwɛɛngy,* 1, 2.	See section V, Crafts, item *41.*	Luba origin.
2. statue: *ipíng,* 7, 8.	Luba: *lúpingú,* 11, 10. Tetela: *luhingú,* 11, 10. Luba Shaba: *ḿpingo,* 9, 10, amulet. Luba Shaba: *-fingú,* to curse.	CS 1534 ("omen, fetish, charm") and 1557 ("to curse"), but the verb has opposite tone and may not be related. The Kuba form is related to the noun. Luba origin.
3. cult statue: *ishak ndweemy.*	See section X, Religion, item *18.*	Luba origin.
4. drawing: *bwiin,* 14 (also means pattern).	See section V, Crafts, item *1.*	Luba origin.
5. mask (a specific type): *nyɛɛng,* 9, 10.	Pende: *muniyaangi,* 3, 4 (De Sousberghe, *Art pende,* p. 156).	Pende origin.

Notes

Full bibliographical information for the shortened references used in these notes is given in the Reference List following the notes.

Chapter 1. " 'The People of the King"

1 Sheppard, "Heart of Africa," p. 185b.
2 Frobenius, *Kulturgeschichte,* pp. 14–15. Recently his description of these people, "civilized to the core," was reprinted on the jacket of Georges Balandier's book *La vie quotidienne dans le royaume de Congo* (Paris, 1965).
3 Sheppard, p. 187c: "What has made the Bakuba so superior do you think?" "I don't know. Perhaps they got their civilization from the Egyptians—or the Egyptians theirs from the Bakuba (!)."
4 Torday and Joyce, *Notes ethnographiques... les Bushongo* (henceforth cited as *Bushongo*), pp. 13, 60. The very fact that Torday placed the analogies at the level of Augustan Rome and imperial Japan is significant. This admiration pervades all his works about the Kuba and their king.
5 This calculation is very rough. It assumes that about half of the Kuba died in the epidemics that racked the country from 1893 to 1921, but this proportion may in fact be higher. In the 1890s only conjectures were available; they put the population around 250,000. See Sheppard, p. 182a, although this figure was for the Bakuba proper—i.e., the Bushoong.
6 See note 3, above; Wharton, *Leopard,* pp. 79–80.
7 Vansina, *Geschiedenis,* pp. 10–12.
8 Calculated from population figures of 1950. See Vansina, *Royaume kuba,* p. 8.
9 Ibid., pp. 54–55.
10 Religious practice was more uniform in the kingdom than was social organization.
11 Douglas, *Lele Economy.*
12 Vansina, *Geschiedenis.* To translate the data this book contains would as much as quadruple the size of this volume.
13 Vansina, "Recording the Oral History of the Bakuba."
14 Braudel, *Ecrits.*

Chapter 2. The Kuba and Their History

1 The names of known Kuba rulers and their order of succession are presented in Appendix A.
2 Brown Edmiston, *Grammar,* has "instructors of dance" (p. 512).
3 Frobenius, "Tagebuch"; Jacobs and Vansina, *"Nshoong atoot."*
4 Brown Edmiston, *Grammar,* p. 517.

5 Ibid., p. 528. It also means "large debt."

6 Vansina, *Geschiedenis,* pp. 26–27. For the expletives, see Vansina, *Esquisse de grammaire,* form No. 78. All the grammatical evidence can be found in that work.

7 Burridge, *Mambu,* pp. 32–34, 150–55.

8 See Rodney Needham, *Belief, Language and Experience* (Oxford, 1972), for a broad discussion of belief and truth. My own grammar and vocabulary also has *aloong*—"want, love, obey, accept, submit"—as a synonym for "to believe." But *yiimsh* is used in historical discussions. Of course, the impact of basic notions on testimony is as pronounced in literary sources as it is in oral sources. But when such notions change over time, oral sources are reworked, whereas written data, if preserved, remain unaltered.

9 Goody and Watt, "The Consequences of Literacy," in Goody, ed., *Literacy,* pp. 27–34, argue that homeostasis is the result of a total "structural amnesia," which makes certain that no discrepancies exist between existing institutions or values and history. Oral traditions would therefore only reflect the present. I do not accept this, and it can be shown that Goody and Watt exaggerate the point. But clearly the Kuba notion of "truth" works toward structural amnesia and their notion of cause, by being fairly static, encourages structural amnesia. That these processes are not completely efficient is due to the fact that people may and do remember previous "truths," and to the fact that homeostasis applies only to official traditions of the type that consciously attempts to transmit a view of the past.

10 Vansina, *Geschiedenis,* pp. 24–25. The year begins with the dry season, when agricultural operations are initiated. The names of the first months relate to this· Brown Edmiston, *Grammar,* claims that the term used for "year" is "a season" (pp. 498, 421), because there was no conception concerning a whole year in the 1920s, when she gathered her data, and in counting, "rainy season" was used. This claim is doubtful. In the 1950s, at any rate, "rainy season" was never used for time computation and the special term *nci* (nominal classes 3 and 4), year, was in common use.

11 The length of the week has remained uncertain from the time of Sheppard down to and including my fieldwork. For some, the week counted only three days. Verner, *Pioneering,* p. 285, mentions that markets were held every sixth day at Ibaanc in 1897. Sheppard, *Presbyterian Pioneers,* p. 72, gives three names but speaks of four days. Our informants gave four names.

12 Delivré, *Histoire des rois,* pp. 179–83, 190; but see also p. 285.

13 Vansina, *Esquisse de grammaire,* p. 60, and No. 58, p. 32. This is identical to No. 51, form 3, followed by No. 50, form 2.

14 Ibid., No. 68, No. 77.

15 Ibid., No. 77.

16 Gossen, *Chamulas,* pp. 29–30.

17 Right and left are also important. This duality is pronounced in the organization of space inside the village and the house. It also involves political titles. It is not, however, much used in a historical context. Right is the superior side, although in political organization the heads of the left halves of villages take precedence. But this is *left* when looking from upstream to downstream, as we conventionally do,

and *right* if one looks in the opposite direction, which is the Bushoong starting position. On right and left in general, see Rodney Needham, ed., *Right and Left: Essays on Dual Symbolic Classification* (Chicago, 1973). See Vansina, *Esquisse de grammaire,* No. 88 (locative) and Nos. 28–30, for three series of demonstratives. A fourth has since been identified.

18 Vansina, *Geschiedenis,* pp. 31–32. Add a 9a, "tales of Genesis," to the classification.

19 Ibid., pp. 35–36.

20 Ibid., pp. 37–38, 315–16.

21 Ibid., pp. 38–40 and passim in Part III for each reign. Clan mottoes were deposited in 1957 at the Musée royal de l'Afrique centrale at Tervuren. All the mottoes of all the sections in the realm are included.

22 Ibid., pp. 91–224 for most of them.

23 Ibid., pp. 215–16.

24 Ibid., pp. 41–44, 215–18 for clear cases. Kete traditions must belong to this type, since they are organized only by village.

25 See Wharton, *Leopard,* pp. 40–41, for the mwaaddy.

26 See Vansina, *Geschiedenis,* pp. 44–47, for tales. See also Vansina, "Traditions of Genesis and "Influence du mode de compréhension."

27 See Vansina, *Geschiedenis,* p. 330, for an example. The campaign can be dated to November 1908: see Torday, *On the Trail,* pp. 147–48, 158–60; and De Grunne, letter of April 12, 1909, to commissaire de district from Luebo, in Achten, "Dossier 493 bis." The royal forces were beaten off and the appearance of government soldiers led by De Grunne saved the situation. The basis for the lodging episode remains unknown.

28 Delivré, *Histoire des rois,* esp. Part I, pp. 27–112, and pp. 291–340.

29 Torday and Joyce, *Bushongo,* pp. 4–5; Achten, "Dossier 394 bis."

30 On kuum, see Vansina, *Geschiedenis,* pp. 29–31. On the muyum as keeper of traditions, see Brown Edmiston, *Grammar,* p. 567: "The one who relates or enumerates all the traditions and history of the tribe. While doing this he stands at a distance with back to the king who never sees his face." Her information probably stemmed from fellow missionaries who attended the enthronement in 1919–20.

31 Jacobs and Vansina, *"Nshoong atoot."*

32 See Frobenius, *Dichtkunst,* p. 157, for instances of Kakashi Kakulu stories.

33 Sperber, *Rethinking Symbolism,* pp. 79–81. See also the sources cited there, and pp. 104–5 ("truth"). Leach, *Genesis,* is an illustration of an approach that has become influential. An example of this influence in dealing with African data is Atkinson, "Traditions." Leach's approach differs substantially from that of Lévi-Strauss or de Heusch, *Roi ivre.*

34 Vansina, "History in the Field."

35 See Vansina, *Geschiedenis,* pp. 50–79 and 228–42 for information about informants and clans, p. 139 for the places of gathering; see also Map 2 there. All the narrative sources personally gathered are cited in extenso in the *Geschiedenis.* Short village histories and the praise names for clans are not given there, and the maps of movements within the kingdom, which exist for each clan, are not repro-

duced. In 1957 the maps were deposited, along with the praise names and some information about the villages, in the ethnographic section of the Musée royal de l'Afrique centrale.

Chapter 3. Kuba Genesis

1 "Myth" is here taken in its broad sense: a true, traditional story of the "timeless past"; it is used in this chapter to refer to stories of origin and migration. See Kirk, *Myth,* pp. 39–41.

De Heusch, *Roi ivre,* pp. 112–77 and 218–21 (myths 9–19, 24) takes stories relating to the past before the reign of King Shyaam [1] to be myths because he feels that their framework is progressive-regressive, whereas with Shyaam we are in the "authentically historical, and history occurs in a progressive framework" (p. 128). His point is that Kuba myths cannot be reduced only to their ideological function, valid as this may be. Their symbolic system *(symbolique)* makes up a single, huge corpus of familial, political, and cosmogonic traditions shared with those of the neighboring (he means the whole Luba-Lunda area) populations, and it is this common system that his book attempts to elucidate (pp. 127–29). He used, however, only a part of the available stories; and, more important, we cannot accept a priori an artificial distinction between "mythical" and "historical." On this score, Leach's remarks in "The Legitimacy of Solomon" *(Genesis,* pp. 27–31) are preferable.

Moreover, traditions as myths must first be placed within the framework of the Kuba symbolic mechanisms. A full treatment of the data and their symbolism would require a long study, which is unnecessary here, insofar as the elucidation of this subject does not affect the validity of traditions as history. The symbolic mechanism does indeed shape myths by *selecting* events or situations among the innumerable happenings of the past because these data are "good to remember." While this must be kept in mind, it does not greatly affect the veracity of each item selected. The operation of symbolic mechanisms may affect the data treated in this chapter more than that treated in others, and it may "distort" the original events. But most of the data I see as having come about from speculation about the existence of the world, mankind, peculiarities of society and culture, rather in the manner proposed by Horton, "African Traditional Thought" (see esp. pp. 66–71). As speculation, most of the data in this chapter do not have historical validity, and it is therefore unnecessary to describe in full the symbolic mechanisms at work, which can be left for another study. I believe that I have, however, acquired a working knowledge of Kuba symbols, or rather imagery, and make use of them when appropriate.

2 Vansina, *Geschiedenis,* pp. 81–83; de Heusch, *Roi ivre,* pp. 156–61.

3 Eighteen is two times nine, "the perfect number." The children correspond to a duality of nine as do the eighteen aristocratic clans among the Bushoong. The duality is made explicit by the references "x of Mboom" "y of Ngaan." See also note 4, below.

4 Vansina, *Geschiedenis,* p. 314 and esp. p. 322. Wharton, *Leopard,* p. 81, makes them part of a trinity, which is certainly wrong. De Heusch did not use this story,

which for the Kuba evokes twins—a figure that appears Janus-like when drawn in the sand—plasticity, and silence. These three evocations occur in other manifestations, and other resonances are also possible. Among all of these only the Janus evocation might have a connection with the notion of fate.

5 See Frobenius, *Dichtkunst*, p. 101, and Baumann, *Schöpfung*, p. 78, on Kakashi Kakulu.

6 Called *kombeem* and *kongweemy*, and associated with right and left. Mboom and Ngaan reflect this duality, among others. I do not know who was associated with which side, but I believe Ngaan went with the left.

7 Vansina, *Geschiedenis*, pp. 91-92, 82; de Heusch, *Roi ivre*, pp. 155-56.

8 Vansina, *Geschiedenis*, p. 83. He is considered as such by all the central Kuba as well as by the Ngeende and Ngongo. To translate the name as "man" is not acceptable because the tone of "Woto," "man," in Lia, Ekonda, and Shoowa is contrary to the tone of Woot, the personal name among the Kuba.

9 Ibid., p. 86, BS 10 (i.e., Bushoong informant no. 10) and BS 12. BS 10 only stresses the androgynous nature. BS 12 has the first man and woman (Woot and Mweel) come out of the broken calabash. De Heusch, *Roi ivre*, p. 197, relates that Nkongolo was supposed to be androgynous but does not treat the Imbidinginy myth. The story is widespread among the Kuba.

10 Sheppard, *Presbyterian Pioneers*, p. 114; Vansina *Geschiedenis*, p. 229. This is a widespread theme. Compare Baumann, *Schöpfung*, pp. 206-13, esp. "Heavenly ladder," p. 209, and p. 78. The closest relation is a Luba (Lulua) story; see Frobenius, *Dichtkunst*, pp. 110-11. In this tale the ancestor came down a spider's thread (the common motif). He went in the forest and left a box, from which his children, whom he had procreated with his sister, appeared. He left, telling them not to open the box. They disobeyed, and the birds informed him. He returned to the village, called all the people, and returned to heaven. The box contained a star, the heirloom of the clan. Some other clan sections also claimed descent from heaven.

11 Vansina, *Geschiedenis*, p. 83. This story was also not used by de Heusch, *Roi ivre*.

12 Nzambi mpungu, in Kikongo. The distribution of the term Nzambi (of which Ncyeem is the regular correspondence in Bushoong) has been given by Baumann, *Schöpfung*, pp. 96-106. It suggests a Western origin. Among the Kongo it is attested by the first written documents relating to the 1491 visit to their capital by the Portuguese. See Vansina, *Geschiedenis*, pp. 16, 83.

13 Vansina, *Geschiedenis*, p. 82. The two terms that have no meaning in Bushoong mean "digger" and "making water flow" in Mongo, which clearly indicates the origin of the tale, whether it be old or new. See de Heusch, *Roi ivre*, pp. 147-55.

14 This, then, is a myth about the origin of death as well. See Baumann, *Schöpfung*, p. 303; Torday and Joyce, *Bushongo*, p. 38. Another story about the origin of death was recorded from the Kete: a dog brought death to punish a woman who had betrayed his secret (Frobenius, *Dichtkunst*, pp. 86-87).

15 Vansina, *Geschiedenis*, p. 83. Another story used the tale of original sin to account for the dispersal of the wild animals, which fled into the bush. Paradise, "where the lion lay with the lamb," was thereby lost.

16 See Hulstaert, *Mongo,* p. 48; Mamet, *Langue ntomba* and *Langage des Bolia;* Van Everbroeck, *Mbomb'Ipoku,* p. 54. Baumann, *Schöpfung,* p. 111, has a distribution map, but many more data are now available than in 1936, when the map was published. It is not impossible that Mboom/Mbomba has a relation with the Kongo spirit Mbumba, known especially among the Vili.

17 See note 12, above.

18 Proto-Bantu *-biding:* "to turn," "to roll," is given by Meinhof and Homburger (see A. E. Meeussen, "Bantu Lexical Reconstructions" [Tervuren, 1969], p. 12a) and is clearly the root of *Imbidinginy.* Mongo has *bilingunya:* "to embrace—from all sides and in all directions," and a noun *mbilingi* (nominal classes 9, 10): "many objects on the ground and without any order or care." In the other name, *Shongl* corresponds to Mongo *songola:* "to start," applied to the rain only. Only one informant used this form (BS 10).

19 See note 8, above.

20 Ngaan in the sense of crocodile differs from Mongo. It is a loan from Luba *ngandu,* related to CS 783 in Guthrie, *Comparative Bantu.* The "archaic" use is of interest. The term never replaced the traditional name for crocodile, but competed with it and was finally dropped. This is intriguing in that it suggests that the term was readily adopted because Ngaan already was seen as a creator associated with water.

21 Vansina, *Geschiedenis,* pp. 161, 173.

22 Frobenius, *Dichtkunst,* pp. 182–83. Iselenge's role in this version is that of Mweel in others. See note 45, below.

23 Vansina, *Geschiedenis,* pp. 160, 154. There is also a man with the same name (p. 156 and n. 382), where he is equated with Selenge.

24 Ibid., pp. 84–91, 136–37, 143, 147–48, 150, 151, 154, 155, 156–61, 186, 193. De Heusch, *Roi ivre,* pp. 112–76, analyzes him as a mythical figure. Frobenius, *Dichtkunst,* p. 182, identifies him with the sun itself, which corresponds to the tale of the cycle he deals with, myth 10 of de Heusch (pp. 114–15). The personage is much more complex than that.

25 Vansina, *Geschiedenis,* p. 186.

26 Ibid., p. 158, first two diagrams.

27 Ibid., pp. 87–89.

28 Ibid., pp. 90, 129–30.

29 Ibid., pp. 91, 134.

30 Ibid., pp. 89–90.

31 Ibid., p. 126. When Woot had left, someone was sent after him to announce that his child was born. He returned to see it before he left for good—hence the name.

32 Ibid., p. 90; Vansina, "Handelingen," p. 300.

33 Vansina, *Geschiedenis,* pp. 136–37. This is the Kakashi Kakulu of the Luba and the Kaniok.

34 Ibid., pp. 156–61.

35 Ibid. This implies that the Ngongo were southern Mongo.

36 Ibid., p. 177.

37 Ibid., p. 173.

38 Ibid., p. 206. This is given in three villages out of nine.

39 Ibid.: for Mweel, see pp. 147, 151 in two chiefdoms; for Selenge, see pp. 147, 150

in two chiefdoms; for Mweelu mu Kol or Iweel, see p. 150 in one chiefdom. Iweel is Mweel; the difference is in the prefix, as in Iselenge versus Nselenge.

40 Ibid., p. 154.

41 Ibid., p. 178, n. 512; pp. 180, 181.

42 Wharton, *Leopard,* p. 77; Vansina, *Geschiedenis,* pp. 333–34 (where the paddle is mentioned).

43 This is further elaborated by mentioning that when Mweel went downstream, Mboom fled to heaven and Ngaan fled in the water, thus giving direction to the world.

44 Vansina, *Geschiedenis,* p. 83, n. 12; p. 94, n. 71; pp. 93, 94–95. De Heusch, *Roi ivre,* pp. 114–17, pp. 121–32.

45 Frobenius, *Dichtkunst,* pp. 182–83. The story also corresponds to de Heusch's myth 10, and it is found among the Songye (Frobenius, p. 101), where the creator made people and animals but only the night. People sent the buffalo to find the day, then they sent the elephant, and then the dog, with a set of birds that sang early in the morning. When they sang the sun rose. This is also the point of the Kuba story: Woot put a spell on the birds that call forth the morning. That the call of the cuckoo and especially of the rooster causes the sun to rise, and not the reverse, was still ritually expressed with full awareness in Kuba thought when an epidemic struck the capital in 1919. Wharton, *Leopard,* pp. 65–66, has yet another version in which instead of animals, men were sent; they became the titleholders *kikaam, cikl, ipaancl, nyaang, nyimishoong,* and *nyibit.*

46 Vansina, *Geschiedenis,* pp. 93–94; de Heusch, *Roi ivre,* pp. 121, 129–30.

47 Vansina, "Initiation Rituals," pp. 141 ff.

48 Vansina, *Geschiedenis,* p. 99, where the boulders dropped by Woot are named by three Ngeende sources *kiidy a Woot;* pp. 101–2, for *Itaangwa dika:* "the sun overhead." I now believe that this is a corruption for Tanganyika and a recently added element. Because of the strong connection between Woot and the sun, the element thus treated would fit, albeit only partly, since the sun at its zenith does not stand east.

49 According to commentary about the praise name for brass. Mweel was a minor culture hero who established the tattooing patterns for women. Like Woot, she did not die. The association of brass and water is derived from the association of brass with Europeans. The latter were still believed by the Biombo in 1896 to have come from under the sea. See Verner, *Pioneering,* pp. 178, 163.

50 Vansina, *Geschiedenis,* pp. 96–97.

51 Ibid., pp. 97–98.

52 Ibid., pp. 95–97.

53 Wharton, *Leopard,* p. 80. Woot, seen drunk by his sons, cursed them and they became black. The tale is also given by Mbop Louis (Vansina, *Geschiedenis,* p. 96) and Achten ("Geschiedenis der Bakuba," p. 191). The Noah theme is used in initiation to explain matrilinearity.

54 Vansina, *Geschiedenis,* pp. 95–98, 137–38, 150, 162, 172, 174.

55 Ibid., pp. 97–98. On the Imbangala, see Miller, *Kings and Kinsmen,* and "Imbangala," p. 561, map facing p. 568; Heintze, "König von Banguela," pp. 190, 199–200.

56 Some armor was still worn in the sixteenth century (Vansina, *Geschiedenis*, p. 96, n. 82), and helmets even later. Note that the entry "helmet, *mpu a utari*," in the Van Geel dictionary (c. 1651) as given in Van Wing and Penders, *Dictionnaire bantu*, cannot be trusted because its basis was a Latin-Spanish dictionary in which the term appears.

57 Vergiat, *Manjas*, p. 100, top left drawing and bottom left: *penga*. The type and name correspond closely to the Kuba examples and name *(mpengdy)*. The Bushoong is probably derived from the Mongo *fengola*, "to turn around, to avoid," but the latter may have a connection with penga.

58 Vansina, *Geschiedenis*, p. 97; p. 100, n. 104; p. 95, n. 77; pp. 108, 141, 196–202.

59 Swartenbroeckx, "Dictionnaire kiyanzi," 2:15, 75, 81; Vansina, *Geschiedenis*, p. 98, n. 100; p. 137.

60 Vansina, *Geschiedenis*, pp. 98–99, n. 102; pp. 137, 162, 172, 182, 194. As early a source as Frobenius, "Tagebuch," p. 7, has *Mbuba*.

61 Vansina, *Geschiedenis*, p. 150, n. 344; pp. 151, 152, and n. 357; p. 154 and n. 366; pp. 162, 172, 174, 228.

62 Ibid., p. 148 and nn. 320 and 321; pp. 151 (SH 101), 180, 182, 183–85, 188, 217, 238.

63 Ibid., pp. 150 (SH 103), 162 (NO 131), 228.

64 Ibid., p. 98, n. 101.

65 Jacobs and Vansina, *"Nshoong atoot,"* pp. 6–7.

66 Ibid., pp. 6–33.

67 Ibid., pp. 97–111, 138–42, 143–44, 146, 148–52, 154, 155, 162–70, 172–74, 178–92, 195–202.

68 Frobenius, "Tagebuch," p. 7. The text dates from 1905. The informant was Mishaamilyeeng, a son of Kot aMbweeky II [14], who in 1905 was not old but was very influential. The language used was Ciluba. Except for the Luidi reference, the text includes names known from other sources, but not this early. Origins somewhere north of the Sankuru are not hidden in this story.

69 Jacobs and Vansina, *"Nshoong atoot,"* pp. 12–15. The ellipsis points represent hesitation. Paragraphs are separated by a shout from the king and the answer by the public.

70 Vansina, *Geschiedenis*, p. 114. Torday and Joyce equate "Pil" with the sun *(Bushongo*, p. 213).

71 Vansina, *Geschiedenis*, p. 106, n. 144.

72 Pers. comm. from Ndjond'a Ngele, March 31, 1975, concerning the Ikolombe (southern Mongo on the northern bank of the Sankuru, opposite the Bushoong). The Ngongo recall a complex set of movements north of the Sankuru and upstream all the way to Lusambo, where they left the Isambo. See Vansina, *Geschiedenis*, pp. 162–70 and Map 9.

73 Vansina, *Geschiedenis*, pp. 114–15; Van der Kerken, *Ethnie mongo*, 1:344, 2:709, 671, 660, 673–74, 675. One of the old capitals was Tom aNdoong. Some of the Van der Kerken data may be influenced by administrative pressure on the Ndengese testimonies.

74 Pers. comm. from Daniel Goemaere, August 18, 1974, whose information stems from the period 1934–51; and from Joseph Cornet, 1974.

75 Van der Kerken, *Ethnie mongo*, 2:622–29.
76 Ibid., 2:658, 661, 664; Brausch, "Associations prénuptiales," p. 102–3.
77 Vansina, *Geschiedenis*, p. 333, n. 506. Cited in the praise name of the capital of Mbop Mabiinc maMbeky [21].
78 Ibid., p. 110; Vansina, "Handelingen," p. 279.
79 Sheppard, *Presbyterian Pioneers*, p. 114.
80 Vansina, *Geschiedenis*, pp. 110–11.
81 Ibid., pp. 178–205, and 215–52 for the whole population.
82 Ibid., p. 115, n. 198.
83 Ibid., pp. 212–13 for a summary.
84 Ibid., Map 14, showing locations of recent southern Mongo clan sections.
85 Van der Kerken, *Ethnie mongo*, 2:654, 661, 671–74 (but see Hulstaert, "Lecture critique," on Van der Kerken); Boelaert, "Bushong," passim.
86 Douglas, "Animals" (manuscript version); Mukenge, "Croyances," pp. 17, 26, and see also p. 55.
87 Or perhaps "coming from downstream" may hint to a period of two thousand years ago or more when the ancestors of all the C-speaking Bantu (i.e., those of Guthrie's zone C) went upstream from the vicinity of the Pool. These are clearly just speculations. The idea that they came from downstream is also well established among the northern riparians along the Sankuru. See Van Laere, *Basongo-Bankutu*, pp. 14–15, who recorded (before 1900) a tradition that the Nkucu came from the "downstream" and the Binji preceded them. This is why the Nkucu of Bena Dibele at that time still buried their dead with the head facing downstream. All this shows is the prevalence and *perhaps* the antiquity of this conviction among southern Mongo.

Chapter 4. Tales about the Kings

1 This summarizes the more detailed information in Vansina, *Geschiedenis*, pp. 286–324.
2 Henige, *Chronology of Oral Tradition*, pp. 27–38; Roberts, *History of the Bemba*, p. 23.
3 Wolf, "Wolf's Bericht," pp. 241–42.
4 Sheppard, *Presbyterian Pioneers*, p. 112.
5 Vansina, *Geschiedenis*, pp. 111–14.
6 According to a Pyaang source—the official history of the Pyaang Nnem, given by the spokesman in the presence of the council and the chief.
7 These are all the colors used in Kuba ritual, but not all the colors known to them.
8 Other sources and variants disagree mostly about the participants in the contest; see Vansina, *Geschiedenis*, pp. 112, 118. That a war did follow is also implied by the versions of the Pyaang Makesh and the Ngeende of the Bushyaang area, which claim that Mboong [C] threw his hammer before them. Because they did not throw it, they were not subject to the Bushoong. A war broke out when the Bushoong asked tribute from them. For the Bieeng version, see Vansina, "Handelingen," pp. 285–86.
9 Vansina, "Initiation Rituals," p. 144; Wharton, *Leopard*, p. 81; de Heusch, *Roi*

ivre, p. 112. The title of that book and of de Heusch's article, "What Shall We Do with the Drunken King?," refers to this myth.

10 Vansina, *Geschiedenis,* pp. 117, 236.

11 Vansina, "Handelingen," pp. 286–94.

12 Vansina, *Geschiedenis,* pp. 122–36; on the Pyaang and Kete, see pp. 124 and 128, and on the Pyaang chief who was the son of a Ngeende man, p. 122.

13 Ibid., pp. 118–19.

14 Ibid., p. 119. The clan Iyop is of Pyaang origin; see p. 236.

15 Ibid., p. 120.

16 Ibid., p. 120–21.

17 Ibid., p. 121.

18 Vansina, "Handelingen," pp. 281, 300. The name Mbobobo is an unusual construction; it may be a reduplication.

19 Vansina, *Geschiedenis,* p. 126; Denolf, *Dibese,* 1:360.

20 For the other peripheral Kuba groups, the Kete, Coofa, Cwa, and Mbeengi, see Vansina, *Geschiedenis,* pp. 136–214.

21 Ibid., pp. 290–91. Labaam is considered to be the ancestress of the Leele. The praise name is "She who repaired the paddles and the boats." Her location is near the confluence of the Kasai and the Sankuru.

22 See de Heusch, *Roi ivre,* pp. 178–95, concerning Lueji (Rweej) of the Lunda. He discusses the symbolic value of menstrual blood on pp. 178–229. The Kuba version is more explicit. See also Musambachime Mwelwa, "Changing Roles": the Chisinga elders tell a similar tale to explain how Chief Nkuba took over from the Bwilile while his wife had her menses.

23 Vansina, *Geschiedenis,* pp. 291–93. On the numbers of Lashyaang [E], see pp. 255–66, esp. 261. See also p. 36, n. 40.

24 Ibid., p. 118.

25 Frobenius, "Tagebuch," pp. 7–8, 9. His informant, MishaaMilyeeng, was the son of Kot aMbweeky [14] and played an important political role at the court from about 1892 to 1896. This is therefore an informed version.

26 Vansina, *Geschiedenis,* p. 291.

27 Ibid., p. 292. Normally residences were given names before they were abandoned, but pp. 215–16 show that when a village moved to another site, a new name might be given to the abandoned site. The permanent name of the village usually was transferred to the new location. In this tale, then, Lashyaang's residence is treated like an ordinary village.

28 Ibid., pp. 292–93.

29 Frobenius, "Tagebuch," p. 9.

30 Vansina, *Geschiedenis,* p. 293.

31 See Appendix B, *mbyeeng.* The title appears in the cliché about the division of an original settlement into two halves. See Vansina, *Geschiedenis,* p. 128 (Pyaang), p. 130 (Ngeende), p. 178 (Kete), p. 180 (Kete). The cliché is common among these groups. I was told that formerly a mock war was held, for amusement, between the two halves of the capital to commemorate their rivalry, but no separation of groups was tied to this.

32 Vansina, *Geschiedenis,* pp. 293–94. The whole sequence can be compared to the
    hunter kings, founders of dynasties among the Luba and Lunda. They too were
    "uncivilized." But de Heusch, *Roi ivre,* has not made the connection. Within the
    Kuba corpus itself the opposition between the peace-loving and palm-wine-
    drinking Ngup aShyaang and his more active or warlike brother recurs several
    times. These tales deal with the two aspects of kingship: life-giving and destruc-
    tive. In reality the new dynasty did not come from the Leele but from the east and
    was, we suspect, Pyaang in origin.

33 The fierceness of the pepper corresponds to the wildness of the king. Pepper was an
    American cultigen (see Murdock, *Africa,* p. 23). In the woman's title the last part,
    "diviner" *(angwoom),* is a term that originated west of the Loange River, the area
    from which all American cultigens were to come. Pepper is the first one mentioned
    by the traditions.

34 Frobenius, "Tagebuch," p. 10.

35 Vansina, *Geschiedenis,* pp. 294–303; Torday and Joyce, *Bushongo,* pp. 25–26;
    and mottoes about the ancestry of Shyaam [1]. One section of the clan Ikweemy
    claims that the father of Shyaam belonged to their clan. He was Nnaang a Yoom-
    booy, who married Shakady, a member of the royal clan. Their child was Shyaam.
    He placed his father's clan section at the village Matwiimy so that it would not be
    very far from his capital. This is the only source that makes this claim. It is
    interesting to note that Yoombooy does recur in the song of the queen mothers, but
    it is denied that it represents a personal name. Mbul aNgoong appears there as the
    mother of Shyaam. See *Geschiedenis,* pp. 279–80, where Shakady, the putative
    mother of Shyaam, recalls the other name of Shyaam: Lashyaang laKady andek. It
    also recalls Shankadi, a common name for the Luba of Katanga. The tradition
    seems wholly fictitious if only because the name Mbul aNgoong does not appear.
    Perhaps there was a link to another king, such as Kot aMbweeky *(ikoongl),* whose
    mother was Kady (ibid., p. 313), a name that was later reattributed to Shyaam. But
    because this name only partially corresponds to the Shakady mentioned, I hesitate
    to attribute this tale to that reign. No other clan anecdote claims to go back this far
    into the past. The earliest other similar anecdotes (and there are some) go back to
    Miko miMbul [11], the reign before c. 1835.

36 Ibid., p. 154.

37 Ibid., p. 295.

38 The tradition among the southwestern Mongo that chiefs are chosen by the spirits
    who send miracles to them should be noted in this connection. This event is a
    criterion of Shyaam's legitimacy. See Vansina, *Kingdoms of the Savanna,* p. 100.

39 Despite the hesitation in traditions between a Pende and a Mbuun origin, the latter
    not only is better attested but the linguistic innovations can only have come from a
    language of the Yans-Dzing-Mbuun group and not from Pende. Moreover, the
    Pende did not then live in the area south and southeast of the Mbuun.

40 See Chapter 10, p. 187.

41 The shesh in 1953–56 was one of my most accurate informants. He was one of two
    who checked Torday's text with me in the presence of Torday's informant, Shyaam
    aShyaam.

42 Did he really exist? In Vansina, *Geschiedenis,* p. 201, a Cwa informant designates a person with the same name as an ancestor of the Cwa who was killed by the Ngeende.

43 Frobenius, "Tagebuch," p. 10, claims that while Shyaam was traveling, his "brother" Mancu maShyaam [A] wanted to proclaim himself king. The people called Shyaam back and his brother was killed. This may be a reference to Mboongl a Shimy. It is more likely that this short passage summarizes the struggles of Shyaam to gain the throne and that the "brother" was Mishe miShyaang Matuun [F].

44 The drum is indeed of a Nkucu type and is a signal drum. The nkolakol ritual was still performed at funerals of major officials in the 1950s. It still implied that the king had not killed the notable through sorcery or any other means.

45 Vansina, *Geschiedenis,* p. 304. The forces came from the chiefdom whose capital was Misumba. The guilty son, Lambeengdy, fled to the farthest Ngongo village, Ishongaam, where he remained unmolested, indicating that Mboong aLeeng's campaign did not reach that far.

46 Ibid., pp. 175, 304–5.

47 Ibid., p. 305. The power of the kaolin egg was still accepted at court in 1953–56.

48 Ibid., pp. 124–25, 127.

49 Ibid., p. 305; n. 283 on that page lists the Binji groups who are their supposed descendants.

50 Ibid., pp. 306–8. P. 307, n. 294, provides information concerning Tooml aKwey, who was the best known of all magicians in 1953–56, and Shyaam aNdoong, whose major fame rests on the story of this war only.

51 Ibid., p. 306.

52 Ibid., pp. 306, 308, 332.

53 Ibid., pp. 306–8.

54 Frobenius, "Tagebuch": "30–40 Jahre" on p. 6, "40 Jahre" on p. 10. All sources agreed on his longevity, which provides the motive for the best-known anecdote about him, but no other source gave an estimate in years of rule.

55 Vansina, *Geschiedenis,* pp. 309–11. The MboMboosh story conclusively shows that at this time a king could no longer be deposed.

56 Ibid., pp. 311–22.

57 This story does not explain the name "ivory forks" at all. Note, however, that here the traditions give us the motif of the king who killed his mother. A similar motif is well known from the ancient kingdom of Kongo, where it appeared during the seventeenth century and has remained ever since. King Affonso killed his mother, we are told, because she had relapsed into paganism (Randles, *Royaume du Congo,* p. 99).

58 Vansina, *Geschiedenis,* p. 122.

59 Ibid. The story as told by the shesh was usually, but I believe erroneously, attributed to MboMboosh [3]; ibid., p. 310.

60 Why was this remembered?

61 The number has a general, symbolic meaning; cf. the seventy sons of Mancu maShyaang [C] who went to Leele country to find a king. Perhaps it means "many."

62 This is typical in Bushoong law. When a person was condemned to death by the court he was given palm wine and efforts were exerted to convince him to commit suicide by hanging.

63 The folktale from which this episode was taken has not yet been identified.

64 How such a story could arise is well illustrated in Torday, *On the Trail,* pp. 102–3, where the main diviner at Misumba pretended to throw lightning into the bush just as it struck a tree close by.

65 Vansina, "Du royaume kuba," pp. 6, 9; Frobenius, "Tagebuch," p. 6. When von Wissmann passed through Luebo early in 1886 the king had already died. The most likely date for his death is 1885.

66 Frobenius, "Tagebuch," pp. 110–11; Torday and Joyce, *Bushongo,* p. 32; Vansina, *Geschiedenis,* pp. 321–24.

67 The arrangements reached between Mbop Kyeen [16] and the Compagnie were still remembered in 1905 as part of a story explaining the king's death; see Frobenius, "Tagebuch," p. 11. For the other accounts see Vansina, "Du royaume kuba," p. 17.

Chapter 5. The Means of Interpretation

1 Bontinck, "Histoire du royaume," pp. 63, 133–34; Brasio, *Monumenta missionaria,* 4:491–92; Sousa Dias, "Viagem a Cassange," p. 29.

2 Silva Porto, "Novas jornadas." Part of Porto's diary remains unpublished and probably has more data about the Kuba. His relation breaks off in Kuba country.

3 Wolf, "Wolf's Bericht," pp. 235–38, 251–53.

4 Sheppard's *Presbyterian Pioneers* is based on notes made when he went on a lecture tour in 1893, after his first visit to the Kuba. His "Into the Heart of Africa" is therefore a more direct source. Most of the notes which went into writing that article are lost, however.

5 See De Macar, Verner, Landbeck, Fox-Bourne, and Shaloff in the Reference List. More data are certainly recoverable, especially from the archives of the missionary congregation Scheut.

6 An introduction to the Kuba during the colonial period can be found in Vansina, "Du royaume kuba," "Les Kuba et l'administration territoriale," and "Mouvements religieux kuba"; see also the references in those articles. The main archives still to be explored are those of the Compagnie du Kasai (since 1901), those of the missions after 1900, the collections of papers of Torday and his companions, and many administrative documents. The file for Achten is "Dossier 394 bis."

7 Wharton, *Leopard,* pp. 16, 51. He visited Torday in 1919 in London. Page 73 reveals his contacts with Sheppard. His own book is constantly referred to in the later American Presbyterian Christian Mission publications. The influence on early administrators before Achten's inquiries is clear in the case of Lardot (see Matagne in Reference List). Lardot was in the area from c. 1904 to c. 1918. The articles based on his notes are practically copies from Torday's 1910 publication. Or perhaps Torday received the notes from Lardot, which is less credible. Torday's book attracted the attention of Brussels and of the central administration of the

Congo, where its influence lasted for almost the whole colonial period. As far as we know today, Catholic missionaries were little influenced by his reports.

8 See Denolf, *Dibese,* which reworks the materials he published starting in 1932 and collected in the years preceding 1932.

9 Maes, "Vocabulaire," p. 210.

10 Brown Edmiston, *Grammar,* p. viii, and on the final vowel question, pp. 6–7, 20. The final vowel she heard was a *shwa.*

11 Hulstaert, "Langues de la cuvette," p. 24, and *Carte linguistique,* p. 29; Guthrie, *Bantu Languages,* p. 36; Van Bulck, *Recherches linguistiques,* pp. 503–6, 531–33, and *Carte linguistique;* Hulstaert, *Sujet des deux cartes linguistiques,* pp. 39–40, and "Quelques langues bantoues," p. 57.

12 Daeleman, "Vergelijkende Studie," pp. 18, 20–24.

13 Evrard, "Etude statistique"; Vansina, "Langues bantoues."

14 Torday and Joyce, *Bushongo,* pp. 43, 255–57. Johnston also used specimens in his *Comparative Study.* See also Van Bulck, *Recherches linguistiques,* p. 506.

15 Brown Edmiston, *Grammar,* p. 2, n. 1.

16 One example among many of such striking continuities are the descriptions in David, *Journal.*

17 See works by Maquet, Laurenty, Boone, Nicolas, Knosp, Miracle, Loir, Olbrechts Maesen, and Boelaert, in the Reference List, for examples of available distribution studies. In general, see Vansina, "Use of Ethnographic Data."

18 Wharton, *Leopold,* p. 65; Torday and Joyce, *Bushongo,* pp. 22, 46.

19 Douglas, "Lele Economy"; Vansina, "Use of Process Models," pp. 375, 389.

20 See Brausch, De Jonghe, De Langhe, Van der Kerken, and Van Laere in the Reference List.

21 See Stritzl, "Raffiaplüsche"; Vansina, "Ndop."

22 Hiernaux, "Bushong et Cwa."

23 Vansina, "Power of Systematic Doubt," pp. 110–15.

24 Shaloff, *Reform,* pp. 32–44, 158–77.

25 Henige, *Chronology of Oral Tradition,* is the only in-depth study devoted to the problem. My "Kuba Chronology Revisited" resulted from his prompting. Miller, *Kings and Kinsmen,* deals with the Imbangala.

26 Marrou, *Connaissance historique,* pp. 52–67.

Chapter 6. The Forebears

1 See Appendix B. The linguistic data are convincing and are reinforced by corresponding ethnographic materials. They form the backbone of our source material. More is known about the material side of life than about any other, and the image that results is consequently skewed. In this chapter, unsupported ethnographic data are introduced in my description when institutions or cultural features that cannot be omitted from any sketch are involved. They consist of comparisons among Kuba, Leele, Ooli, Yajima, Ndengese, and Nkucu. This device has been used only when absolutely necessary. The ethnography of the southern Mongo is still all too scanty, which means that only a portion of what will be one day available was been used here. Moreover, only evidence that seems incontrovertible—and that is only a

portion of what is extant—has been used. The base line "in a sort of ethnographic present" to be constructed is so important that I have deemed it better to err on the side of caution.

2 Robyns, *Carte des territoires;* Bultot, *Carte des zones.*

3 The poison was *lalyeeng; lulengo* in Nkucu. See Van Laere, *Basongo-Bankutu.* Poisoned arrows are not confirmed for the Ndengese and Yajima.

4 Some ground beans are definitely of African origin. See Allan, *African Husbandman,* p. 69.

5 Not only is there great similarity in these tools and in the bells, but all three items are regalia ascribed to the earliest days among the Kuba. North of the Lokenye, among the Yajima as among the Bushoong, the double bell is a major item in the shrine of leaders and is called Itoci, the title given to the first remembered leader north of the Sankuru by the central Kuba. I am grateful to Joseph Cornet for the Yajima information, supplied in 1974.

6 Allan, *African Husbandsman,* pp. 38–48, esp. p. 38. See Bartholomew and Birdsell, "Ecology," on "Leibig's law" (calculation of needs).

7 Much more detail could be given about the mode of production; the sketch presented here is sufficient to serve the purpose.

8 Torday and Joyce, *Bushongo,* p. 268.

9 Yet Torday and Joyce, p. 268, insist that salt was an export among the Ohindu. This is surprising since it was made from the male inflorescence of the oil palm. This yields an inferior product compared to the use of ashes from salt-rich marsh grass, which is and was a specialty of the area between the Sankuru and the Lulua. For camwood, see Denolf, *Dibese,* 1:137.

10 Needham, *"Remarks,"* pp. 8–9, 16, 19–20.

11 Hulstaert, *Mongo,* pp. 16–17, and *Mariage nkundo,* pp. 29–30 and passim. Van der Kerken, *Ethnie mongo,* pp. 668, 671–72, claims that even in early times political succession was matrilineal among the southern Mongo, but evidence is lacking. The assertions of Brausch tracing bilateral characteristics to the influence of early matrilineal Kuba groups in the Nkucu area cannot be substantiated: see "Associations prénuptiales," p. 127; "Famille," pp. 178–87; and "Groepsethnologie," pp. 22, 28, 39. See also de Heusch, "Système de parenté," pp. 1020–27.

12 See Doutreloux, *Ombre des fétiches,* p. 89, and "Introduction," p. 125, for the Kongo. Lineages can be ten generations deep; see de Sousberghe, "Les Pende," pp. 23, 35, 76–78, and table. Lineages are commonly five to six generations deep and exhibit alternation in generations. Further discussion of the transition from patrilinearity to matrilinearity follows in the first section of the next chapter.

13 Information from Joseph Cornet after his 1974 visit to the Yajima.

14 The term literally means "the skin," by implication "of the leopard," the main emblem of political authority. In Bushoong the same root with a different plural prefix, *mikop,* 4, "double bell," refers to a major emblem, perhaps the main one at one time in the past, among the Bushoong and the Yajima. These bells are almost four feet tall, the Bushoong one being attributed to "Woot" and the Yajima one "is" Itoci. Yajima information is from Cornet.

15 *Bokapa ekopo:* "division of the skin"; *Bukap:* "division." On the distribution of

ekopo (ekofo), see Van der Kerken, *Ethnie mongo,* Vol. 2, index, *ekofo,* p. 1089a; Vansina, *Geschiedenis,* pp. 148–49, 150, 151 (n. 351), 152, 155, 165 (Bokap and variations).

16 Van der Kerken, *Ethnie mongo,* 2:662–64, 672–74; Boelaert, *"Bushong,"* pp. 5–6.

17 For the Sengele see Van Everbroeck, *Mbomb'Ipoku,* p. 15: *Etoti,* from root *-tot-.* This is perhaps linked to the Mongo *totsa,* "to inquire." This would correspond to Itoci in the southern Mongo area. Van Everbroeck, p. 27, has Yeli, corresponding to the Ngongo (Kuba) title Iyeli; see his p. 16 for Lokwa among the Ooli. See also Van der Kerken, *Ethnie mongo,* 2:653, 654, 666–69 for Longomo, Lokwa, Elome, Etoci, Welo. Elome is not a title but a common noun: "medicine man, diviner." For Lakoin among the Yajima and in the royal tradition of the Bushoong, see Jacobs and Vansina, *"Nshoong atoot,"* pp. 12–13. For chiefly titles among the Kuba, see Vansina, *Royaume kuba,* p. 171, n. 1, for examples. In each ethnic group there was at least one special title of paramountcy. The title *nyim,* "king," began no doubt as the title of the Bushoong and Bieeng chiefs. Boelaert, "Bushong," p. 3, adds Ilanga.

18 The meaning "subject chiefdom" in Bushoong is linked to the root *-bil-,* the term being *bubil.* Mongo has *bobila* for village, and the villages were composed of kin, which in Mongo is *mbila,* still with the root *-bil-.* The terminology indicates an intimate link with kinship, consonant with the view that the earliest "chiefs" were patriarchs, having mainly authority over their kin and kin of kin.

19 On styles see Maesen, "Zones de répartition," pp. 184–86. The so-called diamond-shaped pattern of decoration in pottery has been attributed great antiquity on the grounds that it is also found in the Lungebungo tradition. See Phillipson, "Iron Age History," pp. 11–12. One could perhaps better compare Kuba pottery with the decorations of Kingabwa ware, which presents an extremely rich variety of patterns, but this also is at best tenuous evidence. Kingabwa may date from the sixteenth or seventeenth centuries. See Van Moorsel, *Atlas de préhistoire,* pp. 224–77.

20 Informant from Tyeen aMbaangi, named Ikweemy, acting as headman of this settlement.

21 Vansina, "Note sur les Twa."

22 Hiernaux, "Bushong et Cwa"; Torday and Joyce, *Bushongo,* p. 52; Vansina, *Geschiedenis,* pp. 201–2.

23 In 1956 I saw a Cwa headrest carved in a flowing naturalistic style, very different from the "normal" Kuba styles. In 1905 Frobenius reported naturalistic drawing in the sand by neighboring Cwa (among the Pyaang); see Frobenius, *Leo Frobenius,* pp. 62–63.

24 Vansina, *Geschiedenis,* p. 201.

25 Ibid., p. 202; Denolf, *Dibese,* p. 579; Torday and Joyce, *Bushongo,* pp. 235–36.

26 These statements were made by the spokesman for all the Ngeende chiefs in 1953. It was the official view. This attitude clearly betrays some of the same stereotypes that Europeans used to apply to Africans.

27 Vansina, *Geschiedenis,* pp. 201–2.

28 Ibid., pp. 112, 119, 178 on the smithy at Iyool. Wauters, *Esotérie,* pp. 173–75,

quotes the cikl of 1938 to the effect that the Kuba (called Gongo Bampila!) brought improvements in smithing, which for the Songye "came" from west of the San-kuru among the Koto group. See also Moeller, *Grandes lignes,* p. 450 (from Wauters, but before 1938). In this area (Songye? Tetela?) the coming of the first smith is a cliché; see pp. 452, 454, 455, 456, 460. Ethnographic and linguistic evidence ties the Kuba tools and terminology to the Mongo area: see Maquet, *Outils de forge,* plates 1 and 4, pp. 5–26, 35–36, 90–94, Map 1. The tradition cited by Wauters refers really to smelting furnaces. But the cikl seems to distinguish between early iron age and later iron age! If so, the chronology of this tradition is probably unacceptable.

As far as weaving is concerned, the looms are better now than Mongo looms and the bits of extant terminology indicate a Kete origin (south of the Lulua, a Kete origin is postulated). Concerning salt, the ethnographic evidence and Lulua data are overwhelming.

29 See Mukenge, "Croyances religieuses," pp. 44–45 (*lupetu lua biupu*) and 62–64, for a recent exposition.
30 See Maesen, "Zones de répartition," p. 184, n. 1.
31 See note 19, above.

Chapter 7. The Age of Chiefs

1 Douglas, *Lele of Kasai,* pp. 12–13. Current Leele tradition is clear in claiming an origin farther to the south (as do the Bieeng). But there also is no doubt that they are so closely related to the Kuba in language and many details of culture that they are, as the Kuba and the Leele claim, a branch of the proto-Kuba. Wongo can be derived from Kongo with loss of the initial *k,* a frequent phenomenon for which Appendix B provides examples. The Kuba were known to the Ndengese as Kongo.
2 Guthrie, *Comparative Bantu,* Vol. 3, CS 714.
3 The Mongo form for "my mother," *nyango,* is probably preserved as an expletive without meaning, as in Jacobs and Vansina, *"Nshoong atoot,"* e.g., p. 4, last line. It serves as a filler to allow a speaker to regain the thread to his argument.
4 The same root occurs in the Kuba, Mongo, and Luba languages. Mongo and Luba have the same tone; Bushoong has the opposite tone. This proves that it was borrowed from Luba, since all Bushoong borrowings from Luba reverse the tones, and if the term was derived from Mongo it should not have the tone opposite to Mongo.
5 The general term for affine is *bokilo,* a nominal form derived from the verbal root *-kil-,* "to avoid." The derivation is passive, hence, "those to be avoided."
6 See Vansina, *Royaume kuba,* pp. 31–34, for bridewealth. The functional utility of involving four clans rather than two is that it spreads the web created by the alliance. This is no proof of great age, however; it can be a simple metathesis of function.
7 A female pawn, *ngady,* derives from Mongo *wali,* "wife" (cf. Leele *ngal,* "wife"). Restricting the meaning of the term made it necessary to coin a new term for wife: *mwaamsh.*
8 Douglas, "Matriliny and pawnship."

9 As in Shyaam aNce, "Tooml aKwey i Kot aMbo," the tale of the marriage of Tooml aKwey. He acquired by trade the camwood blocks with which he paid bridewealth. Other data are in Vansina, "Trade and Markets," p. 195; Sheppard, *Presbyterian Pioneers,* pp. 123–24 (bridewealth paid in mats and cowries); and Sheppard, "Heart of Africa," p. 187b (bridewealth consisting of two large mats, cakes of salt, and up to 15,000 cowries).

10 De Plaen, *Structures d'autorité,* p. 77; De Decker, "Etude du mariage," pp. 125–46; Mertens, *Badzing,* 1:211.

11 Mpase, *Evolution,* pp. 85–88 (Ntomba, Sengele); Van Everbroeck, *Mbomb'Ipoku,* pp. 127–31; Focquet and Van der Kerken, "Populations indigènes," pp. 149–52; Tonnoir, *Giribuma,* pp. 273–79. This development is not unique: a similar calculation over several generations is reported from the Natchez. See e.g. Radin, *American Indian,* pp. 218–20. There probably exist at least several other cases in other culture areas.

12 Vansina, *Royaume kuba,* pp. 58–63, 54–55. In 1953, 53.5 percent of the population were ordinary villagers living in the husband's mother's brother's village; 43.5 percent of the population lived at the capital.

13 The largest clans, Ndoong, Boon, and Ibady, are found everywhere. Their variations with regard to numbers of sections exhibit a characteristic inverse J curve. Ndoong had 86 sections, many others only one each. For detailed figures see Vansina, *Geschiedenis,* pp. 230–42.

14 See ibid., pp. 215–16, for village histories. In time, kinship groups lost much of their significance and almost all their corporate functions, partially excepting only the localized clan section. Villages took the place of descent groups and became the basic units in matters of land tenure, local defense, and other political organization. The village became the cornerstone of the sociopolitical organization. For the Kuba, see Vansina, *Royaume kuba,* pp. 83–97; for the Leele, Douglas, *Lele of Kasai,* pp. 68–84, 168–219, and passim.

15 Douglas, *Lele of Kasai,* pp. 71–72.

16 Ndaywell, "Organisation sociale," 2:443.

17 *Ilumbi* is the official diviner in the Leele village. See Douglas, *Lele of Kasai,* pp. 213, 230ff. The Mongo have the same term, *elombe,* with the meanings intrepid persons, leaders, judges, warrior leaders. Among the Bushoong the term came to be applied only to warrior leaders and "magicians." These were also diviners, as they were among the Mongo. Whether or not all villages had ilweemy during the proto-Kuba period is unclear. Certainly all chiefs had some, but there may have been more of these specialists than there were chiefs.

18 See e.g. Jaspan, "Patriliny to Matriliny," Chaps. 6 and 7 (Redjang Sumatra), Chap. 8 (comparison and theory).

19 Braudel, *Ecrits,* pp. 50–54, 73.

20 Jacobs and Vansina, *"Nshoong atoot,"* pp. 12–13. His deposition does not, however, match in detail with the other accounts. Yet he clearly knew about them, given the declarations of the territorial commissioner *(administrateur)* in the 1930s. See Vansina, *Geschiedenis,* p. 113. His account sounds like the answer he had then given to the evidence from Dekese that at one time the Bushoong had been part of the Ndengese society.

21 Jacobs and Vansina, *"Nshoong atoot,"* pp. 16–17; Vansina, *Geschiedenis,* pp. 133–35, 215, 217, 145 (a clear example of the Iyool cliché in village history), 228 (clan history).

22 Some Bushoong sources, however, claim that these groups were also involved. See Vansina, *Geschiedenis,* pp. 112–13.

23 Pers. comm., Ndjond' a Ngele, March 3, 1975. I thank Mr. Ngele for the information.

24 According to the account of Daniel Goemaere, August 18, 1974. I thank Father Goemaere for this information, which he collected between 1934 and 1951 from Ndengese on the north bank of the Sankuru, who had it in part from Ndengese on the south bank (group Ngele: two villages). It was also mentioned that formerly Kuba and Ndengese married among each other. The history may in fact relate only to the past of the two Ndengese villages of the Ngele group and their relations with their immediate neighbors. The cliché of sudden attack during a celebration is quite common in southern Zaire, but is usually more elaborate.

25 Vansina, *Royaume kuba,* p. 181.

26 The term apparently survives only in the name for the double bell, *mikop.* Similar terms are Kop, the Bushoong ethnic spirit, and the term for palace enclosure, but these two differ in vowel quality or tone from ekopo or mikop.

27 See Vansina, *Geschiedenis,* p. 207, for a case in which mbaangt clans clearly were "invented."

28 Ibid., p. 243.

29 See ibid., pp. 92–93, 303, concerning Mitoom clan, according to one informant the earliest ruling clan, even before the Bieeng ruling clan took over. In another version this clan was a mbaangt. It lost that status.

The aristocratic clans were as important in establishing the individuality of a chiefdom as was the ruling clan itself. Yet some clusters from different ethnic groups shared some mbaangt clans. Originally, perhaps, such clans had been present in areas where the different chiefdoms were founded and were in a powerful position so that they became mbaangt. See ibid., pp. 242–43. The clearest case is that of the Ndoong clan, the largest Kuba clan which is mbaangt among the Bieeng, the Pyaang, the Maluk, and the Ngeende. Why did such a large group resign itself to being only mbaangt and not become a ruling clan itself? Some Kuba have speculated about this, and the main Bieeng source (ibid., p. 114) claims that at one time the Ndoong were the Bieeng ruling clan. But the evidence for this is unsupported and clearly speculative.

Moreover, the shift from patrilinearity to matrilinearity considerably obscures the evidence (ibid., p. 226). It is uncertain whether the patrilineal descent-group names were preserved when matrilineal clans emerged. The names may all come from preexisting matrilineal Kete clans if the first central Kuba girls were assigned (by the Kuba) to the clan names of their husbands. Evidence showing that the patriclan name was inherited by the children of such girls is really only attested for later patrilineal immigrants such as the Coofa, in cases dating c. 1800.

Another solution that could explain the spread of the Ndoong name over such a large area would be that the Kete lumped the former patriclans together under this designation because it was the ethnic name of an incoming group.

A single, united Ndoong clan may never have existed. Some evidence supports this. By 1953 all the Cwa of the eastern region were supposed to belong to clans and had assumed clan names, even though clans were nonexistent among them, since their descent system is bilateral. One of these was Ndoong. The clan sections here comprised many more "members" than in other parts of the kingdom. Instead of some eighteen members per section there are hundreds. See Vansina, *Royaume kuba,* pp. 59, 163. Sociologically, the labels were meaningless. Patrilineal Coofa villages also had very large sections. In fact, the addition of Kete and Cwa figures to the Kuba universe doubles the average of about eighteen per section to thirty-six. Even some matrilineal Kete clan sections are so large as to suggest that the system was artificially imposed here, as in the case of the BwaaTombe, where the average is about fifty. See ibid., p. 163.

The name Ndoong may therefore never have stood for a single social unit, and the "power question" of supposed numbers would be a false issue. The same clearly applies to the third largest Kuba clan, the Boon (see Vansina, *Geschiedenis,* pp. 68, 76–77), who are supposed autochthons and comprise perhaps half of the population among the eastern Cwa. The second largest clan, Ibady (ibid., pp. 69, 77), also may never have been a single unified group. Several synonyms of the clan name point to its possibly composite character (p. 221), as is the case for other relatively large clans: Kot-Keem, Bukoy, Bwaay, and perhaps Bushaang (a ruling clan). On close inspection the problem posed by mbaangt clans belonging to different clusters vanishes, as does the mystery created by the apparent presence of a few huge and widely spread clans in the territory. Both problems are mirages.

On the number of mbaangt, see ibid., p. 115, n. 198, for the Bushoong.

30 See ibid., p. 122, concerning the stability of the early Pyaang chiefdom. The argument does not apply as well to the early Ngeende.

31 Vansina, *Royaume kuba,* pp. 119–20.

32 See note 30, above.

33 Because the details of rivalries and alliances are unknown, we cannot tell why a given chiefdom did or did not break up. Concerning fission, see *Geschiedenis,* pp. 130, 131, 178, 180 (the cliché of mbeem and mbyeeng).

34 Ibid., pp. 126–28 (Pyaang); 129, 131–32, Maps 4–5 (Ngeende); 141–43 (Kel).

35 Ibid., pp. 147–53 (Shoowa), 176–77 (Ngoombe), 193–205 (Cwa), 205–7 (Mbeengi). For Cwa society and culture, see Vansina, "Note sur les Twa."

36 Vansina, *Geschiedenis,* p. 21: *mel* (or *mell*) plus *ibaanc.*

37 Vansina, *Royaume kuba,* pp. 128–30. *Matuk* in the title is the plural for ituk, which corresponds to Mongo *etuka.* Translating *ituk* as "corner" (as of house, mat, or yard) makes little sense since these kolm did not live at the corners of the villages or of the residences of chiefs.

38 Ibid., pp. 131–32; Vansina, *Geschiedenis,* pp. 120–21; Van Everbroeck, *Mbomb'Ipoku,* p. 148, for *botikala,* the acting chief after the chief's death, the term being derived from *-tik-,* "to put," by extension, "to remain." Note, however, that a cikala existed among the Ohindu, who may have borrowed it from the Kuba (if it were Mongo it should have been *cikela).* See Torday and Joyce, *Bushongo,* p. 265. Both the Kuba and ultimately the Ohindu may have derived the

term from Luba, specifically the Luba north of the Kaniok, near the upper San-kuru. See note 39, below.

39 Vansina, *Geschiedenis*, pp. 119, 337; Torday and Joyce, *Bushongo*, p. 265 (*epancula:* Ohindu); Frobenius; *Dichtkunst*, pp. 205–6 (*epancula:* Kuba Isambo of Lusambo). This may have been the title of their "paramount chief." See Huys-man, "Bakubas," p. 383, about the Isambo, who show strong Luba or Songye influences on their technology and way of life. For the Luba see Weydert, *Balubas*, pp. 3–4; Luba data in Appendix B of this book.

40 See Vansina, *Royaume kuba*, pp. 132, 161, where the nyaang is missing; Torday and Joyce, *Bushongo*, pp. 68–70, where both are missing from the Ngeende list, and pp. 66–68, where both are missing from the Ngongo list.

41 Vansina, *Geschiedenis*, pp. 219, 291 (mbaan); Denolf, *Dibese,* 1:224 (katyeeng); Vansina, *Royaume kuba,* pp. 129, 161 (mbeem, mbyeeng). For the cliché concern-ing this division of a village in halves, see *Geschiedenis*, pp. 128, 130, 178, 180. Iyol is quite old. In the motto of the Bushoong itself, its plural is used to describe the Bushoong as emissaries of Itoc.

42 Vansina, *Geschiedenis*, pp. 112–13, n. 185; pp. 117, 92.

43 Ibid., p. 120 (tataam), p. 114 (iyok pyeemy), p. 115 (fetching kaolin).

44 Vansina, *Royaume kuba*, pp. 113–15.

45 Vansina, *Geschiedenis*, pp. 288–89 and nn. 139, 140; p. 139.

46 Vansina, *Royaume kuba*, p. 148 (canes supposedly named after Woot's mother). If the mwaandaan belt was broken on purpose, the person who had caused the ngwoom incyaam to act in this fashion was reduced to slavery. See Vansina, *Geschiedenis,* p. 308, for the curse of the Bieeng; Torday and Joyce, *Bushongo*, pp. 71–72, for the importance of the canes south and north of the Sankuru. In the east, at that time, the canes had to come from beyond this river.

47 As has been stated, the double bell may have been the most important among these, judging by the objects in the national shrine and among the Yajima. Hence it is not surprising that the Kuba designate it with a term whose stem corresponds to ekopo, nor that the Yajima call it Itoci.

48 Most probably this lake acquired its name, which means "chief among lakes," only later. The name is not related to its size, for it is quite small, especially when compared with But aPoong.

49 Vansina, *Geschiedenis*, pp. 120–21.

50 Ibid., p. 291; Frobenius, "Tagebuch," p. 9 (in Frobenius's version, one of the two Lashyaang was killed, not deposed).

51 In Kete, *pangula,* "to take away by force, to make come out by force," seems to be the verb from which this noun is derived.

52 Vansina, *Geschiedenis,* p. 306.

53 Vansina, *Royaume kuba,* pp. 137–38 and accompanying map. It is significant that the titles nyaang and nyimishoong are new formations and are not found in most other Kuba chiefdoms. They probably are relatively younger than the titles cikl and ipaancl. These nyaang and nyimishoong titles may specifically have been created once the practice of establishing provinces *(shin)* had occurred. Nyimishoong's shin is called Lwaay Bushoong, "the thousand Bushoong," and the parallel "the

thousand Bushoong" and "king of the Bushoong [region]," which is the meaning of this title, is probably not coincidental.

54 The king's name, Mishe miShyaang Matuun, presumably has two matronyms (Shyaang and Matuun), or else one matronym (Shyaang) and a nickname (Matuun), as in other cases. The second part (Matuun) was probably only added after another Mishe miShyaang came to the throne; he was distinguished by the ma-Mbul, the name of his grandmother. In still later times the name of the first king was reinterpreted as Mishe miShyaang maTuun (rather than Matuun). Tuun (Tundu) is the "ruling" clan of the Leele, giving rise to a speculative connection, which turned into tradition. This connection cannot be correct because grammatically the name should be Mishe miShyaang miTuun or Mishe miShyaang Tuun. Hence the concept of Leele origin must be rejected.

55 See Vansina, Geschiedenis, pp. 118-77, for detail.

Chapter 8. The Age of Kings: Administrative History

1 See works by Sheppard, Torday, and Torday and Joyce in the Reference List. Earlier reports include those by Wolf and a few items in Silva Porto and von Wissmann. For further data on this period, see Vansina, "Du royaume kuba." Although a treaty was signed ceding sovereignty to the Congo Independent State early in 1885, this had no impact at all on the kingdom until 1897. The old order collapsed with the taking of the capital by government forces in 1900.

2 See Delivré, Histoire des rois, pp. 199-234. A similar case is one of Mukenge Kalamba, founder of the Lulua kingdom. Despite the fact that the traditions tend to fuse the actions of three different persons of two successive generations into the one Kalamba founding figure, Kalamba was the effective founder and the most remarkable of the three. See Ntambwe, "Luluwa," pp. 63-75.

3 See Vansina, Geschiedenis, pp. 310, 314. The attribution to MboMboosh does not agree with the best-informed source.

4 Ibid., pp. 296, 305. See also Chapter 5, above.

5 Torday and Joyce, Bushongo, pp. 59-60.

6 See Chapter 5, above; cf. Vansina, "Croyances religieuses," pp. 737-39.

7 Vansina, Royaume kuba, p. 101.

8 Ibid., p. 104. An analysis of the traditions about kings in which kingship is described reveals the same paradox.

9 Wharton, Leopard, pp. 71-72.

10 Vansina, Royaume kuba, pp. 111-16.

11 The dynastic statues are described in Chapter 12, below.

12 Vansina, Royaume kuba, pp. 102, 170.

13 Sperber, Rethinking Symbolism, pp. 115-49, treats symbolic mechanisms as evocations. How these happen to be collective rather than individual is an as yet unsolved problem.

14 Vansina, Geschiedenis, pp. 297 (note 208 is missing), 308.

15 An example of this was our informant, the shesh Bushoong, who was also a ngwoom incyaam. He claimed, however, that the ngwoom incyaam had stopped meeting. He felt that, even before, the position of shesh was more important that

that of ngwoom incyaam. This stands in sharp contrast to the southeastern Kuba, where the *bin apaang* (equivalent of ngwoom incyaam) really ruled the chiefdoms. See Harroy, "Bakuba," pp. 174-77.

16 See Smith, "Segmentary Lineage Systems," for the principles involved, and Southhall, *Alur Society,* for a case where the structure at each level mirrored all other levels.

17 Vansina, *Royaume kuba,* p. 127.

18 Ibid., pp. 131-33; Torday, *On the Trail,* p. 122; Torday and Joyce, *Bushongo,* p. 53.

19 See Vansina, *Royaume kuba,* pp. 129-34, concerning the kum ashin.

20 Nkwoonc may once have meant "leader." See Appendix B, group II.

21 These two titles were no doubt in use at the settlement where the court stayed, as they were in all other villages, but he enhanced their authority and regulated their succession: mbeem was to be the child of a king and mbyeeng a grandchild. See Vansina, *Geschiedenis,* pp. 293, 302.

22 Ibid., p. 313. This is mentioned in his own praise name.

23 Vansina, *Geschiedenis,* p. 316.

24 Ibid., p. 313.

25 See Vansina, "Negentiende-eeuwse stad."

26 Vansina, *Geschiedenis,* pp. 311-12. A type of weaverbird *(ncuunc)* designated in which capital he was to spend the night by flocking to a tree at the site.

27 Carvalho, *Expedição,* pp. 223-26, 227. For the Kongo, see Bontinck, *Brève relation,* pp. 113-14.

28 See Chapter 10, pp. 187-91.

29 Weekx, "Ambundu," p. 24.

30 Vansina, *Geschiedenis,* p. 305. Iloong corresponds to Ilunga in the Luba languages, or in Locwa. This name refers to "Ilunga the hunter," because he is a pygmy; perhaps we have here a faint echo of the tale of Ilunga the hunter told among both the Lunda and Luba, where they are foundation myths about the kingdoms. See ibid., pp. 305-7, for the organization by Mboong aLeeng of different types of dependent villages.

31 Ibid., pp. 302, 306. Royal wives in mbweengy could bear children fathered by anyone while the king remained the sociological father. They were called *mwaan mumweeny.* The introduction of the custom is attributed to Shyaam, who decided, it is said, that the mbeem should be such a child.

32 Ibid., pp. 310-11. The street received this name because it was along it that he escaped from his burning palace. See Chapter 5, above.

33 Kot aMbul occupied [10] two in succession, one of which may have been his mother's when she acted as a regent. See ibid., p. 318. Frobenius, "Tagebuch," pp. 7, 10, gives seven capitals to Mbop Mabiinc maMbul. His information, collected in 1905, shows that traditions tend to be uncertain on this, although it is of interest that the only other figure he cites is nine capitals for Mboong aLeeng, a number that later sources attribute to MboMboosh. I have only included capitals whose names are remembered.

34 See Vansina, *Geschiedenis,* p. 331, for a case; and Vansina, *Royaume kuba,* pp. 94, 139, 89.

35 Vansina, *Geschiedenis,* pp. 301, 303. The evidence for the creation of the institution by Shyaam derives from the killing of the son of the previous king.

36 Ibid., p. 306.

37 Vansina, *Royaume kuba,* p. 95.

38 Concerning bubaang villages, Vansina, *Geschiedenis,* pp. 306-7, gives examples dealing with the settlement by prisoners of war *(matwiingy)* and the declaration of bubaang status on a trifling charge. Lineage sections in bubaang villages were known as *mbimbil.* For initiation, see Vansina, "Initiation Rituals," pp. 138-39, 146, 152.

39 Only the single case of Baaking is a hereditary endowment. It went to a mbaangt clan, Iyeeng.

40 See Sheppard, *Presbyterian Pioneers,* pp. 133-34; Vansina, *Royaume kuba,* p. 140.

41 Jacobs and Vansina, "*Nshoong atoot,*" pp. 16-17. By the 1950s tribute was a very delicate topic and people were secretive about it. The colonial administration attempted to estimate the cash value of the tribute in kind in the 1930s and imposed a low evaluation in 1951, which angered the king.

42 The title "nyimancok" means "king of the elephants"; these duties were to make certain that all ivory went to the king. The importance of the tithe was obviously linked to the fortunes of the ivory trade. It must have been highly significant in the second half of the nineteenth century. Whether or not this official had control over the different cells of the Itwiimy, the elephant-hunting association, is not known.

43 Eric Wolf, *Peasants,* pp. 51-52, points out that this sort of arrangement disguised the exploitive nature of the labor and led to feelings of good will between patron and laborer at very little cost.

44 Vansina, *Royaume kuba,* p. 142.

45 Sheppard, *Presbyterian Pioneers,* p. 119. This was observed in 1892, before the colonial era imposed its changes.

46 See ibid., pp. 139-40, concerning the mace, and Vansina, *Royaume kuba,* p. 121, for the titles and ranking of the king's wives.

47 See Smith, *Government in Zazzau,* pp. 85-86, 133-34, 157-58, 233, and 251-52 for a similar development. Torday and Joyce, *Bushongo,* pp. 55-56, do not mention guilds, although Torday, *On the Trail,* p. 157, does. The implications of the latter work are unfortunate: his statement that the guild decided who was to be its representative is incorrect; his assumption that the representative was always "the cleverest craftsman" is unwarranted; and p. 146 misrepresents the nature of the offices.

48 Vansina, *Royaume kuba,* pp. 216, 219-20. A clan section tells how Mingiin miNaang settled near the capital, not in Kel country, because King Miko MiMbul [11] wanted him nearby. So the man lived in Matwiimy, a free village and the village of his wife. Such control of movement probably was the exception for free villages but was the rule in matoon villages with their mbimbil clans. Miko miMbul died before 1835, for when Halley's comet passed in that year, Mbop Mabiinc maMbul was king.

49 See Vansina, "Kuba et l'administration territoriale," pp. 289-91 for examples,

from 1923 to 1926, where excessive oppression by a paangl led to rebellion. A portrait from 1897 is given in Verner, *Pioneering,* pp. 288–90.

50 Vansina, *Royaume kuba,* pp. 19–20, 167; Sheppard, *Presbyterian Pioneers,* pp. 132–33.

51 Vansina, *Royaume kuba,* pp. 109, 117 n. 25. The list may be longer, including other felines and waterbuck.

52 This was an expedition led by the king against four Ngeende chiefs. At the same time an expedition by soldiers of the state was in operation there. See Torday, *On the Trail,* pp. 147, 153, 158–60.

53 Vansina, *Geschiedenis,* pp. 149, 317.

54 Ibid., pp. 306–7, 315. Vansina, "Handelingen," p. 285, describes the declaration of war as involving the ceremonial killing of a person, but whether the person killed was one of the enemy or one of their own men is unclear.

55 This I infer from the overall size of the group of the Bena Cishiba, but it is only inference.

56 Vansina, *Geschiedenis,* p. 305.

57 Ibid., p. 319.

58 Ibid. This is a village tradition rather than a dynastic one. The custom of bringing the hands of slain enemies is also attested by the explanations given for wooden carved hands, which were said to be insignia for iyol who had killed enemies. The custom of cutting off hands, a feature that was so prominent during the Congo Reform Campaign, antedated the foundation of the Independent State here, and probably was common in Equateur province.

59 Torday, *On the Trail,* pp. 158–60.

60 Vansina, *Geschiedenis,* p. 315.

61 Vansina, *Royaume kuba,* pp. 140, 169. An expedition of this nature took place around 1907 or 1908. See Van der Linden, *Congo,* pp. 229–30.

62 Sheppard, "Heart of Africa," p. 184a, 184c. One case cited dealt with the theft of a tusk by a son of the king. See also Sheppard, *Presbyterian Pioneers,* pp. 99–100, 139–40.

63 Vansina, *Royaume kuba,* p. 148.

64 Torday and Joyce, *Bushongo,* p. 60. For a concrete instance, see Torday, *On the Trail,* p. 114.

65 Mbyeemy sat also as a justice in the senior half of ibaam when it acted as a court. The *nyoom,* representative of the men of the royal lineage, was a member of ishyaaml, but the title seems to have been created only between 1902 and 1916.

66 Vansina, *Royaume kuba,* p. 149.

67 Ibid., p. 153.

68 Tribute is *nnaam,* but has the same root as ilaam. Because of the nasal prefix of nominal classes 3 and 4, the *l* changes to *n.*

69 The fact that twins born in Bushoong country were supposed to come and live at the capital was, it is said, decided by Shyaam, who had actually induced a twin birth. See Vansina, *Geschiedenis,* p. 298. The title of muyesh was also *mwaan aNcedy iNyony,* which refers to the mythical twins, Nyony aNgaan and Kop aNgaan. Kop aNgaan is identified with the king; hence muyesh is seen as a twin of the ruling

king. See Vansina, *Royaume kuba,* pp. 101, 117 n. 11; and *Geschiedenis,* p. 82, and the royal mottoes.

70 Jacobs and Vansina, *"Nshoong atoot";* Vansina, *Royaume kuba,* p. 151.
71 Vansina, *Royaume kuba,* pp. 151-52.
72 Ibid., pp. 152-53.
73 Sheppard, *Presbyterian Pioneers,* pp. 133-34. This meeting fell into disuse in this century. In 1951 the district commissioner hinted that something like it had existed once and that he believed that all eagle-feather chiefs attended. For its own convenience, the administration wanted such a council to be recreated. But then and during my fieldwork (1953-54) everyone denied its existence. The point is of interest because it shows the impact of practical administration on historical or anthropological inquiry. Were it not for Sheppard's testimony, we probably would not know that such a custom existed. Eagle-feather chiefs clearly did not attend.
74 Vansina, *Royaume kuba,* pp. 160-63.
75 Vansina, "Traditional Legal System."
76 Torday, *On the Trail,* p. 155 *(baang).* Cases of adultery were numerous.
77 Vansina, *Geschiedenis,* p. 119.
78 Ibid., p. 330. Fines were instituted by Kot aPe [18].
79 The execution of the death penalty was the duty of the *iyol ankong* (crow feather). For the *nkukuun* (condemned to die at the king's death), see Vansina, *Royaume kuba,* pp. 112-13.
80 See Vansina, *Geschiedenis,* p. 311.
81 Sheppard, *Presbyterian Pioneers,* p. 99; there, however, the village headman was to be tried. See Wharton, *Leopard,* pp. 71-72, concerning *ishyeeng itaan:* "fifteen," from the number of cowries associated with the practice by which a king informed a person that he should kill himself because he was insubordinate (nkeket). The victim could protest by handing fifteen cowries to the messenger, and this usually led to a trial. Highhanded action by the king is well documented for the first half of the twentieth century, when, for example, a village headman at Kosh was blinded because his village had converted to Protestantism without permission. See Kellersberger, *Life for the Congo,* pp. 93-94.
82 Douglas, *Witchcraft Confessions,* p. xxix; Vansina, "Bushong Poison Ordeal," pp. 246-48 (pp. 258-59 compare this with the fate of nkukuun and with other deaths).
83 Vansina, *Royaume kuba,* p. 168.

Chapter 9. The Age of Kings: Power and Politics

1 Smith, "Segmentary Lineage Systems."
2 The theoretical perspective in this chapter stems from Bailey, *Stratagems and Spoils.*
3 Compare the approach in Vansina, *Geschiedenis,* pp. 253-86, with that in Vansina, "Kuba Chronology Revisited."
4 For the data summarized here, see Vansina, *Geschiedenis,* pp. 268-69, 302-3, 308-9, 312-13, 318; Belepe, "Conflits de succession," p. 16. MishaaPelyeeng killed his brother Mbo Pelyeeng aNce and died soon after. The aNce case is

enshrined in a song sung when the masks come out at the capital. See Belepe, "Etude," pp. 115–18.

5 Wharton, *Leopard*, p. 72; Vansina, *Geschiedenis*, p. 302; Vansina, *Royaume kuba*, pp. 129–30.

6 Vansina, *Royaume kuba*, p. 102.

7 Vansina, "Kuba Chronology Revisited," p. 135 and tables, pp. 139–40. We do not know whether the story of Mbakam's murder of his mother is historic or not because the theme of a king murdering his mother existed, for example, in seventeenth-century Kongo, where it was claimed that King Affonso I had killed his mother, a claim that does not seem to be correct. This theme, like that of royal incest, emphasizes the loneliness of kingship: the king is the only person without kin. It is of interest that the pretext for the supposed killing was an alleged plot between the mother and Mbakam's brother. The story is in Vansina, *Geschiedenis*, p. 312.

8 Data in Vansina, *Geschiedenis*, p. 293, n. 168; p. 302. Informants were unusually divided about the attribution of the modes of succession to this office: some attributed the "invention" of mbyeeng to Woot; one did not attribute the story to any named king; three senior informants placed it during the reign of Lashyaang [E], and one placed it just after this reign. The testimonies pit Mbop Louis' version against that of Nyimiloong, the oldest and one of the most knowledgeable informants in other matters. Nyimiloong claimed the institution dates from just after Lashyaang's reign.

9 Ibid., pp. 298–300, 303.

10 As happened to some of the king's favorites from the 1920s to the early 1950s.

11 Vansina, *Geschiedenis*, pp. 300–301, 304, 310–11.

12 Ibid., pp. 313–14; p. 310, n. 319. The shesh Bushoong is the preferred source concerning the Ngel aMbiim (p. 172). On the royal sons, see pp. 315, 316–17.

13 Ibid., pp. 317, 320–22.

14 Ibid., p. 314; Vansina, *Royaume kuba*, pp. 155–58.

15 Vansina, *Royaume kuba*, pp. 157–58, "case two."

16 Vansina, *Geschiedenis*, p. 301; Torday and Joyce, *Bushongo*, pp. 26–27.

17 Vansina, *Geschiedenis*, p. 298, n. 217. Douglas, *Lele of Kasai*, p. 14, notes the Leele term for slave: *badinga* (pl.), *ninga* (sing.).

18 Vansina, *Geschiedenis*, p. 301.

19 Ibid., p. 297, n. 202.

20 Ibid., p. 299; Sheppard, *Presbyterian Pioneers*, p. 99. The traders had informed the king that Sheppard was coming.

21 Vansina, *Geschiedenis*, pp. 304–8.

22 Ibid., pp. 122–27, 306.

23 Ibid., pp. 297, 302. Changes in Kuba weaponry included a decline in importance of the throwing knife, if indeed it ever had been used on a large scale in war; a change in type of arrow as indicated by the term *pwoonc;* and a change in the knife carried at the belt for beauty and occasional use. The affinities are with shapes west of the Loange, but the name remained Mongo. The Luba and the Kuba used very similar weaponry, although Kuba swords were probably more efficient. See Westerdijk, *Ijzerwerk*, pp. 61, 69, 96.

24 Vansina, *Geschiedenis,* p. 122.
25 Ibid., p. 134. By the reign of Kot aNce at the latest the southern and southeastern areas of the realm were under firm control, so the chronology of these wars cannot be far off.
26 Ibid., pp. 148–50, 310. One source attributes this to Mboong aLeeng.
27 Ibid., p. 315.
28 Ibid., p. 318; p. 126, n. 247.
29 Shaloff, *Reform,* pp. 74–83, esp. 76–78; Vansina, "Du royaume kuba," pp. 15–18; Van der Linden, *Congo,* p. 234.
30 Harroy, "Bakuba," pp. 174–77.
31 Vansina, *Geschiedenis,* p. 245.
32 Ibid., p. 305.
33 The Binji speak a language closely related to Ciluba.
34 See Vansina, *Geschiedenis,* Map 14, which indicates recent settlement from outside by clan section or, along the Sankuru, by village. This was the situation in the 1950s. The infiltrations date presumably from after the arrival of the Coofa—i.e., mostly from the nineteenth century.
35 "Slave" and "Kete" are the same term in Bushoong, and a play on these words was often heard from informants. See also De Jonghe, *Formes d'asservissement,* p. 40.
36 Vansina, *Geschiedenis,* p. 319; and *Royaume kuba,* p. 96, n. 3. The average number of inhabitants per village in the 1950s was 174, and may have been less before. In 1885 villages probably were not very different in size from what they were in the 1950s, to judge by Wolf's report and later Sheppard's. There are, however, too few data to make even a reasonable estimate.
37 Vansina, *Geschiedenis,* pp. 318, 320. Selective terror was still in use in the beginning of this century, as shown in the case of Kosh and its headman as well as in the rebellions provoked by harsh treatment inflicted by paangl. The headman of Kosh was blinded because his villagers had become Christian. From c. 1902 to 1908 the Kuba were subjected to very harsh treatment by agents of the rubber company, which backed the king and was backed by him. See Vansina, "Du royaume kuba," pp. 18–54.
38 Douglas, *Witchcraft Confessions,* pp. xxix.
39 Sheppard, "Heart of Africa," pp. 186a, 187a; De Jonghe, *Formes d'asservissement,* pp. 74, 79–80 (*mitwingy* were prisoners of war, not slaves), p. 84 (*ngady akan* were not slaves), pp. 105, 114, 139, 158, 161–62, 167. Page 181, No. 88, shows that the data are from René Van Deuren, the territorial administrator, and can therefore be dated between 1933 and 1941.
40 This is evident in the tale of Tooml aKwey, as recorded by Shyaam aNce, "Tooml aKwey."
41 Rumor had it in the 1950s that the ruling king, Mbop Mabiinc maMbeky, had a grandfather who was a slave and therefore would not tell his full genealogy. True or false, it shows how little this status weighed on descendants in the second generation, for if the possibility had not been conceivable the gossip would not have been told.
42 Mishaamilyeeng had already become one of the major advisers, perhaps the major

one, to his father, the king. Yet his wealth was quite modest, although he did have a few slaves. See Sheppard, *Presbyterian Pioneers,* p. 116.

43 The image of the king as sun was still so vivid in the 1950s that one young man dreamt of the king as the sun. The image can be traced back to the collective memory about Mboong. See Vansina, *Geschiedenis,* pp. 288–89.

44 Ibid., p. 306.

45 Wharton, *Leopard,* p. 26; Vansina, "Negentiende-eeuwse stad," Part 1.

46 Sheppard, *Presbyterian Pioneers,* pp. 116–17.

47 Vansina, *Royaume kuba,* pp. 122–26 (*itul* and *ncec* feasts); pp. 111–16 (royal ceremonies); pp. 120, 121 (funerals).

48 Vansina, "Valeurs culturelles," pp. 905–9.

Chapter 10. The Hoe and the Cowrie: Economics

1 See Denolf, *Dibese,* 1:9–15.

2 Vansina, "Régime foncier."

3 Vansina, *Geschiedenis,* pp. 333–34. Indications of the central position of fishing in early Kuba life include the burial of the king in a coffin shaped like a canoe, or supposed to be a canoe; the presence, over the door of one of the entries of the palace, of a miniature canoe used as a charm to prevent lightning; the association of this charm with the "first" king; and the paddle that is preserved in the national shrine of the muyum as a symbol of the kingdom.

4 Evidence for all borrowing from the Kete is mainly linguistic; see Appendix B. Concerning hogs, see Epstein, *Origin of Domestic Animals,* 2:337, 346–47. None were kept by people of the equatorial forest.

5 Vansina, *Geschiedenis,* pp. 98, 334. Note, however, Ntambwe, "Luluwa," p. 101. The Lulua claim that raffia cloth was of Kuba or Tetela origin (p. 57). Raffia weaving and "certain fibers," *mapela,* were introduced by the people of Kapuku on the Mwanzangoma River, just south of the easternmost Pyaang. *Mapel* is the the Kuba designation for a man's dress. The loan may have gone from Kuba to Luba or the reverse. It is unclear from this reference just what mapela is among the Lulua: a fiber, or a cloth woven from that fiber, or bark cloth. See Loir, *Tissage,* pp. 51, 55, Maps 2 and 3. All of this weakens the case for a borrowing from Kete, who could have borrowed all the terms from Bushoong. Perhaps the improvement of the loom was a gradual technical achievement of a later date and consisted of the replacement of the vertical by the slanted loom.

6 Vansina, *Geschiedenis,* p. 98, n. 100. The borrowing of sugarcane may be less surprising than it would seem at first. An unbroken forest environment is not suitable for this plant.

7 See Denolf, *Dibese,* 1:25; Torday and Joyce, *Bushongo,* pp. 22, 133–34, Plate 17, and p. 236. Ntambwe, "Luluwa," p. 57, calls this type of salt *luepo lua mbanda,* and states on p. 90 that this salt was used as currency (hence the Kuba word for price, *mbaan*). Among the Lulua the specialists were the Bena Ngoshi. See also Sheppard, "Heart of Africa," p. 187b.

8 Each producing unit was probably an extended family of some type, whose goal

was to fill its own needs and no more. Families with a few dependents might produce a little more, but this would still be much less than they could have produced, whereas families with many dependents probably did not make ends meet. For the general rule formulated by Chayanov concerning this level of production and deviations from it, see Sahlins, *Stone Age Economics*, pp. 87–90, 102–15, giving the analysis of a case from the Tonga Valley at Mazulu and the impact of the village; see esp. p. 114, par. 3.

9 De Jonghe, *Formes d'asservissement*, p. 74, states that the name for slave was derived from *laket*, the noun meaning hat, and adds that it recalls the name of Kete (see also p. 40). This information comes from René Van Deuren, territorial administrator from 1933 to 1941, and can best be explained by the tradition that the Kete "invented" hats. All Kuba men wore hats; there is no reason to link this with slavery.

10 This argument is based on the similarity of Kuba style with those of the carvings along the upper part of the middle Kasai. See Maesen, "Zones de répartition," pp. 184–86, and Cornet, *Art of Africa*.

11 See Wauters, *Esotérie*, p. 173 (data from a Kuba source) and Chap. 6, n. 28, above. Westerdijk, *Ijzerwerk*, pp. 68–69 and 96, and his Group 12, pp. 49 and 54, has stylistic analogies in several forms of iron objects. Ntambwe, "Luluwa," p. 57, cites the Bashila Kasanga and Bakwa Kasansu of the Mwanzangoma area, just south of the Pyaang smiths, as the great Lulua producers of iron. The distribution clearly depended on the quality of the available ore and not so much on cultural tradition. The claim that the Kuba did bring more efficient tools or a more efficient furnace is not to be dismissed out of hand, but is not substantiated by the available data.

12 See Vansina, *Geschiedenis*, p. 311, where cassava is said to have been introduced in the reign of MboMboosh, who must have died before 1680, when Mbakam was king.

13 Beans derive their necessary nitrogen from the air and therefore are not as demanding of the soil as other crops, and their nutritional value is high. It is possible that varieties of American beans were added along with other crops of the American complex, even though the groundbean is an Old World pulse. But unless and until detailed studies are undertaken in the field by a specialist, this point cannot be cleared up. It is an important point, for the introduction of beans with a higher yield or a lower demand on soil nutrients exerts effects on nutrition and indirectly on population size and perhaps population increase.

14 Vansina, *Geschiedenis*, p. 294.

15 The first mention appears to me to be Brun, *Schiffarten*, p. 8, dating from 1612 (Loango, on the coast of the modern People's Republic of Congo). To reach the Kuba before 1680, cassava must have spread very fast. Hence the tradition that dates its introduction after the reign of Shyaam, as most sources have done, is certainly more credible than the few variants that ascribe its introduction (like everything else) to Shyaam's reign, for that would mean an introduction in the 1620s or 1630s.

16 See Randles, *Royaume de Congo*, p. 188; Brun, *Schiffarten*, p. 27 (stating that tobacco was common in Sonyo in 1612); D'Atri, "Relation," p. 64, fol. 321

(indicating that tobacco was not commonly grown there in 1698, since it was suitable as a gift to the local lord).

17 Bananas lend themselves to the intensive agriculture practiced in the interlacustrine area. They must be planted in groves, which must be tended over several years. The shift from fields to the small gardens behind the houses may have raised the productivity of the crop, but it was no longer a staple and no large stands were cultivated. The Kuba chose to develop maize rather than to intensify labor and cultivate banana groves—which would have been required to increase the yield enough to permit them to keep this food—because they did not have the technical knowledge possessed by interlacustrine people to deal with groves. Still, by putting them in the small gardens they provided some fertilizer for the trees.

18 Miracle, *Maize,* pp. 15–17, 207–8, and passim.

19 The tale of Shyaam "creating" cassava as a means to end a famine is mentioned in Chapter 4, above. The association between famine and cassava is the significant item here, not the historicity of the event narrated.

20 Rogers and Shoemaker, *Communication of Innovation,* pp. 176–96, 352–76, and propositions 5–1 to 5–32.

21 Sheppard, *Presbyterian Pioneers,* p. 123 (cultivation of millet); Wolf, "Wolf's Bericht," p. 248 (cultivation of sorghum or millet).

22 Delivré, *Histoire des rois,* pp. 181–83.

23 Vansina, *Geschiedenis,* pp. 297–98; Torday and Joyce, *Bushongo,* pp. 23, 131.

24 Murdock, *Africa,* p. 23.

25 Torday and Joyce, *Bushongo,* pp. 235–36, 244. See de Heusch, *Roi ivre,* pp. 218–21, for a a structural analysis of traditions about palm wine.

26 Douglas, "Lele Economy," p. 222.

27 Sheppard, *Presbyterian Pioneers,* p. 97. He even brought an ear of maize back to Hampton. See also Sheppard, "Heart of Africa," p. 186a.

28 Miracle, *Maize,* pp. 15–17, 107–8.

29 Sheppard, *Presbyterian Pioneers,* p. 97; Wolf, "Wolf's Bericht," p. 248 (describes three harvests of maize).

30 Vansina, *Geschiedenis,* p. 316. The truthfulness of the tale is of less interest than the fact that it was preserved. Another king is remembered for having been a good blacksmith and an excellent farmer.

31 Wolf, "Wolf's Bericht," p. 248, estimated the density in the area he saw at about four per sq km (or two hundred per square *Meil*). The Kuba population was estimated at about the same density by the 1950s. See Gourou, *Carte de densité,* which is based on the 1948 census. Given what we know about epidemics after 1892, the population must have been from one and a half to two times higher than in 1948. The density should therefore be from six to a maximum of eight per sq km. See Vansina, *Royaume kuba,* p. 11, and "Régime foncier," p. 902.

32 De Langhe, "Congo belge," p. 205 (c. 1914).

33 Vansina, *Geschiedenis,* p. 315.

34 See note 8, above.

35 Vansina, *Tribus Ba-Kuba,* p. 30. The source is Achten; during my fieldwork, later, this was repeated. But none of the sources before 1920 (Wolf, Sheppard, Frobenius, Torday) mentions anything other than bridewealth. The requirement of

cultivating a field may have been a standard that was never met—an obligation convertible into bridewealth payments.

36 The ethnographic map for the division of labor in Central Africa shows the Kuba to be practically the only group (south of the northern savanna) where men participated in all agricultural work except for some weeding. It is therefore a Kuba innovation for men to work in the fields as much as they do. For the hats, see Sheppard, "Heart of Africa," p. 187b. The boys were urged to begin right away and build themselves a house. Their age is judged by Sheppard to be fifteen. I do not think that such young boys really started work in the fields in earnest. Vansina, *Geschiedenis,* p. 305, tells that Mboong aLeeng "invented" the initiation drum, and hence invented initiation, and that during a ceremony half of the camp ran away and became Binji. This is a typical descending anachronism, in Delivré's terminology (*Histoire des rois,* pp. 181–83).

37 A connection with slavery west of the Loange is indicated by the similarity in designations for slave *(nsho)* and the fact that this is one of two synonyms in Kuba. The other term probably was older. This indicates that the Kuba either exported or imported slaves from that area, which accounts for the similarity in names. Given the stress on labor and later practice, imports are more likely.

38 Vansina, *Geschiedenis,* p. 319.

39 The estimate was essentially based on one village in the southern half of the kingdom; there were certainly more slave descendants at the capital. In 1886 several caravans from Bihe were said to be en route for the Kuba, carrying up to eight hundred slaves each for sale. See Carvalho, *O Lubuco,* pp. 46–48.

40 Sheppard, *Presbyterian Pioneers,* pp. 129–31, and "Heart of Africa," pp. 186a–b. Over a thousand slaves from the villages "all around" the capital were said to have been sacrificed for the funeral of Kot aMbweeky's mother.

41 By 1885 the competition between the newly arrived Congo Independent State personnel and the Luso-African traders lowered prices on imports, but the slave trade went on practically unchecked. Even in 1897 Verner saw slaves openly sold: Verner, *Pioneering,* pp. 286–87 (Ibaanc), p. 291 (Kampungu).

42 Sheppard, *Presbyterian Pioneers,* p. 134; Torday, *On the Trail,* pp. 186–87.

43 Vansina, *Geschiedenis,* p. 314.

44 Denolf, *Dibese,* 1:44, 49, 64–66.

45 Vansina, *Geschiedenis,* pp. 245–46, documents this in terms of clan sections.

46 No reliable absolute population figures are extant. By 1892 the population may be estimated at between 120,000 and 160,000, far above Wolf's estimate of 80,000 ("Wolf's Bericht," p. 248) and far below the figure Sheppard gave in 1893 as 250,000 or more ("Heart of Africa," p. 187a). My figures are based on the assumption that half, or at least one quarter, of the population was lost in the epidemic-filled years from 1893 to 1920.

47 Vansina, *Geschiedenis,* p. 309. Some say that his mother invented smithing.

48 Torday and Joyce, *Bushongo,* p. 179.

49 Vansina, *Geschiedenis,* p. 306.

50 Wharton, *Leopard,* pp. 52–53.

51 At the Mwabe River. Despite the victories of Kot aNce, the area was later lost by the

Pyaang, for the Luba occupied it when the Europeans arrived. See Vansina, *Geschiedenis*, p. 315.

52 The Kuba jealously guarded the secret of some of their inventions, such as dyeing in blue or yellow: see Wolf, "Wolf's Bericht," p. 247. This is not surprising in view of the fact that they exported cloth dyed in these colors to neighboring peoples (ibid.).

53 Sheppard, *Presbyterian Pioneers*, pp. 103–4.

54 Douglas, "Lele Economy," p. 233.

55 Allan, *African Husbandsman*, pp. 38–48.

56 Vansina, "Initiation Rituals," pp. 141–47.

57 As argued by Hagen, *Social Change;* Pye, *Politics, Personality;* and McClelland and Winter, *Motivating Economic Achievement,* personality factors are causes—or at least necessary, if not sufficient, conditions. In this case the work-ethic aspect of the "core personality" is best explained as an effect, but other aspects may well have facilitated political and economic change. There is no way of proving or disproving such a position.

58 The reverse has been argued most eloquently by the archaeologist Gordon Childe. Whether the notion of surplus itself makes sense has been argued by Leclair Schneider, *Economic Anthropology*, pp. 469–70; Harris, "Economy"; and Dalton, "Economic Surplus." For the neoclassical school, demand and supply are always in equilibrium and there is never a surplus. For the substantivist, there is no surplus because it is impossible to measure surplus. For Marxists, there is surplus; and, I believe, it is measurable. My view is supported by Sahlins, *Stone Age Economics,* p. 140, and Godelier, *Rationalité,* Part II, pp. 158–61.

59 Finley, *World of Odysseus,* shows the same mechanism for Homeric Greece.

60 Jacobs and Vansina, "*Nshoong atoot,*" pp. 16–17.

61 Vansina, *Geschiedenis,* p. 309.

62 Sheppard, *Presbyterian Pioneers*, p. 116. Mishaamilyeeng's treasure consisted of ivory, camwood, and balls of copper and iron. He was one of the king's most influential advisers and perhaps had already become his right arm.

63 For such feasts, see Vansina, *Royaume kuba,* pp. 122–26. The display of wealth increased power as much here as it did in Louis XIV's France, where Fouquet provoked a major crisis because his splendor was too great. He was a menace to the Sun King, and had to be destroyed.

64 Sheppard, *Presbyterian Pioneers*, p. 106, mentions that brass and for some time European clothes were reserved to royalty. Page 116 gives information concerning regulations on dress to be worn on different occasions by different patrician groups.

65 This is evident when inventories of Kuba items were compared with the goods commonly found in the houses of neighboring peoples. The nature of the goods cannot be strictly attributed, however, to the demand by the elite at Nsheng, for the Ngongo along the Sankuru and even the Mbeengi (e.g., at Butala as late as 1956) had the same range and similar numbers of commodities. We can explain this by assuming that the court acted as a trigger: the standard of living rose among the Bushoong first, then among other Kuba who imitated them and who were able to

do so because the volume and diversity of the regional trade had grown so much. Even so, I believe that the people of Butala, to take an example, had far fewer slaves than most Bushoong villages.

66 "Price," *mbaan,* is related to and derived from *mbanda,* the cake of salt made by the Lulua. See Ntambwe, "Luluwa," pp. 57, 90. The Ndjari were the fishermen on the Kasai River, downstream from the Loange-Kasai confluence. For a discussion of the term, see Appendix B, group II, *ncal,* note.

67 Vansina, "Langues bantoues," pp. 178, 181.

68 For Okanga, see Randles, *Royaume du Congo,* pp. 23, 133. First mentioned as a market in 1595, it flourished at least until the Dutch period, 1640–48. For Rafael de Castro, see Bontinck, "Histoire du royaume," pp. 22–23 (concerning the date), p. 133. Songo, or Tsong, was a name also used, however, for the Yans. Lamal, *Basuku et Bayaka,* pp. 89–90, mentions Hungaan settlements along part of this trade route from the Inzia (midway between the Kwango and Kwilu) in the east to Kongo country (Lumene) beyond the Kwango in the west.

69 Fehderau, *Origin and Development,* pp. 98–100 and passim.

70 In De Decker, *Clans Ambuun,* pp. 27, 42, one of the Mbuun clans recalls the Ngongo (of Kwilu) traders located between them and the Kongo.

71 Vansina, "Probing the Past," pp. 349–53.

72 Van Wing and Penders, *Dictionnaire Bantu.* Warri became *lwele* in later Kikongo, and is *leel* or *lyeel* among the Kuba, who interpreted the *lw* as a prefix of class 11. Lyeel is a free variant of leel, so the Kuba borrowed it after the term had appeared. The term for cloth is ncak. See Stritzl, "Raffiaplüsche," p. 45.

73 See Douglas, *Lele of Kasai,* pp. 73–76.

74 Brasio, *Monumenta missionaria,* 4:400, 403; the date of the reference is 1584.

75 Vansina, "Probing the Past," pp. 351–52. Only *nkila* has a Kuba form: *nkil.*

76 The term occurs in Kongo, Yaka, Ovimbundu, as well as Mbuun and other Kwilu languages. In Yaka the term is *mbadi,* and Plancquaert supposed that Yimbadi, an area corresponding to a part of the old Okanga, is linked to the etymology. See Plancquaert, *Yaka,* pp. 56–57.

77 Torday and Joyce, *Bushongo,* p. 9. The very praise name of Bushoong begins: "Bambal, Bambal of Woot and Itoc." Van Bulck, *Recherches linguistiques,* p. 506, believes the name Bambal refers to the "substratum" that existed before the Bushoong arrived, but there is no reason to accept this either. On balance I believe that it is a nickname given to the Bushoong because they were exporters of large quantities of mbal, and therefore the nickname arose at a later date than the name Bushoong. The reference in the praise name would therefore be anachronistic. Clearly there is no proof for this or any other view.

78 Vansina, *Geschiedenis,* p. 306; Sheppard, *Presbyterian Pioneers,* p. 106; but Wolf, "Wolf's Bericht," p. 236, noted that "Lukengo-Muana" (probably Kot aMbweeky) was wearing brass although he was not yet king, being at best the acting ruler.

79 Sousa Dias, "Viagem a Cassange," p. 24; the traveler Leitão, whose report is published there, found that people from the Kwango River went to the Kasai in the region of the Luba ("nâs partes das naçoes Quilubas"), where the Kasai was very wide and where there were falls. This clearly refers to the middle Kasai and

could be either the area of the Kikasa ferry near Mai Munene or, farther north, the region of the Belinge ferry near Djoko Punda, quite close to the Bieeng. In the nineteenth century there were still routes from both places to Mwata Kumbana on the Loange River and from there either to the Yaka capital or the lands upstream. Mai Munene was a Lunda state, ruling over mostly Luba. The date of its foundation is uncertain. See Vansina, *Kingdoms of the Savanna,* pp. 93–96. After 1850 these Kwango-to-Kuba routes could still be used. Mwata Kumbana as well as Mai Munene was then also directly linked to the main caravan route, which ran to Kimbundu: see Ntambwe, "Luluwa," p. 78. Certain Imbangala caravans went straight from the upper Kwango to the Bieeng via Mwata Kumbana, as they and the Holo presumably did in Leitão's time. Others took perhaps the route Silva Porto followed in 1880, straight north to the last falls (in the area of Belinge), although later most traffic between Belinge and Kikasa, and both ferries there, were in Pende hands. On the east bank no one monopolized the road from the Kuba to either Belinge or Mai Munene. It is further to be noted that cowries did "come with the Imbangala," or at least the latter are associated with them. For "Imbaangl of the cowries" see Vansina, *Geschiedenis,* p. 137. For routes, see Verner, *Pioneering,* pp. 179, 183, 201, 204, and p. 89 (Bena Makima to Bieeng and Belinge).

80 Von Wissmann, *Unter deutsche Flagge,* p. 77, reports meeting Kuba traders at Muketeba village, on the road to Mai Munene. The older Pende connection ran mostly via Belinge. It is attested by the association with such trading goods as pottery or velvet cloth. In fact, the Bena Makima–Belinge passage may have been used since the first Mbuun-Kuba contacts.

81 Verner, *Pioneering,* p. 185.

82 Vansina, *Geschiedenis,* p. 316.

83 See Vellut, "Notes sur les Lunda," pp. 121–23 (concerning routes); Ntambwe, "Luluwa," pp. 55–60 (map 59), 75–92.

84 Van Overbergh, *Basonge,* p. 428; Wauters, *Esotérie,* p. 175; Loir, *Tissage,* p. 58. The first Congo Independent State posts were founded to control this Kuba-Songye trade. The Songye specifically called the Isambo Kuba "Kuba." For the Sankuru, see Wolf, "Exploration," pp. 30–35; von Wissmann, *Im Innern Afrikas,* p. 365 (mentions the first trade goods on the Kasai below Kuba country, among Basongo Mino [Ngwi?]; the Ngwi blocked the river). Wolf, "Wolf's Bericht," p. 240, gives trader's information about rivers: on the Sankuru to near Lusambo, on the Kasai to the Loange and beyond. It was known that the Lokenye flowed ultimately into the Kasai and the latter into the Zaire. This last point may be hearsay, but still indicates some indirect contact. It is astonishing that the geographical knowledge of the Kuba went this far. That the Zaire and the Mbu (the ocean) were not identical is shown by the fact that the informant drew the rivers in the sand for Wolf, who therefore did not rely only on his Kuba-Luba-Portuguese translation. Von Wissmann, *Unter deutsche Flagge,* pp. 131–35, mentions Isambo raids.

85 Vansina, *Royaume kuba,* pp. 22–23; Douglas, *Lele of Kasai,* pp. 13–14.

86 Ntambwe, "Luluwa," pp. 57, 82–83, 86–88. The frequency of the markets among the Lulua varied between three and four days "according to the region" (p. 82). For the Kuba, frequencies of three and four are those most often given, but six and five also occur in data recorded between 1885 and 1908. See Hilton Simpson,

Kasai, p. 201; Wolf, "Wolf's Bericht," p. 252; Verner, *Pioneering,* p. 285; Torday and Joyce, *Bushongo,* p. 92; Sheppard, *Presbyterian Pioneers,* p. 72; Vansina, *Geschiedenis,* p. 25; Vansina, *Royaume kuba,* p. 27, n. 6.

87 Ivory collected in Kuba country, however, went to the king. Only ivory in transit trade from north of the Sankuru could be sold by individuals. Elephant hunters' associations existed among the Ndengese (pers. comm., Njond' a Ngele) and among the Ooli. The songs pertaining to Itwiimy show that its aim was to kill elephants without harm to the hunters.

88 Vansina, *Royaume kuba,* pp. 19-20, 22-23.

89 Sheppard, "Heart of Africa," p. 186a, reported that two to three hundred men rallied to go to buy ivory. They stayed away four to six months. See also Sheppard, *Presbyterian Pioneers,* pp. 87, 99; Wolf, "Wolf's Bericht," pp. 240 (mentions a trader for the king), 249 (mentions that all local ivory belongs to the king, who is one of the main dealers in Central Africa). Ntambwe, "Luluwa," p. 88, can be understood if only slaves were accepted for ivory in areas beyond the Sankuru, whereas for the Kuba ivory, cowries, and copper crosses were acceptable. The ordinary people sold their ivory only for slaves, but the king sold his for currency and other goods. The Songo Meno sold theirs only for slaves, which is contradicted by Kuba oral tradition. See Vansina, "Trade and Markets," p. 195; and Wolf, "Wolf's Bericht," p. 249 (reports that ivory was traded for slaves, copper, brass, beads, cowries, and red and blue flannelstuff).

90 Von Wissmann, *Unter deutsche Flagge,* p. 77; Ntambwe, "Luluwa," pp. 83, 77.

91 In Wolf's time the limit of penetration was still Kabao. Later the main market moved to Ibaanc, as the Kuba could no longer prevent traders from advancing. This was so by 1897, when in fact much of the middleman position was lost after the 1886 ascent of the Sankuru. By 1896-97 Zappo Zap traders had settled on the road to Ibaanc with impunity, aiming at cutting direct trade between the Kuba and the Luebo. See Verner, *Pioneering,* pp. 359-63 (esp. p. 362: Kasendi's settlement near Kabao).

92 Vansina, "Trade and Markets," p. 195.

93 Sheppard, *Presbyterian Pioneers,* pp. 132-33, 124, and "Heart of Africa," p. 187. Wolf, "Wolf's Bericht," p. 253, mentions as currencies cowries, *almandrilha* beads, copper, and brass [*sic*]; pp. 253-54 mention fines and market fees in cowries; pp. 250-51 mention judicial fines in cowries; p. 243 mentions bridewealth in cowries.

94 Bohannan and Dalton, *Markets in Africa,* pp. 7-9.

95 Tymowski, *Développement et régression,* pp. 7, 105-6, and passim.

Chapter 11. White Porcelain Clay: Religion

1 Religion as understood here is the concern of individuals and groups with ultimate reality as it affects them. Aspects include both preternatural beings and forces inherent in the nature of persons or objects. For the general concept, see De Craemer, Vansina, and Fox, "Religious Movements."

2 The concept of diffused religion is used by C. K. Yang, "Role of Religion," pp. 644-45. His prime examples are ancestor worship and worship of heaven, the latter

having its subordinate set of naturalistic deities, divination, and sacrifice. Classical religion, as opposed to Buddhism or Taoism, largely diffused into secular social institutions, especially the family and the state. The term does not preclude the presence of specialists, such as diviners. The Kuba have no ancestor worship and probably never knew it in a way similar to the Chinese system, but the worship of heaven is comparable in some ways. Kuba classical religion is linked to village and state and really may be more comparable to early Japanese Shinto than to the worship of heaven.

3 The first definition given in *Webster's New World Dictionary,* concise edition, 1960, as "a set or arrangement of things so related as to form an organic whole: as a solar *system,* supply *system,*" does not fit Kuba religion. Its sixth definition, "... order; method," is more relevant but still inadequate. Lalande's first definition, "a set of elements, material or not, reciprocally dependent on one another, so as to form an organized whole" (in *Vocabulaire technique*), is more precise than *Webster's* first, but is still inapplicable. There is no reciprocal dependence in Kuba thought; the Kuba did not have a single, all-inclusive paradigm concerning preternatural beings and forces. See Vansina, "Religions et sociétés," pp. 99–101. The researcher, not the Kuba, is the systematizer.

4 De Craemer, Vansina, and Fox, "Religious Movements," p. 475.

5 Vansina, "Mouvements religieux kuba."

6 MacGaffey, *The Religious Commissions of the Bakongo.*

7 Sheppard, *Presbyterian Pioneers,* pp. 101, 107–8. The etymology of nshaang is identical with the French *revenant:* "someone returning from the dead."

8 Vansina, *Geschiedenis,* p. 122.

9 See Brown Edmiston, *Grammar,* p. 572, verb: *nkala;* Douglas, *Lele of Kasai,* pp. 221, 228–29; Baumann, *Schöpfung,* pp. 109–11; and Appendix B of this book, group X, "Religion." In Jacobs and Vansina, *"Nshoong atoot,"* pp. 6–7, 11, Nshyaang aMboom is a spirit who rules the sky—i.e., Mboom's double.

10 Even in 1953 Ngaan's name appeared in the stereotyped exclamations that lace a royal speech; see Jacobs and Vansina, *"Nshoong atoot,"* pp. 4–5. Mboom's name also appeared, as mentioned in note 9, above.

11 Brasio, *Monumenta missionaria,* 5:611 (1610), 6:417 (1619), 8:444–45 (1640); Bontinck, *"Histoire du royaume,"* p. 59 (1624). Okanga had a parish and resident priest before 1610. Some time after 1624, but before 1631, the post was not occupied and at some time before 1640 a new curate was sent and a new mission established. No references either to trade or to missions in Okanga exist after 1640. The trade clearly declined and the parish was probably abandoned in the 1640s or 1650s. The texts of 1610 and 1640 stress preaching, and in 1610 the parish priest is reported to have left the mission each year during Lent to do his rounds in the countryside. In his preaching this story of Noah and Ham probably came up fairly frequently.

On the distribution of the term Nzambi, see Baumann, *Völker Afrikas,* p. 616, map 32, and pp. 614–15.

12 This hypothesis for the growth of monotheism is Horton's, in "Rationality of African Conversion," pp. 223–34, and "African Conversion," pp. 101–3.

13 Vansina, "Croyances religieuses," pp. 737–39.

14　Douglas, *Lele of Kasai,* pp. 206–19. The Kuba and southern Mongo data are from my own field notes.

15　Thomas, "Itombwa."

16　Vansina, *Geschiedenis,* p. 316.

17　Ibid., p. 298, n. 139. The names of the spirits in the sun do not correspond to those of the ethnic spirits.

18　Ibid., pp. 307–8, 315, 319, 322.

19　Thomas, "Itombwa," pp. 78–83; Torday, *On the Trail,* pp. 109–10.

20　Vansina, "Bushong Poison Ordeal," pp. 258–60.

21　Vansina, "Bushong Poison Ordeal," p. 248; Torday and Joyce, *Bushongo,* p. 78, fig. 57, and p. 54.

22　Nnyeeng occurs in Wolf, "Wolf's Bericht," p. 237, and is the only religious term there. Douglas, *Lele of Kasai,* p. 205, remarks that among the Leele the kindred *nengu* is sometimes "medicine," sometimes "rite." This applies to the Kuba in the expression "to make," *nnyeeng,* i.e., to perform a ritual with objects.

23　Starr, "Ethnographic Notes," pp. 100–101.

24　Sheppard, *Presbyterian Pioneers,* p. 113, contains the earliest mention of sacrifice. In the 1950s only a very rare sacrifice of fowl was acknowledged.

25　Vansina, *Geschiedenis,* p. 299.

26　Vansina, "Mouvements religieux kuba," p. 161. The hunting charm Piip was the core of the movement, which existed before 1893 or 1892—i.e., before any Europeans (including Sheppard) were in that area. The cult flourished in the center of the kingdom.

27　Vansina, *Geschiedenis,* p. 305. More precisely he invented the initiation friction drum "and hence the initiation." See Torday and Joyce, *Bushongo,* p. 89, for an earlier report of a Kete origin for initiation of boys.

28　Vansina, *Geschiedenis,* p. 305; Vansina, "Initiation Rituals."

29　See de Heusch, *Roi ivre,* pp. 112–14 (M9); de Heusch, "What Shall We Do with the Drunken King?", pp. 370–76. For connections with the Luba and the Ludna, see *Roi ivre,* index entries *ivresse* and *ivrogne.* Concerning Okanga, see note 11, above. Matrilinearity was not the only outcome of the Noah tale: for some it explains why the Kuba are black (Vansina, *Geschiedenis,* p. 97); for others why they are poor and the whites rich (p. 174). Diffusion of the Noah theme and the varying etiological explanations derived from it was already evident to Dammann, *Religionen Afrikas,* p. 144, n. 45.

30　Torday and Joyce, *Bushongo,* pp. 81–89, have a description that cannot apply to a ceremony more recent than 1902 at the earliest, because the king ruling at that time had not yet held an initiation. See Torday, *On the Trail,* p. 185 (an account follows on pp. 185–92). The two previous reigns were probably too short, being each less than one year, so that the last regular initiation at the capital dates at the latest from 1899 and presumably from the dry seasons before—i.e., 1898. Changes in a boy's initiation ritual are a focus of the superb study by Droogers, *Gevaarlijke reis.*

31　Sheppard, "Heart of Africa," p. 187b; Sheppard, *Presbyterian Pioneers,* pp. 123–24. The rite-of-passage aspect in dying was exceptionally strong (*Presbyterian Pioneers,* pp. 134–37), but Sheppard's description of funeral ceremonies is so general that it tells us little. They too changed. Many dances were associated with funerals, among them a war dance, *mpik,* whose introduction is attributed to Mboong aLeeng (Vansina, *Geschiedenis,* p. 309). Other mourning dances no doubt were perfected at different times, but again the whole ritual is lost to us.

32 We do not know when the Kuba began to replace goats with people for the funeral sacrifice, nor are we certain that they did sacrifice goats. See Sheppard, *Presbyterian Pioneers,* p. 131. Wolf, "Wolf's Bericht," mentions human sacrifice at funerals (p. 243) and the custom of letting criminals or persons charged with ishyeeng itaan (the sign of the king's displeasure) live to be sacrificed at the king's death (p. 244). But when did this last custom develop?

33 Sheppard, *Presbyterian Pioneers,* p. 113, mentions a royal house for charms. Is this the "house of the spirits" mentioned in the Bieeng account? See Vansina, "Handelingen," p. 283.

34 Vansina, *Royaume kuba,* p. 108. Van der Linden, *Congo,* p. 234, mentions the kingship objects but says only that they were kept by the keeper of the royal graves, without specifying if there was a special building for them.

35 Vansina, *Geschiedenis,* p. 316.

36 The Yajima data are from Joseph Cornet in a personal communication of 1974.

37 Vansina, *Geschiedenis,* p. 318, n. 400; Jacobs and Vansina, *"Nshoong atoot,"* pp. 28–29.

38 Van Everbroeck, *Mbomb'Ipoku,* pp. 149–52.

39 Vansina, *Geschiedenis,* pp. 302, 303.

40 Vansina, *Royaume kuba,* p. 101.

41 This term still exists in Bobangi as *mokonzi.*

42 Vansina, *Geschiedenis,* p. 312: "Kop and God, their word is identical," is a part of Mbakam's motto. In Jacobs and Vansina, *"Nshoong atoot,"* pp. 4–5, "When Kop roars today, listen!" is called out before the kings begins to speak.

43 Vansina, *Geschiedenis,* p. 314.

44 Ibid., p. 316.

45 Vansina, *Royaume kuba,* pp. 100–101. For the date, see the discussion of statues in Chap. 12.

46 Sheppard, *Presbyterian Pioneers,* p. 113. See also Vansina, *Royaume kuba,* p. 99, where the secret rite performed by the *bangwoom incyaam* may allude to this sacrifice.

47 Vansina, *Royaume kuba,* p. 99. The burial is not exactly similar to that of the king, who was buried with more pomp and wore all the feathers of rank. The ngwoom incyaam wore only the eagle's feather, making him equal to eagle-feather chiefs.

48 Kellersberger, *Life for the Congo,* pp. 123–24.

49 Sheppard, *Presbyterian Pioneers,* p. 72; Vansina, *Royaume kuba,* p. 99.

50 Sheppard, *Presbyterian Pioneers,* pp. 73, 128–30; Vansina, *Royaume kuba,* p. 100. Sheppard graphically describes a specialized medicine man, at the Kete village Bena Kasenga, who claimed to be a rainmaker and to stop lightning. The king had similar but superior powers.

51 Vansina, *Royaume kuba,* p. 100. The education of Mishe miShyaang Matuun [F] concerned those rules; see Vansina, *Geschiedenis,* p. 294. Sex represents fertility, and eating was an activity complementary to sex. See also Torday, *On the Trail,* p. 117.

52 See Vansina, *Geschiedenis,* p. 300, concerning blessing by spitting; Vansina, *Royaume kuba,* pp. 101–3, concerning the debate between "believers" and "skeptics."

53 See Jacobs and Vansina, *"Nshoong atoot,"* pp. 36–39, for the king's opinions, and pp. 32–33 for his claim of pollution; in the second passage "hunger" probably should read "river," an image used in royal language for kings. The last image in the paragraph refers to the woodborer, which also appears in a myth about the search for the sun.

54 Vansina, *Geschiedenis,* p. 303. Lack of knowledge about pitch and vowel quality does not allow us to conclude whether the Leele *nkolokol,* "ordinary [uninitiated] person," is identical with the Kuba term or not. See Douglas, *Lele of Kasai,* p. 209.

Chapter 12. Shapes in the Past: The Visual Arts

1 The early study by Torday and Joyce, *Bushongo,* pp. 179–234, is still the most outstanding. The Kuba are no exception, however: it is surprising how little genuine art history has been recorded in Africa and how few studies of ateliers, and even fewer attempts at dating, have been conducted.

2 Sheppard, "Heart of Africa," p. 185b.

3 Two were supposed to be the drums of Mbo Pelyeeng aNce [9] and MishaaPelyeeng aNce [8]. I do not know their present location.

4 Sheppard, *Presbyterian Pioneers,* p. 90; Starr, *Congo Natives,* Plate 11 (Kete figure, Ndombe) and Plate 12 (Kete, a Janus figure, Ndombe, in a style strongly different from those found among the Kuba). Ndombe is the title of the chief of the Bieeng and is used for his chiefdom. Some Kete villages belonged to it.

5 J. Desmond Clark specifies in a letter of April 21, 1976, that the object was found in 1967 at Tumbica I on the Kwango River, at about lat. 8°45' S, long. 17°58' E. The specimen is 1.38 m long (quite within the Kete range) and 22 cms thick (fairly thin by Kete standards). It was embedded in gravel. It is undated but belongs to the Iron Age. The "stream gravel" farther east range between 130 B.C. (±89 years) and 1070 A.D. (±80 years). The statue probably dates from the first millennium A.D. or perhaps the first centuries of the second millennium. As stated in the text, its style is similar to the Kete pole statues and to Pende objects. Before c. 1600 Pende were living in that area. This gives substance to the map of styles drawn by Albert Maesen ("Zones de répartition"), which unites Kuba styles to those of the middle Kasai and extends the area to the upper Kwango. See below, note 17.

6 Sheppard, *Presbyterian Pioneers,* p. 113. This is not to be confused with later statues in Songye style carved for King Kot aPe [18] in 1902.

7 Frobenius, *Kulturgeschichte,* Plate 75.

8 Sheppard, *Presbyterian Pioneers,* p. 112. There were still statues at Nsheng in 1900, but Drion, who reported this and described them as "busts," did not indicate the number (see Van der Linden, *Congo,* p. 234). Torday acquired four statues and identified a fifth: compare Torday and Joyce, *Bushongo,* p. 31, with Torday, *On the Trail,* pp. 148–50. In each case he describes four but they are not entirely identical, and the total number so described is five. They include one with a board

game as its emblem, one with an anvil as its emblem, one with a woman as its emblem, and two with drums as their emblems. Three are in the British Museum and two are at the Musée royal de l'Afrique centrale at Tervuren, Belgium, where they arrived before 1913. One more statue with a drum emblem and of the same general style attributed to a king but not mentioned by Torday exists today. It was given in 1909 to the visiting Belgian minister, Renkin, only months after Torday left. It is said to represent MboMboosh and is in the Brooklyn Museum. According to the traditional attributions six statues should have existed in Sheppard's time, in 1892. The one with the board game as emblem and the one with the anvil emblem he certainly saw. Which of the others he saw is an insoluble question.

9 The 1913 date is from Fagg, *Art of Central Africa*, p. 17.

10 Dechamps, "Première note," p. 80. Kot aMbul's statue, one of the group brought back by Torday, was tested.

11 Rosenwald, "Kuba King Figures."

12 Van der Linden, *Congo*, p. 234; Shaloff, *Reform*, pp. 159–60. His claim to the throne had to be backed by government force, and by the support of the Société anonyme des produits végétaux du Haut Kasai, represented by Drion. See also Frobenius, "Tagebuch," p. 11 (an account given by Mbop Kyeen's main antagonist). It seems very unlikely that Mbop Kyeen had a statue carved during his short and turbulent rule, living as he did with the refugees from the capital in a site where he barely completed the outline of his own capital.

13 See the discussion of style in Rosenwald, "Kuba King Figures," and Vansina, "Ndop."

14 Rosenwald, "Kuba King Figures," p. 30c. But she remains cautious, rejecting direct contact on chronological grounds. Still, mintadi continued to be made until perhaps the early nineteenth century. The geographical distance is a more serious handicap, and the styles are not very close.

15 See Torday and Joyce, *Bushongo*, p. 81 (Fig. 58), pp. 82, 237–38; Vansina, *Geschiedenis*, pp. 300, 297 (concerning the origin of mukyeeng). Torday and Joyce, pp. 24–25, attributed the invention of bwoom to Shyaam aTul, who was hydrocephalous and who lived during the reign of an unknown king.

16 Vansina, *Geschiedenis*, pp. 315–16. Mwaash aMbooy masks have faces made of leopard skin and are lavishly decorated with cowries and beads; the royal knot pattern appears on the back of the head in a pattern of beads. Formerly they had a face made out of the hide of an elephant (they represented an elephant) and a headcover out of perhaps plain raffia or velvet raffia cloth. Similar remarks for Luba masks of the Kasai are in Ntambwe, "Luluwa," p. 100.

17 In a story of Kot aPe (ruled 1902–16), the appearance of a bwoom mask near a river made onlookers believe they had seen a ngesh. Concerning style, see the comparison with the Pende *mazumbudi* mask in de Sousberghe, "Noms donnés," p. 84, Fig. 1.

18 Maesen, "Zones de répartition," pp. 184–87.

19 Vansina, "Initiation Rituals"; Torday and Joyce, *Bushongo*, pp. 81–86; Torday, *On the Trail*, pp. 185–91.

20 Dechamps, "Première note," p. 81.

21 Olbrechts, *Arts plastiques*, pp. 52–62. The stylistic characteristics of the ndop are

also found in the nnoon, which stem from the Pyaang area in the southeast, and some of them may have been traded from the Lulua. The important fact is that ndop share similar features on masks, which strengthens the feeling that kings are ngesh. There is, then, no evidence for a distinct court style, but since the court was the main patron of the arts and attracted presumably the best sculptors there did exist a court influence in taste. Kuba art is an aristocratic art.

22 For illustrations, see Claerhout, "Kuba statuettes," pp. 60–64. Torday, *On the Trail*, p. 138, claims that these were objects that had recently (1908) passed into the hands of a Belgian officer, which indicates that they were acquired between 1900 and 1907.

23 In 1953–56 a number of such iron sculptures were used among the Bieeng and the Bushoong as clan keepsakes.

24 Thomas, "Itombwa."

25 Van Noten, "Plus ancienne sculpture."

26 Loir, *Tissage*, p. 21, Fig. 3.

27 Wolf, "Wolf's Bericht," p. 247; Torday, *On the Trail*, p. 27.

28 Vansina, *Geschiedenis*, p. 298.

29 Stritzl, "Raffiaplüsche," pp. 38, 50.

30 Ibid., pp. 41, 42, 37, and passim.

31 Vansina, *Kingdoms of the Savanna*, p. 95.

32 I am grateful to Albert Maesen of the Musée royal de l'Afrique centrale at Tervuren for having allowed me to examine photographs of items at London and Copenhagen; the items at Ulm are described in Stritzl, "Raffiaplüsche." The London and Copenhagen items came from the collections of the duke of Gottorp, and are attested as dating before 1666. One was acquired for the Royal Curiosity Cabinet of Denmark before 1674 and one was acquired before 1737, as indicated by letter from the museum at Copenhagen to Maesen. It is probable that some of these reached Europe via the Dutch West Indies Company in the late 1630s and 1640s as gifts to the prince of Orange from Soyo and Kongo. See Stritzl, p. 38.

33 Torday and Joyce, *Bushongo*, p. 190. Torday discusses Kuba textiles on pp. 183–91. In *On the Trail*, p. 208, he claims an early-eighteenth-century date for some specimens, without strong supporting evidence. No effort has been made to try to obtain dates by the use of physical methods, and it may be impossible at this time to date raffia objects.

34 The *Encyclopaedia of Needlework* (New York, 1963) states that the height of popularity of Richelieu embroidery was reached in the seventeenth century. Italy was the country where it was the most extensively used by the peasantry and for clerical vestments. In 1645 the first Italian Capuchins arrived in the kingdom of Kongo, and of course the embroidery may have been used for church vestments even before. An indirect acquisition, perhaps via the Pende, is not to be excluded, as the route to Okanga fell into relative disuse soon after 1648 (at least as far as we know). This type of embroidery is best exhibited in a textile at the Musée royal de l'Afrique centrale at Tervuren. Lesser characteristics (such as buttonhole stitches and ladder stitches) are also shown in the plates of Torday and Joyce, *Bushongo*, p. xxvii, which Torday attributes to the eighteenth century. Stritzl's dissertation, "Die Gestickte Raffiaplüsche," was unfortunately unavailable to me, but her

article, "Raffiaplüsche," does not mention embroidery. The extant textiles from seventeenth-century Kongo are velvets.

35 Wharton, *Leopard,* pp. 43–44.

36 On names, see Torday, *On the Trail,* p. 204; Torday and Joyce, *Bushongo,* pp. 203, 216. Decorative patterns also are named in Kikongo, and the term for a pattern or drawing, *bwiin,* among the Kuba happens to be identical to the term in Mayombe (see Bittremieux, *Mayombsch Idioticon,* 2:795, 1:72), provided the tones are identical. Bittremieux gives no tonal patterns. For the geometrical aspect, see Crowe, "Geometry."

37 Torday and Joyce, *Bushongo,* pp. 208–26; Crowe, "Geometry," p. 5.

38 This was a figure derived from Christ on the cross that had under it a sign imitating a beetle, called *ncyeem,* homophone of the term for God. Leyder, "Graphisme et magie," pp. 111–20, argues that Kuba decorative patterns were on the brink of being used as a script, a point of view I do not share. The only ensemble I found that was meant to be "read" was the set of patterns on the paddle in the national shrine of the muyum, where each ethnic group was represented by its pattern of scarification. Even this is better looked upon as a kind of rebus representation rather than the beginnings of a script—e.g., there was no order in which they were supposed to be read.

39 For Kingabwa pottery, see Van Moorsel, *Atlas de préhistoire,* pp. 224, 277. He suggests a date in the seventeenth century. David Cahen, who reexamined the site, feels that an earlier date is not to be excluded (pers. comm., 1975). Concerning Lungebungu ware, which has been compared to Kuba pottery, see Phillipson, *"Iron Age History,"* p. 12. The similarity in decorative patterns is unconvincing to me. The solution to the problem will only become clearer through excavation of pottery sites on the Sankuru and Lokenye as well as along the Lulua and Kasai.

40 Torday and Joyce, *Bushongo,* pp. 208–9.

41 Delange, *Art and Peoples,* pp. 207, 210.

42 Vansina, "Valeurs culturelles," pp. 905–9.

43 Sheppard, *Presbyterian Pioneers,* pp. 105, 116. For the capital, see Mattelaer, "Mushenge"; Vansina, "Negentiende-eeuwse stad."

Chapter 13. Reflections

1 On the process of selection, see Finley, "Myth," pp. 292–97, 283. On structuralism, see Leach, *Genesis,* p. 27: "I seek to demonstrate the creation of a myth as the precipitate of the development of an historical tradition." Nathhorst, *Formal or Structural Studies,* pp. 60–70, presents a telling critique of Leach's approach following an equally telling criticism of Lévi-Strauss on pp. 37–59.

2 Vansina, *Geschiedenis,* p. 297.

3 Van der Linden, *Congo,* p. 234.

4 Shaloff, *Reform,* p. 160; Vansina, *Geschiedenis,* pp. 328–29.

5 "The snake on the calabash: if you kill the snake, you break the calabash; if you leave the calabash, the snake escapes." King Kot aPe said this to his heir apparent, who was about to attack the European who came to arrest the king at gunpoint.

6 Because MboMboosh is credited with having set fixed amounts as fines in cases involving children of kings.

7 Vansina, "Du royaume kuba," "Kuba et l'administration territoriale," and "Mouvements religieux kuba."

8 Garlake, *Great Zimbabwe,* p. 198.

9 Ryder, *Benin,* pp. 113–18, 134–35; Bradbury, *Benin Studies,* pp. 28–29.

10 See Claessen, *Politieke Antropologie,* pp. 111–26, for a survey of current theories. The list summarizes the concerns of all the recent authors.

11 Sahlins, *Stone Age Economics,* pp. 141–48.

12 Wolf, "Wolf's Bericht," pp. 231, 235.

13 Culbert, *Lost Civilization,* pp. 37–51, deals with the mode of production.

14 See Stevenson, *Population and Political Systems,* and my review of that work in the *Canadian Journal of African Studies* 2 (1968):241–44.

15 See Service, *Primitive Social Organization,* and Fried, *Evolution of Political Society,* both of whom stress that societies move from one level to the next by "mutation"—i.e., rather suddenly. The beginning of the kingdom would be stressed in this context. Carneiro, "Scale Analysis," presupposes a continuing, gradual development. He would see the Age of Chiefs as preparatory to the "mutation." But even in his view, the creation of a new society and culture from the blending of proto-Kuba and proto-Kete would not be significant. The basic multilinear evolutionary theory as set forth in Sahlins and Service, *Evolution and Culture,* is accepted by most evolutionary anthropologists today.

16 The previous transformation was lateral. It did not lead to any change in level unless heavy stress is laid on definitions such that proto-Kuba and proto-Kete would be "tribes" and the early Kuba culture and society would consist of "chiefdoms." But such stress is highly artificial, and there are not enough data available to support it. The case does show that the preoccupation with "levels" of progress or with complexity cripples a theory whose processual aspects often are illuminating.

Reference List

Abbreviations

ARSOM: Académie royale des sciences d'outre-mer (Brussels). Unless otherwise noted, the primary series title for works cited with this abbreviation is Memoirs, Division of Moral and Political Science. The secondary, specific series designation is given with each title in the Reference List. From 1955 to 1960 the institution's title was Académie royale des sciences coloniales. Before 1955 it was the Institut royal colonial belge. In 1955 a new numbering of the Memoirs series began.

MRAC: Musée royal de l'Afrique centrale (Tervuren). Unless otherwise noted, the primary series title for works cited with this abbreviation is Human Sciences, Annals. The secondary, specific series designation is given with each title in the Reference List.

Archives

Frobenius-Institut, Frankfurt.
  Frobenius, Leo. "Tagebuch, Diafe I, Ethnographie III (Kasai)," pp. 6–10. 1905.
Musée royale de l'Afrique centrale, Tervuren.
  Achten, Lode. Dossiers ethnographiques. "Dossier 394 bis." [1921].
  Kafungu, Bwantsa. Section de linguistique. "Vocabulaire mbuun" (on cards). [1968–70].
  Le Bussy, Roger. Dossiers du Bureau de documentation. "Rapport d'enquête sur la tribu Basengere." Territoire Inongo, 1927.
  Motte. Dossiers du Bureau de documentation. "Enquête sur la tribu Booli." Territoire Oshwe, 1926.
  Simon, M. Dossiers du Bureau de documentation. "Juridictions indigènes en territoire Basakata." Territoire de Kutu, 1928.

Theses and Manuscripts

Belepe, Bope M. "Les conflits de succession au trône dans le royaume kuba." 31 pages. Typescript. Lubumbashi, 1977.
———. "Etude socio-morphologique des masques 'bwoom' des kuba." M.A. thesis, Univ. nationale du Zaïre. Lubumbashi, 1974.
Boelaert, Edmond. "De Bushong in de traditie der Mongo." 8 pages. 1956. Manuscript in possession of Jan Vansina.

Daeleman, Jan. "Vergelijkende studie over enkele noordwestelijke Bantoetalen."
M.A. Thesis, Katolieke Univ. Louvain. 1956.
Devisch, Renaat. "L'institution rituelle khita chez les Yaka au Kwaango du nord: Une
analyse séméiologique." 3 vols. Ph.D. diss., Katolieke Univ. Louvain. 1976.
Hoover, Jeffrey. Personal notes on a number of languages, 1976–77.
Jaspan, M. A. "From Patriliny to Matriliny: Structural Change among the Redjang of
Southwest Sumatra." Ph.D. diss., National Univ. Australia. Canberra, 1964.
Kanyinda Lusanga, T. "Pouvoir traditionnel et institutions politiques modernes chez
les Baluba du Sud-Kasai." M.A. thesis, Univ. Lovanium. Kinshasa, 1968.
Meeussen, Albert E. "Bantu Lexical Recontructions." Mimeo. Tervuren, 1969.
Musambachime Mwelwa. "Changing Roles: The History of the Development and
Disintegration of the Nkuba Shila State to 1740." M.A. thesis, Univ. Wisconsin.
Madison, 1976.
Ndaywell Enziem. "Organisation sociale et histoire: Les Ngwii et les Ding." 2 vols.
Ph.D. diss., Univ. Paris I: Sorbonne. Paris, 1973.
Shyaam aNce. "Tooml aKwey i Kot aMbo." 165 pages. 1960. Manuscript in posses-
sion of Jan Vansina.
Swartenbroeckx, P. "Dictionnaire kiyanzi ou kiyey: Langage des Bayanzi ou Bayey
du territoire de Banningville (District du Lac Léopold II) au Congo belge." 2 vols.
Mimeo. Brussels, 1948.

Published Works

Achten, Lode. "Over de geschiedenis der Bakuba." *Congo* 1 (1929):189–205.
Allan, William. *The African Husbandman.* London, 1965.
Atkinson, R. R. "The Traditions of the Early Kings of Buganda: Myth, History and
Structural Analysis." *History in Africa* 2 (1975):17–57.
Baeyens, M. "Les Lesa." *La revue congolaise* 4 (1913–14):129–43, 193–206, 257–
70, 321–36.
Bailey, Frederick George. *Stratagems and Spoils.* Oxford, 1969.
Bal, Willy, trans. and ed. *Description du royaume de Congo et des contrées environ-
nantes,* by Filippo Pigafetta and Duarte Lopes. Paris, 1965. (Orig. pub. 1591.)
Bartholomew, George A., and Birdsell, J. B. "Ecology and the Protohominids."
American Anthropologist 55 (1953):481–98.
Bastin, Yvonne. *Bibliographie bantoue selective.* MRAC, Archives of Anthropology,
No. 24. Tervuren, 1975.
Baumann, Hermann. *Schöpfung und Urzeit des Menschen im Mythus der afrikani-
schen Völker.* Berlin, 1936.
———. *Die Völker Afrikas und ihre traditionellen Kulturen.* 2 vols. Wiesbaden,
1975.
Bentley, Hohman. *Dictionary and Grammar of the Kongo Language.* London, 1887.
Bittremieux, Leo. *Mayombsch Idioticon.* 3 vols. Gent, 1923; Brussels, 1927.
Boelaert, Edmond. "Coups de sonde." *Aequatoria* 2 (1942):26–30.
Bohannan, Paul, and Dalton, George, eds. *Markets in Africa.* Evanston, Ill., 1962.
Bontinck, François, ed. *Brève relation de la fondation de la mission des Frères
mineurs Capucins au royaume de Congo et des particularités coutumes et façons de*

vivre des habitants de ce royaume, by Gian Francesco de Roma. Paris, 1964. (Orig. pub. 1648.)

———. "Histoire du royaume du Congo (c. 1624): Traduction annotée." *Etudes d'histoire africaine* 4 (1972):5–145.

Boone, Olga. *Carte ethnique de la République du Zaïre: Quart sud-ouest.* MRAC, Anthropology and Ethnography, Ser. in 8°, No. 78. Tervuren, 1973.

———. *Carte ethnique du Congo: Quart sud-est.* MRAC, Anthropology and Ethnography, Ser. in 8°, No. 37. Tervuren, 1961.

———. *Les tambours du Congo belge et du Ruanda-Urundi.* MRAC, Anthropology and Ethnography, New Ser. in 4°, No. 1. Tervuren, 1951.

———. *Les xylophones du Congo belge.* MRAC, Anthropology and Ethnography, Ser. in 4°, Ser. 3, Vol. 3, No. 2. Brussels, 1936.

Bradbury, R. E. *Benin Studies.* London, 1973.

Brasio, António. *Monumenta Missionaria africana: Africa ocidental.* 13 vols. to date. Lisbon, 1952–65.

Braudel, Fernand. *Ecrits sur l' histoire.* 2nd ed. Paris, 1969. (1st ed. 1958.)

Brausch, Georges. "Les associations prénuptiales dans la Haute Lukenyie." *Bulletin des juridictions indigènes et du droit coutumier congolais* 15 (1947):102–31.

———. "La famille dans la Haute Lukenie." *Bulletin des juridictions indigènes et du droit coutumier congolais* 15 (1947):178–89.

———. "Groepsethnologie. De maatschappelijke groep als scheppende synthese." *Kongo Overzee* 10/11 (1944/1945):20–48.

———. "Quelques aspects psychologiques de l'organisation sociale nkutshu." *Problèmes d'Afrique centrale* 1 (1952):3–10.

Brown Edmiston, Althea. *Grammar and Dictionary of the Bushonga or Bukuba Language as spoken by the Bushonga or Bukuba Tribe Who Dwell in the Upper Kasai District, Belgian Congo, Central Africa.* [Luebo, 1929].

Brun, Samuel. *Schiffarten welche er in etliche newe Lander und Insulen zu Fünff unterschiedlichen Malen mit Gottes hülff gethan.* Basel, 1969 (reprint ed.; first published 1624).

Bultot, Franz. *Carte des zones climatiques.* ARSOM, General Atlas of the Congo, Ser. in 4°. Brussels, 1955.

Burridge, Kenelm. *Mambu: A Study of Melanesian Cargo Movements and Their Social and Ideological Background.* New York, 1970.

Bylin, Eric Basakata. *Le peuple du pays de l'entre fleuves Lukenie-Kasai.* Studia Ethnographica Upsaliensia 25. Lund, 1966.

Calloc'h, J. *Vocabulaire français-ifumu (batéké) précédé d'éléments de grammaire.* Paris, 1911.

Carneiro, Robert. "Scale Analysis: Evolutionary Sequences and Rating of Cultures." In *A Handbook of Method in Cultural Anthropology,* ed. Raoul Naroll and Ronald Cohen. 2nd ed. New York, 1973.

Carvalho, Henrique A., Dias de. *Expedição ao Muatiânvua: Ethnographia e história dos povos da Lunda.* Lisbon, 1890.

———. *O Lubuco.* Lisbon, 1889.

Claerhout, Adriaan. "Two Kuba Wrought-Iron Statuettes." *African Arts* 9 (1976):60–64, 92.

Claessen, Henri J. M. *Politieke Antropologie*. Assen, 1974.

Colle, R. P. *Les Baluba*. Collection de monographies ethnographiques, Vols. 10, 11. Brussels, 1913.

Cornet, Joseph. *Art of Africa: Treasures from the Congo*. New York, 1971.

Crowe, Donald W. "The Geometry of African Art: I. Bakuba Art." *Journal of Geometry* 1 (1971):169–82.

Culbert, T. Patrick. *The Lost Civilization: The Story of the Classic Maya*. New York, 1974.

Cuvelier, Jean, and Jadin, Louis. *L'ancien Congo d'après les archives romaines (1518–1640)*. ARSOM, Coll. in 8°, Vol. 36, No. 2. Brussels, 1954.

Dalton, George. "Economic Surplus Once Again." *American Anthropologist* 65 (1963):389–94.

Dammann, Ernest. *Die Religionen Afrikas*. Stuttgart, 1963.

Dartevelle, Edmond. *Les "nzimbu," monnaie du royaume de Congo*. Mémoire de la société royale belge d'anthropologie et de préhistoire, New Ser., first division, Vol. 64. Brussels, 1953.

D'Atri, Marcellino. "Relation sur le royaume de Congo: 1690–1700." *Cahiers ngonge*. No. 5. 1960. (This is a summary, in a provisional translation by François Bontinck, of an important account.)

David, Pierre. *Journal d'un voiage fait en Bambouc en 1744*. Ed. André Delcourt. Paris, 1974.

de Beaucorps, Rémi. *Les Basongo de la Luniungu et de la Gobari*. ARSOM, Coll. in 8°, Vol. 10, No. 3. Brussels, 1941.

De Bouveignes, Olivier, and Cuvelier, Jean. *Jérôme de Montesarchio*. Namur, 1951.

Dechamps, R. "Première note concernant l'identification anatomique de bois utilisés pour des sculptures en Afrique (note liminaire par Albert Maesen)." *Africa-Tervuren* 16 (1970):77–82.

De Clercq, Auguste, and Willems, Emiel. *Dictionnaire tshiluba-français*. Leopoldville, 1960.

De Craemer, Willy; Vansina, Jan; and Fox, Renée. "Religious Movements in Central Africa: A Theoretical Study." *Comparative Studies in Society and History* 18 (1976):458–75.

De Decker, J.M. *Les clans Ambuun (Bambunda) d'après leur littérature orale*. ARSOM, Coll. in 8°, Vol. 20, No. 1. Brussels, 1950.

———. "Contribution à l'étude du mariage chez les Bambunda." *Bulletin des juridictions indigènes et du droit coutumier congolais*. 10 (1942):125–46.

de Heusch, Luc. *Porquoi l' épouser*. Paris, 1971.

———. *Le roi ivre, ou l'origine de l'état*, Paris, 1972.

———. "Un système de parenté insolite: Les Onga." *Zaïre* 9 (1955):1011–27.

———. "What Shall We Do with the Drunken King?" *Africa* 45 (1975):363–72.

De Jonghe, Edouard. *Les formes d'asservissement dans les sociétés indigènes du Congo belge*. ARSOM, Coll. in 8°, Vol. 19, No. 1. Brussels 1949.

Delange, Jacqueline. *The Art and Peoples of Black Africa*. New York, 1974.

De Langhe, Herman. "Au Congo belge: Quelques notes sur la vie des indigènes." *Revue d'anthropologie* 27 (1917):72–80, 204–11.

Delivré, Alain. *L'histoire des rois d'Imerina: Interprétation d'une tradition orale.* Paris, 1974.

De Macar, Ghislain. "Chez les Bakuba." *Le Congo illustré* 4 (1895):172-74.

────. "Coutumes des Bakuba." *Le mouvement géographique* (1893):103, 109-10.

Denis, Jules. "Notes sur l'organisation de quelques tribus aux environs du lac Léopold II." *Anthropos* 35-36 (1940-41):815-29.

Denolf, Prosper. *Aan de rand van de Dibese.* ARSOM, Coll. in 8°, Vol. 34, No. 1. Brussels, 1954.

De Plaen, Guy. *Les structures d'autorité des Bayanzi.* Paris, 1974.

De Rijk, Maurice. *Les Lalia-Ngolu: Origines, histoire, moeurs, coutumes, institutions, vie économique, artistique et intellectuelle des Mongandu d' Ikela (district de la Tshuapa).* Antwerp, 1937.

de Sousberghe, Léon. *L' Art pende.* Brussels, 1958.

────. "Forgerons et fondeurs de fer chez les Ba-Pende et leurs voisins." *Zaïre* 9 (1955):25-31.

────. "Noms donnés aux Pygmées et souvenirs laissés par eux chez les Pende et Lunda de la Loange." *Congo-Tervuren* 6 (1960):84-86.

────. "Les Pende: Aspects des structures sociales et politiques." In *Miscellanea Ethnographica.* MRAC, Anthropology and Ethnography, Ser. in 8°, No. 46. Tervuren, 1963.

De Witte, P. *Taalstudie bij de Basakata.* MRAC, Anthropology and Ethnography, Ser. in 8°, No. 15, Ling. 10. Tervuren, 1955.

Dias de Carvalho, Henrique A. *See* Carvalho, Dias de

Douglas, Mary. "Alternate Generations among the Lele of the Kasai (Southwest Congo)." *Africa* 21 (1951):59-65.

────. "Animals in the Religious Symbolism of the Lele." *Africa* 27 (1957):46-58. (I also used a manuscript version of this article.)

────. "Lele Economy Compared with the Bushong." In *Markets in Africa,* ed. Paul Bohannan and George Dalton. Evanston, Ill., 1962.

────. *The Lele of the Kasai.* London, 1963.

────. "Matriliny and Pawnship in Central Africa." *Africa* 34 (1964):301-13.

────, ed. *Witchcraft Confessions and Accusations.* London, 1970.

Doutreloux, Albert. "Introduction à la culture Kongo." In *Miscellanea Ethnographica.* MRAC, Anthropology and Ethnography, Ser. in 8°, No. 46. Tervuren, 1963.

────. *L'ombre des fétiches.* Louvain, 1967.

Droogers, André. *De gevaarlijke reis: Jongensinitiatie bij de Wagenia van Kisangani (Zaïre).* Amsterdam, 1974.

Empain, A. "Les Bakela de la Loto." *Bulletin de la société royale belge de géographie* 46 (1922):206-65.

Encyclopaedia of Needlework. New York, 1963.

Epstein, Hellmut. *The Origin of the Domestic Animals of Africa.* 2 vols. New York, 1971.

Evrard, E. "Etude statistique sur les affinités de cinquante-huit dialectes bantous." In *Statistique et analyse linguistique.* Paris, 1966.

Fagg, William. *The Art of Central Africa*. New York, 1967.

Fehderau, Harold W. *The Origin and Development of Kituba (Lingua franca Kikongo)*. Kisangani, 1967.

Finley, M. I. "Myth, Memory and History." *History and Theory* 4 (1965):281–302.

———. *The World of Odysseus*. New York. 1954.

Finnegan, Ruth. *Oral Literature in Africa*. Oxford, 1970.

Fisher, M. K. *English-Lunda (Ndembu) Abridged Dictionary*. Mutshatsa [Zaire], [c. 1967].

Focquet, René, and Van der Kerken, Georges. "Les populations indigènes des territoires de Kutu et de Nsontin." *Congo* 2 (1924):129–71.

Fox-Bourne, H. R. *Civilisation in Congoland*. London, 1903.

Fried, Morton. *The Evolution of Political Society*. New York, 1967.

Frobenius, Leo. *Dichtkunst der Kassaiden*. Atlantis, Vol. 12. Jena, 1928.

———. *Im Schatten des Kongostaates*. Berlin, 1907.

———. *Kulturgeschichte Afrikas*. 2nd ed. Zurich, 1954.

———. *Leo Frobenius, 1873–1973: An Anthology*. Ed. Eike Haberland. Bonn, 1973.

Garlake, Peter S. *Great Zimbabwe*. London, 1973.

Gerard, R. P. *La langue lebeo*. Brussels, 1924.

Godelier, Maurice. *Rationalité et irrationalité en économie*. Paris, 1969.

Goody, Jack. *Literacy in Traditional Societies*. Cambridge, 1968.

Gossen, Gary H. *Chamulas in the World of the Sun*. Harvard, 1974.

Gourou, Pierre. *Carte de la densité des populations*. ARSOM, General Atlas of the Congo, Ser. in 4°, Brussels, 1951.

Gusimana, Barthélémy. *Dictionnaire pende-français*.Bonn, 1972.

Guthrie, Malcolm. *The Classification of Bantu Languages*. London, 1948.

———. *Comparative Bantu*. 4 vols. Farnborough, 1967–70.

Hagen, Everett. *On the Theory of Social Change*. Homewood, Ill., 1962.

Hagendorens, T. *Dictionnaire français-otetela*. Tshumbe, 1956.

———. *Dictionnaire otetela-français*. Tshumbe, 1957.

Harris, Marvin. "The Economy Has No Surplus?" *American Anthropologist* 61 (1959):185–200.

Harroy, Ferdinand. "Les Bakuba." *Bulletin de la société belge de géographie* 21 (1907):171–92, 234–55. This is the first part of a 45-page typescript by Moroni, "Souvenirs du Congo, 1905–1908."

Heintze, Beatrix. "Wer war der König von Banguela?" In *In Memoriam Antonio Jorge Dias,* 1:184–202. Lisbon, 1974.

Henige, David. *The Chronology of Oral Tradition: Quest for a Chimera*. Oxford, 1974.

Hiernaux, Jean. "Les Bushong et les Cwa du royaume Kuba (Congo Kinshasa): Pygmées, pygmoides et pygméisation; anthropologie, linguistique et expansion bantoue." *Bulletin et mémoires de la société d'anthropologie de Paris,* Ser. 9, Fasc. 11 (1966), pp. 299–336.

Hilton Simpson, M. N. *Land and Peoples of the Kasai*. London, 1911.

Hochegger, Hermann. *Dictionnaire Buma-français avec un aperçu grammatical,* CEEBA (Centre d'études ethnologiques Bandundu), Ser. 3, No. 3. Bandundu, 1972.

Homburger, Louise. *Le groupe sud-ouest des langues bantoues: Mission Rohan-Chabot.* Vol. 3, No. 1. Paris, 1925.

Horton, Robin. "African Conversion." *Africa* 41 (1971):85–108.

―――. "African Traditional Thought and Western Science," *Africa* 37 (1967):50–71, 155–87.

―――. "On the Rationality of African Conversion." *Africa* 45 (1975):219–35, 373–99.

Hulstaert, Gustaaf. *Au sujet de deux cartes linguistiques du Congo belge.* ARSOM, Coll. in 8°, Vol. 38, No. 1. Brussels, 1954.

―――. *Carte linguistique du Congo belge.* ARSOM, Coll. in 8°, Vol. 19, No. 5. Brussels, 1950.

―――. *Dictionnaire lomongo-français.* 2 vols. MRAC, Anthropology and Ethnography, Ser. in 8°, Nos. 21, 22 (Ling. 16, 1–2). Tervuren, 1957.

―――. *Les Mongo: Aperçu général,* MRAC, Archives of Anthropology, No. 1. Tervuren, 1961.

―――. "Les langues de la cuvette centrale congolaise." *Aequatoria* 14 (1951):18–24.

―――. "Une lecture critique de *L'ethnie mongo,* de G. Van der Kerken." *Etudes d'histoire africaine* 3 (1972):27–60.

―――. *Le mariage des Nkundo.* ARSOM, Coll. in 8°, Vol. 8. Brussels, 1938.

―――. *Notes de botanique mongo.* ARSOM, Division of Natural and Medical Science, New Ser., Vol. 15, No. 3. Brussels, 1966.

―――. "Sur quelques langues bantoues du Congo." *Aequatoria* 24 (1961):53–58.

Huysman, R. P. "Les Bakubas." *Bulletin de la société royale belge de géographie* 28 (1904):379–87.

Jacobs, John, and Vansina, Jan. "*Nshoong atoot:* Het koninklijk epos der Bushong." *Kongo Overzee* 22 (1956):1–39.

Johnston, Harry. *A Comparative Study of the Bantu and Semi-Bantu Languages.* 2 vols. Oxford, 1919.

Kellersberger, Julia. *A Life for the Congo: The Story of Althea Brown Edmiston.* New York, 1947.

Kirk, Geoffrey S. *Myth: Its Meaning and Functions in Ancient and Other Cultures.* London, 1970.

[Knosp.] *Enquête sur la vie musicale au Congo belge, 1934–1935 (Questionnaire Knosp).* 3 vols. MRAC, Archives of Anthropology, Nos. 11–13. Tervuren, 1968.

Lalande, André. *Vocabulaire technique et critique de la philosophie.* 11th ed. Paris, 1972.

Lamal, F. *Basuku et Bayaka des districts Kwango et Kwilu au Congo.* MRAC, Anthropology and Ethnography, Ser. in 8°, No. 56. Tervuren, 1965.

Laman, Karl E. *Dictionnaire kikongo-français, français-kikongo.* ARSOM, Coll. in 8°, Vol. 2. Brussels, 1936.

Landbeck, Paul. *Malu Malu: Erlebnisse aus der Sturm und Drang periode des Kongo-staates.* Berlin, 1930.

Lapsley, Samuel N. *Life and Letters of Samuel Norvell Lapsley, Missionary to the Congo Valley, West Africa, 1866–1892.* Richmond, Va., 1893.

Laurenty, Jean-Sébastien. *Les cordophones du Congo belge et du Ruanda-Urundi.* MRAC, Anthropology and Ethnography, New Ser. in 4°, No. 2. Tervuren, 1960.

——. *Les sanza du Congo.* 2 vols. MRAC, Anthropology and Ethnography, New Ser. in 4°, No. 3. Tervuren, 1962.

——. *La systématique des aérophones de l'Afrique centrale.* 2 vols. MRAC, Anthropology and Ethnography, New Ser. in 4°, No. 7. Tervuren, 1974.

——. *Les tambours à fente de l'Afrique centrale.* 2 vols. MRAC, Anthropology and Ethnography, New Ser. in 4°, No. 6. Tervuren, 1968.

Leach, Edmund. *Genesis as Myth and Other Essays.* London, 1969.

LeClair, Edward, and Schneider, Harold K. *Economic Anthropology: Readings in Theory and Analysis.* New York, 1968.

Leyder, Jean. "Graphisme et magie chez quelques peuplades au Congo belge." In *Recueil des exposés fait à la semaine universitaire de pédagogie.* Brussels, 1935.

Livingstone, David. *Missionary Travels and Researches in South Africa.* London, 1857.

Loir, Hélène. *Le tissage du raphia au Congo belge.* MRAC, Anthropology and Ethnography, Ser. in 4°, Ser. 3, Vol. 3, No. 1. Brussels, 1935.

Lopes, Duarte. *See* Bal, Willy

McClelland, David C., and Winter, David G. *Motivating Economic Development.* New York, 1969.

MacGaffey, Wyatt. "The Religious Commissions of the Bakongo." *Man,* New Ser. 5 (1970):27–38.

Maes, Joseph. "Vocabulaire des populations de la région du Kasai-Lulua-Sankuru." *Journal de la société des africanistes* 4 (1934):209–67.

[Maesen, Albert.] "Les zones de répartition des styles de l'art congolais traditionnel; Les styles et l'art traditionnel congolais." In *Le Congo belge,* 2:184–87. Brussels, 1959. The source of the data is the ethnographic section of the Musée royal du Congo belge, then headed by Maesen, who is the presumed author.

Mamet, M. *Le langage des Bolia (lac Léopold II).* MRAC, Anthropology and Ethnography, Ser. in 8°, No. 33. Tervuren, 1960.

——. *La langue ntomba telle qu'elle est parlée au lac Tumba et dans la région avoisinante (Afrique centrale).* MRAC, Anthropology and Ethnography, Ser. in 8°, No. 16 (Ling. 11). Tervuren, 1955.

Maquet, Emma. *Outils de forge du Congo, du Rwanda et du Burundi.* MRAC, Anthropology and Ethnography, New Ser. in 4°, No. 5. Tervuren, 1965.

Marrou, Henri I. *De la connaissance historique.* 6th ed. Paris, 1973.

Matagne, Antoine. "Comment étaient choisis les chefs coutumiers à l'époque de l'occupation par nos pionniers." *Revue congolaise illustrée* 31, No. 1 (1960):13–16.

——. "La constitution et les lois de certaines peuplades du Congo." *Revue congolaise illustrée* 31, No. 2 (1960):15–18.

Mattelaer, Victor. "Mushenge, village royal des Bakubas." *Jeune Afrique* 25 (1957):23–24.

Merriam, Alan P. *Culture History of the Basongye.* Bloomington, Ind., 1975.

Mertens, Joseph. *Les Badzing de la Kamtsha.* 3 vols. ARSOM, Coll. in 8°, Vol. 4.

Brussels, 1935–39. (The first volume is an ethnography, the second a grammar, the third a dictionary.)

Miller, Joseph C. "The Imbangala and the Chronology of Early Central African History." *Journal of African History* 13 (1972):549–74.

———. *Kings and Kinsmen: Early Mbundu States in Angola.* Oxford, 1976.

Miracle, Marvin P. *Maize in Tropical Africa.* Madison, 1966.

Moeller, Alfred. *Les grandes lignes des migrations des Bantous de la Province Orientale du Congo belge.* ARSOM, Coll. in 8°, Vol. 6. Brussels, 1936.

Moroni. *See* Harroy, Ferdinand

Mpase, Mpeti N. *L'évolution de la solidarité traditionnelle en milieu rural et urbain au Zaïre.* Kinshasa, 1974.

Mukenge, Léonard. "Croyances religieuses et structures socio-familiales en société luba: 'Buena Muntu,' 'Bakishi,' 'Milambu.' " *Cahiers économiques et sociaux* 5 (1967):3–94.

Murdock, George Peter. *Africa.* New York, 1959.

Nathhorst, Bertil. *Formal or Structural Studies of Traditional Tales.* Stockholm Series in Comparative Religion, No. 9. Bromma, 1969.

Ndolo, Pius, and Malasi, Florence. *Vocabulaire mbala.* MRAC, Archives of Anthropology, No. 18. Tervuren, 1972.

Needham, Rodney. "Remarks on the Analysis of Kinship and Marriage." In *Rethinking Kinship and Marriage.* London, 1971.

Nicolas, François J. "Origine et valeur du vocabulaire désignant les xylophones africains." *Zaïre* 11 (1957):69–89.

Ntambwe, Luadia Luadia. "Les Luluwa et le commerce luso-africain." *Etudes d'histoire africaine* 6 (1974):55–104.

Olbrechts, Frans. *Les arts plastiques du Congo belge.* Brussels, 1959.

Phillipson, D. W. "Iron Age History and Archaeology in Zambia." *Journal of African History* 15 (1974):1–25.

Pigafetta. *See* Bal, Willy

Plancquaert, M. *Les Yaka: Essai d'histoire.* MRAC, Anthropology and Ethnography, Ser. in 8°, No. 71. Tervuren, 1971.

Pye, Lucian W. *Politics, Personality, and Nation Building: Burma's Search for Security.* New Haven, 1962.

Radin, Paul. *The Story of the American Indian.* 2nd ed. New York, 1937.

Randles, W. G. L. *L'ancien royaume du Congo des origines à la fin du 19ᵉ siècle.* Paris, 1968.

Richards, Audrey. "African Kings and Their Royal Relatives." *Journal of the Royal Anthropological Institute* 21 (1961):135–60.

Roberts, Andrew. *A History of the Bemba.* London, 1973.

Robyns, Walter. *Carte des territoires phytogéographiques.* ARSOM, General Atlas of the Congo, Ser. in 4°. Brussels, 1948.

Rogers, Everett M., and Shoemaker, F. Floyd. *Communication of Innovation.* Glencoe, Ill., 1971.

Rood, N. *Ngombe-Nederlands-Frans woordenboek.* MRAC, Anthropology and Ethnography, Ser. in 8°, No. 27. Tervuren, 1958.

Rosenwald, Jean B. "Kuba King Figures." *African Arts* 7 (1974):26–31, 92.

Ryder, Alan. *Benin and the Europeans: 1585–1897.* London, 1969.

Sahlins, Marshall. *Stone Age Economics.* Chicago, 1972.

Sahlins, Marshall, and Service, Elman R. *Evolution and Culture.* Ann Arbor, 1960.

Samain, Alidor. *La langue kisonge: Grammaire-vocabulaire-proverbes.* Bibliothèque Congo, No. 14. Brussels, [1923].

Service, Elman R. *Primitive Social Organization.* 2nd ed. New York, 1971.

Shaloff, Stanley. *Reform in Leopold's Congo.* Richmond, Va., 1970.

————. "William Henry Sheppard: Congo Pioneer," in *Education for Life in a Multi-Cultural Society.* Hampton, Va., 1968.

Sheppard, William. "Into the Heart of Africa." *Southern Workman* 22 (1893):182–87.

————. *Presbyterian Pioneers.* Hampton, Va., [1917].

Silva Porto, António da. "Novas jornadas nas sertões africanos." *Boletim da sociedade de geografia de Lisboa.* Ser. 6a. Lisbon, 1885–86.

Sims, Aaron. *Vocabulary of the Kiteke as Spoken by the Bateke and Kindred Tribes on the Upper-Congo: Kiteke English.* London, 1888.

Smith, Michael G. *Government in Zazzau.* London, 1960.

————. "On Segmentary Lineage Systems." *Journal of the Royal Anthropological Institute* 86 (1956):39–80.

Sousa Dias, Gastão. "Uma Viagem a Cassange nos meados do seculo XVIII." *Boletim da sociedade de geografia de Lisboa.* Ser. 56a. Lisbon, 1938.

Southall, Aidan. *Alur Society.* London, 1956.

Sperber, Dan. *Rethinking Symbolism.* Cambridge, 1975.

Starr, Frederick. *Congo Natives: An Ethnographic Album.* Chicago, 1912.

————. "Ethnographic Notes from the Congo Free State: An African Miscellany." *Proceedings of the Davenport Academy of Sciences* 12 (1909):95–222.

Stevenson, Robert F. *Population and Political Systems in Tropical Africa.* New York, 1968.

Stritzl, Angelika. "Raffiaplüsche aus dem Königreich Kongo." *Wiener ethnohistorische Blätter* 3 (1971):37–55.

Thomas, Thérèse. "Les Itombwa, objets divinatoires sculptés conservés au Musée royal du Congo belge." *Congo-Tervuren* 6 (1960):78–83.

Tonnoir, René. *Giribuma. Contribution à l'histoire et à la petite histoire du Congo equatorial.* MRAC, Archives of Anthropology, No. 14. 1970.

Torday, Emil. "The Influence of the Kingdom of Kongo on Central Africa." *Africa* 1 (1928):157–69.

————. *On the Trail of the Bushongo.* London, 1925.

Torday, Emil, and Joyce, T. A. *Notes ethnographiques sur les peuples communément appelés Bakuba, ainsi que sur les peuplades apparentées: Les Bushongo.* MRAC, Anthropology and Ethnography, Ser. in 4°, Ser. 4, No. 2. Brussels, 1910.

Tymowski, Michal. *Le développement et la régression chez les peuples de la boucle du Niger à l'époque précoloniale.* Warsaw, 1974.

Van Avermaet, E. *Dictionnaire kiluba-français.* MRAC, Anthropology and Ethnography, Ser. in 8°, No. 12. Tervuren, 1954.

Van Bulck, Gaston. *Carte linguistique.* ARSOM, General Atlas of the Congo, Ser. in 4°. Brussels, 1954.

———. *Les recherches linguistiques au Congo belge.* ARSOM, Coll. in 8°, Vol. 16. Brussels, 1948.

Van der Kerken, Georges. *L'ethnie mongo.* 2 vols. ARSOM, Coll. in 8°, Vol. 13. Brussels, 1944.

Van der Linden, Fritz. *Le Congo, les noirs et nous.* Paris, 1910.

Van Everbroeck, Nestor. *Mbomb'Ipoku: Le seigneur de l'abîme.* MRAC, Archives of Anthropology, No. 3. Tervuren, 1961.

———. *Religie en magie onder de Basakata.* ARSOM, Coll. in 8°, Vol. 24, No. 1. Brussels, 1952.

Van Laere, Adolphe. *Les Basongo-Bankutu: Notes sur leur organisation domestique, sociale et politique.* Antwerp, 1900.

Van Moorsel, Hendrik. *Atlas de préhistoire de la plaine de Kinshasa.* Kinshasa, 1968.

Van Noten, Francis. "La plus ancienne sculpture sur bois de l'Afrique centrale?" *Africa-Tervuren* 18 (1972):133–36.

Van Overbergh, Cyrille. *Les Basonge.* Brussels, 1908.

Vansina, Jan. "The Bushoong Poison Ordeal." In *Man in Africa,* ed. Mary Douglas and Phyllis Kaberry. London, 1969.

———. "La chanson lyrique kuba." *Jeune Afrique* 27 (1958):31–35.

———. "Comment: Traditions of Genesis." *Journal of African History* 15 (1974):317–22.

———. "Les croyances religieuses des Kuba." *Zaïre* 12 (1958):725–58.

———. *Esquisse de grammaire bushong.* MRAC, Anthropology and Ethnography, Ser. in 8°, No. 29 (Ling. 23). Tervuren, 1959.

———. *Geschiedenis van de Kuba van ongeveer 1500 tot 1904.* MRAC, Anthropology and Ethnography, Ser. in 8°, No. 44. Tervuren, 1963.

———. "La hache et la houe." In *Problèmes de l'enseignement supérieur et de développement en Afrique centrale: Recueil d'études en l'honneur de Guy Malengreau.* Paris, 1975.

———. "De handelingen der voorouders: Een handschrift waarin de genesis der Bieng verhaald wordt." *Kongo Overzee* 22 (1956):257–300.

———. "History in the Field." In *Anthropologists in the Field,* ed. D. G. Jongmans and Peter C. W. Gutkind. Assen, 1967.

———. "L'influence du mode de compréhension historique d'une civilisation sur ses traditions d'origine: L'exemple kuba." *Bulletin de l'académie royale des sciences d'Outre-mer,* New Ser. 19 (1973):220–40.

———. "Initiation Rituals of the Bushong" *Africa* 25 (1955):138–153.

———. *Kingdoms of the Savanna.* Madison, 1966.

———. "Kuba Chronology Revisited." *Paideuma* 21 (1975):134–50.

———. "Les Kuba et l'administration territoriale de 1919 à 1960." *Cultures et développement* 4 (1972):275–325.

———. "Les langues bantoues et l'histoire: Le cas kuba." In *Perspectives nouvelles sur le passé de l'Afrique noire et de Madagascar: Mélanges offerts à R. H. Deschamps.* Paris, 1974.

———. "Les mouvements religieux kuba (Kasai) à l'époque coloniale." *Etudes d'histoire africaine* 2 (1971):157–89.

———. "Ndop: Royal Statues among the Kuba." In *African Art and Leadership,* ed. Douglas Fraser and Herbert M. Cole. Madison, 1972.

———. "Een negentiende-eeuwse stad in Central Afrika: Nsheng." *Africa-Tervuren* 22 (1976):47–56.

———. "Note sur les Twa du territoire de Mweka (Kasai)." *Zaïre* 8 (1954): 729–32.

———. "The Power of Systematic Doubt in Historical Enquiry." *History in Africa* 1 (1974):109–27.

———. "Probing the Past of the Lower Kwilu Peoples." *Paideuma* 19/20 (1973/1974):332–64.

———. "Recording the Oral History of the Bakuba." *Journal of African History* 1 (1960):45–54, 257–70.

———. "Le régime foncier dans la société kuba." *Zaïre* 9 (1955):899–926.

———. "Religions et sociétés en Afrique centrale: Religions Bushong et Tio." *Cahiers des religions africaines* 2 (1968):95–107.

———. *Le royaume kuba.* MRAC, Anthropology and Ethnography, Ser. in 8°, No. 49. Tervuren, 1964.

———. "Du royaume kuba au territoire des Bakuba." *Etudes congolaises* 12 (1969):3–54.

———. "Trade and Markets among the Kuba." In *Markets in Africa,* ed. Paul Bohannan and George Dalton. Evanston, Ill., 1962.

———. "A Traditional Legal System: The Kuba." In *Man in Adaptation: The Structural Framework,* ed. Yehudi Cohen. Chicago, 1971.

———. *Les tribus Ba-Kuba et les peuplades apparentées.* MRAC, Ethnographic Monographs, No. 1. Tervuren, 1954.

———. "The Use of Ethnographic Data as Sources for History." In *Emerging Themes of African History,* ed. Terence O. Ranger. Dar es Salaam, 1968.

———. "The Use of Process Models in African History." In *The Historian in Tropical Africa,* ed. Jan Vansina, Raymond Mauny, and Louis Vincent Thomas. London, 1964.

———. "Les valeurs culturelles des Bushong." *Zaïre* 8 (1954):899–910.

Van Wing, Joseph, and C. Penders, eds. *Le plus ancien dictionnaire bantu: Vocabularium P. Georgii Gelensis.* Louvain, 1928.

Vellut, Jean-Luc. "Notes sur les Lunda et la frontière luso-africaine (1700–1900)." *Etudes d'histoire africaine* 3 (1972):61–166.

Vergiat, A. M. *Moeurs et coutumes des Manjas.* Paris, 1937.

Verly, Robert. "Les Mintadi: La statuaire de pierre du Bas-Congo." *Zaïre* 8 (1955):5–83.

Verner, Samuel. *Pioneering in Central Africa.* Richmond, Va., 1903.

von Wissmann, Hermann, et al. *Im innern Afrikas.* Leipzig, 1888.

———. *Meine zweite Durchquerung aequatorial Afrikas vom Congo zum Zanzibar.* Frankfurt, 1890.

———. *Unter deutsche Flagge: Quer durch Afrika.* 6th ed. Berlin, 1890.

Wauters, C. *L'ésoterie des noirs dévoilée.* Brussels, 1949.

Weekx, G. "La peuplade des Ambundu." *Congo* (1937), 1:353–73, 2:13–35.

Westerdijk, H. *Ijzerwerk van Centraal Afrika.* Lochem, 1975.

Weydert, Jean J. *Les Balubas chez eux.* Luxemburg, 1938.

Wharton, Conway T. *The Leopard Hunts Alone.* New York, 1927.

Wharton, E. T. *Led in Triumph: Sixty Years of Southern Presbyterian Missions in the Belgian Congo.* London, 1952.

Wolf, Eric R. *Peasants.* Englewood Cliffs, N.J., 1966.

Wolf, Ludwig. "Exploration sur le Kasai et sur le Sankuru." *Bulletin de la société belge de géographie* 12 (1888):26–43.

———. "Wolf's Bericht über seine Reise in das Land der Bakuba." In *Im innern Afrikas,* by Hermann Von Wissman et al. Leipzig, 1888.

Yang, C. K. "The Role of Religion in Chinese Society." In *An Introduction to Chinese Civilization,* ed. J. T. Meskill. New York, 1973.

Glossary

Only the Bushoong and Kete terms mentioned in the text more than once are listed here. Numbers indicate nominal classes; *t* indicates tone unknown. The forms given in brackets are the correct forms; if no form occurs in brackets, the single form given is the correct one.

apoom: to divine
baang, 1a, 2: an official
bakon: see *nkon*
bubaang, 14: a tributary village
bubil, 14, 6: a tributary chiefdom
bukaang, 14: an oracle
bulaam, 14: a local historian, a dance instructor
bulungu [búlungu], 14: matrician, matrilineage (Kete)
bulup, 14, *t:* the drum used for dances
bweemy [bwéémy], 1a, 2: the heir apparent to the king
bwiin, 14: a pattern, a drawing
bwoom [bwɔɔ́m], 14: the most common type of mask
cikl [cíkl], 1a, 2: an official
cwaal, 1a, 2: the heir apparent to the king's heir apparent
dweey [dweéy, pl. *moóy],* 5, 6: word
dyaash, 5, 6, *t:* the spirit of individual pride
ibaam, 7, 6: the crown council
ibaanc [ibáánc], 7, 6: the general council
ibwoon [ibwɔɔn], 7, 6: a tribute collector
ikaam, 7, 6: word; also, business, "because"
ikul, 7, 6: a ceremonial knife
iloonc, 7, 6: a tree (*Crossopterix febrifuga*); plural denotes staffs made from that tree
iloonc, 7, 6: matriclan, matrilineage (may be the same term as the above)
ilweemy, 7, 8: a religious specialist; also, the place where the dead go
ipaancl, 7, 8: an official
iping [ipíng], 7, 8: a statue
ipweemy, 7, 6: the poison ordeal; the tree from which the poison is made
ishak ndweemy, 7, 8: a type of statue
ishyaaml, 7, 6: a council of officials

377

ishyeeng itaan, 7: a type of fine imposed by the king (literally, fifteen)
ishyeen imaalul, t: a type of mask
ituk [*itúk*], 7, 6: a corner
iyok pyeemy [*iyok pyéémy*]: the king's first wife
iyol, 7, 8; 1a, 2: a warrior, a military official
iyol ankong, 1a, 2: a police official
iyoot [*iyɔɔt*], 7: a square within the palace grounds; a type of council
kalyengl, 12?, *t:* a type of mask
katyeeng [*katyɛɛ́ng*], 1a, 2: an official (woman)
kibanza [*kíbànzà*]: a council (Kete)
kiin [*kíín*], 9, 10: the main village charm, a small garden
kikaam, 1a, 2: the highest official
kin mimbaangt: the leader of the *kolm* (the term was later replaced by *kikaam*)
kolm [*kɔ́lm*], 1a, 2: an official (generic term)
kol mat [*kól mát*], 1a, 2: a police official
kolm matuk mabol [*kɔ́lm mátuk mábol*]: "notables of the corners of the village"; an
      important group of officials in the twentieth century
kombeem [*kɔmbɛɛ́m*], 1a, 2: the right half of the capital or of a village
kongweemy [*kɔngweemy*], 1a, 2: the left half of the capital or of a village
kubol [*kúbol*], 1a, 2: a Kuba village headman
kum [*kúm*], 1a, 2: a chief
kum adweengy [*kúm ádwéèngy*], 1a, 2: the harem chief (woman)
kum apoong [*kúm ápóóng*], 1a, 2: a tributary chief (literally, "eagle-feather chief")
kum ashin [*kúm áshin*], 1a, 2: a provincial chief
kum mabaanc [*kúm mábáánc*], 1a, 2: main officials (generic term)
kuum, 9, 10: a closed meeting, a secret
kyeemk ngel ambiidy [*kyeemk ngɛ́l ámbíídy*]: a type of market official
lalyeeng [*lalyɛɛng*], 11, 10: a poison for arrows
lambil, 11, 10: the old or provincial language (derived from *bubil*)
lashyaang [*lashyááng*], 11, 10: a seed
latoot [*latɔɔt*], 11, 10: a noise, a speech
lyeel [*lyɛɛl*], 11, 10, *t:* a type of board game
maan, 6: palm wine
maash [*maásh*], 6: water
makaan [*makáán*], 1a, 2: an official
makieky [*makiɛ́ky*], 6, *t:* a type of dance
malaang, 6: a council (of a village or chiefdom)
mapel, 6: man's dress
mashingady angady ngwoom [*mashingády angády ngwɔɔm*], 6: an official (woman)
matoon [*matóón*], 6: servile villages; also, a royal clan name
mbaan, 1a, 2: an official (woman)
mbaan, 3, 4: price
mbaang, 9, 10: a corner
mbaangt [*mbáángt*], 3, 4: an aristocratic clan
mbal, 9, 10: a raffia square
mbeem [*mbɛɛ́m*], 1a, 2: an official in the capital city

mbey [*mbɛy*], 1a, 2: a comrade

mbimbil, 3, 4: a servile lineage or clan (derived from *bubil*)

mbok ilaam [*mbók íláám*]: a council of king and officials

mbweengy [*mbwɛɛngy*]: a specific quarter of the capital

mbyeemy, 1a, 2: an official

mbyeeng, 1a, 2: an official in the capital city

mel ibaanc [*mel ibáánc*], 1a, 2 (*t* for *mel*): the highest official

mell, 1a, *t:* the highest official (alternate term for *mel ibáánc*)

men mbweengy [*men mbwɛɛngy*], 1a, 2: the official in charge of *mbwɛɛngy*

meshoosh, 1a, 2: a tribute collector

mikop [*mikóp*], 4: a double bell

minyiing, 4, *t:* a type of mask

mitwiingy [*mitwííngy*] (tone uncertain): a prisoner of war

mooy mawalawal [*mooy máwaláwal*], 6: history

mpengdy, 9, 10, *t:* a throwing knife

mpik, 9, 10 *t:* a war dance

mukyeeng [*mukyɛɛng*], 3, 4?, *t:* a type of mask

muyesh [*muyésh*], 1a: a spokesman for the king

muyum, 1a: the highest religious official

mwaaddy, 1, 2: an official (the oldest of the king's sons)

mwaan [*mwaán*], 1, 2: a child

mwaandaan, 3, 4: an official belt

mwaash aMbooy [*mwaash aMbóóy*], 3, 4: a type of mask

mwana [*mwànà*], 1, 2: a type of statue

mwepy ngom [*mwɛpy ngóm*], 1a, 2: an official

ncak [*ncák*], 9, 10: woman's dress

nci [*ncí*], 3, 4: a year

ncik, 3, 4: a tale

ncok, 9, 10, *t:* a type of song

ncyaam [*ncyáám*], 9, 10: a royal basket (with charms); the royal genealogy

ncyeem [*ncyéém*], 1a, 2: God; a royal charm; a species of beetle

ncyeem ingesh [*ncyéém ingésh*], 9, 10: songs for the nature spirits, ritual songs

ncyeem nkwoonc [*ncyéém nkwoonc*], 1a, 2: a royal title (literally, "God on earth")

ndop, 9, 10: a royal statue

ngaan, 9, 10: a crocodile

ngady akan [*ngády ákán*], 1a, 2: a pawn wife

ngady mwaash aMbooy [*ngády mwaash aMbóóy*], 1a, 2: a type of mask

ngel [*ngɛl*], 9: downstream

ngesh [*ngésh*], 3, 4: nature spirit

nget (sing.), *byeet* (pl.) [*ngɛ́t byɛɛ́t*], 1a, 2: a slave

ngo [*ngó*], invariable: thus

ngoosh [*ngɔ́ɔ́sh*], invariable: thus

ngwoom [*ngwɔɔm*], 1a, 2: a diviner

ngwoom incyaam [*ngwɔɔm incyáám*], 1a, 2: a member of the crown council

ngwoong anbaang [*ngwɔ́ɔ́ng ambaang*]: ordinary people

nkaan, 3, 4: the boys' initiation; a secret

nkolakol [*nkolákól*], 9, 10: a ritual and the drum associated with it
nkon, 1a, 2: a villager, an uncouth person
nkop [*nkóp*], 9, 10: a royal enclosure
nkweemy nyeeng, 1a, 2: an official
nkwoon, 3, 4: a proverb, a saying
nkwoonc, 3, 4: a hill; the world
nkyeenc makaam [*nkyɛɛnc makaam*], 1a, 2: an official
nnaam [*nnáám*], 3, 4: tribute
nnoon, 3, 4, *t:* a type of statue
nnup [*nnúp*], 3, 4: a type of mask
nnyeeng, 3, 4: a charm, medicine
nshaam, 1a, 2: a male in-law of the same generation
nshaang, 3, 4, *t:* ghosts reborn as humans
nsheeng [*nshɛ́ɛ́ng*], 3, 4: the capital city
nsho [*nshɔ́*], 1a, 2: a slave
nyaang, 1a, 2: an official
nyabashoong, 1a, 2: an official
nyeeng, 9, 10, *t:* a type of mask
nyibiin, 1a, 2: an official (literally, "king of patterns")
nyibit, 1a, 2: a military official (literally, "king of war")
nyibit idüing, 1a, 2: a military official (literally, "king of war for the slave quarter"
nyim, 1a, 2: king
nyim ancok [*nyim áncok*]: an official (literally, "king of elephants")
nyim ashing, 1a, 2: an official (literally, "king of the rope")
nyimishoong [*nyimishɔ́ɔ́ng*], 1a, 2: an official
nyim lakaang, 1a, 2: an official (literally, "king of the oil press")
nyimmwaan, 1a, 2: the head of the Cwa groups (literally, "king of the vine")
nyim sheky [*nyim shɛky*], 1a, 2: the guardian of the poison ordeal
nyoom [*nyóóm*], 1a, 2: an official
paangl, 1a, 2: a tribute collector
pel ambish [*pél ámbísh*], 9, 10: the royal drum
pok ibaan, 1a, 2: an official
poom [*pɔ́ɔ́m*], 1a: a European
pwoonc, 9, 10: an arrow
shaash, 9, 10: adultery
shanshenge, 1a, 2: the Kete village headman
shash anyim [*shásh anyim*], 9, 10: a field whose produce was reserved for the king
shesh [*shɛ́sh*], 1a, 2: a military official
shoosh [*shɔɔsh*], 9, 10: a praise name
shyaam [*shyáám*], 9, 10: the African oil palm
tancoon [*tancóón*], 1a, 2: an official
tataam, 1a, 2: an official
wal, invariable: long ago

Index

Achten, Lode, 79
Adam, in genesis story, 31
Affonso, king of Kongo, 330 *n57,* 345 *n7*
Africa: states, 3, 4, 238; history, 11; people, 36, 37
—Central (Equatorial): historiography, 3, 242; descent, 83, 105; art, 170, 219; religion, 197, 208; languages, 234; trade, 236; social stratification, 238; kingdoms, 241
—West: 189, 240
Agriculture, 92–93, 174–79, 320 *n10. See also* Crops
Albinos, 37
Almandrilha beads, 354 *n93*
Anachronism, 178, 186, 230–31, 233; and war, 44, 191; and chiefs, 54, 161; and titles, 55, 58, 99; and trade, 70, 187; and politics, 74; and tribute, 143; and crops, 177; and sacrifice, 203; and boy's initiation, 204, 356 *n30;* mentioned, 37, 121
Ancestors, 99, 198, 200, 208
Andrianampoinimerina, 127
Anecdote, 227–34; as a form of tradition, 18, 24, 26, 27; and performance, 47, 186
Angola: and missionary influence, 37; and Kuba art, 84, 102, 212; and trade, 192, 193, 195
Annales, French school of, 11, 235
Antwerp, ethnographic museum of, 218
Archaeology: as a source, 10, 11, 78, 84, 88, 221; and sites to be excavated, 49, 137, 181; early Kuba and, 90, 102–3; and trade, 193
Architecture, 141, 223–24
Archival data, 10, 85, 235; feedback into, 79
Aristocratic clans, 44, 115; gave wives to the king, 67; loss or gain of privileges, 131, 159–60, 164; and royal succession, 157. *See also* Ilyeeng; *Mbaangt;* Ndoong
Arts, visual, 11, 17, 99, 170, 211–24. *See also* Architecture; Decorative patterns; Masks; Statues
Asante (state), 238
Atlantic Ocean, 83, 241
Atlantic trade, 63, 105, 189, 236
Augustus (emperor), 3
Autochthons. *See* Kete; Cwa
Axum (state), 241

Baaking (village), 66
Baambooyi (village), 49
Baang (title), 151
Baashween (village), 140
Babindi Bakusu (people), 165
Bakon (villagers), 168, 169
Bakongo (people), 42
Bakuba (people), 34. *See also* Kuba
Bakwa Kubale (people), 165
Bakwa Mputu (people), 165
Bambal, as term for Kuba, 191
Banana: large (plantain), 38, 92–93, 173–74; small, 57, 173–74
Band, as form of Cwa social structure, 100
Bantu languages, 18, 80–82, 111, 234. *See also* Language
Bapende, 35. *See also* Pende
Bark cloth, 55, 94
Beads, as trade item, 70, 192, 193, 194, 216
Beans, 54, 84, 85, 93, 175
Belgium, 3, 25, 42, 79, 213
Belinge (village), 191, 192
Bell, double, 93, 122, 337 *n26,* 339 *n47*
Bemba (people), 241
Bena Cishiba (people), 70
Bena Dibele (settlement), 40
Benin kingdom, 237, 239, 242
Bibokl (person), 158
Bieeng (ethnic group), 5, 33, 70; as chiefdom, 7, 84, 119, 121, 122; links with Kel and Ngongo, 26–27, 32, 34, 125; wars with Bushoong, 35, 51, 52, 54, 55, 113, 114, 123–24; origin, 43, 56; war with Mboong aLeeng, 65, 66–67, 124, 144, 161–62; and cassava, 68, 176; and Kuba kingdom, 69, 73, 158; war with Mbop Mabiinc maMbul, 72; titles, 150; and the Bulaang, 163; trade route, 191, 192. *See also* Bikenge
Bihe kingdom, 350 *n39*
Bijengele (village), 40
Bikenge (people), 49, 50. *See also* Bieeng
Bingi (people), 7. *See also* Binji
Bini (people), 237, 238, 242
Binji (people), 7, 84; origins of, 66, 165, 204, 327 *n87*
Biology, as source for Kuba history, 84–85
Bit aNgom (person), 33

DESIGNED BY GARY GORE
COMPOSED BY THE COMPOSING ROOM, INC.
GRAND RAPIDS, MICHIGAN
MANUFACTURED BY GEORGE BANTA COMPANY, INC.
MENASHA, WISCONSIN
TEXT AND DISPLAY LINES ARE SET IN TIMES ROMAN

Library of Congress Cataloging in Publication Data
Vansina, Jan.
The children of Woot.
Includes bibliographical references and index.
1.   Kuba (Bantu tribe)—History.   I.   Title.
DT650.K83V36   967.5′1′004963   77-91061
ISBN 0-299-07490-0